Superheroes and Gods

Superheroes and Gods

A Comparative Study from Babylonia to Batman

Don LoCicero

McFarland & Company, Inc., Publishers
Jefferson, North Carolina, and London

LIBRARY OF CONGRESS ONLINE CATALOG

LoCicero, Don.
Superheroes and Gods : a comparative study from Babylonia to
Batman / Don LoCicero.
p.   cm.
Includes bibliographical references and index.

ISBN 978-0-7864-3184-7
softcover : 50# alkaline paper ∞

1. Heroes — History.   2. Heroes — Mythology.
3. Hero worship — History.
BL325.H46L63   2008   202'.1 — dc22   2007035228

British Library cataloguing data are available

Cover image ©2007 Brand X Pictures.

Manufactured in the United States of America

*McFarland & Company, Inc., Publishers
Box 611, Jefferson, North Carolina 28640
www.mcfarlandpub.com*

Table of Contents

For Cecelia: my wife,
my best friend and a super person

Preface

In the early 1970s, Cedar Crest College introduced a four-week semester, inviting professors to develop innovative courses, not necessarily within their major fields. I volunteered to take part in the experimental program. The course that I developed was entitled The Superhero in World Literature, later shortened to The Superhero. It was to become one of the most popular courses in the program, to the extent that it was quickly elevated to full-course status as part of the regular liberal arts curriculum. As such, it invariably enjoyed robust enrollment, often requiring a lengthy waiting list. In keeping with the times, moreover, I eventually developed another original course entitled The Female Hero. This latter offering was enthusiastically welcomed by the students of Cedar Crest as it is a women's college.

As the word got out, I was asked to offer The Superhero at Lehigh University as part of the LVAIC (Lehigh Valley Association of Independent Colleges) consortium's visiting scholar series. *Superheroes and Gods: A Comparative Study from Babylonia to Batman* is the product of more than three decades of study, teaching and intermittent writing on the subject of the superhero. In the work, I select a number of mythological superheroes from varied time periods and cultures and demonstrate how they all follow archetypal patterns. It becomes clear as the work progresses that very often those beings referred to as "gods" are merely heightened versions of the human superheroes. Whether in an ancient Greek, Roman, Babylonian, Indian, Egyptian, Persian, or Finnish heroic epic poem, or in a modern American comic, it becomes evident that the various superheroes are essentially far more alike than is obvious at first glance. Indeed, they share similar mythological DNA. In addition, the great villains of mythology also prove to be cut from the same archetypal timber as their mirror image, heroic brothers and sisters.

Over the course of the years, I continued to work on my manuscript, adding areas that could not be covered in the classroom because of the time limits of an academic semester. While not intended as a reference work on the superhero, this work could very well serve that purpose. Anyone fascinated by the larger-than-life figures who have awed and intrigued the human imagination from ancient times to the present will be able to retrace the extraordinary exploits of their favorites in the following pages.

1

Introduction

Throughout the ages, heroes have occupied an exalted position in the lore of virtually every recorded society. When not enjoying the favor of the gods, in ancient times the hero was often viewed as a divinity, or at least as semidivine. Moreover, in some cultures the line between hero and god was so vague as to be nonexistent. The mythology of Ancient Egypt is a case in point. For example, while Osiris, Isis, Seth, Horus and the other Egyptian "divinities" are clearly superior to ordinary humans, they are not omniscient, omnipotent, invulnerable, or immortal, as one would expect gods to be. Thus, Osiris, the leading member of the Egyptian pantheon, lacked the foresight to recognize the deadly trap set for him by his brother, Seth, and this lack cost him his life. Moreover, while his grieving wife/sister, Isis, succeeded in having his corpse impregnate her, she was unable to restore him to life or protect his body from being hacked to pieces by Seth. Her subsequent efforts to resection her mate's remains were only partially successful, further proof of the Egyptian gods' limited powers.

The gods of the ancient Norsemen were also portrayed as human, all too human. They lacked judgment in crucial situations, and at times their behavior can be described as petty. In addition, like the Egyptian deities, they were subject to injury and death at the hands of their enemies. In his wide-ranging history of the Danes, the renowned scholar Saxo recognizes this and goes so far as to deny their divinity outright, asserting that they were merely shrewd old men who fooled the people into believing that they were gods. To be sure, Odin, Thor, Loki and the other leading figures of Norse mythology were extraordinary beings, but hardly more so than the human superheroes in the mythologies of other cultures. The apocalyptic battle known as *Ragnarök* (German: Götterdämmerung, English: Twilight of the Gods) is the final proof that they were not immortal, for all but one of their number is slain.

Unlike the gods of Egyptian and Norse mythology, there is no uncertainty about the divine status of the deities worshiped in Ancient Greece. Zeus and the other Olympians, along with a host of minor divinities whose spheres of influence encompass the rivers, streams, forests, and meadows, are true immortals, in a class far above the greatest human heroes. Moreover, the amazing exploits of Achilles, Odysseus and the other great Greek superheroes would have been impossible without the aid of the gods and goddesses who favored them. In the *Iliad*, at one point Homer describes how Achilles is saved from drowning by Hephaestus, who fights water with fire. And at the end of Homer's epic, had it not

3

been for the intervention of the goddess Athena, the greatest Greek hero of the Trojan War might still be chasing the Trojan superhero, Hector, around the wall of Troy.

Aphrodite, whose area of expertise was erotic love, not war, was also known to intervene in the battlefield action when she saw a favored hero in danger. Aware that Hector's flighty brother, Paris, would not survive a confrontation with Helen's enraged husband, Menelaus, she whisked the young shepherd off to safety just in the nick of time. (In part, this was his reward for having judged her the winner in the most famous beauty contest of all time.) Moreover, this was not the only time that Aphrodite interceded during the Trojan War. On another occasion she transported her son, Aeneas, from the battlefield, thus saving him from certain death at the hands of Achilles. Aware that the Trojan hero was destined one day to found a great new civilization, Zeus also intervened on one occasion to preserve Aeneas' life by granting him the agility to flee from an encounter with Achilles. Had the Thunderer not done so, there is little doubt that Aeneas would not have lived to become the hero of Virgil's great epic poem.

However, while the gods of the ancient Greeks were secure in their divinity, nowhere in any mythology is the dividing line between god and man more indistinct than in the case of the great superhero Heracles (Roman: Hercules), son of Zeus and a mortal woman, Alcmene. In the course of his heralded adventures — twelve labors, each of which could be considered a mission impossible — Heracles' stature rose to that of a god. The Greek lyric poet Pindar recognized this, referring to him as *heroes theos* (hero god).

The Roman gods were also indisputably divine, if not nearly as charismatic as the Greek deities from whom they were cloned. Like their Greek progenitors, they often provided assistance to a favored hero in his time of need. Virgil's *Aeneid*, as derivative from Homer's epics as the Roman gods were from the Greek pantheon, details the ongoing machinations of Jupiter, Juno and the other deities of Rome during Aeneas' struggle to lead the surviving Trojans from his ravaged city in their search for a new homeland. As was the case in Homer's epic poem, the goddess of love (in Roman mythology, Venus) watches over her son. But she is not his only divine benefactor. In spite of his knowledge that Aeneas was the issue of his wife's infidelity with a human, Vulcan gives in to her pleas and provides the future father of Rome with a magnificent shield and set of armor, equipment even more extraordinary than that which Hephaestus (Vulcan's Greek equivalent) had forged for Achilles in the *Iliad*.

While the gods often play a significant role in the national epics of various lands, the human heroes are always the central characters. Idolized by their followers and feared by their equally numerous enemies, those who rise to the status of superheroes are invariably portrayed as far above average in physical size, with extraordinary strength and endurance. These attributes, coupled with remarkable courage, enable them to perform feats that challenge the most fertile human imagination. When facing off against the towering Babylonian hero, Gilgamesh, or the equally awe inspiring Persian giant, Rustam, an adversary is doomed before the first blow is struck. Entire armies fall before the onslaught of the great superhero of India, Rama, and the rivers, streams and fields are scarcely large enough to accommodate the corpses of those unfortunate enough to arouse the ire of Siegfried, Achilles or Aeneas. The gods themselves must have marveled as Heracles took the full weight of our planet from Atlas and bore it on his broad shoulders, or as they watched him defeat Thanatos (death) in a wrestling match.

In addition to their ability to dominate the battlefield through sheer physical strength, the superheroes of ancient lands also demonstrated other talents. Osiris was a super teacher as well as a hero/god. According to Egyptian myth it was he who instructed mankind in the art of agriculture and law, and in so doing civilized mankind.

Väinämöinen, the greatest superhero of Finland, was also more than a traditional warrior-hero. This ancient wizard often subdued his enemies with poetry and music, proving with his conquests that the power of the word can be mightier than that of the sword, and that music can be a more effective weapon than brute force.

The stereotype of the hero as someone who is all brawn and no brains certainly does not apply to Rustam. When not slaughtering his foes on the battlefield, the greatest Persian superhero revealed an introspective, philosophical side. Aware as he was that life was short and glory an illusion, he would have well understood Percy Bysshe Shelley's sonnet *Ozymandius.*

Odysseus is the best example of a multifaceted hero, one who relied more often on his mental acuity than on his considerable physical prowess. The hero of Homer's renowned epic poem bearing his name, he was as adept at constructing a sailing vessel as he was at scheming his way out of the Cyclops' cave and eluding the clutches of the enchantress Circe. He was an excellent singer, a gifted storyteller, beloved by both human and divine females, a master of disguise, and one of the most skillful liars of all time. It is not surprising that, unlike most superheroes, Odysseus managed to live a long life.

No study of the superhero would be complete without a discussion of a number of the world's best known super antiheroes. What becomes clear when one examines these universally feared and hated figures is that they share many of the same traits that we revere in their positive counterparts and are, in a reverse sense, as popular as the latter. The so-called Frankenstein monster and Count Dracula are as much a part of our present day mythology as any superhero.

Modern representatives of the superhero genre are no less impressive than their predecessors in that illustrious fraternity. However, while in antiquity the orally transmitted epic poem was the medium in which tales of heroic exploits were circulated to a limited audience, today the superhero's prowess is readily available worldwide by means of mass produced books, countless moving pictures and television productions and through Internet search engines. Superman, Captain Marvel, Wonder Woman, James Bond — these and other larger-than-life figures are the counterparts of the classic superheroes of the past. While they may differ from the latter in that science, rather than the gods, provided them with their extraordinary gifts, and while they often wear more colorful costumes and speak in other languages, the two groups are far more similar than they appear to be at first glance. Indeed, Achilles and Superman, Rustam and Captain Marvel, the Hulk and the Frankenstein being, Odysseus and James Bond — all are essentially blood brothers, their shared essence derived from a wellspring of motifs that the Swiss psychotherapist Carl Jung (1875–1961) designated with the term *archetypes.*

Jung presented his theory of archetypes in a 1936 lecture, "The Archetype and the Collective Conscious" (*Collected Works*, Vol. 9, 87–110). In his lecture, Jung postulates the existence of a collective unconscious quite separate from the personal unconscious made famous by Sigmund Freud. He explains that while the personal unconscious was at one time a part of an individual's conscious state, for one reason or another its contents are forgotten or repressed with passing time. On the other hand, the collective unconscious was never part of any individual consciousness, but an inherited attribute, "a psychic system of a collective, universal and impersonal nature which is identical in all individuals." This inherited psychic system consists of preexistent forms or, as he calls them, *archetypes.*

In a further discussion of the nature of archetypes, Jung declares that dreams and myths are constellations of archetypal images, not original creations aimed at achieving an artistic or informational purpose. The mythic hero is also an amalgamation of a number of archetypal images, and as such is a part of our species' psychic inheritance, a universal constant that transcends culture and time. In the chapters that follow, a number of the most famous superheroes in world literature and legend from varied cultures and times are examined, with particular emphasis given to the significant archetypes that transcend any differences in geography or chronology.

1

Babylonia

Faster than a speeding bullet. More powerful than a locomotive. Able to leap tall buildings with a single bound. Look, up in the sky! It's a bird. It's a plane. It's Superman! Anyone who grew up in America during the golden age of radio recalls those famous words. The same is true of those following: *Out of the west come the thundering hoof beats of the great horse Silver! The Lone Ranger rides again!*

Superman and the Lone Ranger are two beloved superheroes who are as much a part of American culture as Achilles and Siegfried were of their own cultures. Yet, while we all know and love our superheroes, it is safe to assume that none of us will meet one during our lifetimes. The reason for this is simple: the superhero is a concept rather than a flesh and blood being, an archetype residing in the human psyche where there are no physical, spatial or chronological boundaries. Unlike ordinary humans, these larger-than-life mythical beings perform impossible deeds on a regular basis. In fact, almost everything about them is incredible, including their very origins. In defiance of normal biological procedure, miraculous conceptions and fantastic births are the rule rather than the exception in the world of the superhero. Often, their super powers are already developed in infancy, enabling them to overcome any obstacles that might prevent them from fulfilling their manifest destinies. Some have the ability to become invisible, others fly through the air like eagles (indeed, change into eagles should the situation demand), and almost all perform astounding feats of physical strength. From time to time they even battle and conquer that most powerful nemesis of humanity, death itself.

The French have a saying: "The more things change, the more they stay the same." Such is the case with the superhero. Although appearing in different guises throughout the centuries, the superhero is the archetypal replication of his or her predecessors. Gilgamesh, Rustam, Rama, Achilles, Penthesilea, Siegfried, Batman, Captain Marvel, Superman, and Wonder Woman are but a few of the many identities the superhero has assumed at various times and in diverse lands. Externally, they appear to differ greatly from one another, but in essence they are cleverly disguised clones, a leitmotif in the rich music of our species.

Another reason why their similarities are not readily apparent is that throughout the ages superheroes have been presented to the world in various media. Before the advent of writing, the exploits of a superhero were disseminated solely by word of mouth, often by the poets who had created them from a combination of existing myths and their own fertile imaginations. Audiences in ancient Greece must have been as mesmerized by Homer's musical rendition of the Trojan saga as those in the modern era were as they sat around the family radio and listened to the saga of the Lone Ranger, Superman and the Shadow, or watched their exploits on celluloid in a neighborhood movie theater. And the show goes on. Today, as the world trembles before the onslaught of terrorism and weapons of mass destruction, superheroes are reappearing in force on the giant screen and on television. The old superhero film serials have been remarkably improved by the advent of modern special effects, so that our living rooms and movie theaters now boom out the fantastic feats of our familiar comic book heroes in stereophonic sound and living color. Superman, the Hulk, Spider Man, the Flash, Wonder Woman, Captain Marvel, Batman, and Captain America have been resurrected, joined in recent times by a number of newcomers to the select superhero fraternity.

Yes, indeed, as certainly as there is a Santa Claus, superheroes do exist. To verify this, one need only consult the daily television or theater guide, not to mention the shelves of any local comic book outlet. Or one can journey through the following pages and get an account of some of the greatest representatives of the genre ever to trod the yellow brick road of human imagination, beginning in the ancient land of Babylonia, where the greatest hero of the time made his mark: the mighty Gilgamesh.

As is frequently the case with superheroes of antiquity, we must piece together the epic of Gilgamesh from the diverse fragments that have survived. The task is complicated by the fact that there are several versions of particular episodes and a number of inconsistencies, but these obstacles do not detract from the power and appeal of the basic story, which contains many of the archetypes that characterize the superhero.

Gilgamesh

The main source for the story of Gilgamesh is found in 12 large cuneiform tablets dating from the seventh century B.C. These were rediscovered in the mid nineteenth century,[1] and since that time other source materials have surfaced, some recounting the Babylonian version of the epic, some the Assyrian, and yet others a revised version of the former. The common denominator of these sources is the fragmentary nature of the material. Nevertheless, although there is no complete edition, the story of Gilgamesh has been published in many countries, including the United States.[2]

It is ironic that the country responsible for the ultimate male chauvinist, Gilgamesh, could have named a female as the Universal Prime Mover. According to the Babylonian creation myth, in the beginning there was the great mother, Nammu, the only living being in the boundless waters that made up the universe. By definition there can be no mother without children, and since water, as wonderful as it is, can become tedious if it isn't interrupted by a bit of land here and there, and since even a goddess can become lonely after many eons of divine solitude, who can blame Nammu for deciding to liven things up a bit? After all, what good is being in charge if you have no subordinates to command? Thus, Nammu brought forth two children in human form: *An* and *Ki*. How she conceived or bore them is left to the imagination, but what is certain is that their size at birth would have given an obstetrician a major hernia, not to mention a few slipped discs.

An, the male child, extended from "pole to pole" in the upper regions, while Ki, the female, was equally large and resided below. "Mother" Nammu learned quickly that parenthood is not without its difficulties. One can only guess how she reacted when she witnessed An and Ki, better known to us as sky and earth,[3] engaging in what must have been a most spectacular act of cosmic copulation.[4] Though appalled by her children's incestuous interlude, she nevertheless must have felt the incomparable pride of a new grandparent when a grandson was born.

Enlil, who was to become the great god of the air, proceeded to separate his parents, just as air separates the earth from the sky even to this day. Next, he carried his mother, Ki, away to the privacy of some clouds and from her fashioned all of those things which live on earth: plants, animals, rivers, deserts and, finally, the human species. Since any creation myth beginning with only one male and one female necessitates incest if there is to be a propagation of the species, we must suspend our normal standards and appreciate the wonder of it all.

As a reward for his exertions, Enlil was appointed god of wisdom (perhaps by grandma Nammu). Wasting no time, he began to teach his human offspring how to plant and sow crops and build cities. One can only wonder whether he now regrets having passed on this last skill, in view of the ensuing urban crime rates and pollution. At any rate, as a result of his instruction, the great Babylonian city of Uruk was built, a bustling metropolis made famous by its most celebrated king, Gilgamesh.

One must piece together the fragmentary data to draw a portrait of the Babylonian hero, beginning with his extraordinary conception. This story is provided by the Roman author Claudius Aelianus' (Heidel, 4–5) work from the year A.D. 2. Aelianus tells of a Sumerian king named Seuchoros, who was given a prophecy that his daughter's son would eventually usurp his throne. Since the prospect of becoming an ex-king did not appeal to him, Seuchoros decided to prevent his daughter from engaging in the biological process necessary to produce a son, thus thwarting fate. Since chastity belts would not take their place in the world of moral fashion until the medieval period, the king ordered his guards to make certain that his daughter remained chaste. Unfortunately, these efforts failed and "...without his knowledge ... the girl became a mother by an obscure man." Since guards will be guards, and since they are usually obscure men, we are forced to draw the logical conclusion. Our suspicions are heightened by what happened next. As the pregnancy progressed, the fearful guards agreed that the coming baby had to be eliminated before the king got word of its existence. Lacking originality, they chose a traditional method of infanticide: no sooner had the wails begun when one of them snatched the newborn baby boy up, and threw him from the walls of the acropolis. Ordinarily, that would have been the end of the story, but Gilgamesh was no ordinary baby.

As fate would have it, an eagle happened to be soaring by the acropolis at the time and saw what was happening below. Giving his wings full throttle, he skillfully flew directly beneath the downward hurtling baby and allowed it to gently alight on his feather-cushioned back. Then, satisfied that everything was in order, the eagle proceeded to an orchard and discharged its passenger. The caretaker, one of those sensitive souls who cannot resist taking in stray animals, took one look at baby Gilgamesh and without further ado adopted the future superhero. In keeping with the prophecy, when Gilgamesh (Gilgamos) reached manhood he replaced his grandfather on the throne of Babylonia, where he remained for 126 years.

As is often the case in mythology, however, there is an alternate version of this story. In that account, inscribed by the Sumerian King Utuhegal of Uruk, Gilgamesh's mother was no mortal, but rather the offspring of the goddess Ninsun and the high priest of Kallab. This mixed parentage agrees with what we find written in tablet I, where Gilgamesh is described as "...two thirds god; one who saw and knew everything." In addition to omniscience, he is credited with having built the great wall of Uruk, "...whose brightness is like copper!" and whose "...inner wall none can equal!"[5] While there is no doubt that he was one very exceptional fellow, the story that follows makes it very difficult to view Gilgamesh as omniscient.

Physically, Gilgamesh was a colossus. Ruggedly handsome, he was 11 cubits tall (eighteen feet!), with a chest measurement of more than nine spans (eighty inches) and legs that were like cedar pillars in the palace courtyard. Other physical measurements are also given, one of which is rather cryptic. In view of his insatiable sex drive, one shudders to think what the missing words in the following lines of the Hittite version of tablet I are: "The length of his [...] was three [...]." The added fact that he could hold a mighty war club in one hand and a struggling lion in the other makes it very understandable why his enemies were terrified when they saw him.

Young Gilgamesh was no gentleman. In fact, his escapades in Uruk must have made the task of the Uruk chamber of commerce a nightmare. It is fairly certain that even the beautiful shining wall surrounding their city could not offset the damage done to the tourist trade by the rampaging resident superhero. The terrible truth is that Gilgamesh, at least in his younger years, was a rapist and a killer. There was no safe haven for the maidens of Uruk, not in the streets of the city, not in the marketplace, not even as they held the arm of their bridegrooms on the way to the wedding reception. Insatiable Gilgamesh would snatch them up and carry them off. "Gilgamesh leaves no virgin...," tablet I declares, not once but twice, and adds, "Gilgamesh leaves no son to his father...."

Enkidu

Since they had no David to confront their raging Goliath, the people of Uruk resorted to a communal plea for divine intervention, directing their prayers to Aruru, the goddess of love. Aruru responded by creating a half-human, half-bull creature named Enkidu, a behemoth specifically designed to rival the hated and feared Gilgamesh. He is described in the following manner:

> His whole body is covered with hair.... the hair of his head is like that of a woman.... With the gazelles he eats grass; With the game he presses on to the drinking place; With the animals his heart delights at the water.[6]

Enkidu's swiftness and strength became the talk of Uruk. Gilgamesh's curiosity was piqued when he heard of this potential adversary. He devised a plan to lure Enkidu to the city, a plan based on the subject he knew best: the power of the sex drive. He called in his best hunter and ordered him to bring Enkidu to Uruk. Accompanying the hunter, as ordered by Gilgamesh, was the most accomplished and beautiful of the palace courtesans, scantily dressed and anointed with seductive perfume.

As Gilgamesh expected, Enkidu quickly succumbed to the seductive courtesan's wiles. Finally, after six nights and seven days of almost uninterrupted lovemaking, Enkidu, "sated with the charms" of his instructress, decided to take a break to visit the communal watering hole. As he approached his former animal cohorts, prepared perhaps to engage in a bit of elbow-in-the-ribs macho watering-hole talk (in lieu of a locker room), he learned a universal lesson, namely, that all actuality is bought at the cost of excluded possibility, or, put in simpler terms, everything has a price. Whereas he had previously been extremely popular with the animals, contact with a human woman had tainted him in their eyes (noses?). When they saw him now, "The game of the steppe fled from his presence." Spurned by his former comrades, there was nothing left for Enkidu to do but follow the courtesan to Uruk, where she promised him that he would meet the mighty hero Gilgamesh.

In order to enter the "civilized" world, however, Enkidu had to adjust to its ways. He learned to eat, drink and dress as well as any other human who was half bull. Tablet II describes how he ate bread, drank intoxicating beverages, and "...became like a human being...."[7]

The first encounter between Gilgamesh and Enkidu had the elements of an American wild-west showdown. The crowds greeted Enkidu enthusiastically as he made his way to the gate of the city's market place, the site chosen for the arranged meeting.[8] The inhabitants of Uruk were hopeful that he would be able to take the measure of their tormentor, Gilgamesh. As he walked along the street some whispered, "He looks like Gilgamesh...." Others added, "He is shorter ... but stronger." All seemed to agree, however, that "For Gilgamesh an equal like a god has arisen."

The battle began immediately, a wrestling match of titanic proportions. Doorposts were shattered and buildings shaken to their foundations by the lengthy, violent battle. At last, Gilgamesh managed to score a narrow victory. While the winner was not the one they had hoped for, however, the people of Uruk benefited in the long run. For, due to each gladiator's respect for the other's strength and bravery, the two became inseparable, loyal sidekicks[9] who agreed to set forth from Uruk together in order to seek adventure in the wider world. With Gilgamesh gone, brides and bridegrooms no longer had to look over their shoulders as they made their way to the wedding reception or to the site they had chosen to sample their anticipated connubial delights. And although we have no source to verify it, we can assume the great fight had a positive effect on the economic and social life of Uruk. Whereas women previously had bought their wares at the first stand in the marketplace and rushed home to escape the giant rapist of Uruk, they were now able to shop for the best sales, thus fostering competition. And they could also socialize once more, exchanging the latest items of gossip as they washed the family laundry at the communal fountain.

Meanwhile, the two heavily armed heroes battled monsters, seduced women, and behaved in traditional superhero fashion. A number of their adventures deserve special mention.

The first and most terrifying adversary they faced was the demon Humbaba, guardian of a gigantic cedar forest far from Uruk. For committing the sin of pride, Humbaba (alias Huwawa) had evoked the anger of the god Enlil. The heroes' journey was long and arduous, but Gilgamesh and Enkidu arrived unscathed, calmly killed the demon's watchman and entered the forest. After a time, they came upon a sacred cedar tree and proceeded to chop it down. Humbaba heard the sounds of their axes and suddenly appeared before them in full fury. The fact that he was quite an imposing figure is attested to by Gilgamesh's response. As brave as the Babylonian hero was, he was so terrified by the sight of Humbaba that "...his tears gushed forth in streams." He prayed to the god of the sun, Shamash, who sent the winds down against the demon. "The storm wind, the chill wind, the hot wind, the tempestuous wind ... eight winds arouse against him. He is unable to go forward. He is unable to turn back."[10] Humbaba surrendered, but it did not save him. Gilgamesh and Enkidu cut off his head and returned in triumph to Uruk.

Fittingly, a female ultimately brought Gilgamesh down: Ishtar, the goddess of love.[11] If hell hath no fury like a woman scorned, it follows that a goddess scorned is even more furious. Upon his return from the Battle of the Cedar Forest, Gilgamesh and Ishtar met. Overwhelmed by his great beauty, the goddess got right to the point: "Be thou my husband and I will be thy wife! I will cause to be harnessed for thee a chariot of lapis lazuli and gold...."[12] To sweeten the pot even more, she offered him unlimited power, fertile goats and sheep, donkeys, horses, oxen, the most fashionable clothes, food and drink — in short, everything but the kitchen sink; she would have offered him that, too, if there had been such things in Ancient Babylonia. But Gilgamesh would not be bribed, perhaps because his macho nature prevented him from entering a relationship that had been initiated by a female. Whatever the case, he rejected her advances. Infuriated, the vengeful goddess supplicated her father, Anu, to send down the bull of heaven to punish Gilgamesh.

A bloodbath followed. The heavenly bull slaughtered hundreds of soldiers before Gilgamesh and Enkidu dispatched it.[13] Thereupon Gilgamesh shouted to the crowds lining the streets of Uruk: "Who is the most glorious among heroes? Who is the most eminent among men?" No fools, the people of the big city gave the expected response: "Gilgamesh is the most glorious among heroes! Gilgamesh is the most eminent among men!" No one, the author of the epic included, seemed to care that Enkidu got no credit for the major role he played in ridding the world of the hellish heavenly bull. In the interest of fairness, therefore, let us offer a belated three cheers for that unheralded hero. Hip hip hoorah for Enkidu! Hip hip hoorah! Hip hip hoorah! Unfortunately, no accolades can change the sad fate that he was to suffer.

In tablet VII, Enkidu dreamed that he was soon going to die. At the same time, the gods Anu, Enlil, Ea and Shamash decided that either Gilgamesh or Enkidu would have to pay with his life for having killed Humbaba and the heavenly bull. Ultimately, Enkidu drew the short straw and succumbed to a divinely induced illness. Gilgamesh was completely shattered. "Wailing like a woman," he gave free reign to his emotion: "He lifted his voice like a lion. Like a lioness robbed of her whelps, he went back and forth before his friend, pulling out his hair and throwing it away, taking off and throwing down his beautiful clothes."[14] Compare this to Homer's description, in the *Iliad*, of Achilles' grief when he hears that his beloved sidekick, Patroklos, has been killed by Hector:

> ... the black cloud closed on Achilleus/ In both hands he caught up the grimy dust, and poured/ it over his head and face, and fouled his handsome countenance/ and the black ashes were scattered over his immortal tunic./ And he himself, mightily in his might, in the dust lay/ at length, and took and tore at his hair with his hands, and defiled it.[15]

Unlike his Greek fellow-superhero, however, Gilgamesh was not driven by anger or desire for revenge, but by fear and grief: fear that he, too, would have to die someday, and grief over the loss of his friend. His only goal from that point on was to find the secret of eternal life. To this end, he sought out the fabled sage Utnapishtim, the Babylonian counterpart of the Old Testament's Noah. Like Noah, the renowned sage Utnapishtim, together with his wife, daughter and boatman, was a survivor of the great flood that had inundated the world.

Gilgamesh pressed on in spite of the threats of the terrifying Scorpion people; ultimately they recognized his divinity and allowed him to pass through the gate of the Mashu Mountains. Nor was he diverted from his course by the goddess Siduri's warning that "...when gods created mankind, they allotted death to mankind."[16] His persistence paid off. Eventually, Siduri provided the location of Utnapishtim's boatman. The anticipated meeting between superhero and super-survivor finally took place. After a long discussion of man's inability to escape death,[17] Utnapishtim realized that Gilgamesh would not relent until

The Babylonian hero Gilgamesh slays the bull of Ishtar. (From a painting by E. Wallcousins.)

his request was granted, and he revealed the secret of immortality to Gilgamesh. There was, he explained, a miraculous plant on the bottom of the sea with the power to return those who have become old to their youth and restore the dead to life.

Gilgamesh immediately sailed out to sea, and when he reached the designated spot he tied heavy stones to his feet and jumped overboard. The thorny flower was right where Utnapishtim said it would be. Sadly, though, the story had a tragic ending. At one point on his return to Uruk, Gilgamesh paused to take a refreshing swim. Without thinking, he placed the flower of immortality on a rock and dived into the refreshing water.

If we had only been there we could have warned him. We could have raised our voices as one and screamed out, "Watch out, Gilgamesh, don't put the flower on that rock! A serpent has been following you!" At any rate, the serpent took advantage of Gilgamesh's mental lapse, snatched up the magic flower, shed its skin (a metaphor for old age) and slithered off beneath the surface as Gilgamesh helplessly watched and wept. Gilgamesh had learned the unhappy truth that the dictates of fate cannot be reversed.

The epic of Gilgamesh ends as he and the boatman (the latter banished by Utnapishtim for having divulged his location to Gilgamesh) sadly make their way back to Uruk.

A variant version of Enkidu's death provides an insight into the ancient Babylonian concept of the afterlife. According to this version, the goddess Innana, queen of heaven, made two wooden objects called pukku and mikku from the wood of a tree Gilgamesh had chopped down for her. These two objects of indeterminate use and appearance fall into the underworld one day. When Enkidu offers to retrieve them, Gilgamesh agrees to let him go, warning him to follow nine basic rules while in the underworld or be condemned to remain there. He was forbidden to do the following:

1. Wear clean clothes
2. Rub himself down with oil
3. Hurl a spear
4. Take a staff in his hands
5. Put sandals on his feet
6. Kiss the wife he loves
7. Strike the wife he hates
8. Kiss the son he loves
9. Strike the son he hates

Enkidu, not one to adhere to rules, proceeds to violate every one of the prohibitions. After rubbing himself down with oil, he dons his finest clothes, puts on his best sandals, clasps a staff in one hand and a spear in the other, hurls the spear as soon as he reaches the underworld, kisses his favorite wife and son, and slaps the wife and son he hates.

As a result of his disregard for Gilgamesh's advice, Enkidu is "seized by the underworld." This version of the epic ends tragically: Enkidu is permitted to ascend to the upper world briefly to see his friend. In somber tones, he informs Gilgamesh how terrible the world of death is.

* * *

While there may have been an actual Babylonian hero by the name of Gilgamesh, the story of his life clearly belongs more to the realm of mythology than that of history. That is not to say, however, that it lacks intrinsic meaning or truth. In fact, the opposite is true. The noted philosopher, Ernst Cassirer, asserts the mythology of a particular people determines that people's history, while Ananda Coomeraswamy states that mythology is "the vehicle of man's profoundest metaphysical insights." Mythology, then, should not be viewed as frivolous, as is sometimes done. Indeed, as one learns more about mythology, one becomes more receptive to the theory of the great Swiss psychologist Carl Jung, who deemed myths to be an expression of a collective unconscious, a means to supply the schematics of existence. He called these schematics *archetypes*. If Jung's theory is valid, one can accept the claim that mythology is more trustworthy than history.[18] The myth of Gilgamesh is a good example of how a work that contains clearly unrealistic action nevertheless also highlights a number of universal truths.

The mythological Babylonian hero is presented to us as an impossible eighteen-feet-tall bully who reigned as king of Uruk for 126 years. Obviously, this Gilgamesh has very little if anything to do with the historical[19] personage who lent him his name; however, this does not detract from the universal constants in the epic tale. The archetypes present there, some more obvious than others, provide a number of important links that serve to connect various cultures and times.

What is the meaning of life? This key question has always intrigued and tortured philosophers, theologians, and others who take time out now and then to ponder the meaning of existence. Reduced to its components, this seemingly simple question yields an endless succession of sub-questions, among which are: Where do we come from? Why do we come from wherever we came from? Is (are) there a God (gods)? Does God (do the gods) determine what happens to us? Why does whoever determines what happens to us make this or that happen to us? What comes after this life? Why does evil exist? Sickness? War? Mythology is one avenue for the exploration of these basic questions. Every culture's mythology contains an account (or more than one) to explain how and why life began. However, while origin myths depict creation, it is in the myth of the hero that we see the ongoing interaction of the human and the divine.

Carl Jung wrote: "The god is by nature wholly supernatural; the hero's nature is human but raised to the limit of the supernatural; he is 'semi-divine.'"[20] The close relationship between hero and god is inherent in the epic of Gilgamesh. In physical strength and stamina the Babylonian hero is clearly "supernatural," his remarkable exploits rightfully earning him a place alongside superheroes such as Achilles, Aeneas and Heracles, who were also said to be of divine heritage.

Even the most extraordinary human beings do not "know all things" and are not "versed in everything," as Gilgamesh was purported to be. In spite of the claim, in Gilgamesh's case there is a great deal of evidence to the contrary.[21] Nevertheless, one account deems him semidivine in that his mother was a goddess. This dual heritage is one of the most interesting and significant aspects of the heroic myth, because it places man within the universal scheme. In the last analysis, Gilgamesh was depicted as a human being with many of the flaws and virtues of the species, albeit greatly magnified. He used his strength and position to terrorize and physically abuse his people, nor did he always act in a heroic fashion when confronted by danger. He showed that he was human when he cowered before the raging Humbaba, and later when he was shaken by the fear of death. His lack of discipline and his inability to reason were demonstrated when he left the flower of immortality unattended in order to take a recreational swim. On the positive side, he proved himself to be supremely courageous time and time again in the course of battle, and was a model friend, ultimately willing to risk his own life to resurrect Enkidu.

The depiction of the man-god gives an insight into the complexity of the human condition. Gilgamesh had serious faults, but due to his divine other nature, he was able to transcend his human limitations and work for a noble cause (friendship). The message of the man-god archetype is a simple one: humans have the potential for both good and evil, and within us there is at least a spark of the divine.

There are numerous other archetypes in the epic of Gilgamesh whose meaning may not be quite as profound as the man-god example above but still supply us with more pieces to the puzzle of our existence. Some are easily explained, while the meaning of others remains open to interpretation. In either case, however, these archetypes appear again and again in the superhero myths of varied cultures and times.

From the very beginning, Gilgamesh follows the archetypal road. Otto Rank, in his work *The Myth of the Birth of a Hero*, gives the following archetypal framework associated with a hero's birth and the events leading up to it:

> The hero is the child of most distinguished parents; usually the son of a king. His origin is preceded by difficulties as continence, or prolonged barrenness, or secret intercourse of the parents due to external prohibition or obstacles. During or before the pregnancy, there is a prophecy in the form of a dream or oracle, cautioning against his birth, and usually threatening danger to the father (or his representative). As a rule he is surrendered to the water, in a box. He is then saved by animals or lowly people (shepherds) and is suckled by a female animal, or by a humble woman. After he is grown up, he finds his distinguished parents in a highly versatile fashion; takes his revenge on his father, on the one hand, and is acknowledged on the other and finally achieves rank and honors.[22]

With one or two exceptions, the above formula fits the myth of Gilgamesh quite well. In accord with Rank's requisites, the Babylonian hero is the son of royalty or a goddess, depending on the version of the story one reads; his conception is the result of a secret liaison, there is a prophecy cautioning against his birth, he is saved by an animal, we can reasonably assume that the orchard keeper's wife suckled him, and he ultimately achieves rank and honor. Thus, Gilgamesh scores a six out of eleven or twelve, depending how one computes Rank's heroic birth archetype formula. Admittedly, there are a few items on the list that seem to be lacking in the Babylonian epic, but their essence is present as follows:

1. Though he is generally credited with only one extraordinary parent (a goddess), as previously cited, there is a version that describes his father as a high priest. While the prophecy cautioning against his birth threatens his grandfather rather than his father, the spirit of this portion of the heroic birth archetype has been met (at any rate, Rank qualified his statement by using the term "usually").
2. The king's guards do not surrender Gilgamesh to the water in order to dispose of him, but by throwing him from the acropolis they surrender him to another element: the air. The essence of this archetype is that a hero is abandoned directly after birth. Thus, Gilgamesh must be included in a select group of famous newborns.[23]
3. Although it is not stated in the tablets, we can assume that the wife or some other female relative, friend or acquaintance of the orchard keeper suckled him. (An orchard keeper is not a shepherd, but they do have similar outdoor jobs.)

Finally, there are the two conditions listed by Rank that are not satisfied by the fragments we have of the Gilgamesh myth:

1. There is no mention of Gilgamesh seeking revenge against his grandfather.
2. We do not know the circumstances of his assumption of power.

The possibility exists that even these two criteria were met in the portions of the myth that have been lost. Even without them, however, on balance Gilgamesh's origin satisfied Rank's standard for the birth of a hero.

Another major archetype present in the Gilgamesh myth is the *monster-slaying* archetype. When Gilgamesh and Enkidu slay Humbaba and other frightful monsters they are merely doing what superheroes of all lands do best. Clyde Kluckhohn, examining all of the sixty culture areas known to history and ethnography, finds the monster-slaying archetype present in thirty-nine of them.[24]

The *destructive female* archetype is also one that occurs in virtually every superhero myth. The only female who has a role of any significance in the Gilgamesh epic, the goddess Ishtar, fulfills this archetype. She is a vindictive temptress who provokes the ultimate tragedy, the counterpart of Eve in Judeo-Christian mythology. As Kluckhohn has pointed out, such a figure is typical of hero myths in varied cultures and time periods. Even today, she is present in literature and myth. Women are frequently portrayed as a necessary evil at best, useful primarily, if not solely, for the sexual satisfaction of the male hero.

On the other end of the spectrum is the chaste, sublime female, the embodiment of all that is pure and good. This can be called the *Virgin Mary* archetype. Although absent in the heroic epic of Gilgamesh, she will make her appearance in many of the myths to follow, often not as a positive but as a subtly negative representative of the female gender, an Eve in Mary's clothing.

The male-male friendship, or *sidekick* archetype is related to that of the destructive female. The close relationship between Gilgamesh and Enkidu, stronger than any male-female relationship in the work, is standard fare for the superhero. One need not search too long to find such examples in the hero myths of many lands, including our own. Achilles and Patroklos, the Lone Ranger and Tonto, Batman and Robin — these are but a few of the famous male teams of heroic mythology. The ties between these men were often so strong that when one died the other was so grief stricken that he could not long survive the loss.

The *man/beast* motif is another familiar archetype in countless myths of the hero. Enkidu is one of a long line of heroes (as well as antiheroes) and divinities who were either part animal or had the ability to transform themselves into animals. From Zeus to Dracula, we see variations of this archetype.[25]

The *deluge and the evil serpent* archetypes (Utnapishtim and the water serpent who steals the flower of immortality) appear in the myths of many lands, but these are more at home in theologically or morally oriented myths (punishment for sins/reward for virtue)[26] than in those of superheroes. Without exception, their appearance in the latter is incidental. This is also true of the *ominous dream* archetype, represented by Enkidu's dream of impending death. Throughout world mythology and literature, we see innumerable manifestations of such dreams.

Enkidu's descent to the underworld is an example of the *superhero vs. death* archetype. In Greek mythology Odysseus and Heracles make such a descent, while the Roman hero, Theseus, and Virgil's Aeneas do likewise. Unlike their Babylonian fellow traveler, however, the Roman and Greek heroes manage to return safely to terra firma.[27] The details of their visits to the underworld will be recounted in later chapters of this work.

2

Persia

The ancient kingdom of Persia (present day Iran), famous for intricately patterned rugs and silky-haired cats, was another home to a world class superhero: Rustam (Rostam; Rustem). A detailed account of his origin and exploits is found in the national poem of Persia, *Shah-nama: The Epic of the Kings*[1] by Abu'l Qasim Mansur (or Hasan), who wrote under the pen name Firdausi (Firdowsi).

The *Shah-nama* is a colossal work covering 3,874 years, from 3223 B.C. to A.D. 651. Firdowsi worked on his epic poem for thirty years, recounting the many colorful legends of the four Persian dynasties. Yet, for all of its scope it is Rustam who is the central, overriding figure in the work. The importance of Firdowsi's poem to the cultural life of Iran is attested to by the fact that even today schoolchildren in Iran are able to recite entire episodes verbatim. If one were to imagine an American epic dealing with the period from 1938 to 5812, concentrated on a great American superhero, one would gain an idea of the enormity of Firdowsi's accomplishment.

Firdowsi states his view of how a hero must conduct himself, in the lines of a short poem:

> The black mass of an army,
>   Which fronts a soldier's eye,
> Should never his brave soul pale
>   Nor make him dread to die;
> He should with stouter heart advance,
>   Recalling there and then,
> That one real warrior is worth
>   A hundred thousand men.[2]

Rustam was a "real warrior" and then some. Most likely, Firdowsi would have assessed this great hero's worth in men not at a hundred thousand, but in seven digits or more. While he was undoubtedly an outstanding individual, however, a close examination of the *Shah-nama* shows that Rustam is cut from familiar, archetypal timber.

As was the case with Gilgamesh, a grandfather plays an extremely important role in Rustam's life. The grandfather, Sam, was a superhero in his own right, made commander of the southeastern part of Shah Minuchir's kingdom as a reward for his unfailing loyalty, unmatched bravery, and consummate skill in battle.

After one of his many successful military campaigns, Sam hears the long awaited news that one of his wives is pregnant. He is ecstatic. At last he will have a son to whom he can pass on the mantle of glory when the time comes for him to retire. Along with Sam, the entire city of Seistan awaits the blessed event, happy for their beloved hero.

If all had gone well, the story of Sam would have taken the following course: a beautiful son would have been born, the mirror image of Sam, and under Sam's expert tutelage the son would have grown up to become a spectacular champion in his own right, eventually replacing Sam as the hero in residence. Then, at the end of a long, successful life, Sam would have been given an elaborate, ultra expensive retirement party complete with laudatory speeches by the Shah and other dignitaries. To top it off, the Shah would have personally presented him with the Persian equivalent of a gold watch, along with the promise of support for any secretarial help Sam might need to write his memoirs. Unfortunately, however, Sam's life did not follow this ideal script.

It started off well. A baby was born, a healthy, strapping baby boy. Unfortunately, though, when the midwife looked more carefully at the newborn son of Sam she saw that something very serious was wrong. While the baby had all of its fingers and toes in the right places, there was a major problem: its hair and eyelashes were as white as an Antarctic landscape. An albino! The son of Sam was an albino, a condition looked upon as a curse at that time.

The midwife and her assistants tore their hair as they attempted to determine what to do. Finally, one who was braver than the others decided to test the old adage that the best defense is a good offense. Her jaw clenched resolutely, she carried the silver-haired baby to the beaming, proud father and announced:

> Fortune prosper Sam the hero.... God has granted what you desired. Embellish your soul with the fulfillment of your wishes. Behind the veil in your place, illustrious prince, a handsome son has been born to your wife; a young paladin with the heart of a lion. Even now, in his baby state, he shows himself to be of sturdy nature; his body is of pure silver, his face like Paradise. You will see no ugly feature in him, his one blemish being that his hair is white....[3]

The ploy failed. Instead of rejoicing at the news, Sam took one look at his bleached offspring and ordered his underlings to take it to some remote place and dispose of it. He then attempted to shut the unpleasant incident out of his mind and get on with his life. And it worked, at least for a good number of years. It might have gone on working, moreover, if one of his wives had been able to produce another son. But this did not happen, leading one to suspect that our hero's sperm count was at a considerably lower level than his military prowess.

What happened next proved that even heroes can suffer the pangs of a guilty conscience. Sam, fast approaching old age, dreamt one night that the son he had ordered abandoned was still alive somewhere in India. As was customary, he related his dream to the priests for an interpretation. Their response was disconcerting. They berated him for having abandoned his child, declaring that even a wild animal would not have been so cruel. To make certain that he realized the graveness of his transgression, they told him that he had to find the abandoned offspring even if it took his entire life to do it. Sam needed no such advice; he had already decided to do just that.

Heroes do not waste time. Gathering a posse of his best men, Sam saddled up and set out for the mountains of India, aware that the odds against success were astronomical. Many years passed in futile search. Sam grew increasingly aware that even if his son were alive, it was unlikely that he would still be on the mountain where he had been discarded. Added to that was the problem of finding the right mountain. But Sam was no ordinary man. The search went on. Then, when it seemed as if they would never succeed, he and his followers came to a towering mountain called the Alborz. On the peak of the mountain they could barely make out a huge bird's nest. It was the eyrie of the fabled, ruby-winged Simurgh. Eagerly, Sam ascended.

That the Simurgh was a fantastic bird was immediately evident to Sam as he approached her. Not only did she have ruby wings, but she also sported very unbirdlike breasts with which to nurse her young. To top it off, she spoke perfect Persian! In itself, this might not seem miraculous, since many varieties of birds have the ability to speak. But as all ornithologists will tell you, while birds may be able to mimic the human voice, they are totally oblivious to any meaning the words contain. The Simurgh, on the other hand, spoke coherently. Moreover, she exhibited a refinement of speech and a sensitivity of spirit often absent in many members of the human species. This became evident as Sam stood and gazed upward, praying for guidance. The Simurgh immediately recognized her visitors. Without any preliminaries, she explained to her incredulous foster son that his father had come to pick him up. (She was probably glad to get rid of him by that time, in view of the fact that he was a full grown man and, unlike her biological offspring, could not fly off on his own.) When the young man hesitated, she motivated him to depart by informing him that he was destined to be the ruler of an empire. That did the trick. She bade him an emotional farewell, and carried him down to his father.

Sam was bubbling over with gratitude. He thanked the Simurgh profusely for having taken care of his son, Zal, during those crucial, formative years. But Zal was not pleased with the turn of events. He voiced his anger in no uncertain terms, accusing the Simurgh of abandoning him just as his father had. In response, the magic bird assured him that this was not the case, and to prove it, she plucked out one of her jeweled, ruby feathers. Handing it over to Zal, she said:

> If ever a difficulty overtakes you or any dispute arises over your actions, good or ill, then cast this feather of mine into the flames and you will at once experience the blessing of my authority. I will come as a black cloud, with speed, and transport you unharmed to this place [Levy 38].

One is tempted to wonder what kind of life Zal had led in the Simurgh's nest. As a hungry baby had he squawked for food like his foster mother's biological offspring, or simply bawled like a human baby until she offered him a breast? What did he do for recreation once he was grown? How did the Simurgh get him to study the Persian language without a textbook or blackboard? Where did she, an Indian bird, learn Persian? Why did she teach it to Zal, unless she knew that one day he would leave the nest and go to join his human family? Was there sibling rivalry in the nest? If not, did the Simurgh suffer from the empty nest syndrome once he was gone? Such questions, of course, are unanswerable, since mythology does not have to concern itself with everyday logic or natural possibility. Still, one wonders....

The return of Sam with his recovered son was a joyous event. Drummers drummed, bells were rung, and clarions trumpeted the glad news that Zal was alive. The Shah, upon hearing the news, immediately sent an array of gifts: horses, jewels, carpets, suits of armor, clothing, weapons — in short, everything a hero could ask for. The beaming daddy, Sam, capped it off by immediately stepping aside to let his son govern the territory while Sam went out to lead a military campaign against the latest enemies of the Shah.

Zal quickly established himself as a worthy successor to his father. In fact, he became so popular that the people suspended their bigotry and overlooked the fact that his hair was snow white. To demonstrate that he was a hands-on leader, one of Zal's first undertakings was to acquaint himself firsthand with the land under his jurisdiction. To this end he took a trip to the renowned city of Kabul, which was ruled at the time by an Assyrian feudal lord named Mihrab. The visit was an unqualified success. Despite their differences, Zal and Mihrab respected each other's leadership abilities. To Zal, moreover, there was something of even greater interest: Mihrab's young daughter, the beautiful, enchanting princess Rudabah. It was a classic case of love-before-first-sight. His young fancy had been aroused by the description one of his followers had given of her.

> From head to foot she is white as ivory; her face is a very paradise and for stature she is as a plane-tree. About her silver shoulders two musky black tresses curl, encircling them with their ends as though they were links in a chain. Her mouth resembles a pomegranate blossom, her lips are cherries and her silver bosom curves out into breasts like pomegranates. Her eyes are like the narcissus in the garden and her lashes draw their blackness from the raven's wing.... If you seek a brilliant moon, it is her face; if you long for the perfume of musk, it lingers in her tresses. From top to toe she is Paradise [Levy 40].

Who can blame young Zal for getting a bit worked up? After all, the only feminine company he has had in his whole life was the Simurgh and a few feathered stepsisters.

Unknown to Zal, the lovely Rudabah had experienced identical stirrings of love when she inadvertently overheard her father describe the dashing, silver-haired Persian hero to her mother. She was already madly in love with Zal before Mihrab finished the following description:

> ... you never saw anyone ... with such arms as his, and for manipulation of the reins and for his seat in the saddle there never existed a horseman to equal him. He has the heart of a lion and an elephant's strength. For generosity he is as bounteous as the Nile ... [Levy 40].

However, the road of love is a rocky one, filled with many bumps and potholes. Such was the case for the two would-be lovers. For one thing, Zal was Persian and Rudabah Assyrian and therefore they had different religions and customs. Add to that the fact that the Shah of Persia despised Mihrab. As the latter put it: "The Shah ... does not even like me to mount my horse." But these obstacles did not faze either Zal or Rudabah; their ardor increased by the hour. Rudabah's servant girls, fearing that any involvement between their lady and the Persian stranger would bring the wrath of the Shah down upon all of them, attempted to make her come to her senses and forget the "white haired bird nursling." However, when Rudabah declared that Zal was the only man "...tall enough and handsome enough for me," the one who "...will bring peace in my body and soul," they consented to play the role of matchmakers. A series of messages was passed through these intermediaries, further inflaming the passions of the two young romantics.

A familiar scenario followed. A rendezvous was arranged and Rudabah, anxious to make everything perfect, had her boudoir decorated meticulously with silk curtains, along with portraits of kings and heroes. She ordered dancers, musicians and sumptuous gourmet dishes, prepared her couch with the softest, most beautiful cushions, and then nervously waited for the Persian hero to appear.

One wonders if Shakespeare was familiar with Firdowsi's poem when he wrote *Romeo and Juliet.* At any rate, the balcony scene in Kabul takes second place to none, including the much more publicized one in Verona. Rudabah must have held her breath as Zal expertly hooked his lasso on the parapet and climbed up to her with the agility of a professional gymnast (probably child's play compared to romping around on a mountain peak). And how her heart must have pounded when he completed his climb. Firdowsi describes their first meeting in the following way:

> As he seated himself on the roof, the maiden came applauding him, and then, with her hand held in his, they went together, intoxicated with love, down from the roof [Levy 45].

The scene fades as they whisper sweet nothings into each other's ears and enter Rudabah's boudoir.

Zal's problems were far from over. Although he had won Rudabah's heart, before the pair could be united permanently he had to get his father's blessing. To this end, he dispatched a messenger to Sam with a letter explaining the situation.

Sam was not pleased. Initially, he believed that his son's lack of experience in the real world left him particularly vulnerable to conniving female wiles, but after consulting his astrologers and receiving a glowing report about the benefits to be derived from a relationship between Zal and Rudabah, he became convinced that the union would be a propitious one. With this in mind, he set off to try to induce the Shah to agree. Since he knew how negatively the Shah viewed Mihrab, he had devised a plan to get the former into the proper frame of mind for a positive response. Sam's plan was simple — he would bribe the Shah by offering him a thousand of the prisoners he had taken during his military campaign.

Meanwhile, back at Mihrab's palace, Rudabah's mother had discovered the liaison between her daughter and Zal. She was terrified. She suspected that if the Shah learned of it they would all be in serious trouble. She was right. When Sam arrived at the Shah's palace and told him of his son's intention to marry the Assyrian princess, the Shah's response was immediate and unambiguous: he ordered Sam to kill Mihrab, Sindukht (Rudabah's mother), and Rudabah, and to burn their palace to the ground. Sam, distraught by this order, saddled up and set out for Kabul, torn between loyalty to the Shah and love for his son.

The situation was desperate. Fortunately, however, Zal was not as naive as someone who had grown up on a mountain peak might have been expected to be. When Sam came to him to explain what the Shah had commanded, Zal used one of the most effective weapons in the human arsenal: guilt. He berated his father for having abandoned him as a baby, and reminded him that he had made a vow to work for his, Zal's, happiness.

The strategy worked. Sam immediately sat down and wrote a letter to the Shah, to be delivered by Zal himself. In the letter, he subtly hinted that if the Shah did not rethink his position about the proposed marriage there might be serious military repercussions.

The plot was also thickening back in Kabul. To make doubly certain that Sam would support his son's marriage to Rudabah, Sindukht convinced her husband to offer him a huge bribe: 300,000 pieces of gold, 30 horses with silver saddles, 60 slaves, an equal number of golden goblets filled with jewels, rare perfumes, 100 camels, 100 mules, a jeweled crown, a gold throne, 4 elephants, a large number of beautiful carpets and a royal supply of the costliest material. Then she disguised herself and personally delivered the small fortune to the Persian hero. Any remaining ambivalence faded when Sam saw what she had brought. To her great relief, he swore an oath to defend her and her husband with his life. So much for his loyalty to the Shah.

All's well that ends well. After he had calmed down, the Shah began to think more logically about the whole situation. He realized that he was risking the support of his greatest champions, Sam and Zal, by opposing their wishes. Probably more to save face than to get advice, he called in his astrologers and asked for a reading. To no one's surprise, the astrologers determined that a marriage between Zal and Rudabah would be in everyone's best interests (including their own, since they knew that this was the result Sam wanted). Thus, by the time Zal arrived with the letter from his father, the Shah had already made up his mind to give his consent. To make it look more official, however, he had Zal take a quickly drawn up IQ test to prove that his years in the Simurgh's nest had not destroyed any gray matter.[4] Zal was able to answer the tricky questions perfectly; the wedding celebration was arranged, and the two were married.

Unlike his father, Zal did not have to wait long for the happy news that his wife was pregnant. Once again, though, nature deviated from the normal script. After nine months, Rudabah was as pregnant as ever with no labor in sight. Vainly, she waited for the contractions to begin, alternately blowing up like a giant beach ball and becoming as thin and pale as an empty envelope. The situation had become very grave; Rudabah was dying.

When he heard that his wife's life was in danger, Zal suddenly remembered the Simurgh's feather. He fetched it quickly, burned it as he had been directed to do, and, lo and behold, his winged stepmother instantly appeared before him in all of her glory. Then, with the assurance of an experienced obstetrician, she proceeded to issue her orders.

> Bring me a poniard of tempered steel.... Let the girl be given a drug to stupefy her and to dull any fear or anxiety in her mind.... The wizard will pierce the frame of the young woman without her awareness of any pain and will draw the lion-child out of her, covering her flank with blood, and will sew together the part he has cut [Levy 48].

Since no one would have dared to disobey a huge, red, articulate bird who had materialized out of thin air, her instructions were immediately followed. Thus, we have the first C-section in recorded history, well before the birth of Caeser. Soon the glad news that a healthy son had been born to Zal and Rudabah was spread throughout the land.

Rustam

That Rustam was no ordinary baby became apparent immediately. Not one but ten wet nurses were needed to satisfy his voracious appetite, and as he grew up the overworked cooks had to prepare five normal portions for him at each meal. To say he was tall would be like saying that the Grand Canyon is deep. Next to him, Gilgamesh was a dwarf. As Firdowsi describes it, "He grew to the height of eight men so that his stature was that of a noble cypress; so high did he grow that it was as though he might become a shining star at which all the world would gaze" (Levy 48). And superior height was not his only attribute; he was handsome, wise, graceful and intelligent, a true superhero in every sense of the word.

But there was trouble brewing in Persia. The enemies of the realm had gained strength, and finally the unthinkable happened: the Shah was captured and killed by his archenemy, the Turanian king Afrasiyab. With the empire on the verge of collapse, only one man could be counted on to save it. The call went out for Zal. Together with his father-in-law, Mihrab, the super albino rode to the rescue, soundly defeating Afrasiyab's forces and driving them out of Persia. The peacock throne was secure; Zal was the hero of the hour. In spite of the pressure exerted on him to accept the office, however, Zal refused to become the new Shah. Following in his father's footsteps, he had decided to take an early retirement. He felt that it was time for his son, Rustam, to take his place.

Rustam was lacking only two items which every superhero needs before embarking on adventures: a weapon worthy of his station and suitable transportation. The first was easily attained from the family's private collection: the famed mace that had been his grandfather's. "When the young hero saw the mace of Sam/ He smiled with pleasure, and his heart rejoiced."[5] It should be noted here that no one but Sam had ever been strong enough to brandish this awesome weapon, not even Zal; but Rustam picked it up and swung it around as if it were a toy.

The second necessary item, transportation, was more difficult to secure. Rustam wanted nothing but the very best. Agonizing much the same way many do today when buying a new automobile, Rustam examined and tested many horses. But none was strong enough to satisfy him: "Whenever Rostam drew a horse towards him he pressed his hand down on its back; each time with potency of his strength its spine yielded until its belly touched the ground" (Levy 50). Finally, one day he saw the horse of his dreams, a huge foal, already the size of its giant mother: "...his eyes were black, but his body was not of a single colour; his tail curved high, his testicles were black and firm, his hoofs of steel. His skin was bright and dappled as though flecked with petals of red roses on saffron" (Levy 51). The old herdsman in charge of the horses warned Rustam that the foal's mother was extremely vicious and had already killed to protect her foal. Rustam was not discouraged. How could he be when the prize was so great? Not only was the foal beautiful, but "At night he was able to see an ant's footprint on a black cloak two leagues away. His strength was that of an elephant, for speed he equaled any racing-camel and for courage any lion..." (Levy 51).

Rustam knew immediately that this was the horse for him, and wasted no time in trying to capture it.

Rustam flings the noose, and suddenly/ Rakhsh secures. Meanwhile the furious mare/ Attacks him, eager with her pointed teeth/ To crush his brain — but, stunned by his loud cry,/ She stops in wonder. Then with clenched hand/ He smites her on the head and neck, and down/ She tumbles, struggling in the pangs of death [Hawthorne 80].

After a fierce struggle, Rustam finally subdued and tamed the wild stallion, which he named Rakhsh. From that day on, man and horse were inseparable companions.

The story of Rustam and Rakhsh is archetypal. Many centuries later, an American superhero experienced a similar situation. In an episode from the radio program of 1958, we learn how the Lone Ranger attained his famous horse, Silver. The hero's previous horse had been shot out from under him by the outlaw, Butch Cavendish. The Lone Ranger stands over the dead animal and laments the loss to his faithful companion, Tonto. As they ride together on one horse they suddenly see an awesome sight: a white stallion and a buffalo in deadly combat. The Lone Ranger is immediately smitten, declaring that he must have the stallion as his own. But the buffalo is stronger, and is about to make the kill. Before he can, however, the Lone Ranger gets off two quick shots and the buffalo falls down dead. What follows is recounted below:

LONE RANGER: "I'd like to have that horse more than anything in the world, but he deserves his freedom...."
TONTO: "Him look like silver."
LONE RANGER: (Calls in a loud voice) "Silver! ... Tonto, he's coming back!"
ANNOUNCER: "Every instinct told him that he must flee at once ... yet he [Silver] stood his ground...."
LONE RANGER: "Now Tonto, the saddle."
TONTO: "Oh, no horse like that ... take saddle."
LONE RANGER: "There never was a horse like this.... "

ANNOUNCER: "The horse was wild ... but the masked man was a kind teacher.... After several days of training he was ready."

LONE RANGER: "Follow me, Tonto! ... Come on, Silver!"

ANNOUNCER: "No hoofs had ever beat the plains like those thundering hoofs of the great horse Silver...."

The ensuing partnership between the "masked man" and his mighty white stallion is an integral part of American mythology, a saga as familiar to Americans as that of Rustam and Rakhsh is to Iranians. That there are differences between the two stories is obvious, but the similarity is remarkable. Separated by so many centuries, the two superheroes and their horses are part and parcel of a common archetype. For want of a better designation, we can label this the *transportation archetype.* In our technologically oriented world the place of Rakhsh and Silver may have been taken by machines, i.e., an automobile, an airplane or a helicopter,[6] but our modern superheroes are as dependent on them as the Lone Ranger and Rustam were on their loyal steeds.

The *Shah-nama* goes on to recount a series of fantastic adventures shared by Rustam and Rakhsh. During the course of many of these, the peerless Persian is repeatedly called upon to save his bumbling Shah, Key Kavus (Kai-Kaus), either from the clutches of the enemy or from his own foolishness.

In one typical episode the Shah has been taken prisoner, and he and his troops blinded during an unsuccessful, badly prepared attack on an enemy city. Rustam rushes to the rescue, killing a lion and a witch along the way as he crosses a desert so hot that all the birds there have turned to powder. He also defeats a dragon and slaughters a powerful demon after a long and violent battle. Once he reaches and liberates the Shah, he uses the blood from the White Demon's heart to restore the latter's eyesight: "The champion brought the Demon's heart/ And squeezed the blood from every part/ Which, dropped upon the injured sight/ Made all things visible and bright..." (Hawthorne 102).

At another time, Rustam demonstrates his incredible strength in full view of his army. The Persian superhero is about to dispatch an enemy wizard-king with his spear when the latter suddenly transforms himself into a giant boulder. The Shah orders the boulder to be brought to him, but the strongest athletes in the army are unable to move it. For Rustam, however, it is an easy task:

> It was then that the giant hero stretched out his arms and, without any aid in that ordeal, lifted the stone with such ease that the troops were left in amazement. He walked with it over the shoulder of a mountain with the crowd roaring at his heels, brought it to the Shah's pavilion and there cast it down ... [Levy 58].

In response to Rustam's threats, the frightened wizard makes the mistake of changing back to human form, whereupon the Shah immediately has him hacked to pieces.

In yet another episode, Rustam is called upon to rescue his Shah from a remote fortress where the latter has been incarcerated by his deceitful father-in-law, the king of Hamavaren. The great superhero not only annihilates the combined armies of several lands, but on his return to Iran defeats the nefarious pretender to the peacock throne, Afrasiyab, who has occupied the country while the Shah was absent. During the course of this episode Rustam demonstrates a characteristic lack of modesty. One of his lieutenants, upset because his leader was out partying before the impending battle with Afrasiyab's army, declares:

> You lion man, Rostam, you must leave this merrymaking, for their army is measureless, their troops cover mountain and plain alike, and the banner of the malevolent Afrasiyab shines out above the dust like the sun [Levy 63].

Undaunted, Rustam answers:

> ... Were there only myself on this plain, with my mace and Rakhsh and my armour, there would be no cause for qualms about Afrasiyab and his numerous army, nor any need for perturbation. Even if there were only one of us on this field of strife, the whole might of Turan would be of no avail against him in battle [Levy 63].

He then proves that he is no idle boaster by completely crushing the enemy. As a reward for his loyalty, the Shah awards Rustam the honorary title *Jahani Pahlvan* (Hero of the People).

On yet another occasion, Rustam is called upon to save his errant Shah in archetypal fashion. One day the devil, Eblis, decides to lead Key Kavus astray. To this end he has a demon convince the Shah that, although he is a great leader on earth, to complete his circle of power he must control the sky as well: "Upon that, he [Key Kavus] hit on a distorted scheme devoid of sense" (Levy 60). The scheme he carries out was as follows: he has his men steal a number of young eagles from their mothers' nests, and for a year and a month feeds the eagles excessively to build up their strength. Next, he constructs a throne, attaches long poles onto each side and ties legs of mutton to them. This is the description of what happens:

> He ... brought four strong eagles and bound them securely to the throne on which he seated himself, with a goblet of wine before him. When the eagles felt the pangs of hunger they sprang towards the mutton, thus lifting the throne from the ground until it rose from the earth's surface into the clouds [Levy 60].

Unfortunately, the unwitting Shah has not thought about the fact that whatever goes up must come down. He learns the truth of this maxim the hard way as the eagles become exhausted and crash-land in a forest somewhere in China. Another SOS is sent out to Rustam, who by this time is fed up with his leader's harebrained escapades. And he is not alone; the other paladins mirror his feelings. One of them expresses the consensus of his peers upon Rustam's return with the rescued Shah:

> ... never, amongst either great or small, have I beheld a man so self-willed as Kavus. Of wisdom he has none, nor has he any faith or judgment, for neither his sense nor his heart is in the right place. You would say he had not a brain in his head, seeing that not a single thought of his has any worth.... Like all lunatics he is bereft of sense and judgment and is moved from his place by every breeze that stirs [Levy 60–61].

To his credit, the Shah listens to these criticisms and agrees that he has been a fool: "He did penance, accustoming himself to pain and toil and giving away much of the treasure he had stored up" (Levy 61). Ultimately, "...the Creator granted him forgiveness."

After the Shah's metamorphosis, Rustam and Rakhsh have numerous adventures together. A memorable one takes place one day while he and Rakhsh are out hunting. After a feast of many "birds and beasts" that he has snared, Rustam lies down to rest while his faithful horse grazes on the plain. He is unaware of the group of Turanians that has been trailing him, determined to steal Rakhsh in order to use him as a stud to strengthen their herds. As soon as Rustam falls asleep they make their move. They gallop up to Rakhsh with lassos at the ready. But the great horse is not to be taken easily: "...as Rakhsh perceived the rope and the horseman he flew into a wild rage. Two of the pursuers he brought down with a kick from his hind legs and he tore off the head of a third with his teeth" (Levy 65). Eventually, however, they manage to overpower Rustam's faithful steed and carry him off.

When Rustam wakes up and discovers that Rakhsh is gone, he is torn by a mixture of grief, anger and pragmatic self-concern: "On foot, running, whither shall I go in my disgrace and with my gloomy spirit, all girt as I am and laden with quiver and battle-axe, a helmet ... my sword and leopard-skin cloak? How shall I traverse the wilderness, and what can I do against any that may attack me?" (65).

Wearily, Rustam makes his way to the city of Samangan. The king, fearing that the Persian giant might turn his anger on him and his countrymen, wines and dines him, and assures him that a horse as famous as Rakhsh will be quickly found. Calmed by the assurances and the large quantities of food and wine, Rustam retires for the night in the elegant sleeping quarters provided for him. But his sleep is interrupted in the middle of the night when:

> ... the door ... was softly opened. Towards the unconscious warrior's pillow stepped a slave with a perfumed candle in her hand, while behind her came a creature lovely as the moon, radiant as the sun and fragrant in her beauty. The colour of her cheeks was that of the corals of Yemen, her mouth small as the heart of a lover contracted with grief. Her soul was ripe wisdom, her body pure spirit uncontaminated by earthly element [Levy 66].

Rustam awakens immediately, more than a little interested in knowing who his beautiful visitor is and why she is there. She answers his questions with great poise, if not modesty: "I am Tahmina.... On earth I have no peer among persons of royal birth; indeed beneath the dome of heaven there rarely exists anyone like me" (Levy 66). She goes on to tell him that no one has ever seen her unveiled, nor has anyone ever heard her voice. Without further preliminaries, she adds, "If you desire me, I yield myself to you, and neither bird nor fish will set eyes on me [hereafter]" (Levy 66).

When Rustam hesitates she tells him that she wants him to father her child, and promises that she will get Rakhsh back for him. Displaying an unusual degree of moral fiber, Rustam calls for a priest who can secure her father's blessing on the union. This is accomplished immediately since the father is more interested in saving his own life than in protecting his daughter's virtue. The remainder of the night "...passed without tedium" (Levy 66).

The rest of the episode is vintage superhero. Morning arrives on schedule and the news is brought to Rustam that Rakhsh has been found. Rustam saddles up quickly, bids a pained farewell to the weeping Tahmina and rides off.

The people of Samangan rejoice nine months later when Tahmina gives birth to a son, whom she names Sohrab. Given Sohrab's genes, it should not surprise anyone that he is a physical phenomenon. At the age of one his chest is as broad as Rustam's, by three he begins to train on the battlefield and at ten he is superior to any warrior in the land.

Sohrab is well aware that he is different from other children his age. When he asks his mother who his father is, she tells him that he is the son of Rustam, a revelation that further inflates the youngster's already enormous ego. He develops a plan that he shares with his mother: he will raise an army, attack and defeat the Shah of Persia, and, this done, he will place his renowned father on the peacock throne. Next, he will turn his army against Turan, defeat King Afrasiyab and make his mother queen of that land. It never occurs to him that Rustam is perfectly capable of fighting his own battles, or that he does not want to be Shah, but since his mother raises no objections to his reckless adventure, he sets off to put it into action.

Sohrab and his army defeat the Persians in a series of battles. He is also victorious in an encounter with the Amazon Gordafarid (Gurdafrid), whom he spares because of her gender. She manages to secure her freedom as follows:

> Expert in wiles each siren-art she knew,/ And thence exposed her blooming face to view/ Raising her full black orbs, serenely bright/ In all her charms she blazed before his sight ... [Hawthorne 125].

The inexperienced young Sohrab is no match for her psychologically:

> Raptured he gazed, her smiles resistless move/ ....Thus vanquished, lost, unconscious of her aim/ And only struggling with his amourous flame/ He rode behind, as if compelled by fate/ And heedless saw her gain the castle gate [126].

Meanwhile, the Shah has received the reports of his armies' defeats at the hands of this mighty stranger, and sends out the call for his number one hero. Rustam does not take the summons seriously, however, and instead of rushing to the Shah's aid, he goes on a drinking binge. The Shah is so infuriated that he orders Rustam to be hanged. Of course, no one is foolish enough to agree to carry out the sentence.

At last, the two are reconciled, but not before the Shah apologizes. Rustam, in his turn, retracts the vow that he will never again lift a finger to fight for the Shah, setting the stage for an archetypal showdown between father and son.

Even in mythology, where logical possibility is regularly transcended, there are attempts to make the action appear realistic. Why, one might ask, would Sohrab fight with his father when his whole purpose was to seat the latter on the throne of Persia? And how could Rustam bring himself to do battle with his young son? The answer, obviously, is that neither is aware of the other's identity. Rustam initially pondered the possibility that Sohrab was his and Tahmina's son, but he discarded this thought fairly quickly, concluding that any child of theirs would have been too young to perform the exploits accredited to the enemy champion. For Sohrab's part, when he tried to get a captured Iranian to point out Rustam to him, the prisoner assured him that Rustam was nowhere in the vicinity. One need not probe too deeply to recognize that this is highly unrealistic. Since both of them were so much taller and stronger than everyone else, it should have been fairly easy for them to deduce the truth upon seeing each other. But they did not. Or did they? The only thing that is clear is that neither Rustam nor Sohrab was certain of the other's identity, but it is also clear that both suspected the truth. These suspicions grew stronger, moreover, as they engaged in their ferocious single combat. If this is so, then, why did they continue to fight? The simple answer to this question is that they were following their destiny; they had no choice.

In comparison, the violent battle between Rustam and Sohrab makes the clash between Gilgamesh and Enkidu look tame. While the Babylonian combatants limited their struggle to brute physical strength, the gigantic father and son use every weapon at their disposal. They hack and slash at each other until both their swords break to pieces; they hammer one another with heavy shafts until the shafts splinter; they jab and stab with spears until their armor begins to break apart, and they pepper each other's shields and shirts of mail with arrows until their supplies run out. The exhausted Rustam tries repeatedly to lift Sohrab from his horse and smash him to the ground as he has done with so many other opponents before, but he cannot do it. His young son is unlike any adversary he has ever come across. For the first time in his life, Rustam begins to fear that he is going to be defeated, and says as much to one of his brothers during a lull in the fighting.

Sohrab, on the other hand, is confident that he will emerge victorious. At one point, he smashes his father's shoulder with a heavy club and laughs at the latter's pain, boasting, "You are a knight, but you cannot withstand the wounds dealt by a warrior, and Rakhsh under you is no better than a donkey" (Levy 74). (It is difficult to ignore the fact that Sohrab could not have known that the horse was Rakhsh without also knowing that the rider was Rustam.)

Finally, unable to sustain such a fierce encounter, the two superheroes turn their horses and gallop back to their respective camps, each slaughtering many soldiers in the opposing armies on the way. As night falls, Rustam pledges to renew the single combat on the following day.

In spite of the fact that one of the soldiers in his camp assures him otherwise, that night Sohrab is troubled by the growing feeling that his opponent is his father, Rustam. He cannot believe that anyone other than Rustam could have survived against him so long. That is why he questions Rustam on the following morning, as the two meet on the battlefield to renew the struggle: "Are you not the son of Dastan [Zal] son of Sam the warrior? Are you not the most elect and famous Rostam of Zabolestan?" (Levy 76). Rustam answers the youngster curtly, telling him in effect to stop talking and start fighting. But the years have caught up to Rustam, and like an athlete who has waited a bit too long to retire, the old hero learns the cruel lesson of time. He is soon brought to the ground by his stronger, more energetic son. As Sohrab is about to cut off his head, however, Rustam resorts to trickery. Speaking calmly, he explains to Sohrab that a respectable warrior may not cut off an opponent's head until he has taken him down twice. Sohrab is not fooled by the ploy, but he "...bowed his head to the older man's argument even though it was not to his liking. This he did first out of gallantry, next because it was destined and again, without doubt, out of generosity" (Levy 77).

The short phrase "because it was destined" is not only the key to understanding this particular incident in the Rustam epic, but is also an essential key to understanding mythology as a whole. They fight because it is their destiny; Rustam escapes death and emerges victorious because it is his destiny. Destiny is the ultimate power, stronger even than the gods, who must also submit to its dictates. Unfortunately, it is no easy or happy destiny that has been allotted to Rustam or his son.

What does a superhero do when defeat seems imminent? That was the problem facing Rustam as he ignominiously made his escape from the scene of his first defeat. In a myth, the answer to the question is not difficult: he turns to the gods for a bit of supernatural assistance. Why not, after all? If we are able to accept the fact that Rustam is as tall as eight men, why not stretch our imaginations a bit further? Firdowsi provides an explanation for what happens next. He tells how Rustam, as a young man, was so powerful that when he walked along normally his feet sank into the stones beneath them. (That must have been both uncomfortable and embarrassing, not to mention the expense in overtime wages the Shah had to pay his road crews for filling the potholes Rustam's footsteps made in the streets.) To alleviate this problem, young Rustam had prayed to the Creator to diminish his strength somewhat, enough at least to enable him to walk along without leaving a trail of destruction in his wake. And his prayers had been answered. Now, facing death, he prays again, this time for the return of his original super-super strength.

Once again, his prayer is granted. The Rustam who returns to battle on the following morning is not the same man whom Sohrab had given a sound drubbing just a short time before. Even so, it takes the last ounce of Rustam's strength to gain the final victory:

... Rostam angrily stretched out his arm to encircle his opponent's head and shoulders, but he fought like a leopard and bent him low until he was at the end of his strength. Swiftly then he drew a dagger from his girdle and with it cleft the chest of his bold-spirited son [Levy 78].

Just before he succumbs to his wounds, Sohrab discloses his identity to Rustam. Rustam is horrified by this revelation, but he clings to the hope that the young man before him is either lying or mistaken. When Sohrab produces a signet ring that his mother has given him as an amulet, Rustam's hope fades; he recognizes it as the one he left with Tahmina after their fateful night of love. In desperation, he sends a messenger to the Shah to beg him to provide the secret elixir that can cure Sohrab. Unmoved by Rustam's sorrow, however, the Shah refuses to help, bitterly castigating the young enemy who had dared to covet his throne. At any rate, it is too late. Sohrab has already "...breathed the last expiring groan" (Hawthorne 153).

In all of literature there is no despair deeper than that suffered by a superhero who has lost a loved one. Rustam's grief is as extreme as his exploits on the battlefield. "He beat his burning breast, his hair he tore.... A shower of ashes o'er his head he threw; 'In my old age,' he cried, 'What have I done? Why have I slain my son, my innocent son?'" (Hawthorne 153). It is only with great effort that he is prevented from committing suicide. As terrible as his anguish is, however, Tahmina's is even greater. When she hears of her son's death, she loses all control: "With frenzied hands deformed her beauteous face; The musky locks her polished temples crowned/ Furious she tore, and flung upon the ground" and "At length worn out from earthly anguish riven/ The mother's spirit joined her child in Heaven" (Hawthorne 135,136).

In spite of his advancing age, Rustam engages in a number of further adventures before he dies. The most significant of these is his clash with the young prince, Esfandiyar (Isfendiyar), son of the Shah, Goshstasp (Gushtasp), and a rising star in the superhero firmament. It is one of the most difficult encounters of Rustam's entire life, and but for some last-minute magic might well have been his last. Esfandiyar's story provides the backdrop for the fierce battle.

Some time before, Shah Goshstasp had promised to step aside and yield the peacock throne to Esfandiyar, but when one of his subordinates warns him that the latter is becoming more powerful than he, the Shah has second thoughts. Finally, his fears grow so great that he has Esfandiyar thrown into prison. Meanwhile, the enemies of Iran are growing stronger and the Shah realizes that he needs his son's military prowess to save the country from defeat. Since he is more pragmatic than principled, he goes to Esfandiyar, apologizes for his lack of trust and renews his pledge to give over the throne to him if he would defeat the enemy. Released from prison, the young superhero once again saves the kingdom. Shah Goshstasp, overwhelmed by suspicion and fear, breaks his word and delays his son's succession to the throne. Dejected over his father's refusal to keep his end of the bargain, Esfandiyar complains to his mother, Kitabun. Her advice is as follows:

The gold and jewels, the imperial sway/ The crown, the throne, the army, all he owns/ Will presently be thine; then wait in patience/ And reign in time, the monarch of the world [Hawthorne 290].

But patience is not in Esfandiyar's emotional makeup. Instead of waiting, he confronts his father and repeats his complaint.

The Shah, who has become even more envious and fearful, consults a soothsayer to learn what the future has in store for Esfandiyar. Told that none other than the great Rustam would kill the latter in battle, Goshstasp conceives a wicked plot to hasten his son's fate. Playing on Esfandiyar's patriotism, he fabricates a story to the effect that Rustam is becoming increasingly disrespectful of the throne and has already gained far too much territory and power. If the famed superhero were allowed to go on this way, he explains, his, Esfandiyar's, ascension to power will be threatened. Esfandiyar listens intently and is eventually persuaded to follow his father's plan to go to Rustam and convince the latter to demonstrate his loyalty by returning to the palace as a symbolic prisoner.

For the second time Esfandiyar disregards his mother's advice to abort what she considers a suicidal mission. Instead, he leads his army to Sistan. He does not turn back, moreover, when one of his camels refuses to move, an obvious omen of disaster. Instead, he slaughters the beast and continues.

At last they meet: the old and the young superhero. What begins as an amiable meeting marked by mutual respect very quickly turns sour. Rustam firmly rejects the Shah's demands. He reminds Esfandiyar of the many victories he has won on the battlefield in service of the peacock throne. Esfandiyar, a typically arrogant hero himself, is annoyed by Rustam's egotism and proceeds to insult the latter's heritage, taunting him with the accusation that his father, Zal, was a Demon. A deadly game of one-upmanship ensues, culminating in Rustam's challenge to combat, which is readily accepted by the younger, more confident Esfandiyar.

The fight on the following day is bloody and one-sided. Rustam is badly out of shape and no match for the energetic youngster. Very soon, Rakhsh is wounded so severely that Rustam has to dismount and continue alone, although he, too, is bleeding profusely from numerous arrows that have hit their mark. In contrast, Esfandiyar remains unscathed. He taunts the old superhero as the latter attempts to drag himself away in defeat: "Is this the valiant Rustem, the renowned/ Quitting the field of battle? Where is now/ The raging tiger, the victorious chief?/ What has become of all thy valour now?" (Hawthorne 303). Short of a miracle, it is obvious that Rustam is finished.

More dead than alive, Rustam makes his way to his father, Zal, who is aghast when he sees how seriously hurt his son is. But Zal is no quitter. He binds his son's wounds as well as he can and refuses to consider the possibility that the battle is already lost. The old albino has one trump card left to play. He excuses himself for a few minutes and when he returns he has a beautiful red feather in his hand!

What happens next is the miracle Rustam needs. Within minutes after Zal sets fire to the beautiful feather, the Simurgh appears in all her glory. Nor does she waste any time before dealing with the most pressing problems at hand. Combining medicine and magic, she quickly heals Rustam's and Rakhsh's wounds. At this point, the plot thickens. The problem of how to have Rustam defeat Esfandiyar is not an easy one to solve since Esfandiyar is also protected by Simurgh magic. We learn that he managed to kill a Simurgh during one of his adventures, and by bathing in the blood of the dead bird had become invulnerable. Or at least almost invulnerable. His eyes never came into contact with the blood and were therefore unprotected by the magic.

The Simurgh leads Rustam to a remote area where an unusual tree is growing. Then she plucks out one of her feathers, rubs it across his eyes, and has him carve a forked arrow from one of the branches of the Kazu tree. If Esfandiyar is to be defeated, she explains, the poisoned arrow has to be shot into his eyes. But, she warns, there is a catch: should Rustam be successful in defeating his opponent, he will suffer calamity during his whole life" (Hawthorne 306).

The ensuing conflict is short and deadly. Esfandiyar is amazed to see Rustam and

Rakhsh return to the battlefield on the following day, both healthy and eager for battle. Before he is able to ponder the situation, however, Rustam strings his bow and fires the deadly arrow. His aim is perfect. Before he dies, Esfandiyar absolves Rustam of any guilt in his death, ascribing it to fate. And to prove that he holds no grudge, he gives over his son, Bashutan, to Rustam's care. What he does not know is that the old superhero will soon follow him into the next world.

Earlier, Rustam had angered the king of Kabul by demanding more than the usual tribute from Kabul that year. The king complains to Rustam's brother, Shughad, knowing that the latter hates his famed sibling. The two conspirators devise a deadly scheme: the king pretends to insult Shughad publicly and Shughad then asks Rustam to return to Kabul to redress the wrong. In the meantime, large pits are dug all along the road, sharpened swords placed in them, and the pits covered up so as to be unnoticeable.

Everything goes like clockwork until the very end. Rustam returns to Kabul, the king apologizes, Rustam agrees to take part in a conciliatory sporting contest, is steered into the pits, and eventually falls onto the swords. But Shughad does not get to enjoy his success. Rustam, mortally wounded, turns to his brother and makes a dying request:

> Now that misfortune has come on me, withdraw my bow from its covering and apply that gift of mine to use. String it and place it before me with two arrows. It must not befall that some prowling lion shall catch sight of me and injury come upon me from him [Levy 217].

Foolishly, Shughad grants Rustam's final request. He immediately realizes that it was a mistake, however, and runs for cover behind a tree as Rustam strings his bow and looses an arrow at him. A tree is no shelter when Rustam is the archer: "The arrow pierced both the tree and him, and they/ Were thus transfixed together...." (Hawthorne 313). Rustam thanks the Creator for allowing him to exact revenge on his murderer, and dies relatively happily.

* * *

Strictly speaking, Rustam meets only two of the criteria for the birth of the hero as outlined by Otto Rank:[7]

1. His parents, Zal and Rudabah, are of royal blood.
2. He and Rudabah have to overcome extreme difficulties (religion, enmity of the Shah, I.Q. test, etc.) in order to become man and wife.

As for the other criteria:

1. There was no prophecy warning his father or any representative against his birth.
2. He was not abandoned as a baby and thus was not saved by animals or lowly people.
3. He was not suckled by a female animal or a humble woman.
4. He had no need to exact revenge on, nor any need to regain acknowledgment by, his father.
5. Rank and honors were his from the beginning.

Nevertheless, if one looks more carefully, one can see that all of Rank's criteria for the hero are satisfied within the larger story of Rustam, not by the superhero himself, but by his father. Zal was abandoned as a baby, saved and suckled by the Simurgh (nonhuman in spite of her eloquence and magical powers), and eventually reconciled with his father and awarded rank and honor. But these criteria apply just to the initial phase of a superhero's life. The story of Rustam contains many other archetypes commonly associated with the ensuing stages of a hero's development.

The *love-before-first-sight* archetype is often encountered in myths of the hero. In the *Sha-nama*, Zal and Rudabah were deeply in love before they had even seen each other. The same was true of Tahmina, who unashamedly revealed to Rustam that she had waited her whole life for him. In both instances, this "pre-facto" love was not only confirmed but strengthened when the principals finally did come together. As later chapters in this work will illustrate, Egyptian, Indian, Norse, and Greek heroic myths also contain examples of this archetype.

Frequently, a hero must undergo some kind of test in order to win his lady. The test that Zal had to pass before gaining the Shah's final approval of his union with Rudabah is an example of this, and can be included under the rubric of the *suitor's-test* archetype. In Zal's case, the test consisted of a series of very difficult and tricky questions that he had to answer before Rudabah could become his wife.[8] Although a test of intelligence was not unique to the Rustam myth, it is more usual for the test to center on the hero's physical superiority. This is the case with Rama (*Ramayana*), Gunther (actually Siegfried) (*Nibelungenlied*), and Odysseus (*Odyssey*), to name three major examples. One can view such tests in two ways: a woman is denigrated to the status of a "prize," an award for the winner of a contest, presented by one man (the father) to another (the would-be husband). On the other hand, such an exercise can be seen as a means of elevating the station of a woman, in that a man must prove himself worthy of her before he wins her over. In either case, however, the woman plays a passive role, the man an active role.

As significant as they are in their own right, the above two archetypes, the *love-before-first-sight* and the *suitor's-test*, are subordinate to the more encompassing archetype we can call the *chosen one* archetype. This latter archetype is a ubiquitous resident in heroic literature and a potent expression of the deterministic essence of mythology. What it reveals to us is that fate is the supreme power, that there are those who are selected by destiny to share particular relationships, come into possession of certain objects, perform particular tasks, etc. Thus, Zal and Rudabah found each other because they were destined to do so. Similarly, no one but Zal could have given the correct responses to the test that he breezed through so easily, nor could Tahmina have loved anyone but Rustam. In each instance fate was the matchmaker.

The *chosen one* archetype was also in effect when Rustam was seeking a proper weapon for his adventures. As already reported, the mace of his grandfather, Sam, had remained unused for many years after the latter's death. There was more than super strength involved in Rustam's ability to brandish the mace effortlessly. In fact, strength was a secondary factor. Had Rustam not been destined to wield his grandfather's awesome weapon, no amount of strength would have enabled him to do it. Put simply, he was the *chosen one*. Parallels are to be found in other mythologies. In Celtic mythology, for example, King Arthur was *chosen* to gain possession of the legendary sword, Excalibur (Escalibore). The strongest knights in the kingdom had tried to remove it from the stone in which it was miraculously embedded, but no one could budge it. Yet, Arthur, a young squire to Sir Kay at the time, removed it "with great ease."[9] In the next chapter, we shall see how the Indian superhero, Rama, also obtained remarkable weapons through the offices of the gods and fate.

Weapons, however, are not the only acquisitions destined for a particular hero. For example, in Wolfram von Eschenbach's great German medieval epic, *Parzival*, there is an article of quite a different sort involved, one that is more powerful than any sword or mace: the Holy Grail. Parzival did not ultimately succeed in his quest to locate and secure the Grail because of his strength or perseverance; he succeeded because he had been *chosen* to become the future Grail King. The fact that it was God rather than fate that made this selection does not alter the basic essence of the archetype, since the two are often used interchangeably.

Several other archetypes common to heroic myths are present in the *Sha-nama*. The bloody battle between Rustam and Sohrab is one such illustration. Variations of this *father-son conflict* archetype are commonplace throughout mythology, extending from the myths of heroes to those of the gods themselves. In Greek mythology, for example, there is a double illustration of this conflict at the highest divine level. Cronus became the number one deity by defeating and castrating his father, Uranus, and was in turn conquered and imprisoned in Tartarus by his son and successor, Zeus.[10] The myth of King Oedipus is merely a variation of this archetype, though some consider it to be "prototypical of all human myths" (Murray 53).

A later version of the generational conflict, though with an outcome different from those in the Greek myths mentioned above, can be found in the German epic poem *The Song of Hildebrand* (*Hildebrandslied*). The fragment of the work that has been preserved begins with a battlefield confrontation between two heroes: Hildebrand, the seasoned old vassal of the great king, Dietrich von Bern (Theodoric), and his son, young Hadubrand. The ensuing action is strikingly similar to that which took place between Rustam and Sohrab. For one thing, the two Germanic warriors do not know the other's identity as they face each other, although Hildebrand suspects from the start that the opponent before him may be the son he deserted as a baby (*abandonment* archetype). To test his suspicion, he asks the young man to reveal his identity. Hadubrand complies without hesitation, proudly identifying himself as the son of the great Hildebrand, "who was always in the front ranks of his army." His suspicions confirmed, the older man discloses his own identity and offers gifts to his long-lost son; but there is no happy reunion. Hadubrand gruffly refuses to accept the peace offering.

"The way to take gifts is with spears, point against point!" he scoffs, and then accuses Hildebrand of being a cunning old Hun using trickery to avoid a fight. He adds that he was told that his father died in battle. Finally, Hildebrand reluctantly agrees to fight, since not to do so would have stained the honor of each. We do not learn from the original poem who wins the combat, since the conclusion is missing. The fragment of the poem we retain ends as they hurl spears at each other and hack each other's shields to pieces with their swords. From later sources, however, we learn that after a long and bloody struggle Hildebrand delivers the death blow to his son, another parallel with the Rustam epic.

In both of these deadly contests between fathers and sons there is fertile ground for philosophical and psychological speculation. Of the four heroes, the only one who was certain of his adversary's identity was Hildebrand; nonetheless, it is hinted that the other combatants were merely feigning ignorance. In addition to the fact that they fought each other to the death because it was their destinies, there is a broader possible interpretation. By battling each other, these fathers and sons fulfill not only their own destinies, but the destinies of all living beings. Their struggle is the archetypal struggle between past and present, one of the basic laws of existence. Today replaces yesterday, to be replaced in turn by tomorrow. One might observe that this is true in the case of Uranus, Cronus and Zeus, but the exact reverse is evident in the myths of Rustam and Hildebrand. After all, if we follow the above analogy they are the yesterdays and yet they defeat their sons, who represent the todays. Why is this so? The answer to this question is psychological rather than philosophical, and can be surmised rather than logically proved. Since the writers of these works were older men, is it not possible that they brought to their works a personal bias against the young? Could it not be that through their literary creations they sought to, if not deny, at least delay the truth of time that applied to themselves as well as the characters in their stories? But, one might interject, why was this not then the case with Uranus and Zeus? A possible explanation: they were gods, not men, and therefore, paradoxically, ageless. Perhaps Uranus, Cronus and Zeus are still out there somewhere in a celestial retirement home for gods, shaking their heads at the mess their successors have made of the world.

In the *Shah-nama* we see the opposite of the *sidekick* archetype, but one that is equally common and equally important: the archetype of the *archenemy*. Rustam had no Enkidu to accompany him on his expeditions, nor a Tonto to grunt in the background when things became difficult. The only one close to him during all of his adventures was Rakhsh, who was undoubtedly one of the greatest super horses of all time, and could be considered a *sidekick* if one expanded the concept to include other species. Even if one rejects this liberal interpretation, however, the gap left by the absence of an Enkidu or Tonto is at least partially filled by the villain of the piece, Afrasiyab. The latter is a variation on the many notorious nemeses found in heroic myths throughout world literature and popular culture. Although negative in essence, these characters are necessary to validate the powers of the superhero. Teleologically speaking, one might say that the archenemy is to the superhero what Satan is to God, a necessary (d)evil.

Yet another archetype present in the myth of Rustam is the *divine intervention* archetype. The authors of mythical tales regularly employ this device when the going gets really rough for the hero. The rescuer can be a god(dess), a magical being, or a human who happens to have a magic elixir. What is consistent in all such myths is that without this intervention the hero would be defeated.

Rustam is aided by two of the three archetypal rescuers. In the showdown with Esfandiyar, the Simurgh heals him and provides the winning battle plan, while it is the Creator who provides him with the extra strength necessary to defeat Sohrab. He would have had a human savior to add to the others, moreover, if he had not refused the elixir offered him by the contrite king of Kabul as he lay dying.[11] As we shall see later, modern superhero epics often contain a version of this archetype, replacing the anthropomorphized supernatural with scientific hardware or modern medicine. This substitution mirrors the modern shift in emphasis from religion to science and technology.

Rustam is a universal representative of the superhero genre. One can relate very well to him even today, because in spite of all of his superhuman attributes he remained throughout human-all-too-human. He could be insufferably arrogant, stubborn, short tempered, and cruel to his enemies, but at times he also demonstrated profundity and sensitivity. As is the case with many superheroes, he constantly boasted to one and all that he was unbeatable, yet he was often shown as an introspective, philosophical thinker. During those introspective interludes he often contemplated his place in the great scheme of the universe and felt a deep sense of personal insignificance. "We are all dust," Rustam asserted more than once, and not just for effect. He also displayed extreme bravery in the direst of circumstances. Before his final encounter with Sohrab, which he was certain would be his last, he sent a message to his mother telling her not to weep over his death because "No man can live forever." In spite of this fatalistic stance, however, he had his weak moments. During the initial stage of his clash with Esfandiyar he was terrified, and at a crucial point in his death struggle with Sohrab he retreated ingloriously. But he returned both times to win victories.

His complex nature is illustrated very clearly in the scene where he flees the battlefield, afraid that Sohrab will kill him if he continues to fight. As he rides away, he cruelly slaughters scores of Sohrab's followers without giving their deaths a second thought. Yet, when Sohrab himself dies, Rustam thinks of the pain it will cause Tahmina when she hears of it, and is himself reduced to a despair so deep that it prompts him to attempt suicide. Like any memorable superhero, Rustam was a multidimensional man, if not a perfect one.

3

India

In the *Bhagavadgita*, a leading source of information on the essence of Hinduism, the god Krishna, "Supreme Brahman and Godhead," explains his essence to his disciple, Arjuna.[1] "Of weapons I am the thunderbolt.... Of procreators I am Kandarpa, the god of love.... I am Yama, lord of death."[2] He adds, "Of all creations I am the beginning and the end, and also the middle.... Of letters I am the letter A.... I am also inexhaustible time, and of creators I am Brahma.... I am all-devouring death, and I am the generator of all things yet to be" (Prabhupada 173). Within this ongoing list of superlatives he includes the following: "...of wielders of weapons I am *Rama*" (173).

Rama, recognized by Krishna as the "supreme wielder of weapons," is indisputably the greatest of all Indian superheroes. But he is far more than a simple warrior-hero dependent on physical strength alone to achieve success, and is still considered by many in India today to be the perfect human being. In Rama, the people of India see the fusion of the three major components of life: action, devotion and knowledge, otherwise known as Yoga. For all of his seeming uniqueness, however, Rama is not unique. Rather, he is the archetypal brother of Gilgamesh, Rustam[3] and many other superheroes of world literature and mythology.

In order to better understand Rama, one must look at the mythological framework in which he exists. In Indian mythology, Vishnu is the preserver god, the god who embodies the qualities of mercy and goodness. Because Vishnu never asserts his superiority (the essence of goodness is alien to such a concept), he is considered the supreme god, worshiped rather than feared. Moreover, as the preserver god his being is linked with the relatively late belief in reincarnation (samsara), the belief that every person is repeatedly reborn to live again according to his or her previous incarnation. One might think of it as a cosmic merit system. Those who have lived good lives continue an upward spiral of growth during each new incarnation, finally becoming gods. Those who do not perform their duties well take the opposite path, ultimately winding up as demons.

During those times when the balance between good and evil shifts in favor of the latter, Vishnu may find it necessary to return to earth in human form. Although there is no agreement on how many times he has had to make the journey (estimates vary from twenty-two to the infinite), it is generally agreed that the hero, Rama (Ramachandra), was Vishnu's seventh incarnation (avatar). His story, as recounted below, appears in two great Indian epic works: the *Mahabarata (c.300 B.C.–A.D.300)* and the *Ramayana (c.200 B.C.–A.D.200)*.

37

Rama

The earth was in trouble again. The super demon, Ravana, was running amok and the gods were unable to stop his rampage because of a wish that Brahma, the god of creation, had granted Ravana: the power never to be killed by "gods, celestial beings, elements or other powers on earth."[4] It appeared that this terrifying "breaker of all laws and ... ravisher of other men's wives"[5] was about to lead his hordes of grotesque followers to the final triumph of evil. Needless to say, it was a serious situation. The super villain with ten heads and twenty eyes was so terrifying that he could make the sun itself become cold, while fear of him brought the winds and oceans to a standstill. One might think that someone who could break off mountaintops and stir up oceans as easily as one stirs a cup of coffee would be rather dense, but Ravana was brilliant, a learned demon whose father was a Brahmin.

The gods could not defeat Ravana. Due to his invulnerability, their mighty weapons were incapable of putting an end to him; even Indra's thunderbolt could only scar him slightly. During one of their many encounters, Ravana not only triumphed but was able to capture their entire divine kingdom and enslave all of them, including the top three gods: Brahma, Vishnu and Shiva. The divine trio eventually managed to escape, but not before Ravana had humiliated them repeatedly by forcing them to do menial chores. The situation was unacceptable. The gods knew that Ravana had to be neutralized if they were ever to feel secure again, and so they decided to hold a brainstorming session. Putting their godly heads together, they realized that there was a serious chink in Ravana's armor that they had overlooked, namely, while he could not be killed by gods or demons, he had no immunity against termination by a human being. The fatal flaw in his invulnerability was the result of his boundless vanity. It seems that when Brahma asked him if he wanted his indestructibility to apply to attack from humans, Ravana had scoffed at the idea, calling human beings mere worms who were worthy of nothing but pity and contempt.

Once they realized they had a chance to rid themselves of the super demon, the gods began to discuss strategy. It was decided that Vishnu would undergo yet another incarnation: he would destroy Ravana by becoming a human being once more (Ions 54). The only question was who he would be in his seventh incarnation. The answer was not long in coming. He would return as a prince.

Dasaratha, a powerful maharaja in the capital city of Ayodhya, had three favorite wives.[6] Rama's mother was the beautiful Kausalya, while three other male children, Bharata, Laksmana and Satrughna, were sons of the maharaja's two other wives. Bharata was the son of Kaikeyi, the other two were from his union with Sumitra.[7] Although Rama was more intelligent, stronger, better looking and braver than his half-brothers, they were not jealous. In fact, he was their favorite.

During their youth, Rama and his closest brother, Laksmana, engaged in many adventures and became particularly adept at killing demons. This served as preparation for the colossal battle they would have to fight in the future. While these adventures are interesting, the story of how Rama met and won his wife is a key to the understanding of his strength and character.

One day, the ruler of a neighboring kingdom announced that he would hold a competition for the hand in marriage of his eldest daughter, the beautiful princess Sita.[8] In the full flush of youth, Rama and his brothers set out together to King Janaka's domain.

The contest involved a single task: the prince who was able to bend a fabled bow would be the victor. This was easier said than done, however, since the bow in question was no ordinary one; it had been given to King Janaka by the god Shiva, and up till then no one had been able to bend it.

Rama was confident. He had no sooner arrived at the court when he asked to be shown the fabled bow. Before the whole court the monstrous bow was hauled into the audience chamber: "Stalwart men of ample stature pulled the mighty iron car/ In which rested all-inviolate Janaka's dreaded bow of war."[9] If Rama had been an ordinary person, he would have made some excuse or other and taken his leave when he saw how impossible it was to bend such a bow; but he was a superhero, and the reincarnation of a god. Therefore, without a moment's hesitation:

> Rama lifted high the weapon on his stalwart arms displayed,/ Wond'ring gazed the kings assembled as the son of Raghu's race/ Proudly raised the bow of Rudra with a warrior's stately grace,/ Proudly strung the bow of Rudra which the kings had tried in vain/ Drew the cord with force resistless till the weapon snapped in twain! [Ions 4].

A delighted Sita thus became Rama's bride.

About a month and a half after the happy couple's wedding, Dasaratha decided to step down to let Rama assume the role of leadership. Everyone was elated. At least, almost everyone. While Rama was being hailed by the throngs as the bravest, kindest, most learned and just of men, a maid of Queen Kaikeyi had other ideas. Like a giant, two-legged mosquito, she buzzed her vitriol into the Queen's ear, namely, that Kaikeyi's son, Bharata, and not Rama should become king. Kaikeyi resisted at first, but was finally convinced to act. As fate would have it, she had a trump card to play: an old debt owed her by Dasaratha. It seems that at one time in the distant past she had treated two of the latter's battlefield wounds, wounds that would have been fatal had she not possessed special healing skills. In repayment for her service, he had agreed to grant her two favors at any time in the future she might choose to ask for them.

The unsuspecting old king assured Kaikeyi that he would stand by his vow when she approached and told him she had two requests to make of him. But he was not prepared for the bombshells she dropped: "Let my Bharat, and not Rama, be anointed Regent King," she demanded. Then she added, "Fourteen years in Dandak's forests let the elder Rama dwell..." (Dutt 26).

Dasaratha was caught on the horns of a dilemma. He had to abide by his word, but how could he tell Rama that his brother was going to be made king in his place? Moreover, even if he managed to get those hard words out, what possible reason could he give Rama for sentencing him to a fourteen year exile in the jungle? After a period of excruciating mental agony, he was still unable to do it, and so the task fell to Rama's mother.

Rama took the unpleasant news as only a perfect superhero could: "Calmly Rama heard the mandate, grief nor anger touched his heart/ Calmly from his father's empire and his home prepared to part" (Dutt 31). Moreover, when he saw how distraught his father was, Rama assured him that he was only too happy to obey unquestioningly. Then he packed his bags with jungle survival gear and matter-of-factly informed Sita that she was not going to become queen after all, and that he would be going into the jungle for fourteen years, so she should not wait supper for him. He also gave her some parting instructions:

> Keep thy fasts and vigils, Sita, while thy Rama is away/ Faith in Gods and faith in virtue on thy bosom hold their sway/ ....To my mother, Queen Kausalya, is thy dearest attendance due/ Offer her thy consolation, be a daughter fond and true! [Dutt 33].

He further instructed her to honor not only his father and mother, but also Kaikeyi and Bharat!

To put it mildly, Sita was less than delighted by the prospect of her husband going to the jungle for fourteen years. Under the circumstances, though, she must be given credit for handling it as well as she did. She neither ranted nor raved; she did not advise Rama to disobey his father, nor did she hatch a sinister plot against Bharata or Kaikeyi. But she did make one request: that she be allowed to accompany him in exile. At first he rejected this idea vigorously. After all, he pointed out, a jungle was no place for a lady, what with all the bothersome insects, poisonous snakes, fierce tigers, etc., etc. Sita was adamant. She persisted until Rama gave in.

While Sita was getting her things ready for the dangerous journey, a weeping Laksmana announced to Rama that he, too, would make the trip into the jungle: "If my elder brother and his lady to the pathless forests wend, Armed with bow and ample quiver Laksmana will on them attend" (Dutt 35). He went on to explain why he would be useful to them in their exile: he would clear the jungle, build them a home, pick berries, fruit and roots, and stand guard while they slept. It was an offer that Rama could not refuse. After a few weak efforts to change Laksmana's mind, he gave his consent.[10]

As Rama, Sita and Laksmana made their way into the jungle, followed by crowds of loudly lamenting citizens, Dasaratha sank into a state of deep depression and died six days later. Meanwhile, Bharata returned from a journey he had been on while all of these events were taking place. When he heard what his mother had done, he had to exercise great self-restraint to keep from killing her. Determined to correct the unjust deed his mother had perpetrated, he, the three queens, and a huge retinue set out into the jungle to find his beloved brother and convince him to come back to Ayodhya as rightful king. (At this point, the people in the kingdom were probably feeling quite insecure as they helplessly watched all of their leaders disappear into the jungle.)

While Bharata did manage to locate Rama, he could not convince him to return as king, since to do so would have been to disobey their father's final command. He told Bharata, "And the deep and darksome jungle shall be Rama's royal hall/ For a righteous father's mandate duteous sons may not recall" (Dutt 62). Although he knew that he could not change Rama's mind, the dejected Bharata was still unwilling to be a part of his mother's unworthy scheme. Therefore, as a symbol of his recognition that his brother was the true ruler, he placed a pair of the latter's sandals on the throne and went off into the wilderness to live as an ascetic. As he put it, "Henceforth Bharat dwells in palace disguised as hermit of the wood/ In the sumptuous hall of feasting wild fruit is his only food" (Dutt 63).

While his sandals quietly did their job in Ayodhya, Rama was facing all kinds of peril in the jungle. As is typical in the heroic epic genre, it was a female who initiated the difficulties for the hero, in this instance the demoness Surpanakha, an ugly creature who was determined to seduce both Rama and Laksmana. With no attempt at subtlety, she made the following proposition to Rama: "Thee I choose as lord and husband; Cast thy human wife aside/ Pale is Sita and misshapen, scarce a warrior's worthy wife/ To a nobler, lordlier female consecrate thy gallant life!" (Dutt 78). Then she added, oblivious to the fact that Sita was present as she spoke, "...weakling Sita I will slay/ Slay that boy thy stripling brother — thee as husband I obey..." (Dutt 78).

Rama not only responded with a firm *no*, but he and Laksmana began to mock the repulsive demoness. Furious at the unexpected response, Surpanakha tried to attack Sita, but Laksmana was too fast for her. More skillfully than a Japanese cook, he flicked his sword several times and before she knew it Surpanakha was minus a nose and ears: "Laksman's anger leaped light lightning as the female hovered near/ With his sword the wrathful warrior cleft her nose and either ear" (Dutt 79). Weeping and wailing, the female Kovalev[11] went to her younger brother, Khara, and pleaded with him to avenge her. Unfortunately for Khara, Rama, having secured the bow of the god Vishnu, the quiver of the thunder god Indra, and the dart of Brahma, was not going to be a pushover.

Khara began his campaign by sending fourteen demons out to eliminate his sister's tormentors, and after Rama effortlessly demolished all of them, Khara personally led an army of fourteen thousand of his best warriors against the Indian superhero. As easily as a shark might deal with a school of attacking minnows, Rama destroyed Khara and his entire army. Rather than concede that it was a lost cause, however, Surpanakha became more determined than ever to exact vengeance. She hastened to her elder brother, Ravana, and related everything to him. The stage was set for the approaching battle, the battle for which Vishnu had reincarnated himself as Rama.

At first Ravana was cool to the idea of avenging his noseless, earless sister, seeing little gain in it for himself. When Surpanakha saw that a call to family loyalty was not working, she decided to use another tactic. Ultimately, she was able to arouse him to action by concentrating on his major area of weakness: his runaway libido. She described Sita's beauty in such a titillating fashion that before long he was convinced that she would be a perfect mate for him. Since she was married to Rama, however, he would have to abduct her.

Aware that Rama was no ordinary adversary, Ravana developed a plan of action. He had one of his underlings[12] transform himself into a golden, bejeweled deer, in order to bait the unsuspecting Sita. It worked perfectly. When Sita saw the enchanted deer she was overcome by the desire to possess it. Using all of her persuasive powers, she induced the reluctant Rama to go out after it and bring it back to her (see note 10). It was just what Ravana wanted. As soon as Sita was alone, he swooped down on her in his flying chariot and carried her off. To his chagrin, however, no matter how he tried he could not get Sita to respond to his amorous advances. Neither charm nor threats to kill her made her waver in her determination to remain faithful to Rama.

Why did Ravana not rape her might be the question of those who still demand a modicum of realism from their myths. There is an explanation, though one that is a bit contrived. We are told that Ravana had heard a prophecy that if he were to force one more woman to make love to him it would cost him his life. For a macho demon used to having his way with women whether they liked it or not, it must have been difficult for Ravana to accept the fact that the only safe sex for him could be of the consensual variety. Nevertheless, his inflated ego enabled him to believe that sooner or later Sita would submit to him of her own free will.

Contrary to Ravana's expectations, Rama did not die of grief when he learned that his wife was missing. A man of action, he set out immediately to search for her. It was not an easy quest. During the course of his travels he learned the details of Sita's abduction from the dying Jatayu, king of the vultures,[13] whom Ravana, having transformed himself into an eagle, had mortally wounded in the ancient counterpart of an aerial dogfight. One can imagine Rama's state of mind as he pondered the situation: his wife was the prisoner of the most terrible demon of them all, he and Laksmana were without allies to direct them to the demon's fortress, and now to top it off he had to bury a giant buzzard. As noble as he was, one can only imagine the psychological pain Rama felt every time he thought of how unfair life was. While he had to suffer in steamy, insect-infested jungles, his sandals sat on a comfortable throne. What was the solution? He thought and thought until he had a sudden flash of insight, one similar to that which Tarzan experienced some years later in a different jungle. It was a simple plan, but one Rama knew would work. He would get himself a reliable monkey as an ally![14]

Fortunately, on the day following Jatayu's burial Rama's path crossed that of the famed monkey king, Sugriva. In spite of their differing species, the two discovered that they had something in common. Sugriva expressed it in the following way: "Equal is our fateful fortune — I have lost a queenly wife/ Banished from Kiskindha's empire, here I lead a forest life…" (Dutt 90). Sugriva explained that his wife, Tara, had been recently abducted by his brother, the evil giant Bali. As a result of their similar plights, Rama and Sugriva joined forces.

The first half of their goal was achieved within a day. Having located Bali, Sugriva engaged him in single combat. Although the monkey king did his best, however, it was soon obvious that Bali was too strong for him. Rama intervened just in time to save his simian friend. With a single arrow, he killed the gigantic ape.

Meanwhile, Sugriva's monkey army turned up some promising clues to Sita's whereabouts. The heroic ape-warrior, Hanuman, chief counselor to the reinstated king Sugriva, found several articles of Sita's clothing and a number of her trinkets. In Hansel and Gretel fashion, she had left these things behind at various intervals to mark the trail of her kidnapper.

It was Hanuman's turn to demonstrate heroism. Employing his miraculous ability to change size at will, he performed some remarkable feats during a daring reconnaissance mission behind the enemy lines. First he became a giant and leaped easily across the ocean separating India from Lanka. Once in Ravana's lively city, he reduced himself to the size of an organ grinder's monkey in order to gather information without being noticed. He eventually located Sita, seated alone in a secluded area in the vicinity of Ravana's palace. Perched in a tree above her, he attempted to gain her attention, but she paid him no heed, suspecting that it was just another one of Ravana's magic tricks. It was only after he had sung the entire story of Rama's life that she would even look up at him. When she indicated that she still did not believe that her husband had sent him, Hanuman produced Rama's ruby ring, the ring Sita had given him to use as proof of its bearer's authenticity. Finally, convinced he was who he claimed to be, she exchanged the sacred jewel from her forehead for the ring, and asked Hanuman to assure Rama that she had been faithful to him.

Monkeys will be monkeys, though, so before returning to Rama with his news, Hanuman decided to have a little fun. He uprooted numerous trees in Ravana's favorite park, leveled hillsides, and in general made the area look as if it had been hit by a hurricane. Ravana sent out his troops to put an end to the destructive monkey business, but Hanuman slaughtered them with huge boulders, pieces of buildings, and anything else he could find to hurl at them. Ravana was finally forced to send his greatest fighter to deal with the situation: his son Indrajit. Indrajit was up to the task; he quickly subdued Hanuman by striking him with a dart of Brahma. Ravana would have finished him off right then and there, moreover, had not his brother, Vivhishana, talked him out of it.[15] As a compromise, the angry demon ordered his men to set fire to Hanuman's tail and drag him through the streets so that the people could ridicule him. The sentence was carried out, but because he was under divine protection Hanuman remained uninjured and had the last laugh. Tiring of the game, he shrank himself so that he could slip out of his bonds and, using his burning tail as a torch, set fire to the entire city. Then, satisfied with his pyromaniacal handiwork, Hanuman went back to report to Rama.

The showdown was approaching. On the one side Rama, Hanuman and thousands of monkey warriors, on the other, Ravana, Indrajit, another cast of thousands and an enormous, secret weapon. The only obstacle separating them was the seemingly impassable ocean.

Rama had a problem. What does one do when one has to cross an ocean with thousands of monkeys and no ships? Since the Indian hero was very pious, he began with a three-day period of fasting and prayer. (We will try to overlook the fact that he was himself a god, the incarnation of Vishnu.) This done, he sternly ordered the ocean to part so that he and his army could ride across. But nothing happened. Since Moses was not on his staff of advisors, Rama found his own solution to the dilemma: he shot a number of his magic arrows into the sea and warned that more would follow if his wishes were disregarded. When the sea god looked around and saw that practically all the fish and other forms of life in his domain had been killed by Rama's arrows, his attention was piqued. Rising to the surface, the god began to explain why he could not meet Rama's demands. To do so, he said, would be in opposition to the laws of nature and therefore beyond his power. Fearing that Rama would reach into his quiver and let loose another volley of murderous shafts, he suggested another course of action: he would help them build a bridge to Lanka. Rama agreed immediately and, with the sea god himself directing the construction, within a very short time Rama and his monkey army were scampering over the crude but functional bridge they had erected across the ocean.

The colossal battle began. A besieged Ravana tried everything he could to defeat the fierce simian hordes, but they kept advancing steadily. Neither magic nor his attempts to bribe Rama's followers to defect could stem the tide. Ravana's hopes for victory soared, however, when his son, Indrajit, managed to render Rama and Laksmana unconscious with his magic darts. When Sita heard what had happened, she began to weep and asked to see her husband.

"Soon they harnessed royal coursers and they took the weeping wife/ Where her Rama, pierced and bleeding, seemed bereft of sense and life/ Brother lay beside his brother with their shattered mail and bow/ Arrows thick and dark with red blood spake the conquest of the foe..." (Dutt 119).

Ravana's elation and Sita's grief were cut short by the intervention of the great eagle Garuda who brought a magic potion that neutralized the effect of the darts: "...by the winged Garuda's skill/ Rama and the valiant Laksman lived to fight their foemen still!" (Dutt 121).

With the return of Rama and Laksmana to the battlefield, the situation became so desperate that Ravana had to suit up and enter the fray. After a heated exchange of arrows, the super demon wounded Laksmana, forcing him to leave the battlefield. But Ravana's success was short-lived. Carried on the shoulders of Hanuman, Rama met Ravana head-on and dealt him a severe wound. The wounded demon retreated in panic as he contemplated defeat for the first time in his life. But there was still a chance to turn the tide of battle. He would use his secret weapon: his brother, the sleeping giant Kumbhakarna. The explanation for Kumbhakarna's extended sleep can be found in the episode where Ravana was granted the power of indestructibility by Brahma. At that time, Kumbhakarna was a fellow penitent of Ravana's. Unlike his brother, though, he had only one head and therefore could not match his brother's spectacular self-decapitation routine every thousand years.[16] At any rate, he, too, had propitiated Brahma sufficiently and thereby earned the right to have one wish granted. This presented the gods with a serious problem. It was obvious to everyone that were Kumbhakarna to wish for limitless powers, he would be a menace to the entire world, gods included. Brahma was faced with a divine dilemma: according to the rules he had to grant the giant's behest, but to do so would be catastrophic. Gods, it appears, do not have it as easy as one might think.

Fortunately, there is a clever goddess behind every god, and so it was with Brahma. His wife, Saraswati, the goddess of learning and speech, caused Kumbhakarna to become tongue-tied when he was about to state his wish. As a result, no matter what he tried to say it always came out as "I want to sleep — without interruption."[17] Therefore, when Brahma asked him to make his wish, he uttered that sentence. Brahma was happy to accommodate him, and so from that day onward, the giant spent all of his time sleeping instead of creating difficulties.

In a scene bordering on slapstick comedy, Ravana's followers were ordered to wake Kumbhakarna from his deep sleep and request his aid in the battle with Rama. It was a dangerous assignment, and many paid the supreme price for their efforts. Periodically, the giant awoke as they played trumpets, beat drums, poked, prodded, and pulled at him. Each time he woke up, he would grab as many of his tormentors as he could lay his hands on and swallow them whole. They were persistent, however, and at last someone hit upon the brilliant idea of using elephants to wake him. While this new approach to the problem worked, it was not without a huge cost. Kumbhakarna, they learned to their horror, was very hungry after his long sleep. Finally sated after devouring more than an entire regiment, he went to Ravana and offered his services, promising his brother that he would bring him "Rama's head on a platter."

At first, Rama's army, along with Hanuman and King Sugriva, was forced to retreat under the new onslaught. Rama, however, did not give ground. In response to Kumbhakarna's challenge, the superhero appeared to face him one on one. It was no contest. Rama shot off a quick flurry of arrows and, presto, the giant's arms and legs were gone! A final flaming shaft and Kumbhakarna's head no longer had a neck to sit on:

> Deadly arrows keen and flaming from the hero's weapon broke/ Kumbha-karna, faint and bleeding felt his death at every stroke/ Last an arrow pierced his armor, from his shoulders smote his head/ Kumbha-karna, lifeless, headless, rolled upon the gory bed ... [Dutt 125].

Rama then lifted the huge, dead torso (it must have weighed tons considering what Kumbhakarna had just eaten) and threw it into the sea, causing a severe tidal wave.

With his uncle dead, it was Indrajit's turn to take the lead against Rama's armies. Ravana's son was a formidable opponent, since he had the ability to become invisible. Using this power, plus a host of other magic tricks, he wreaked havoc on the monkeys.[18] Things looked very bad for Rama. Fortunately, however, Vibhishana, who had defected to Rama earlier on in the battle, provided Laksmana with the method of penetrating Indrajit's magic cloud of invisibility. Once he had done this, Laksmana was able to engage Ravana's son in single combat:

> Lakshman with his hurtling arrows pierced the Raksha's (demon's) golden mail/ Shattered by the Raksha's weapons Lakshman's useless armor fell.... Till with more than human valour Lakshman drew his bow amain/ Slayed the Raksha's steeds and driver, severed too his bow in twain/ On the field of Nikumbhila, Lakshman's foeman headless rolled! [Dutt 129–130].

Left with no one to assist him, Ravana climbed into his golden chariot, Pushpak, and rode to the battlefield. To counter this, the god Indra loaned Rama a swan-drawn chariot:

"Rama mounted on the chariot clad in arms of heavenly sheen/ And he mingled in a contest mortal eyes have never seen!" (Dutt 135). The two began to fight. As was typical, the combat was short and decisive: Rama ended Ravana's life with a perfectly aimed Brahman dart to the heart. Good had triumphed once more, but that was not the end of the story. The faithful Sita was yet to be reunited with her hero husband. One would anticipate their reunion to be the happiest moment in the *Ramayana*. Alas, though, that was not the case.

What happened next is extremely difficult for someone raised in western culture to understand, and thus has given rise to some negative views of Rama in a number of critical studies. Instead of rushing up to his wife, embracing her and shedding a joyful tear or two, as Sita approached him Rama stood there like a stone carving, refusing to make eye contact. Sita was crushed. She knew that his silence meant that he doubted her fidelity. With a heavy heart, she requested Laksmana to prepare a funeral pyre: "When a righteous lord and husband turns his cold averted eyes/ Funeral flame dispels suspicion, honour lives when woman dies!" (Dutt 139). Did Rama then relent? Was he horrified at the thought of his beautiful wife being consumed by flames? The answer to both questions is an unqualified *no*: "Dark was Rama's gloomy visage and his lips were firmly sealed/ And his eye betrayed no weakness, word disclosed no thought concealed" (Dutt 139).

Sita's dismayed brother-in-law reluctantly obeyed her wishes. A huge funeral pyre was quickly built and, weeping uncontrollably, Laksmana set it on fire. Everyone watched in horror as the beautiful queen stepped into the flames as calmly as if she were entering her parlor. The only one in the entire crowd who remained dry eyed and silent was Rama. The flames continued to roar; the crowd continued to weep and moan. Suddenly, however, to everyone's delight the fire god, Agni, appeared above the funeral pyre, reached into the raging inferno and lifted the unscathed Sita gently out:

Slow the red flames rolled asunder, God of Fire incarnate came/ Holding in his radiant bosom fair Videha's sinless dame/ Not a curl upon her tresses, not a blossom on her brow/ Not a fiber of her mantle did with tarnished lustre glow! [Dutt 140].

Elated by this proof of Sita's innocence, Rama took her home in the swan-drawn chariot. Bharat, who had returned to Ayodhya to greet his returning brothers and sister-in-law, received them with the largest party the city of Ayodhya had ever seen:

Joy! joy! in bright Ayodhya gladness filled the hearts of all/ Joy! joy! as lofty music sounded in the royal hall/ Fourteen years of woe were ended, Rama now assumed his own/ And they placed the weary wand'rer on his father's ancient throne ... [Dutt 144].

So ends the *Ramayana*, the story of India's greatest mythical hero. He was so great, in fact, that with the passage of time, Valmiki, the author of Rama's exploits, himself became the subject of myth. According to one story, as a young man Valmiki was a heartless thief who was eventually converted to goodness by seven wise men, the Seven Sages. His transformation from brigand to holy man took an indeterminate number of years, perhaps thousands (time in mythology is more an idea than a reality), and was brought about by the constant repetition of the single word *Mara*. Somewhere along the line, however, instead of *Mara, Mara, Mara* he began to intone *Rama, Rama, Rama*. He later learned from yet another wise man that the person whose name he had been chanting endlessly was:

... a perfect man, possessing strength, aware of obligations, truthful in an absolute way, firm in the execution of vows, compassionate, learned, attractive, self-possessed, powerful, free from anger and envy but terror striking when roused....[19]

Today, this evaluation of Rama is open to question. Does a perfect person treat a loved one as badly as Rama treated his wife? What kind of learning and compassion did he demonstrate by blaming Sita for having been carried off by a raging madman? Would a perfect, compassionate, learned man have worried more about his own reputation than about his wife's well-being? Was it not callous to refuse to acknowledge her? How could he have allowed her to walk into a blazing fire? The explanation that is offered by those sympathetic to Rama is that he had no doubt she would come through the ordeal of fire unscathed, and only allowed her to do what she did to prove her innocence to everyone else. Unfortunately, this explanation does not appease the modern audience. It would be closer to the truth to say that Rama was a product of a society that looked upon women as possessions, disposable items easily replaced when they were no longer useful. Rama's own words add credence to this view. When Laksmana was wounded, he made the revealing statement that while he could find another wife equal to Sita he would never find a brother equal to Laksmana.[20] Moreover, in a sequel to the story told in the *Ramayana*, Rama eventually banishes Sita (who was pregnant at the time) because of the persistent rumors that she was unfaithful to him while with Ravana. In this later work, he has second thoughts and asks the poet, Valmiki, to bring her back to him. She returns, but her spirit has been broken by Rama's unjust suspicions, and the gods answer her prayers for death. Apparently, the author of this sequel did not consider Rama to be a model of perfection.

Whether or not one agrees with Valmiki that Rama was perfect, compassionate and learned, it is indisputable that he was an archetypal superhero. Moreover, his major flaw is less a character flaw than a defect in the cultural and literary milieus to which he was confined.[21] The hard truth is that treating women as equals, indeed, treating them as human beings, is not a requisite for entry into the circle of superheroes. Gilgamesh regarded rape as the preferred way of dealing with members of the opposite sex,[22] while Rustam, though no brutalizer of women, was more comfortable with one-night stands than with a loving, lasting relationship. It is the nature of the beast. A superhero craves adventure, not a comfortable little hut in the country, complete with fireplace and a favorite pair of slippers. His primary occupation is smashing down walls and butchering the enemy, not sharing his hopes and fears with a beloved mate. Many of our present day superheroes realize this, and as a result never marry. Imagine the Lone Ranger, Superman, Batman, or James Bond taking out the garbage or repairing a leaky faucet. Indeed, with few exceptions the heroes of old who did get married could not be considered ideal husbands, even by the most relaxed standards of their day. It was not unusual for them to leave their wives (and families) for periods of up to twenty years, as Odysseus did, and expect their wives to wait faithfully for them to return home.[23] Rama was not a bad person; he was, to use modern American idiom, simply a good old boy doing the superhero thing.

* * *

Using Otto Rank's criteria for the birth of a superhero as a starting point, it is possible to examine those factors that earn Rama the title of superhero.

1. When it comes to *miraculous births*, Rama's was second to none. Very few babies are simultaneously the incarnation of a god and the offspring of a king.
2. It is not necessary to stretch a point very far to assert that in one sense his conception was the result of a secret liaison; for, while Dasaratha and Kausalya are the biological parents, his birth was decided upon by a top-secret divine committee.

3. There was a prophecy warning that Rama's birth would result in tragedy — not for Rama's father or grandfather, but for the demon Ravana. The latter had been told that a monkey, a woman and a member of Ikshvahu lineage would be the cause of his death.[24] The monkey and the woman were respectively Hanuman and Sita and, since Rama was a member of the Ikshvahu clan, the prophecy was ultimately fulfilled.

4. Dasaratha did not banish Rama for selfish reasons, nor was Rama a baby when it took place; however, the act of sending Rama to the jungle for fourteen years can be properly viewed as a variation of the abandonment archetype.

5. Rama was saved by an animal twice, though not as a baby. In two instances during the war in Ceylon, Hanuman had to fetch magic herbs from the Himalayas to heal wounds that Ravana had inflicted on him.

6. There was no reconciliation necessary between Rama and his father, nor ever any question of revenge. At any rate, Dasaratha's premature, grief-induced death makes this a moot point.

7. Rama ultimately does achieve the rank and honor destined for him.

All in all, the myth of Rama satisfies most of the standards set by Rank for a hero's birth. Furthermore, as was true with the myths of Gilgamesh and Rustam, there are many other archetypal themes present, some already familiar. We know, for instance, that even before his birth, Rama was a *chosen one*. In his case it is a bit more complex, since he was not only chosen by the gods, but was himself a god in human form. As a dual being (the incarnation of Vishnu and the superhero Rama), he was a representative of yet another common archetype, that of the *man/god*. Gilgamesh also represents this archetype. As the offspring of a human and a divine parent, he, like Rama, shared both natures. Variations of this general archetype are also to be found in Greek, Roman, Norse and other mythologies, where gods and goddesses regularly appear on earth in the guise of humans. Jesus of Nazareth, viewed by Christians simultaneously as God and the son of God (man), also fits the *man/god* paradigm, as does Heracles, son of mighty Zeus and a mortal woman.

In Ravana, the myth of Rama offers a prime example of the nemesis, or *archenemy*, archetype. Critics have labeled the battle between Rama and Ravana an epic struggle between good and evil. While it is true, however, that Ravana was an awesome, worthy adversary, he was nevertheless an ambiguous representative of pure evil. After all, he did earn his indestructibility by performing unbelievably lengthy and painful penance, and this is scarcely the activity of a devil. It is also told that he married a young woman named Mandodari, and that he was a very good husband. In fact, "...It was the happiest marriage known" (Narayan 103). Hardly the kind of relationship one would expect a fiend to have. It is only on a simplistic level, then, that the struggle between Ravana and Rama can be considered a classic battle of good versus evil. The reason for the difficulty is that in Hindu philosophy the distinction between gods and demons is not clear-cut. As Wendy Doniger O'Flaherty writes:

> Gods and demons are "separate but equal," rather like two separate castes; each has his own job to do — the gods to encourage sacrifice, the demons to destroy it — but there is no immorality in the demons; they are merely doing their job.[25]

This view of the gods and demons places no moral superiority in either camp: "...it is only through battle that they can be made distinct, and the distinction consists no more and no less than that quality which distinguishes winners from losers" (O'Flaherty 62).

The complexity becomes even more apparent when one examines the reasons why this opposition between the two camps has always existed. What we do know is that in these myths the gods always win, although there is never a true end to the war. O'Flaherty points out that each myth begins with a battle between the gods and demons, a battle which very often seems to be going in favor of the latter. No matter how badly they are being beaten, however, the gods manage to develop the formula necessary to score an ultimate victory. But their victory is only a temporary one; in the subsequent myths the demons have regrouped and a new battle begins. Anyone who is familiar with horror films (from *Frankenstein* to *Friday the 13th*) recognizes this familiar scenario: the evil one (be it human or supernatural) is seemingly destroyed at the end, only to return in the sequel(s) with renewed and increased malevolence. In the last analysis, Hinduism is as hard put to solve the enigma of good and evil as are all other religious and philosophical schools.

The *sidekick* archetype is quite prominent in the epic of Rama, although in this case it is not a friend but a brother who fills the role. Laksmana is the ideal sidekick for a superhero, willing to subordinate his entire life to his leader and able to accept the latter's superiority in all areas without ever exhibiting an iota of jealousy. If, indeed, he did love Sita in more than a filial fashion, he certainly never gave any outward evidence of this. His declaration that Rama and Sita were like father and mother to him is very believable (Brockington 163). Even the most skeptical among us must accept at least the possibility that all of the sacrifices he made were made out of love and respect for his brother, not for any personal gain. That he is a magnificent warrior in his own right is also typical of the superhero sidekick. It is he who finally defeats and kills the rampaging Indrajit, who was second only to Ravana in stature on the opposing side. The degree of love between Rama and Laksmana is also characteristic of the superhero-sidekick relationship; that they were brothers merely intensifies this. The sidekick is a form of alter-ego or Doppelgänger, without whom the hero is not fully alive.[26]

Rama engaged in heroic adventures very early on in his life. Together with Laksmana, he rid the countryside of a number of destructive demons (Ions 54). This is the equivalent of the *monster-slaying* archetype, in spite of the fact that the designations *monster* and *demon* are not necessarily synonymous. Both categories share fantastic destructive powers, powers that no ordinary human could hope to successfully combat. The destruction of a fire-breathing dragon, therefore, cannot be viewed as a more heroic feat than the demolition of a super demon with magical powers (Ravana). When he defeated the voracious giant Khumbhakarna, moreover, Rama rid the world of a traditional monster.

A *transportation* archetype is not prominent in the myth of Rama. He never tamed a wild horse, as did Rustam and the Lone Ranger; he had no special jet-propelled vines that could zip him through the jungle faster than Tarzan and he would have had little use for a Ramamobile in the thick underbrush of the jungle. He is basically a super infantryman, dependent on his feet for locomotion. The incident that comes closest to representing the transportation archetype happens toward the end of the *Ramayana*, when the god Indra loans Rama his swan-drawn chariot for the final combat with Ravana. There is little doubt, however, that whether he had a swan chariot or not, Rama would have found a way to run rings around Pushpak, Ravana's renowned vehicle.

While he had no super transportation, however, Rama was equipped with not one but three *super weapons*. Neither Gilgamesh's huge battering club nor Rustam's mighty mace of Sam could compare with Rama's bow of Vishnu, quiver of Indra, or dart of Brahma. Armed with these, Rama was virtually an army unto himself.

There is no work in which the *suitor's test* archetype is more powerful than the example found in the *Ramayana*. The ease with which Rama shatters the colossal bow to win Sita's hand also makes it clear that Rama is the *chosen one* in the contest. There was never any doubt that Rama would succeed where so many other princes had failed.

Few female characters in mythology fit the *destructive female* archetype more aptly than the demoness Surpanakha. She has all of the necessary attributes: she is as vicious as an angry pit bull and meaner than Cinderella's stepmother. It was she who set the wheels in motion for the titanic battle between Ravana's demon armies and the man/monkey alliance led by Rama. As is often the case in the heroic myth, her desire to destroy Rama stems from his rejection of her crude advances. Thus, he joins Gilgamesh and Enkidu, who also learned how dangerous it could be to reject a determined female's advances.[27] Nor, as we shall see in later chapters, were they the only superheroes to feel the fury of a woman scorned.

The demoness, Surpanakha, is not the only example of the *destructive* female archetype in the *Ramayana*. Both Kaikeyi's maid and Kaikeyi herself share this negative distinction. The former instigates and the latter directs the scenario that results in Rama's banishment, thus setting the stage for the terrible events that follow. In their defense, however, it must be pointed out that neither of these women can be viewed as a demoness; at worst they are flawed human beings whose jealous natures indirectly led to bloodshed.

In a certain sense, Sita could also be classified as a *destructive female*. By abducting her, Ravana set the stage for his own destruction. However, she is no more guilty of the death and devastation that resulted from the war to recover her than one of Gilgamesh's rape victims would have been for the latter's death if he had died of a heart attack during a violent sexual assault. Sita is a victim, not a destroyer. It would be more accurate, therefore, to place her, alongside Helen of Troy, under a subheading in this archetype, which we will call the *abducted beauty* archetype.

Sita also occupies a second archetypal frame: the *faithful wife*. She and Odysseus' wife, Penelope, are the most famous mythical representatives of this group.

Two more archetypal motifs associated with the superhero are present in the *Ramayana*. The *journey to the realm of death* is one of them, although this perilous journey was made by the demon, Ravana, and not Rama. Ravana, a prime representative of the antihero, visited the other world and lived to tell the story. Unlike Enkidu, however, he was protected by the god, Brahma. This protection made it impossible for Yama, the god of the dead, to prevent Ravana from returning to the world of the living. Thus, as a result of his successful round trip, Ravana joins an elite circle of those who, at least temporarily, conquered death.[28]

The *transformation* archetype, the ability to assume the form of other beings, appears throughout the myth of Rama. Vishnu's reincarnation as Rama, Hanuman's frequent change of size, Maricha's transformation into an enchanted deer, Ravana and Indrajit's constant appearances in other forms — all of these are variations of this archetype. Indrajit's ability to become invisible is also related to the *transformation* archetype, although it is in itself a distinct category. In the ensuing chapters, Zeus, Odin, Väinämöinen and others will also demonstrate their mastery of metamorphosis.

In conclusion, while Rama may not be the perfect man some claim him to be, he meets the criteria for inclusion in the fraternity of superheroes and is a leading representative of the genre.

4

Egypt

World War II was raging in Europe. The jack-booted, swastika-adorned forces of evil seemed unstoppable. Almost daily, a stunned world read of overwhelming Nazi victories. America sat on the sidelines, rooting for the underdogs and wondering when it, too, would be put to the test of steel and fire. It was a dismal time for democracy. More champions for the cause of good were desperately needed. Superman, who had made his debut some two years before, could not do it alone. Fortunately, help was on the way.

In 1940, the comic book became the birthplace of a number of fascinating superheroes. Among them was an exotic figure called the Hawkman, alias Carter Hall, the reincarnation of an Egyptian Prince named Khufu. Written by Gardner Fox and drawn by Dennis Neville, the Hawkman began a career which, although interrupted several times by the vicissitudes of the marketplace, continues to this day. The heroic birdman was no shrinking violet. Garbed in a costume consisting of a pair of huge wings, a hawk mask, and what has been described as resembling a red bathing suit over bright green pantyhose, the Hawkman flew into American mythology by means of an antigravity belt made of "ninth" metal.

As this new superhero's character developed, alterations and additions were made. Carter Hall developed the ability to communicate with birds, and eventually acquired a female feathered sidekick, aptly named Hawkgirl (later promoted to Hawkwoman). The story line is that she is the reincarnation of Princess Shiera, lover of Prince Khufu.

Increasingly, there was an attempt on the part of the producers of the strip to introduce Egyptian elements into the story line, but these were rather primitive and more often than not inaccurate.[1] Following the cue of a famous winged ancestor, the Phoenix, Hawkman was discontinued, only to make several comebacks from comic book limbo. He appeared as a member of the Justice League of America in *All Star Comics* until 1951, and then, after being retired once more, he was returned to active duty in 1961, but with some very interesting changes. Reflecting the keen interest in space exploration that characterized the sixties, Hawkman was no longer cast as a reincarnated Egyptian prince, but as a visiting policeman from the planet Thanagar, with headquarters on an orbiting spaceship. This time, the winged superhero lasted until 1968, accompanied by his sidekick, Hawkgirl, who had also been resurrected. By 1968, however, the second American superhero era had passed, and Hawkman was demoted from a feature strip to a part-time player in a short-lived publication called *Atom and Hawkman*.

He was down, but not out. For a time, Hawkman rejoined the Justice League, and after another hiatus he was brought back again in the 1990s, this time as Carter Hall, originally from Egypt but reincarnated many times. The empowering substance originally called 9th metal became Nth metal in the new series and was imbued with even greater powers.[2]

While the creators of Hawkman made a superficial connection between their superhero and Egypt, it is obvious they did not do their homework as well as they might have. This is evidenced by the fact that they equated Hawkman with the canine god Anubis, rather than with the god they had in mind, the avenging hawk-god, Horus. Whatever the flaws, the Hawkman embodies a number of heroic archetypes. A reincarnation of the god Horus, Carter Hall, alias Prince Kufu, satisfies four hero archetypal categories: the *resurrection, chosen one, man/god,* and *miraculous birth* archetypes. In addition, he has an unusual kind of *super-transportation*: he is able to fly because of the gravity-defeating substance called seventh metal. During the course of his adventures, he wields many *super weapons,* including maces, crossbows, axes, swords, etc., and is often opposed by *archenemies,* the most prominent of whom is an exotically dressed villain called the Ghost. He also slays numerous *monsters,* as any good superhero must. The *transformation* archetype is also evident in the story of Hawkman, as it is in every story where the superhero has a mundane alter ego. It is only when Carter Hall dons his colorful costume and wings that he becomes the dreaded crime fighter, a combination *man-beast* such as those that are found frequently in ancient mythologies. The *love before first sight* archetype is satisfied by his relationship with the beautiful Shiera, whom he had known in a previous life. Moreover, from time to time the winged crusader is the beneficiary of *divine intervention*. As was true with his Egyptian ancestors, however, Hawkman has no *sidekick,* and undergoes no *suitor's test*.

How is it, though, that Egypt, the land of the beautiful and mysterious Nile, the mighty pharaohs, the incomparable pyramids and the sphinx, the land of Cleopatra, the land that produced the outstanding institution of learning at Heliopolis[3]— how is it that such a land cannot lay claim to a national superhero with the stature of a Gilgamesh, Rustam or Rama? The answer is a semantic one: whereas in other lands the superheroes were like gods, in Egypt the gods were the superheroes.

In his translation of the Egyptian funerary texts, *The Book of the Dead,* E.A. Wallis Budge discusses problem of defining the Egyptian gods. The difficulty centers on the translation of the word *neter*. In English, the translation of *neter* ranges all the way from "strong" to "God."[4] Unlike the gods in many other mythologies, the Egyptian gods, "...although held to be 'divine,'" were at the same time finite and mortal, and were endowed by the Egyptians with "love, hatred, and passions of every sort and kind..." (100).

At a later point in the texts, Budge makes the observation that, in spite of the fact that they had an entire pantheon of divinities,[5] the Egyptians were essentially monotheistic. Their belief in a single god was complicated, however, by the acceptance of a group of very powerful beings whom they called "gods." In spite of this seeming contradiction, they "...made in their minds a clear distinction between God and the 'gods'" (113). In this sense, the "gods" of Ancient Egypt were the superheroes of that culture, beings far more powerful than ordinary humans, but at the same time neither omniscient, omnipotent nor immortal. Who were these "gods"?

The Hawkman. Flash Comics, February 1940.

Creation Myth and Major Gods

The philosophers and theologians of Ancient Egypt had as much difficulty explaining the origin of the universe as did those of other cultures. The attempt to establish and define a prime creator has always led to further questions such as "Where was this creator before the creation?" and the classic inquiry "Who created the creator?" The Egyptian answers are as ambiguous as they are imaginative.

Scholars have determined that in approximately 1600 B.C. the Egyptians believed that in the beginning only the god Tem (Tum, Atum) existed. According to myth, by sheer effort of will Tem created the heavens, the earth, the gods, humans and every other living creature. If asked where Tem was when he began creation, the priests at Heliopolis most likely would have answered that he was in Nun (Nu), the designation for the primordial ocean (the equivalent of the Greek chaos). While Nun is designated in some texts as the father of the gods, he was more a concept than a personal god and "...he had neither temples nor worshippers."[6] As time passed, moreover, the sun god, Ra, replaced Nun as father of the gods. In chapter eight of *The Book of the Dead*, the following entry appears: "I have delivered the Eye of Horus which shineth with splendor on the brow of Ra, the Father of the gods" (Budge 479). Ra, as the father-god, was eventually also given credit for creation. This is how the creative process under the directorship of Ra has been described:

> He enclosed himself in the bud of the lotus until the day when, weary of his own impersonality, he rose by an effort of will from the abyss and appeared in glittering splendor under the name of Ra. He then bore Shu and Tefnut who, in their turn, gave birth to Geb and Nut, from whom issued Osiris and Isis, Set and Nephthys [Larousse 11].

The fraternal twins Shu and Tefnut (the latter in particular) and their children, Geb and Nut, were also more conceptual than anthropomorphic. Shu was the god of air, an Atlas-like figure whose job it was to hold up his daughter, Nut, who represented the sky. Tefnut was Shu's twin, wife, and constant companion, the goddess of dew and rain. Geb was the god of earth, the twin and mate of Nut. According to myth, Geb and Nut (sky and earth) were united at one time, but Ra was angered by their union and ordered Shu to force himself between them.[7] Eventually, Nut became king of earth, taking his father's place. (Shu had succeeded Ra.)

In spite of all his accomplishments, Ra himself does not fit into the category of superhero, for while he begins as an energetic, mighty, creative force, before long we see him depicted as a pitiful old man with spittle running down the side of his mouth. He became a tired, senile god, so disillusioned by the evils of humans that, although their creator, he wanted nothing further to do with them. He was carried each morning on the back of the goddess Nut (who changed herself into a cow to accommodate him); he then rode across the heavens from east to west, born each morning as a young child and dying each evening as an old man. It is not until some three generations after Ra that Egypt produced gods who can be considered superheroes.

Ra's great-grandchildren, Osiris, Isis, Seth and Nephthys, display the archetypes that are found in heroic epics. Indeed, there was an actual historical connection, vague to be sure, between at least two of these "gods" and actual historical personalities. According to historians, in approximately 7500 B.C Egypt was invaded by Asiatic hordes under the leadership of a warrior named Seth. The invasion was halted and its army defeated by an Egyptian king named Osiris. It is fairly certain that the god Osiris evolved from this human

monarch and was eventually promoted to the status of god by time and legend. He is often referred to as the fourth man/god (Pharaoh) of Egypt. Similarly, the historical Seth became the leading antihero of Egyptian mythology.

Osiris was indisputably the greatest of the Egyptian gods; he was born in Thebes on the first day,[8] to the accompaniment of a mysterious voice that proclaimed him to be the "Universal Lord." Ra, who had cursed his granddaughter for marrying her twin brother, rejoiced at the birth of his first great-grandchild and immediately designated him as his successor. Osiris lived up to that trust. In later texts, the relative newcomer is said to have surpassed the sun god in stature so that "...the priests of Ra were obliged to acknowledge the supremacy of Osiris..." (Budge 1). One had only to look at Osiris to know that he was worthy of this stature. This is how he was described:

> He was a tall man and slender, as all devout Egyptians longed to be so that their bodies might fit lightly around their immortal souls. On his head he wore the lofty white crown of Egypt with an ostrich feather on each side of it because these feathers are as light as the truth. A beautiful plaited beard fell from his chin as befitted a great and powerful ruler. Around his neck and shoulders he wore a white collar like necklace of precious gems, ivory and symbolic beads. Wherever he stepped grew a lily.... His naked body from ankles to wrists was beautifully decorated with crimson painted flowers. He was powerful and black, for black is the color of youth.[9]

Osiris quickly demonstrated that he was also a super teacher. He not only led his people away from the prevalent practice of cannibalism, but also taught them to farm the land with agricultural tools he had personally designed. Very soon his human pupils were able to produce bread, wine and beer, and through his instruction they also learned the rules of religious ritual. The great Greek writer, Plutarch, describes what Osiris accomplished:

"And they say that Osiris, when he was king of Egypt, drew them [the Egyptians] off from a beggarly and bestial way of living, by showing them the use of grain, and by making them laws, and teaching them to honor the Gods...."[10] But Osiris was not satisfied with teaching alone. He went on to prove the falsity of the saying "Those who can, do; those who can't, teach" by inventing two types of flute, building many towns and cities, and providing a legal code for the people. At one point in his life, in true superhero fashion he decided that it was time to seek adventure. His conquests, however, were quite different from those of the superhero warriors whom we have already examined. Osiris' weapons were not maces, bows and arrows, magic darts, or huge clubs, but because of their unusual nature they were even more impressive. We learn that "Osiris was the enemy of all violence and it was by gentleness alone that he subjected country after country, winning and disarming their inhabitants by songs and the playing of various musical instruments" (Larousse 16). By means of these unorthodox "weapons," Osiris was able to spread civilization not only through Asia but across the entire earth. Several of his adventures are worth recounting here, as they provide us with a fuller portrait of this gentle conqueror.

Before Osiris set out on his proselytizing mission he assigned the task of running the government to his twin and wife, the beautiful goddess Isis, whom "...you could see in the golden light of sunrise, clothed in the brilliant green robes of a new day, the lady bountiful who fills one's fields with crops and one's cradle with a newborn son" (Goodrich 27). The remarkable relationship between Osiris and Isis is underlined by the fact that they had made love while both were fetuses in their mother's (the sky) womb, a unique event in any mythology.

Opposite: **Egyptian Creation — The creation of the world.**

When he returned from his world tour, Osiris immediately learned that his trust in Isis had not been misplaced. Under her capable regency, Egypt had flourished. But all was not well; there was trouble brewing in the land on the Nile. The evil, red-haired Seth, from whom all of the discord and destructive forces on earth stem,[11] had made his decision to destroy his brother, Osiris. Why did he come to such a decision? There are two primary reasons offered.

The first myth attributes Seth's hatred for Osiris to his suspicion that Osiris had impregnated Nephthys, his wife and sister to both gods. And his suspicion was not unfounded. Osiris and Nephthys, the latter previously thought to be barren, had made love during one of Osiris' adventures. As a result of this interlude, Nephthys became pregnant and eventually gave birth to the god Anubis, who came to the world in the form of a dog. Undoubtedly, poor Nephthys was very surprised when she saw her unusual offspring, but her fear of Seth's reaction if he were to discover her transgression was even greater than her surprise and so "...in her terror of her husband Seth [she] had exposed the child among the reeds and left him to die" (Goodrich 30). Contrary to expectations, however, Anubis did not die. The abandoned puppy-god was eventually discovered and rescued by his aunt, Isis.

What does one do when one finds an abandoned puppy who also happens to be the illegitimate son of one's mate? At best, it would be a severe emotional shock. Isis, however, not only remained calm, but "...she brought it up; and he afterwards became her guardsman and follower, being named Anubis, and reported to guard the Gods as dogs do men" (Plutarch 77).

Anubis eventually learned to speak, and after proper training became a very successful medical doctor and embalmer, a canine combination of Digger O'Dell and Doctor Welby.[12]

The second and more powerful reason for Seth's decision to eliminate his brother was his desire to rule in Osiris' place. Unlike Rama's loyal brothers who had no designs on his throne, Seth was tired of living in his brother's shadow, and so he devised a simple but very deadly plot. First, he gathered together seventy-three accomplices, among whom was an Ethiopian queen. Then he announced that he was having a gala dinner party and invited Osiris.

At the party, there was excessive eating and drinking, much spirited conversation and, to liven up the evening even more, Seth suggested they play a game. The game he had in mind was one he had devised specifically for that occasion, one with a deadly outcome.

Osiris was probably quite impressed and interested when his brother brought out the beautiful hand-carved cedar chest ornamented in gold and jewels and shaped like a human figure. Perhaps if the setting had been different, he would have noticed that the ornate chest was strikingly similar to a coffin; but it was a party, and death was far from his thoughts. At any rate, when Seth explained how the game was played, Osiris eagerly agreed to play along.

The rules of the game were simple: each player had to climb into the chest and stretch out comfortably. The one who best fit into it would win it as a prize. One after the other the coconspirators took their turns, but none seemed to fit into the enclosure very well. Finally, it was Osiris' turn. Gently, he eased himself into the chest and, wonder of wonders, he fit perfectly! He was the undisputed winner of the game.

Osiris never suspected that the coffin was custom made. Plutarch writes: "Having pri-

***Opposite:* The Number One Egyptian god, Osiris.**

vately taken the measure of Osiris' body Seth framed a curious ark, very finely beautified and just of the size of his body..." (Plutarch 76). This was no Cinderella story, and the beautiful cedar receptacle certainly no glass slipper. As soon as Osiris made himself comfortable in the coffin, Seth and his accomplices nailed down the lid. Next, they sealed the seams with molten lead to make certain that their victim would suffocate, and when they were satisfied with their handiwork they carried the coffin to the Nile and unceremoniously threw it into the churning water. Thus, Osiris went to sleep with the fishes. But not for long.

Poor pregnant Isis was probably worried sick as she waited for her husband to come home, fearing perhaps that he had imbibed too much Egyptian beer at the party and gotten into a chariot accident. Her worst fears were dwarfed, however, when she was told that Osiris had been assassinated by their brother, Seth, and his body thrown into the Nile. In an outburst of grief that dwarfed similar displays by Gilgamesh and Achilles upon the deaths of their friends, Isis wept and wailed and tore her hair; she moaned and groaned until her voice began to fail. But she was not one to passively accept the unacceptable, and when she had no more tears to shed, she set out to find her husband's body.

After a long and arduous search (it was during this time that she found and rescued her nephew-stepson, Anubis), the distraught widow finally located the coffin containing Osiris' body. Having washed up onto land, it was embedded in the trunk of a tamarisk tree that had been used to prop up the palace roof of the Phonecian king Malcander.[13] Isis' grief upon discovering her husband's coffin is described by Plutarch: "...she threw herself down upon the chest, and her lamentations were so loud, that the younger of the king's two sons died for very fear..." (Plutarch 78). What transpired next was miraculous.

Isis was so emotionally wrought up when she discovered her husband's corpse that she began to embrace it again and again, bathing it in her tears. Gradually, a change took place. Whereas at first utter despair and bottomless pain characterized her embraces, before long she was hugging Osiris more in passion than grief. She fondled her dead husband so passionately that he was "...miraculously re-animated by her charms" (Larousse 19). The eventual outcome of Osiris' reanimation was predictable. Without going into the details, suffice it to say that Osiris must be placed in the record book as the first and only individual who ever made love both before his birth and after his death. When the allotted amount of time following this necrophilic interlude had passed, a child was born, one as extraordinary as might be expected given the circumstances of his conception.

The difficult birth is described as follows: "...like a plain peasant woman she labored to deliver her child, the child of her love for Osiris. Straining and moaning, the goddess suffered, but the baby could not be born" (Goodrich 33). Unfortunately, Isis had no red Simurgh feather with which to summon the magical Persian bird to perform a C-section, but she was a goddess with divine connections. When it appeared as if the situation was hopeless:

... two gods appeared and smeared her temples with blood, symbol of life. They brought her amulets also.... With the help of their incantations the body of Isis burst open and out sprang her beautiful son, flooding the world with light just as in the darkness before morning the golden sun suddenly appears dazzling and glorious over the eastern rim of a black world. Thus was finally born the son of Osiris, he who was awaited, Horus the hawk, the avenger [Goodrich 33].

In view of the conception and birth described above, one cannot be surprised that the ancestor of America's Hawkman was destined to accomplish extraordinary things during his life.

Opposite: **The Egyptian goddess Isis.**

The Egyptian god Anubis (the Dog God), Son of Osiris and Nephthys.

Had Isis been an ordinary human widow, she would have given Osiris a proper burial and gotten on with her life; but she was a goddess. Since she feared what Seth might do if he learned that she had located Osiris' body, upon her return to Egypt she hid the coffin in the swamp and remained there long enough to bring up her newborn hawk-baby. The situation wasn't perfect, to be sure, but at least she had kept her family together.

Apparently, however, she did not hide Osiris' remains well enough, and after a time Seth found them. Not satisfied by the fact that Osiris was dead, the red-headed devil-god proceeded to cut his body into fourteen pieces. When he had finished his crude dissection, he threw the pieces into the Nile at widely separated locations, certain that this was the end of his hated brother. But he was wrong. He had not counted on Isis' love and determination. "When Isis heard of this she took a boat made of papyrus ... and sailing about she collected the fragments of Osiris's body" (Budge 56). Then, demonstrating skills worthy of a world class microsurgeon, Isis did what all the king's horses and all the king's men were unable to do with Humpty Dumpty: she meticulously reassembled the body of her brother-husband. Unfortunately, however, she had found only thirteen pieces. She was one piece short. One very important piece! The reconstituted Osiris, thanks to the undignified appetite of some Nile fishes, was missing his sexual organ! As Plutarch relates it, "...of all Osiris's members, Isis could never find his private part, for it had been presently flung into the river Nile, and the lepidotus, sea-bream, and pike eating of it, these were for that reason more scrupulously avoided by the Egyptians than any other fish." But Isis remained undaunted: "...in lieu of it, [she] made its effigies, and so consecrated the phallus for which the Egyptians to this day observe a festival" (Plutarch 80). A phallic festival! And some people think that the Oktoberfest in Munich and the Mardi Gras in New Orleans are risqué.

Another account of this episode contends that after Isis had finished putting Osiris back together, she, Nephthys, Anubis, Horus, and Thoth[14] got together and "...performed for the first time in history the rites of embalmment which restored the murdered god to eternal life" (Larousse 18–19). Yet a third version reports that not Isis, but Osiris' son, Horus, pieced him back together:

> Because he was a god who had very special and secret knowledge of both black and white magic, Horus assembled together the parts of his father's body. Slowly and tediously he joined bone to bone and flesh to flesh until there appeared before him the very likeness of the great Osiris.... However, one piece of the body had not been recovered..." [Goodrich 37].

Poor Osiris. No matter which version we accept, he still winds up missing that very important piece.

In the next episode of the Osiris myth one reads of a furious Seth, resolved to find and punish Isis. At one point he ordered a poisonous scorpion to inflict a fatal sting on the baby, Horus. But while the scorpion did manage to locate and sting Horus as ordered, the mission was thwarted by the intervention of the gods Ra and Thoth. To keep the scorpion's poison from killing Horus, Ra halted time long enough for Thoth to teach Isis an antidotal incantation: "As she uttered the incantations the wound on Horus' body opened and the poison oozed out" (Goodrich 36).

At another point, and here the chronology is very unclear, Seth managed to capture Isis and place her in a dark prison. In that instance she was rescued by her nephew/step-son, the dog-god Anubis.

In the meantime, Horus was quickly becoming a full-fledged superhero. As is common in mythology, there are some contradictions evident in this story. For one thing, we

The Bier of Osiris: Anubis ministering to his father, Osiris. At Osiris' head is his sister/wife, Isis, and at his feet, his sister, Nephthys.

have been told that Osiris was against any kind of warfare; yet, in *The Book of the Dead*, Budge says: "But now Horus had grown up, and being encouraged to the use of arms by Osiris, who returned from the other world, he went out to do battle..." (Budge 56). Horus had learned well and was physically suited for the task before him. The avenging hawk had become "...tall like his father, strong in arm and limb, and skilled in the weapons of war..." (Goodrich 36). His first show of strength took place when he and his men rescued a young woman from a huge serpent that was pursuing her. But his conquest of the serpent was child's play compared to two celebrated encounters with his evil uncle, Seth.

The initial battle took place shortly after the restoration of Osiris' body to 92.9 percent (13/14) of its pre-dissected form. After having satisfied himself that his services were no longer needed, Horus began to search for Seth in order to avenge his father. Finally, he located his prey, and "Sharper than a hawk and swifter in his course, the furious Horus pounced down upon the mottled Seth and with his first burst of strength threw him high up in the air, shrieking vengeance..." (Goodrich 38). For three days and nights the two fought continuously, the entire course of action recorded in gory detail by the Ibis-headed scribe, Thoth. At last, Horus overpowered his uncle, chained him up carefully and delivered him to his mother, Isis.

Seth was lucky, considering what might have happened next. Had Isis been anything like Kriemhild, whom we shall get to know in a later chapter dealing with the German epic *Nibelungenlied*[15], she would have made short work of the red-headed murderer who had dissected her husband. But Isis was a soft touch for a hard luck story, and Seth was clever. He used every trick in the book to save his neck. He warned her that Egypt was doomed without him, showed her the wounds he had received in the battle with her son, and when none of that worked he appealed to her feelings of kinship, reminding her that it was not proper for a sister to keep her brother in chains. (He failed to mention the fact that he had killed his brother.) She weakened at this last argument and set him free.

Later, Horus went to check on his prisoner. To say that he became angry when he learned that Isis had set Seth free would be akin to saying that Julius Caesar was peeved by the actions of Brutus and Cassius on the Roman Senate steps. Horus was furious. Livid. So enraged that he "...laid violent hands upon his mother, and plucked off her head!"! (Plutarch 81). Thus the goddess Isis made her exit from life; or at least that is what would have happened had she not been a goddess.

In his description of Isis, Larousse writes the following: "Occasionally ... her head-dress is a disk, set between cow's horns.... Finally we sometimes find her represented with a cow's head on a human body" (Larousse 19). The reason Isis is depicted in that manner is given us by mythology. Fortunately, Thoth was in the vicinity during Isis' decapitation, and before she had time to realize what had happened to her, the god/magician performed an instant head transplant, substituting on Isis' shoulders the head of the ancient cow goddess Hathor. Talk about bovine inspiration! Isis was also fortunate in another way. Since her family included a dog and a hawk (Anubis and Horus), Isis could hardly be rejected because she was a cow. One only wonders what poor Hathor thought of the whole episode, having donated her only head to save another's life. Then again, in her headless state she probably wasn't able to think at all.

The second battle between Horus and Seth was even more ferocious than the first had been. This time Isis aided her son, and it was fortunate for him that she did. Seth fought so fiercely and so well that he was able to tear out one of Horus' eyes. With his mother's help, however, the avenging hawk managed to retrieve his eye and send Seth fleeing for his life. It was over. Horus had avenged his father. According to one myth, Seth was castrated; another myth is kinder, relegating to him the role of god of chaos and thunder after his defeat.

But Horus had one more task to accomplish. Returning to the temple where his father's body lay:

> Reverently he approached Osiris and embraced him, thus transferring to that god some of the power of his double spirit, or ka. In his right hand Horus bore the eye that he had snatched from Seth. Osiris sat on a splendid throne, bearing the scepter of royalty. Gently opening the lips of Osiris, Horus fed him the eye, and Osiris rose from the dead and lived again! [Goodrich 38].

The scene ends with Osiris climbing a ladder to heaven; there he is judged to be pure by the other gods and admitted to their ranks: "As Osiris advanced over the crystal floor of heaven, the Boat of a Million Years came to a slow halt. Its crew of gods hailed him as the Lord of a Million Years. For ever afterward Osiris ruled the earth, crossing it every day in his solar boat and at night crossing the Milky Way of stars" (Goodrich 40). Horus the Hawk[16] becomes his father's successor on earth and the resurrected Osiris assumes the role of god of the dead. It is he who from that time on has judged the souls of the departed, admitting those who are worthy to the Isles of the Blessed.

Ibis the Invincible

In February 1940, just one month after the appearance of Hawkman, Egypt served as the inspiration for a second American comic book superhero: Ibis the Invincible. Created

Horus, the Hawk God, son of Isis and Osiris.

by Bill Parker, Ibis was modeled after the brilliant god Thoth. Whereas most other heroes relied primarily on physical and military strength, Ibis was a master of magic. Possessor of a wondrous device called the Ibisstick, given to him by Thoth, this super magician battled the forces of evil in some one hundred and fifty-five issues of Whiz Comics and in six issues of his own comic book. In addition, he made many guest appearances in other Fawcett publications.

The origin story of Ibis contains a number of the archetypes characteristic of the superhero genre. An ancient Egyptian Prince named Amentep (alias Ibis), was captured by the evil Black Pharaoh, but with the aid of the Ibisstick (a variation of a magic wand), he was able to defeat and destroy his nemesis. Unfortunately, however, the Black Pharaoh had succeeded in placing a four thousand year spell on Princess Taia, the woman Prince Amentep loved. Distraught by the fact that his beloved would not wake up for forty centuries, Prince Amentep used his Ibisstick to put himself to sleep for the same length of time. Ibis first appears in Whiz Comics, February 1940; we learn what happened when he woke up in the year 1940 to begin his superhero career, and how he uses the magical Ibisstick to battle vampires, werewolves, demons, and every other variety of supernatural evil imaginable, as well as human demons such as the Nazis.

In the early 1950s, the appeal of superheroes temporarily diminished, causing Fawcett to discontinue the publication of Ibis and other of their previously popular characters. Two decades later, DC Comics purchased the rights and reintroduced Ibis and Taia as members of the Shazam Squadron of Justice. They and other former Fawcett heroes dwelled on a world called Earth-S. Later, they were included in the Golden Age of DC Universe, along with a number of other war heroes.

Ibis has since enjoyed other incarnations, and most likely in the future the durable Egyptian prince will continue to combat evil with his magic.

* * *

The Egyptian myths, particularly those centered on the ancient Egyptian divine trinity of Isis, Osiris and Horus, incorporate many of the elements familiar to the superhero genre. It has already been noted that although these individuals are designated gods, the Egyptian deities were, in fact, traditional national superheroes. As a starting point, let us look again at the standards set by Otto Rank for the birth of a hero. Rank said of the hero that:

1. He is the child of most distinguished parents.
2. His origin is preceded by difficulties: continence, prolonged barrenness, or secret intercourse of the parents.
3. During or before the pregnancy there is a prophecy warning that his birth threatened danger to his father or to the latter's representative.
4. As a rule he is abandoned.
5. He is saved by animals or lowly people and suckled by a female animal or by a humble woman.
6. When grown, he finds his parents in a highly versatile manner and takes revenge on or is acknowledged by his father.
7. He ultimately achieves rank and honors.

In Egyptian mythology the above criteria are fairly well satisfied by the gods, though not by any one individual. Examining the various leading characters, we come up with the following observations:

Ibis awakens Princess Taia. Origin story of Ibis the Invincible. Fawcett, *Whiz* #2. (DC Comics.)

1. All are children of most distinguished parents, since all have divine parents.
2. All meet this criterion: Geb and Nut conceived Osiris, Isis, Seth and Nephthys secretly, because Ra was against their union; Anubis was also the result of a secret interlude between Osiris and the previously barren Nephthys; Horus' birth is preceded by extreme difficulty; Osiris had to be brought back from the dead so that he could impregnate Isis.
3. There were no prophesies warning of the births of any of the Egyptian superhero/gods, but Ra had initially issued a curse against Nut's offspring (Larousse 16).
4. Anubis was abandoned in the desert by Nephthys.
5. The animal motif takes a different form in Egyptian mythology. The superhero/gods themselves take on the characteristics of animals to one extent or another: Anubis has the physical appearance of a dog; Horus has a hawk's face; Isis eventually sports the head of a cow.
6. Horus first met his father under extremely unusual circumstances (the latter was in fourteen pieces). He attains vengeance not on but for Osiris.
7. Osiris was recognized by Ra as his heir, and in turn recognized Horus as his replacement.

A similar picture emerges as we view other Egyptian archetypes indigenous to the realm of the superhero, although there are notable exceptions. Absent, for example, are any specific *transportation* or *sidekick* archetypes. Neither Osiris, Isis nor their son, Horus, the three who come closest to being traditional representatives of the superhero genre, have any extraordinary means of transportation. We are informed, however, that Horus was well aware of the need for such. Plutarch tells us that after Osiris had "...trained Horus in the discipline of war," he asked his son to name the most useful animal that one could have in a battle. Horus replied that a horse "...would serve best to cut off and disperse a flying enemy" (Plutarch 80–81). But there is no further mention of this, so it is possible that he discovered his wings and no longer had any need for an Egyptian version of Rakhsh or Silver.

The absence of *sidekicks* in Egyptian mythology is due to the fact that the Egyptian superhero/gods are basically loners. Each performs his or her tasks independently of the others. Osiris, for example, goes off alone to civilize the world, while Isis remains home to take care of the country. While it is true that in the final confrontation Horus and Isis fight together as a team against Seth, they do so as mother and son, and can hardly be considered sidekicks.

Another archetype absent in Egyptian god/superhero myths is the *super weapons* archetype. In the case of Osiris there is no reference to offensive weaponry. As has already been pointed out, he was a peaceful conqueror, armed only with poetry and musical instruments, not with anything remotely resembling the mace of Sam or the dart of Brahma. His son, Horus, was well versed in the use of weapons, but there is no mention of any particular super weapon that he used in his battles with Seth. That this lack of destructive hardware is not unique to Egyptian mythology will be seen in the chapter dealing with Finland's great heroic epic.

Two other traditional archetypes generally associated with the superhero are also lacking in Egyptian myths: the *love before first sight* and the *suitor's test* archetypes. One could indulge in semantic gymnastics and assert that by copulating before their birth, Isis and Osiris literally experienced "love before first sight," but this would be more in the letter than in the spirit of the archetype. With regard to a *suitor's test*, this archetype is lacking for one simple reason: all of the couples (Shu/Tefnut; Geb/Nut; Osiris/Isis; Seth/Nephthys) are brother and sister, three of them twins. The other leading characters, Ra, Horus, Anubis and Thoth, were, as far as we know, bachelors.

The *man/god* archetype is at the core of Egyptian mythology. The primary personalities are presented as divinities, and yet it is the human aspect of their beings that is most compelling. The Egyptian gods do not possess two powers that we have come to expect in our celestial beings: omniscience and invulnerability. In fact, they sometimes seem naïve and lack the most elementary defensive skills. For example, Seth was able to deceive and murder Osiris; Isis could not prevent her son from tearing off her head; a severely wounded Seth was chased ignominiously from the battlefield, and Horus lost an eye in battle. But in this respect the "gods" of Egypt differ from those of other cultures only in degree. The Norse gods were at least as limited and flawed as the Egyptian, the Greek gods as essentially human, though with fewer physical limitations,[17] and the gods of Rome merely faded facsimiles of the Greek.

The *archenemy* archetype is alive and well in Egyptian mythology. Osiris' nemesis, Seth, is as much a demon as Ravana. He stands in opposition to the forces of good represented by Osiris, Isis, and Horus, just as Ravana countered the purity of Rama, Sita and Laksmana. And like Ravana, it was a woman who eventually led to his undoing. Both Sita and Isis, although loving, faithful wives, are representative of the *destructive female* archetype in that they were indirectly instrumental in the destruction of their husbands' *archenemies*.

Other familiar archetypes are also evident in the myths of Egypt. While none of their superhero/gods were as active in the area of *monster-slaying* as Gilgamesh, Rustam or Rama were, Horus did indulge in such activity at least once. In fact, the incident was so remarkable that it provided the stimulus for an ancient Egyptian holiday. The myth is as follows:

There was a beautiful young woman named Theuris, who had formerly been the concubine of Seth. When Theuris shifted her loyalty to Horus, Seth sent a huge serpent after her and she would have been killed had the hawk-god not flown to the rescue. With his customary aplomb, Horus dismembered the serpent and rescued the damsel in distress. Plutarch writes that the Egyptians "...still fling a certain cord into the midst of the room and chop it to pieces in memory of the deed" (Plutarch 81).

It seems strange to discuss *divine intervention* in the case of the Egyptian myths, since the superheroes themselves were gods. And yet, this archetype is present. We have already seen at least two instances where gods intervened to save other gods from destruction. When Horus was bitten by a scorpion, Ra stopped time so that Thoth could teach Isis the incantation necessary to save his life. In the second instance, Thoth took charge to save the day when Horus angrily decapitated his mother. There are many such instances in Egyptian mythology, as well as in other mythologies. This clearly demonstrates that the gods are formed in human image.

Two other familiar archetypes are worthy of mention before concluding the discussion of Egyptian superheroes: the *transformation* and the *superhero versus death (resurrection)* archetypes. Although there are many specific myths in which they used this capability, a study of the Egyptian myths informs us that both Osiris and Isis were able to metamorphose into diverse forms. Larousse says of Osiris: "He appeared in the forms of various animals..." (17). As for Isis, during the time she was taking care of Queen Astarte's and King Malcander's baby, she often "...would be turned into a swallow, and in that form would fly around..." (Plutarch 78).

As has already been noted, Osiris conquered death both in the myth where he makes love to Isis while a corpse and when he is *resurrected*. This conquest of death places Osiris in a select company that includes such diverse beings as Heracles, Odysseus, Aeneas, and Jesus of Nazareth.

The American comic book offshoots of the Egyptian superhero/gods also display a number of familiar archetypes.

Ibis the Invincible had a *miraculous birth* (actually, a miraculous *resurrection* after 4,000 years of suspended animation), wielded a *super weapon* par excellence (the Ibisstick), which he alone had been *chosen* to acquire; he was a *monster killer* of the first degree, dispatching as he did hordes of vampires and other supernatural *archenemies*.

What sets Ibis apart from the superheroes we have examined up till now is that he was one of the first superheroes to have an inanimate *sidekick*, in his case the Ibisstick. This phenomenon has been heightened in the present time, with slight variation. Today, the human half of a number of superhero duos is often subordinate to an inanimate sidekick that is a product of technology.[18]

5

Greece

A journey to ancient Greece uncovers the roots of western civilization. After thousands of years, the myths and philosophies that formed the foundation of that great civilization remain as intriguing and profound today as they were at their inception. Virtually every area of our lives, be it psychiatry, medicine, sports, or science,[1] bears the imprint of that time long ago when gods and human beings made love to each other, broke bread together, and at times fought shoulder to shoulder with their human subjects, often against each other, in lengthy, gruesome wars. Greece also produced a number of the most memorable superheroes in human history; but before there can be any meaningful discussion of these, one must first examine the theological framework within which they performed.

Creation Myths

The Ancient Greeks had a number of myths to explain the origins of existence, none as imaginative and psychologically telling as the one that appears in the work of the eighth century B.C. didactic poet, Hesiod. He gives the following account of life's origin:

In the beginning there was a formless void called Chaos, from which sprung Gaea (Earth, often called Ge), Tartarus (a fearsome, underground realm), Erebus (the darkest part of Tartarus, similar in some ways to the Christian hell), Eros (Love), and dark Night. After an unspecified period of time, Night united with Erebus to produce the shining upper atmosphere, called Aether. Not to be outdone, Gaea brought forth Uranus (the heavens), the Mountains, and Pontus (the sea). Then, with the expert assistance of Eros, Gaea mated with Uranus and eventually gave birth to twelve gigantic beings, the Titans: Iapetus, Oceanus, Hyperion, Tethys, Phoebe, Rhea, Themis, Mnemosyne, Coeus, Crius Theia, and, last but not least, Kronos (Cronus). Several of the Titans are worthy of special note.

Hyperion is, in essence, the Greek equivalent of the Egyptian sun god, Ra. Like his Egyptian counterpart, he travels across the sky each day from east to west in a beautiful golden chariot that is drawn by a team of powerful horses. (Poor Ra, mounted on a converted cow, must seethe with envy each morning when he sees Hyperion's luxurious mode of travel.) Hyperion is often confused with his son, Helios, who at times was also referred to as the god of the sun.

By far the most important Titans are the brother/sister, husband/wife team, Kronos and Rhea, since they were the parents of Zeus and his company of divine Olympians. But the titanic lovers were not able to begin their family until they had overcome some very difficult obstacles. Their father, Uranus (heaven), had the annoying routine of seizing his children right after their births and returning them to the depths of their mother, Gaea (earth).

Hesiod gives us the reason for Uranus' seemingly bizarre action. He explains that in addition to the Titans, Gaea had given birth to a number of other "beings" who were less than appealing. When Uranus saw the Cyclopes, each with a single eye in the middle of his forehead, and the Hecatonchires, ugly beings with a hundred arms and hands and fifty heads, he was so shaken that he sent them right back (in)to their mother. Perhaps he did the same with the newly born Titans out of habit; he may have assumed that they were as monstrous as their predecessors and didn't bother to examine them before returning them. Perhaps he simply did not want to have to compete with children for Gaea's affection.

Gaea's maternal instinct made her increasingly upset by her husband's behavior. When she could tolerate it no more, she devised what Hesiod calls a "crafty and evil scheme." Shouting down within herself, she asked for a volunteer among her buried children to punish father Uranus. To her joy, Kronos volunteered. What happened next is enough to make even a god shudder. Out of a new metal she had invented just for that purpose (called gray adamant), Gaea fashioned a huge sickle with jagged teeth and gave it to Kronos. Then, after hiding him carefully, she waited.[2] Since she was familiar with her husband's amorous nature, she knew that she would not have a long wait. Hesiod described what happened next:

> So when ... great Ouranos came and lay on/ Gaia, desiring her love, closely embracing her, stretching/ everywhere over, then his son from where he was hiding/ stretched out his left hand, and with the right hand wielding the sickle/ jagged and long, quickly cut off his father's/ genital parts....[3]

Ouch! Poor Uranus should have known that a mother whose young are threatened is one of the most potent forces in the universe. Not only had he been castrated, but to add insult to injury each drop of blood that fell to the ground from his severed genitals turned into another grotesque offspring: mighty giants and the dreaded Erinnyes.[4] Finally, Kronos seized the bloody genitals that had been his father's and heaved them into the ocean where, instead of sinking or being devoured by hungry fish as one might expect, something miraculous happened.

> ... Then shining white '*aphros*'/ 'foam,' arose from the flesh of the god, and in this a girl/ came into being..../ Gods and men called her by various names: Aphrodite because she came from aphros..../ From the beginning she was allotted both among mortals/ and the immortals the following portion, and these were her honors:/ flirtatious conversations of maidens, smiles and deceits ... [Frazer 36–37].

Thus, Aphrodite, the goddess of love was "born," a divine siren who becomes a leading player in the Golden Age of Greek superheroes.

No people were more astute students of life than were the ancient Greeks. Unfortunately, many of the unpleasant conclusions they reached as a result of their studies are as valid today as they were during their time. Sociologists and psychologists of the present often write and speak as if they have made important new discoveries in the field of human behavior when they produce detailed, jargon-laden papers and lengthy volumes detailing the results of their studies. One such example is in the area of child and spouse abuse. Recent studies indicate that more often than not persons who were abused as children, or came from homes in which violence prevailed, repeat the pattern when they become parents or spouses. There is an ongoing argument between the "experts" who attribute primary blame for these and other personality defects to heredity, and those who see environment as the culprit. However, regardless of which side one takes in this debate, one fact remains: children often repeat the evils of their parents. The ancient Greeks never conducted such studies, but they were well aware of this phenomenon and illustrated it in many of their myths. The story of Kronos is a case in point.

Kronos did not seize each of Rhea's babies as it was born and reinsert it into her as his father had done to his mother. After all, he did not want to suffer the same fate as his father. He had a better idea, although it was actually a variation on the theme. While Uranus had been motivated by aesthetics, Kronos, whose sickle feat had earned him the leadership role among the Titans, was determined to maintain his supremacy, even more so when he became aware of a disturbing prophecy. Hesiod describes it: "For he had learned of the future from Gaia and star-studded Ouranos/ how he was destined to meet with defeat at the hands of his son..." (Frazer 57). In order to prevent the fulfillment of this prophecy, Kronos devoured his children immediately after their births.

As terrible as Kronos' deed was, it could have been much worse. The bad news was, of course, that he devoured his children; the good news was that he apparently did not chew his food. If he had had better eating habits, the course of Greek mythology and literature would have been quite different.

Kronos should have realized that he would not get away with his cannibalistic parenting method for long. He should have listened to his father, Uranus, when the latter warned that his time to suffer was coming. He should have known that Rhea was coming to the end of her patience, that she was sick and tired of going through the difficult process of pregnancy and birthing just so he could have a hearty lunch. But like many tyrants, he closed his eyes to reality.

While Gaea had had no one to advise her what to do when she was faced with her pressing dilemma (she was the offspring of Chaos), Rhea had parents to whom she could turn. Despite an obvious conflict of interests (Kronos was Gaea's favorite son), both she and Uranus "...heeded their daughter's request and did as she asked them/ telling her all that was destined to be, revealing the future..." (Frazer 57). Specifically, they told her that her next child, Zeus, would be the one to overthrow his father, whereupon he would become the new leader of the gods. They then explained what she would have to do to fulfill this prophecy.

Unlike her mother, Gaea did not take out the old sickle and begin to sharpen it. (Kronos was luckier than his father.) Instead, she devised an equally effective but much less gory plan. She secretly whisked Rhea off to the island of Lyktos in Crete where she could give birth to her baby in safe, pleasant surroundings, far away from her insatiable husband. Everything went like clockwork. The newborn baby, Zeus, was given over to his grandmother, who took him to an isolated cave where she "...could nurse him and rear him to manhood" (Frazer 58). Then, following her mother's instructions, Rhea swaddled a huge stone in an equally huge diaper and handed it over to Kronos who, "...having taken it from her, sent it down into his stomach" (58). At this point one would have to say that Kronos' habit of not chewing his food was a plus, since a set of dentures for a Titan would undoubtedly have cost a fortune.

Although Hesiod tells us that Gaea personally nursed Zeus during those early days, other sources give the credit to a she-goat named Amalthea. This latter version of the myth tells that bees provided food for the growing god while a group of young men stood outside the cave rattling their spears on their shields so that Kronos could not hear baby Zeus crying. Whichever the case, little Zeus grew like a divine weed.

Once fully grown, Zeus prepared to fulfill the prophesy of his ascendancy. He was aware that Kronos and his allies would not relinquish power without a fight, and that as things stood they had the upper hand. Therefore, to even things up a bit, he tricked his father into regurgitating his brothers and sisters. Next, he personally released his long-imprisoned uncles, the Cyclopes and Hecatonchires, from the underground prison in which Uranus had placed them. As a token of their gratitude, they give him two mighty super-weapons: "...the crash of the thunder and the smoldering bolt and/ flash of the lightning.../ which are the weapons Zeus uses to rule all immortals and mortals" (Frazer 60–61). At last, Zeus was ready for the approaching battle.

The war between Zeus and his followers and the Titans was a Greek Götterdämmerung:

> The boundless sea terribly echoed/ earth roared loudly, broad heaven above was shaken and groaned, and/ high Olympus was trembling..../ The life-giving earth was everywhere crying,/ burning with fire ... like what one would expect should the earth and the broad sky above/ come crashing together ... [Frazer 72–73].

Ultimately, aided by the Hecatonchires, whose hundred hands gave them the firepower of so many rock-spewing machine guns, and supplied with an inexhaustible supply of thunderbolts by the assembly-line manufacturing capabilities of the Cyclopes, Zeus and his allies subdued his father and the other Titans, tied them up, and imprisoned them in the depths of Tartarus. To reward the two Titans who had defected to his side, Themis and her son Prometheus, Zeus granted them honored guest status on Mt. Olympus, where he and the other gods and goddesses had set up their luxurious living quarters. Atlas, the leading military hero of the defeated Titans, suffered the full wrath of Zeus: he was given the strenuous and boring job of holding up the sky. Who or what had held it up before Atlas assumed the labor remains one of those mythological mysteries we encounter so frequently. In any event, a sweating and straining Atlas will have to wait until the discussion of Heracles before his aching shoulder gets even a brief respite.

The Olympians

1. Zeus, the most powerful of the gods, the god of thunder.
2. Hera, Zeus' wife and sister; Demeter, Zeus' sister, goddess of the harvest.
3. Poseidon, Zeus' brother, the god of the sea; Hephaestus, son of Zeus and Hera, god of fire.
4. Ares, son of Zeus and Hera, god of war and craftsmen.
5. Athena, goddess of wisdom, weaving and reasoned war; Apollo, god of medicine, music and prophecy.
6. Artemis, virgin goddess of the hunt.
7. Hermes, messenger god; god of thieves.
8. Dionysus, god of wine and fornication.
9. Aphrodite, goddess of love.

Hades, the second brother of Zeus, is not included among the Olympians since he rules the kingdom of the dead, called the underworld by the Greeks. It is unclear why Poseidon, whose realm is the ocean, is considered an Olympian. A sister of Zeus, Hestia, is also excluded, probably due to the fact that her primary function was to protect hearth and home; she is rarely involved in any interesting adventures.

Any discussion of the great Greek superheroes would have to include the gods, since the latter often involved themselves directly in the heroes' adventures. It would be very useful, moreover, to begin with a recounting of the ancient Greek myths of humankind's origin.

Not surprisingly, there are differing versions of the creation of man in Greek mythology (and separate ones to explain the origin of woman). One myth, for example, designates Zeus as the sole creator, but this is a later version, most likely added to solidify the "Thunderer's" position as the prime force in the universe.

The Roman poet Ovid awards not Zeus but Prometheus the title of father of mankind: "The son of Iapetus fashioned man after the image of the Gods, who rule over all things.... Thus, that which had been lately rude earth, and without any regular shape ... assumed the form of Man, till then unknown." If anything, Prometheus was too good a father to his human brood; when he stole fire from the gods and gave it to man, Zeus punished him severely. Were it not for Heracles, Prometheus might still be suffering somewhere out there in the Caucasus, chained to a rock with a raven pecking out his continually self-regenerating liver.[5]

Of all the versions of man's origin, Hesiod's account is the most fascinating. In *Works and Days*, he writes, "First of all, the immortals who dwell in Olympian homes/ brought into being the golden race of mortal men" (Frazer 101). According to Hesiod, then (and it is not clear whether he is spreading around the credit or the blame), the creation of man was a group effort. This was not the case with the creation of woman, for whom the "credit" goes to Hephaestos. However, rather than as a result of divine thoughtfulness, or as a reward for male good behavior, Zeus ordered Hephaestos to create a race of women to punish Prometheus for stealing fire from Olympus and giving it to mankind. According to Hesiod, Zeus declared, "I shall give them in payment of fire an evil which all shall/ take to their hearts with delight, an evil to love and embrace" (Frazer 98). Thus came into being the maiden Pandora, lovely beyond compare; but there was a catch: "...enclosed in her breast/ lies and wheedling words and the treacherous ways of a thief" (99). Along with Pandora, Zeus sent men a jar filled with horrible miseries and evils, among which were labor, disease, old age and death. On cue, Pandora opened this jar (more commonly referred to as *Pandora's box*), and released these evils to the world. Only hope remained sealed in the jar.[6]

Hesiod goes on to describe the five periods of human history up to his time: the Golden, Silver, Bronze I, Bronze II, and Iron ages. In effect, with one exception this history details a steady deterioration in the quality of life. In the earliest period of human history, the Golden Age, the world was a Utopia where "...man lived like gods without any care in their hearts ... apart from all evil" (Frazer 101). There was no war or disease, only happiness. It was too good to last. The Silver Age of man saw a race that was "...much worse than the first..." (101), but life at that time was still relatively good compared to what was coming. Men sinned and were punished, but there were still those who earned the blessings of Zeus. The ensuing First Bronze Age saw a marked decline. The men from this age were "...devoted to war's wretched works and acts of hybris" (102). Intent on slaughtering each other, these men won no glory, and at the end of their miserable lives they were sent into Hades to decay forever. It is safe to say that no one regretted the passing of that appalling age. The Second Bronze Age saw a temporary reversal of direction. Men of this time were

"...juster and better/ ... the divine race of heroes" (103). During this period the greatest collection of superheroes the world had ever seen appeared. For ten years of the Second Bronze Age, Achilles, Hector, the two Ajaxes, Diomedes, Odysseus, Agamemnon, Menelaus, Paris and a supporting cast of thousands performed their heroics on the fields in Asia Minor in what has come to be universally known as the Trojan War.

The age that followed this heyday for heroes, the Iron Age, can best be described as atrocious. The words written so long ago by Hesiod, as he viewed his contemporary scene, have an uncomfortably familiar ring today:

> Would that I now were no longer alive in the fifth age of men/ but had died earlier or had been born at a later time/ For we live in the age of the iron race, when men shall never/ cease from labor and woe by day, and never be free from/ anguish at night, for hard are the cares that the gods will be giving..../ And what will be left for mortal men are only the anguishing pains, but no defense against evil [103–104].

With things during his own time in such a dismal state, it is no wonder that Hesiod preferred to write about an earlier, heroic age. That it was an age replete with bloodshed does not seem to have lessened his enthusiasm or poetic skills.

Ironically, it was a gala event that set the events leading to the tragic Trojan War into motion. A wedding reception was taking place in the cave of the Centaur, Chiron, and everyone who was anyone had been invited. If there had been photographers present, the popping flashbulbs would have lit up the sky around Mount Pelion, turning night into day. Anticipation grew as the divine celebrities pulled up in their magnificent chariots and other marvelous conveyances. They were all there, a veritable Who's Who of the gods. Led by the Olympians, all the minor deities of the forests, oceans, lakes and streams were present. Even Hades had taken time out from his heavy schedule of processing the newly arrived dead (shades) in his underworld kingdom; he stood to one side of the celestial reception hall, in animated conversation with his brothers, Zeus and Poseidon. The beautiful tones of Pan's pipes merged with the enchanting lyre music of Apollo and the vocal renditions of the muses, providing incomparable musical accompaniment for the suggestive dancing of scantily clad woodland nymphs and fawns. The nectar flowed in unprecedented volume, distributed to the thirsty participants by Hebe, Ganymede and their celestial serving staff. The hungry, happy guests emptied huge golden plates of delectable ambrosia as quickly as they were set before them.

The groom sat nervously in an isolated corner, waiting with growing impatience for his lovely young bride to appear. He was a strong, handsome fellow, but there was something different about him. He seemed out of place. No wonder, since he was a mere human being! Though not unprecedented, it was rare to see a mortal in the company of so many gods and goddesses, let alone as the center of attention. His name was Peleus, a maternal grandson of Chiron, handpicked by Zeus to become the mate of the stunningly beautiful sea nymph, Thetis.

Small clusters of goddesses gossiped animatedly as they glanced over their shoulders to make certain that they were out of Hera's earshot. Zeus, they whispered, was himself in love with Thetis, and would have eventually cast Hera aside and taken the young nymph as his new wife had it not been prophesied that she was destined to give birth to a son who would surpass his father in glory. The father of the gods was an astute student of divine history, and not about to fall into that old trap. And so he had put his emotions aside and chosen a mortal mate for Thetis.

There was one notable name missing from the guest list, missing by design rather than chance: Eris, the goddess of discord. It was a happy affair, and no one wanted any of the backbiting and pettiness that she always brought with her. Imagine the dismay of all present, then, when the brazen troublemaker walked in and made her way to the head table as if she were the guest of honor. Seated at that table were Zeus, his wife Hera, his favorite daughter Athena,[7] and the seductive goddess of love, Aphrodite. Suddenly, Eris' face twisted in a malicious grin as she produced a golden apple and threw it onto the table in front of the three surprised goddesses. Written on the apple in bold letters was the phrase, *For the Most Beautiful.*

Since humility was not one of the attributes of the Olympian goddesses, each of the three immediately claimed the apple as hers. The situation deteriorated rapidly as they argued, Zeus becoming more uncomfortable with every passing minute. Finally, in a moment of divine inspiration he hit upon a solution: there would be a competition to determine who of the three was the most beautiful. Thus was born the first beauty contest. Everyone agreed that Father Zeus had come up with the ideal way to resolve the dispute. Now all that was needed was a judge.

It must be pointed out here that Zeus was the leading expert in the ancient Greek world when it came to beautiful females. To put it more indelicately, he had a constantly wandering eye (not to mention the other parts of his anatomy which were often where they should not have been), and because of this suffered ongoing friction in his marriage. The numerous children he had sired with various females dotted the celestial and earthly landscape like freckles on a redhead's back, and served as a testament to both his matchless ingenuity and unbridled energy. Nor did he limit his extramarital flings to goddesses. He had fathered offspring with various Titanesses: with Mnemosyne (memory) he had produced the muses,[8] with Themis, the fates[9] and the seasons, with Leto, Apollo and Artemis, and with Atlas' daughter, Maia, Hermes. His liaisons with human females had also resulted in countless progeny, the most notable of whom were Dionysus,[10] Aphrodite, Helen of Troy,[11] and Heracles (whose conception and birth will be discussed at length in the ensuing pages). In view of Zeus' insatiable sexual appetite, then, it is no wonder that countless individuals in Ancient Greece claimed to be either an offspring, a grandchild or in some other way directly related to Zeus.

Although he was the expert in the field, Zeus was too smart to alienate two of the three most powerful females in the universe, and so he recused himself from the upcoming competition. But, while he had no inclination to be the judge, he did have someone in mind whose qualifications were excellent.

Across the Aegean Sea, almost on a straight line from Mt. Olympus, was the rich, beautiful, walled kingdom of Troy, beloved by Zeus because of the unfailing piety and devotion of its inhabitants. The king of the country was Priam, now in the twilight of his life, a man who, in his prime, had fathered fifty sons and an unspecified number of daughters with the hundreds of women in his harem. Together with his number one wife, Hekuba, he was now enjoying a comfortable semiretirement, content with the excellent manner his eldest and favorite son, Hector, was discharging the heavy responsibilities of leadership. If there was one dark cloud in his otherwise clear sky, though, it was another of his sons, the one named Paris.

Even before his birth, Paris had caused King Priam a great deal of worry. It began when Hekuba dreamt that the baby she was carrying within her womb would one day bring ruin to Troy. To prevent the fulfillment of this prophecy, Priam reluctantly ordered one of his men to take the newborn Paris to the top of Mount Ida and leave him there to die. He could not have foreseen that a she-bear would find the baby and nurse him, or that a shepherd would then take him in and raise him as one of his own. At any rate, King Priam and Queen Hekuba suffered pangs of guilt every time they thought of their abandoned son. When they learned years later that he had survived,[12] they welcomed him back to the family, convincing themselves that Hekuba's terrible dream had been a false alarm. Troy was flourishing, and Paris was not the kind of person to become involved in politics. It was clear to them that neither power nor responsibility interested their handsome son; rather, his goal in life seemed to be to seduce every woman he saw. Gilgamesh would have understood. Zeus certainly did, and that was why the Father of the Gods chose the young Trojan shepherd for the extremely difficult task at hand.

Zeus had no telephones, telegraphs or fax machines with which to transmit his messages, nor did he either need or desire any of these technological frills. Who needed electronics when one had Hermes, the ultra-swift son he had fathered with Atlas' daughter, Maia? Because of his swiftness, Hermes could speed departed souls (shades) to the underworld, or carry urgent messages from Zeus and the other gods to the most distant areas of the earth and beyond. His winged shoes and helmet were synonymous with speed. In addition, he was universally popular because of his exceptional sense of humor, matchless oratorical skills, and inventive genius. His popularity among the other gods and goddesses was attested to by the priceless gifts they often gave to him. Hades, for example, had presented him with a magic hat, one which made its wearer invisible; from Apollo he received a golden divining rod in return for the lyre brilliant Hermes had invented on the very day of his birth. Most importantly, Zeus relied on and loved Hermes dearly, in spite of the fact that he was "...a shrewd and coaxing schemer/ a cattle-rustling robber, and a bringer of dreams...."[13]

Hermes' mischievous irreverence sometimes got him into trouble. Once, for example, he was so bold as to hide Zeus' scepter, and at another time he stole Aphrodite's girdle. He had a serious side, though, and a versatility that defied the imagination. His innovations included the lyre, the musical scales, the field of astronomy, and the sports of boxing and gymnastics; he is also given credit for being the first to cultivate the olive tree. We shall soon see, moreover, that the swiftest of the gods was the ancestor of an American comic book and television superhero.

Hermes raced to Troy to relay Zeus' instructions to Paris. The Trojan shepherd listened attentively as the divine messenger described the task Zeus had assigned him. He was intrigued, but frightened. Paris understood female psychology well enough to know how dangerous the role of a judge in such a contest could be. Only when he had received assurances that the losers would not hold a grudge against him (assurances which later proved worthless), did he agree to serve. He also added a term of his own: he would have to see the three goddesses *au naturel* in order to judge accurately. Since Zeus had not given any orders to the contrary, the terms were accepted and the contest began.

Hera was the first to disrobe. Although there is no detailed description of the proceedings, we can confidently assume that Hera, who was not the least bit prudish, turned this way and that to allow Paris to closely examine her ample attributes. To help make his decision easier, moreover, she did what any self-respecting goddess would do under the circumstances — she offered him a bribe. She told him that if he selected her as the winner, she would see to it that he became the richest, most powerful ruler of all Asia. As difficult as it must have been for him to take his eyes off of her (she could not have won Zeus had she not been exceedingly well endowed), Paris finally had to dismiss her and call for the next contestant.

The fact that Athena was willing to take part in such a degrading event was astonishing. One must keep in mind that she was the arch-feminist of all time, a goddess who had never knowingly allowed a male, god or man, to see her without her full suit of armor, let alone minus whatever else she wore under it. But vanity is a powerful force, and so the virgin goddess stripped in as dignified a manner as she could, undoubtedly increasing Paris' pulse rate to the danger point. Next, she demonstrated to the young Trojan that she was no more principled than her father's wife by offering him a bribe of her own. She would, she declared, make him the most handsome, militarily victorious man in the entire world if his vote went to her. Paris thanked her politely for the offer and assured her that he would take it into consideration during his deliberations. He looked her over carefully for a few more minutes and then called for Aphrodite.

As soon as the radiant goddess of love appeared it was obvious that it was really no contest after all. It was not that she was any more beautiful than the others, but seduction was her profession. No one knew better than she what made the male animal tick loudest. Most likely she stepped so close to Paris that they almost touched, and in a throaty voice cautioned him not to miss a single detail. By then, Paris was undoubtedly in a state bordering on narcomania, and so when Aphrodite offered the drug that would satisfy his craving he was powerless to reject it. The drug was the promise of a woman, not just any woman, but the most beautiful of them all: Helen of Sparta. To ensure victory, Aphrodite described Helen's unmatched beauty in vivid detail and promised that the Spartan queen would be his if he awarded her the prize. As excited by this prospect as he must have been, Paris still had the presence of mind to ask how this would be possible, since Helen was the wife of King Menelaus of Sparta. Aphrodite brushed this concern off as easily as one would flick a flake of dandruff from one's shoulder. This was a minuscule problem, she assured; with the help of her son, Eros, Helen would fall so madly in love with him that if she had to she would swim across the Adriatic to give herself to him. Without a further word, Paris handed over the apple to the goddess who had made him the one offer he could not refuse. The stage was now set for the Trojan War, chronicled in Homer's great heroic epic, the *Iliad*.

The *Iliad*

Menelaus should have known better than to leave Helen unchaperoned while he went traipsing off who knows where. The proof that he was well aware of the problems one faced when one had a beautiful wife was evident from the oath he and the other Greek heroes had sworn to Helen's father some years before.[14] One can imagine how upset he was, then, when he returned to Sparta to hear that his wife had sailed off to Troy with a dashing young shepherd. The SOS went out immediately to his elder brother, Agamemnon, King of Mycenae and the ranking Grecian leader of the time. When he heard what had happened, Agamemnon began mobilization for a full-scale invasion of Troy, sending his recruiters out to enlist the leading heroes of the various Greek states.

A man may sometimes commit to a cause in his youth that no longer has as much appeal to him in later years. Such was the case with Odysseus, who probably would have liked to kick himself in the backside for having taken the oath to recover Helen should she be abducted. Agamemnon's call came just when things were going well for him. He was

Georg Pencz. Das Paris-Urteil. (Bartsch 89)

The Judgment of Paris, from a painting by George Pencz. Paris judges who is the most beautiful of the Greek goddesses Hera, Athena and Aphrodite.

happily married to a wonderful woman, Penelope, and had just become the proud father of a strapping baby boy, Telemachus. War was the furthest thing from his mind, particularly a war for the sake of a flighty female like Helen. Hell no, I won't go, was the essence of his thinking, and to that end he improvised a plan to avoid the draft.

Agamemnon was convinced that if the Greeks were to succeed in their mission they would need to have brilliant Odysseus in their expeditionary force. He knew, however, that the Ithacan king would not leave his family and country without some skillful prodding. Therefore the commander in chief chose Palamedes to recruit the reluctant hero.[15]

Odysseus was plowing his fields as someone approached. When he recognized Palamedes, he knew what was afoot and so he put his plan into operation. Rolling his eyes in a practiced manner, he began to strew salt in front of his plow. It was obvious to Palamedes that Odysseus was feigning insanity, but he had prepared for this eventuality. As Odysseus came closer, the sharp plow blade biting hungrily into the soil, Palamedes placed an object on the ground in its path. To his horror, Odysseus saw that it was the baby, Telemachus. Odysseus swerved the plow before it could harm his screaming offspring, and by that act proved that he was in command of his senses. Probably uttering the Greek equivalent of *gotcha*, Palamedes presented Odysseus his draft notice, an action for which, according to at least one later myth, Odysseus later killed him.

Odysseus was not the only unsuccessful would-be draft dodger in Greece, although the second one was following his mother's instructions rather than his own inclinations. He was none other than Achilles, the super-superhero of the Trojan War: Achilles, son of Thetis and Peleus, the beautiful sea nymph and her mortal husband whose wedding reception had set the stage for all of the problems. Why would Thetis so desperately want her son to avoid his duty? The answer once more was in the stars. It seems that shortly after Achilles was born there was a prophecy that he would live a short, glorious life if he were to fight in Troy, but that if he could avoid service there his life would be long and unspectacular. To a mother it was a no-brainer. Thetis was determined to do her best to have Achilles escape induction into the army being assembled by Agamemnon. Her plan was a desperate one: after dressing Achilles as a girl, she whisked him off to the small island of Syros.

As the saying goes, rumor has wings, and so it was not long before Odysseus and Diomedes, chosen to recruit Achilles, heard that he was hiding out on Syros, dressed in drag. Misery loves company, and so they set out to bring him back. Before long, they docked their boat in the island's harbor and began their search. One can only wonder how they were unable to recognize the ultra-masculine Achilles immediately. Perhaps they simply pretended not to, wanting to have a little fun with their transvestite comrade before they drafted him. Cunningly, they passed out some armor and weapons to the group of "maidens," and while the latter were inspecting these items, Odysseus secretly gave the order for the war trumpets to sound. All of the frightened young ladies scattered in fear, but Achilles calmly picked up a weapon and prepared for battle. *Gotcha!* Thus, the greatest of all Greek heroes failed to escape his fate: he was going to Troy. With the major players finally in place, the time for the Greek fleet to set sail was drawing very close.[16]

The *Iliad* is similar to other heroic epics in that the whole of the work is subordinate to its parts. In other words, the individual episodes describing the adventures of the various superheroes are the prime focus, not the overriding plot. The latter can be summarized very briefly as follows: in the tenth year of the war, Achilles withdraws from the battlefield after a petty argument with Agamemnon, and as a result the Trojans begin to slaughter the Greeks. Just when it seems as if the Greeks are about to suffer a crushing defeat, Patroklos dons Achilles' armor and fights fiercely until Hector deals him a death blow. It is the most painful event of Achilles' life. The grief over his best friend's death becomes a burning desire for revenge. Since Hector has stripped Patroklos of the borrowed shield and armor, Achilles implores his mother to have the god, Hephaestos, make him a new set. No sooner said than done. Resplendent in his new armor, Achilles returns to the war, turns the tide of battle, kills Hector in single combat and proceeds to abuse the fallen Trojan hero's corpse. At the end of the work, Hector's father makes the dangerous journey to Achilles' camp and requests his son's body for proper cremation and burial. Achilles takes pity on old Priam, who reminds him of his own father, and grants his wish. The epic ends with the funeral of Hector.

Although only one of a number of world class superheroes in the *Iliad*, Achilles is by far the greatest of them all. It does not detract from his stature as the number one Greek superhero that he never wounded a god or goddess in battle as did Diomedes (aided by Athena), that he did not have an entire work named after him as did Odysseus, or that he was dependent on Agamemnon's generosity when it came to gaining spoils of war. Nor is it unprecedented that the leading hero does not hold the highest rank. One need only look back to Persia to find a parallel. In terms of rank, Rustam was subordinate to the Shah of

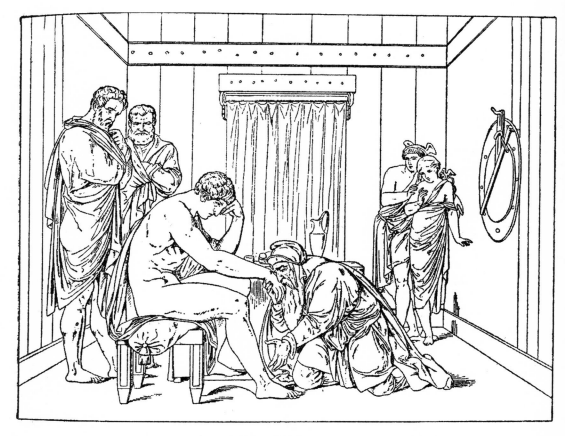

King Priam begs Achilles for the corpse of his son, Hector.

Persia, but no one ever doubted that he was a far greater hero. This is the case with Achilles in the Greek coalition. But there is a difference in their epic stories: while Rustam had as little use for his Shah as Achilles did for Agamemnon, his contempt was limited to words and had no disastrous consequences. Achilles, on the other hand, allowed his excessive pride (Hybris) to translate into near defeat for his fellow Greeks. By refusing to fight on after being humiliated by Agamemnon, he indirectly caused the deaths of many of his countrymen and almost cost them the final victory.

The groundwork for the future crisis was presented at the very beginning of the *Iliad*: the Greek army was in chaos, its ranks depleted by a terrible plague. Agamemnon was informed that Apollo was punishing him for holding captive the beautiful Chryseis, daughter of one of his priests, and that if he did not release her the pestilence would destroy them all. Agamemnon reluctantly agreed to let the girl go, but only on condition that Achilles give him as a replacement Briseis, a young girl whom he had earlier awarded the latter as war spoils. Achilles was furious. He vented his rage at Agamemnon in no uncertain terms, spitting out these words: "O wrapped in shamelessness, with your mind forever on profit/ how shall any one of the Achaians ever obey you/ either to go on a journey or to fight men strongly in battle?"[17] As Achilles continued to rant, it became clear that his negative feelings toward Agamemnon had been festering for a long time. At one point he declares, "To me you are the most hateful of all the kings whom the gods love" (63, line 176). He even goes so far as to question Agamemnon's courage: "You wine sack, with a dog's eyes and a deer's heart. Never/ once have you taken courage in your heart to arm with your people for battle..." (65, lines 225–227).

After his tirade, Achilles stomped off to his camp, but not before informing Agamemnon that while he would not fight him over a woman, neither would he ever again lift a finger to help the Greeks battle against the Trojans. Then, to make certain that Agamemnon understood that he would never give in to him again, Achilles warned: "But of all the other things that are mine.../ you shall take nothing away against my pleasure/ Come then, only try it, that these others may see also/ instantly your own black blood will stain my spear point" (67, lines 300–303). The fact that Agamemnon took such abuse indicates the limitations of his authority over Achilles.

Achilles reluctantly returned the weeping Briseis to Agamemnon, much to the latter's later regret, since without its leading warrior the Greek expeditionary force was pushed to the brink of annihilation. Had Achilles not ultimately relented and returned to the battle, most likely some talented Trojan poet would have written a famous epic work about the great superhero, Hector, who led his armies in a victorious campaign to eject the invading Greeks from Troy. In that scenario, Homer might have remained just another unknown Greek poet with no national triumph to celebrate in his epic poetry. But fate chose a different scenario.

If perfection were a criterion for superherohood, it is clear that Achilles would not have made the grade. From the little we have seen in the above account, it is apparent that he had a tendency to react to adversity more like a brooding teenager than a mature adult. Had the reason for his deep anger been a genuine love for Briseus this might have been excusable, but this was not the case. His words as she is led away to Agamemnon's tent indicate that love was not involved: "Now the son of Atreus, powerful Agamemnon/ has dishonoured me, since he has taken away my prize and keeps it" (68, lines 355–356). Clearly, Achilles considered Briseis a "prize," more a thing than a person. He did not grieve for lost love, but for injured "honor," a totally self-centered reaction. His egocentric anger was so deep, moreover, that he was actually pleased when many of his countrymen were killed and maimed as a result of his absence from the field. His sole aim had become to punish Agamemnon regardless of the cost. He did not even relent when a contrite and panic-stricken Agamemnon attempted to bribe him back to the battlefield with an offer that cannot be refused. Swallowing his pride, the hapless commander in chief offered to return Briseis to him with a sworn oath that he had never "...entered into her bed and never lay with her" (201, line 133). In addition, he would grant Achilles twenty of the loveliest Trojan women, a shipload of gold and bronze, and one of his own daughters, together with a dowry of seven citadels.

Even the usually glib-tongued Odysseus was left speechless when Achilles rejected the lavish bribe. Diomedes expresses the majority attitude when he declares, "...now you have driven him deeper into his pride/ Rather we shall pay him no more attention, whether he comes with us/ or stays away..." (216, lines 700–702). Even his closest comrades viewed Achilles' behavior as disproportionate to the provocation. They saw that his rage had destroyed his ability to think clearly and was leading to a great personal tragedy. A clear thinking Achilles would never have given Patroklos his armor and sent him into the thick of battle against a raging Hector. As Lattimore puts it, "There is no reason why Achilleus should not fight himself. His action makes no sense, and is fatal to Patroklos" (48).

Moreover, instead of learning a lesson from Patroklos' death, Achilles simply redirected his rage from Agamemnon to Hector. This personality trait makes it easier to understand why Achilles had not made any great effort to meet Hector in single combat. In ten years of fighting, he must have had many opportunities to do battle with the indisputable Trojan superhero. Since it was not fear that prevented him, we can only assume that it was simply a lack of any personal motivation. When Hector gave Patroklos the coup de grace, however, everything changed. Obviously, Achilles was not a team player; but then very few superheroes are.

There was never any doubt about the outcome of the final showdown between Achilles and Hector. As is often the case, the short battle proved to be a terrible mismatch, an archetypal wipeout. What Achilles did after dispatching his Trojan foe was hardly admirable: "...he would fasten Hector behind the chariot, so as to drag him/ ... then rest again in his shelter, and throw down the dead man/ and leave him to lie sprawled on his face in the dust..." (475, lines 15, 17–18). Even the gods, themselves often guilty of terrible cruelty, were appalled by Achilles' brutal behavior; finally, Zeus himself had to intervene to put an end to it.[18]

In spite of his faults, however, Achilles remains the leading hero of the *Iliad*, one whose gifts extended beyond extraordinary military prowess. Periodically, we are given glimpses of him that show there was more to him than the spectacular ability to kill the enemy. For instance, when Odysseus, Ajax and Phoenix seek him out to deliver Agamemnon's peace offer "...they found Achilleus delighting his heart in a lyre, clear-sounding ... and singing of men's fame/ as Patroklos was sitting over against him..." (203, lines 186, 189–190). One can claim that this scene provided a model for America's later hero-cowboys like Roy Rogers and Gene Autry, whose prowess with six-shooters was matched by their ability to serenade their audiences.

When not in the grip of his uncontrollable anger, Achilles displayed a keen intelligence. In response to Odysseus' articulate appeal for reconciliation with Agamemnon, he made the following philosophical observation: "Fate is the same for the man who holds back, the same if he fights hard/ We are all held in a single honour, the brave with the weaklings/ A man dies still if he has nothing, as one who has done much" (206, lines 318–320). He also had the capacity to empathize, as we see in the scene where Priam, led to him by Hermes, begs for the return of Hector's corpse: "...as Priam sat huddled/ at the feet of Achilleus and wept close for manslaughtering Hector/ and Achilleus wept now ... in pity for the grey head and the grey beard...." (Priam, in his turn, showed good judgment by leaving in the middle of the night, before Achilles' rage had a chance to reemerge.) In short, Achilles is a flawed human being, which does not detract from his heroic stature.

To many modern readers, Achilles' *archenemy*, Hector, is the most sympathetic character in the *Iliad*. That he was no match for his Greek counterpart was obvious even before their short, deadly encounter. Earlier in the *Iliad*, Hector had two opportunities to defeat Ajax in single combat, and both times he was the loser. In the first of these losing clashes, Ajax wounded him in the neck with his spear and then knocked him down with a huge stone. Only darkness saved the Trojan hero from certain death. The second time they fought was even worse for Hector. That time it took a group of his comrades to save his life. This is how the action is described by Homer:

> First glorious Hector made a cast with his spear at Aias/ ....But as he drew away huge Telamonian Aias/ caught up a rock; there were many, holding-stones for the fast ships/ ... and hit him in the chest next to the throat over his shield rim/ and spun him around like a top with the stroke, so that he staggered/ in a circle..../ so Hector in all his strength dropped suddenly in the dust [305, lines 402, 409–410, 412–413, 417].

The Greek superhero Achilles and his comrades.

Hector was "groaning heavily" as Aeneas and a few other Trojans carried him back to the city. This is not exactly what one would expect from a superhero.

Hector also came out second best in a short exchange with Diomedes during the Trojans' swift advance toward the Greek ships. When it seemed as if there would be no way to stop the onslaught, Diomedes took aim and threw his spear at Hector, hitting the latter's shield dead center. Although the shield was sturdy enough to prevent the spear from killing him, Hector was shaken badly by the close brush with death. Homer writes: "...Hector sprang far away back and merged with his own people/ and dropping to one knee stayed leaning on the ground with his heavy/ hand and a covering of black night came over both eyes" (243, lines 354–356).

Hector's sole major triumph in the *Iliad* is also shown to be tainted. Apollo stuns Patroklos, and a Greek warrior stabs him in the back with a javelin before Hector is able to deal the death blow with his spear. If not a paper tiger, the Hector that we see in Homer's epic poem is something less than the greatest superhero of all time. Given all of this, why do so many readers continue to see him in such a positive light? The answer to this question is a complicated mixture of psychology and logical deduction.

There is little doubt that Hector is the most likeable person in the *Iliad*. He was the favorite of his parents, and a faithful, loving husband and father, as well as a selfless leader. Hector does not fight for personal gain, but because he is compelled by a sense of duty; he leads his people in a war caused by a brother he does not respect, and he fights tirelessly. Much of this is evident in a conversation he has with his wife, Andromache. He has just returned to the walled city during a lull in the fighting. Andromache is overjoyed to see him, but fearful that he will be killed if he returns to the battle, and so she pleads with him not to leave her and their child. In this tender scene, so uncharacteristic of the work, she says:

> Hector, you are father to me, and my honoured mother/ you are my brother, and you it is who are my young husband/ Please take pity upon me then, stay here on the rampart/ that you may not leave your child an orphan, your wife a widow ... [164, lines 429–432].

His response is simple; he tells her that he must fight on because "...I would feel deep shame/ before the Trojans, and the Trojan women with trailing garments/ if like a coward I were to shrink from the fighting..." (165, lines 441–443). Then, in a most human moment, he picks up his infant son, Astynax, and tosses him in the air like any normal, loving father. Such behavior is not only a rarity in Homer's work, but in the superhero genre as a whole.

Even Helen, who has become tired of the superficial Paris and is anxious to return home to Greece, has grown to love Hector. When Priam brings his body back for burial she expresses her deep personal loss. As the mourning women gather to give vent to their grief, only Andromache and Hekuba seem more distraught than Helen:

> Third and last Helen led the song of sorrow among them/ "Hector, of all my lord's brothers dearest by far to my spirit..../ I have never heard a harsh saying from you, nor an insult/ ....There was no other in all the wide Troad [Troy] who was kind to me, and my friend..." [495, lines 762, 767, 774–775].

Like Achilles, then, this was a man, but unlike the Greek superhero, Hector was a man guided by love, not by anger.

The remaining superheroes in the *Iliad*, as great as they are, do not quite measure up in emotional appeal to either Achilles or Hector. The extraordinary battlefield exploits of Diomedes in Book V have already been mentioned, as has his brief, successful encounter with Hector. One other episode in which he played a key role indicates his outstanding valor. In Book X, he and Odysseus undertake a dangerous reconnaissance mission behind the Trojan lines. They not only gain valuable intelligence about the enemy's strength and positions, but also manage to steal Trojan horses (a scene which later became a standard in early Hollywood westerns). In spite of his heroic accomplishments, however, the less charismatic Diomedes remains a supporting actor in the epic tale.

Odysseus' role in the *Iliad* is also a supporting one. He is not yet the "super survivor" of the later *Odyssey*, nor is the full extent of his versatility or intelligence shown. We do get a glimpse of these attributes, however, right from the outset. One example can be found in Book II, where he decisively deals with the troublemaker, Thersites.[19] The latter, upset by the Agamemnon's treatment of Achilles, has publicly unleashed an avalanche of invective against the Commander in Chief. Not long before, when Achilles similarly vented his spleen against Agamemnon, Odysseus judiciously remained silent; but on this occasion he feels forced to intervene. Normally, the brilliant king of Ithaca reasoned with those who held differing opinions, using his eloquence and logic to win the opponent over. However, recognizing that such an approach would not work with a malicious man like Thersites, Odysseus demonstrated his flexibility: "...he [Odysseus] ... dashed the scepter against his [Thersites'] back and/ shoulders, and he doubled over, and a round tear dropped from him/ and a bloody welt stood up between his shoulders under/ the golden scepter's stroke, and he sat down again, frightened..." (83, lines 265–268). Put in the form of an aphorism, his action might be expressed thusly: "When dealing with a bully, force is more effective than reason."

The greatest Trojan hero, Hector.

It is also evident throughout the work that Agamemnon respected Odysseus' brain power. When there was a task involving intelligence, he invariably called on Odysseus, whether it was to seek reconciliation with Achilles, or to reconnoiter the enemy. The seeds of Odysseus' superheroism, germinating in the *Iliad*, would sprout into full bloom in the *Odyssey*.

Ajax (Aias) had neither the flair of Achilles nor the mental power of Odysseus; nevertheless, he was an indispensable member of Agamemnon's military team. Homer says of him: "Among the men [Greeks] by far the best was Telamonian Aias/ while Achilleus stayed angry, since he was far best of all of them..." (96, 768–769). The previously mentioned victories over Hector in single combat, moreover, were not Ajax's greatest accomplishment. In Book XV Homer describes how, virtually single-handedly, he prevented the attacking Trojans from overrunning the Greek ships: "...There he stood and waited for them, and with his pike always/ beat off any Trojan who carried persistent fire from the vessels" (328, lines 730–731). And it is he and his namesake, little Ajax, "...not great in size like the son of Telemon,/ but far slighter..." (90, 528–529), who beat off the Trojans when they attempted to seize the body of Patroklos after Hector slew the latter. In spite of these accomplishments, however, Ajax stands in the shadow of the other Greek heroes. Indeed, he was a great fighter, but primarily a defensive one. He lived up to his nickname, "The Wall," on many occasions, and like a wall he was necessary to hold things up. But the fact of the matter is, a plain, unadorned wall is rather dull, and so was Ajax. In short, like the famous American comedian, Rodney Dangerfield, he did not get the respect he deserved.

The two remaining major Greek heroes, Agamemnon and Menelaus, together with their Trojan counterparts, Paris and Aeneas, form the next heroic level in the epic of the Trojan War. Agamemnon is basically a brave, strong fighter, but, although he kills many Trojans before being superficially wounded in Book II, he does not engage in combat with any of the leading Trojan heroes. He is a complicated, introspective man with a kingly spirit, but not above pettiness and miscalculation. On at least two occasions he is ready to quit the war and return his forces to Greece in defeat, and must be shamed by Diomedes and Odysseus to continue the war. In short, he is an imperfect, but nevertheless competent leader, able to swallow his pride and admit a mistake publicly for the good of his cause. A hero, to be sure, but one who does not rise to superhero status.

Agamemnon's brother, Menelaus, is also a brave and capable warrior, but well below the level of superstars like Achilles, Hector, Ajax or Diomedes. When he volunteers to meet Hector in single combat in Book VII, Agamemnon tells him, "Menelaos ... you are mad;/ you have no need/ to take leave of your senses thus..../ he is far better than you" (171, lines 109–110, 114). Wisely, he follows his brother's advice and lets Ajax take the challenge.

Paris, who provoked the war by abducting Helen, is much more at home in the bedroom than on the battlefield. This is a constant source of irritation to his elder brother. At one point Hector has to deliver a stern lecture in order to get his brother to leave Helen's bed and return to the fighting. His parents, moreover, are also fed up with him, so much so that during one of their conversations they express regret that he survived on Mount Ida.

Homer recounts only one instance where Paris engages in single combat: the encounter he has with Menelaus. It is a short, one-sided fight, and would have ended with Paris' demise had Aphrodite not interceded and whisked the handsome shepherd back to Helen's boudoir. Helen expresses her disdain for him when she sees him there: "So you come back from the fighting. Oh, how I wish you had died there/ beaten down by the stronger man, who was once my husband" (111, lines 428–429). Whatever one thinks of Paris, one has to admire his consistency. Whereas another might have settled for a bath and a good night's sleep after such a harrowing experience and unpleasant welcome, Paris turns to Helen and says, "Come, then, rather let us go to bed and turn to love making/ Never before as now has passion enmeshed my senses" (112, lines 441–442). And so, while a furious Menelaus searches for Paris in order to finish him off, the latter is making passionate love to Helen. Clearly, the Trojan shepherd is a world-class lover, but hardly a superhero.

The second greatest Trojan hero, Aeneas, would have to wait for Virgil to rediscover him before gaining his deserved recognition as a superhero. However, that is not to say that he was a nonentity in the *Iliad*; nothing could be further from the truth. He was, in fact, the only one who was able to face Achilles one-on-one and live to tell about it. And he did it twice. Of course, it might have been quite a different story had Zeus not "...made his knees quick" in Book V, thus permitting him to run away from their first encounter before Achilles could deliver a fatal blow.

In Book XX, we see the second encounter between them. To his credit, Aeneas is undaunted by Achilles' efforts to frighten him. In answer to the latter's reminder of how he had chased him from Mount Ida on their earlier encounter, Aeneas replies, "Son of Peleus, never hope by words to frighten me/ as if I were a baby. I myself understand well enough/ how to speak in vituperation and how to make insults" (409, lines 200–202). He then goes on to give a long dissertation on his genealogy, hinting that his bloodline is superior to Achilles' since his mother was the Olympian Aphrodite while Achilles' was Thetis, a minor deity. What happens next proves that it does pay to have connections in high places, especially when you are facing an Achilles. Just as the latter is about to hack Aeneas to pieces with his sword, Poseidon "...drifted a mist" across his eyes and plucked the Trojan hero out of danger. Luckily for Aeneas, there was no third encounter.

As has already been shown, in the *Iliad* the gods do not sit by quietly and dispassionately while Achilles and the other mortals slaughter each other. They intervene constantly, not only to save a favorite hero or relative, but often to settle old scores with each other. The Greek side is bolstered by the powerful foursome: Hera, Athena, Poseidon and Thetis, while the Trojans field a divine A-Team: Aphrodite, Ares, Apollo and Artemis. The referee is the original father-god himself, Zeus. While these divine beings often demonstrate their phenomenal powers, they just as frequently reveal qualities that are not exactly godlike. They talk behind each other's backs, incessantly belittle and threaten each other, and in more than one instance actually injure each other.[20] The divine first couple, Zeus and Hera, are the original Bickersons,[21] grown expert in the art of marital conflict as a result of eons of practice. We have already seen the extent of Zeus' philandering, but it was also true that Hera does not think it beneath her dignity to use sex as a tool when it is needed to achieve her ends. An excellent example of this can be found in Book IV. In this episode she ensnares Zeus in her web by appealing to his hyperactive libido. Her plan is to get him out of the way temporarily so that she and the other divine allies of the Greeks can reverse the tide of battle. At the time, Agamemnon and his army are on the brink of destruction, weakened as they have been by Achilles' refusal to fight alongside them. The situation is desperate: Zeus has given specific orders that none of the gods are to interfere in the hostilities, but Hera has other ideas. She is not willing to allow a Trojan victory, not even a temporary one. Homer writes:

And now the lady ox-eyed Hera was divided in purpose/ as to how she could beguile the brain in Zeus of the aegis/ And to her mind this thing appeared to be the best counsel/ to array herself in loveliness, and go down to Ida/ and perhaps he might be taken with desire to lie in love with her [298, lines 159–163].

Since they had long since passed that period in their marriage where a suggestive glance was sufficient to propel Zeus to their bedroom, Hera knows that she must make elaborate preparations for the seduction. After washing herself carefully with ambrosia and rubbing olive oil over her whole body, she combs out her hair and puts on her most alluring robe, "...an ambrosial robe that Athene/ had made her carefully" (299, lines 178–179). Next, she selects her best earrings and sandals and strolls over to Aphrodite's house to borrow the latter's legendary bra, a mainstay of the love goddess' line of seductive apparel. Since Aphrodite is on the Trojan side in the war, however, Hera concocts an imaginative story to explain why she needs it.[22] Aphrodite, always happy to be of service to promote lovemaking, agrees immediately: "...from her breasts she unbound the elaborate, pattern-pierced/ zone, and on it are figured all beguilements, and loveliness/ is figured upon it, and passion of sex is there, and the whispered/ endearment that steals the heart away even from the thoughtful" (299–300, lines 214–217).

So equipped, Hera is fairly confident that she will be able to get Zeus into the proper mood, but there is one more thing she must do. Quickly, she sets out for the island of Lemnos: "There she encountered Sleep, brother of Death" (300, line 231). Without preamble she makes her request: "Put to sleep the shining eyes of Zeus under his brows/ as soon as I have lain beside him in love..." (300, line 236). To encourage Sleep to do this little favor for her she offers a bribe: a lovely, golden throne complete with matching footstool, both handmade by her son, Hephaestos. As much in demand as Hephaestos' original creations are, Sleep hesitates, pointing out that he is afraid of what Zeus will do were he to find out that he has been deceived. Hera is ready for this reaction; she chides Sleep gently for his faintheartedness and then sweetens the pot a bit: "Come now, do it, and I will give you one of the younger/ Graces for you to marry, and she shall be called your lady;/ Pasithea, since all your days you have loved her..." (301, lines 266–268). Even Sleep cannot resist such an offer, and so, after extracting an oath from Hera that she will abide by the terms they have discussed, the deal is sealed.

Hera is finally ready to execute the final stage of her plan. She seeks out Zeus in his personal Trojan War box seat on the peak of Mount Ida. His reaction upon seeing her indicates that her plot is working as planned:

> Zeus who gathers the clouds saw her/ and when he saw her desire was a mist about his close heart/ as much as on that time they first went to bed together/ and lay in love and their dear parents knew nothing of it [302, lines 293–296].

After giving him a contrived story to explain why she happened to be passing by, Hera awaits his reply. It comes swiftly; Zeus is the number one god, hence he does not have to be subtle: "...let us now go to bed and turn to love-making.... For never before has love for any goddess or woman/ so melted about the heart inside me as now..." (302, lines 314–317). He then ticks off a list of goddesses and mortal women with whom he has made love in the past, emphasizing that none of them excited him nearly as much as she does at that moment. Hera, who ordinarily goes into paroxysms of fury whenever she thinks of her husband's extracurricular activities, bites her godly tongue to keep from telling him what she thinks of his distorted idea of foreplay. Playing the prude, she explains that she would prefer not to make love there in the open where the other gods can see them, suggesting instead that they go to her place, a cozy chamber built for her by their son, Hephaestos. Zeus has a better idea:

> He ... caught his wife in his arms. There underneath them the divine earth broke into young, fresh/ grass, and into dewy clover, crocus and hyacinth/ so thick and soft it held the hard ground

deep away from them/ There they lay down together and drew about them a golden/ wonderful cloud, and from it the glimmering dew descended [303, lines 346–351].

Although one of the greatest lovers in all mythology, even Zeus has his limits. When he finally satisfies his passion, Sleep drifts down to keep his part of the bargain. While Zeus sleeps on the job, Poseidon rallies the besieged Greek armies and they begin to gain the upper hand again.

Zeus realizes what has happened when he awakes from his unscheduled nap. He is angry, though certainly not as angry as he might have been had he not thoroughly enjoyed the "trick" Hera played on him. Therefore, instead of punishing her he focuses his wrath on his brother, Poseidon, who very actively intervened in the war on the Trojan side. After some initial resistance, the god of the sea buckles under to his brother's threats and agrees not to interfere further. This does not mean, however, that it is the end of divine intervention in the Trojan War. After all, gods will be gods.

In spite of Zeus' standing prohibition throughout the *Iliad*, there are numerous instances where the Olympians intrude in the action. In Book XXI, they unleash vicious attacks on each other while Zeus watches like a benevolent father amused by the antics of his naughty children. The first encounter between two divinities occurs soon after Achilles returns to the fighting. In an unsurpassed killing rampage, the grieving Achilles inundates the river Xanthos with corpses and blood, inducing the angry god of the river to warn him to stop the carnage that is polluting his domain. But Thetis' incensed son ignores the warning and continues to slaughter hordes of Trojans. Finally, in a surrealistic scene the river "...rose against Achilleus, turbulent, boiling/ to a crest, muttering in foam and blood and dead bodies/ until the purple wave of the river fed from the bright sky/ lifted high in its waters the son of Peleus" (427, 424–427). When it seems as if Achilles will drown, Hera asks her son, Hephaestos, to save the Greek superhero. The god of fire eagerly accepts the challenge. He ignites the numerous Trojan corpses Achilles has strewn out across the plain, and spreads the conflagration to all of the trees and bushes lining the banks of the river. Finally, the river itself bursts into flame. His waters boiling violently, Xanthos begs Hera to spare him, promising never to aid the Trojans, not even should the Greeks set fire to Troy. Satisfied by this response, Hera calls her son off.

After the battle between Xanthos and Hephaestos a free-for-all erupts among the gods: "...Zeus heard it/ from where he sat on Olympos, and was amused in his deep heart/ for pleasure, as he watched the gods' collision in conflict" (428, lines 388–390).

To mere humans it may seem rather strange that Father Zeus is amused when he sees Athena smash Ares down with a huge boulder and then lay out Aphrodite with a terrific body punch. How, one might ask, is he able to derive pleasure from watching Hera pummel Artemis until the latter runs crying to Olympus? Who can fathom the gods? Even Poseidon, unaccustomed to combat on land, attempts to get into the fray by challenging Apollo. To his credit, Apollo refuses to be drawn into the escalating family strife. His response to Poseidon explains why he is called the god of reason:

Shaker of the earth, you would have me be as one without prudence/ if I am to fight you even for the sake of insignificant/ mortals, who are as leaves are, and now flourish and grow warm/ with life, and feed on what the ground gives, but then again/ fade away and are dead ... [430, lines 462–466].

From the standpoint of the Trojans, the most costly divine intervention takes place in Book XXII. The famous clash between Achilles and Hector has an unexpected beginning.

Hector, the superhero of Troy, loses his nerve as Achilles advances: "...the shivers took hold of Hector when he saw him, and he could no longer/ stand his ground there, but left the gates behind, and fled, frightened..." (438, 136–137). As his terrified countrymen watch from the wall above, he circles the entire wall of Troy three times with Achilles in hot pursuit.[23] We are left with the impression that had there been no divine intervention, Hector might still be running to this very day. But Athena, anxious to see a Greek victory, suddenly appears at the frightened Trojan hero's side in the form of his favorite brother, Deiphobos, and offers to fight with him against Achilles. Completely deceived by the goddess, Hector stops his retreat and prepares to do battle.

Had Athena simply drawn back at that point and let them fight it out on even terms, one might be justified in refusing to call this a major intercession. But she did not. When Achilles misses with his first spear cast, she picks up the spear and gives it back to him. It is at this crucial point that Hector acquits himself like a true superhero. Aware at last that Athena has tricked him, he stands his ground and fights bravely. Achilles vanquishes Hector quickly by thrusting his spear into the Trojan hero's throat.

Although Hector's death marks the end of the military action in the *Iliad*, the gods continue to take part in the proceedings until the very end of the work. Ironically, once it is certain that the Trojans have lost the war (without Hector they had no chance to win), any divine interventions that take place are on their side. They are appalled at Achilles' defilement of Hector's corpse. In his fury, the son of Thetis repeatedly stabs his defeated foe and drags the body behind his chariot as he circles the wall. In spite of such cruel abuse, however, Hector' body remains unmarked due to Apollo's intercession. Finally, Zeus has had enough. He sends Thetis down to order her son to release Hector's body to Priam, and then gives Hermes the mission of providing safe conduct for Priam on his journey to Achilles' camp. The *Iliad* ends as Achilles allows Priam to take his son's body back with him in order to perform the proper funeral rites.

* * *

The heroes depicted by Homer in the *Iliad* are more limited physically than those already discussed in previous chapters, and they do not always fit into the standard heroic mold. In actuality, the Greek gods satisfy the archetypal paradigm for the superhero better than do the human heroes.

The *miraculous birth* archetype can be applied to several of the divinities of Ancient Greece, one more incredible than the next. It would be difficult to find more miraculous births than those of Aphrodite (born from the discarded genitals of Kronos), Athena (entered the world from Zeus' head, in full armor), and Dionysus (delivered from Zeus' thigh after the Thunderer served as a surrogate mother, having sewed the six month old fetus into his thigh when Dionysus' mother, Semele, was killed by lightning). In Greek mythology, however, the award for the birth most in keeping with Otto Rank's criteria for the birth of a hero has to go to Zeus. In fact, it was almost as if Rank had the leader of Olympus in mind when he set down his requirement. He was born of distinguished parents, his birth was preceded by many difficulties, there was a prophecy before his birth warning his father of danger, he was abandoned (hidden) in a cave, an animal nursed him (and bees fed him), and when grown to maturity he took his revenge on his father and achieved top rank and honors among the gods.

In spite of the above, Achilles and Hector are always placed at the top of the superhero list in Greek mythology, notwithstanding that neither experienced a *miraculous birth*, nor was either *abandoned* at birth to be *saved and nursed by an animal*.[24] Moreover, while both were exceptional warriors, neither had supernatural powers. The Achilles of Homer's work was not the same hero we see in later myths, the one whose only vulnerable spot was on one heel. Had he been so nearly invulnerable in the *Iliad*, he would not have feared being drowned by an angry river god, nor would he have needed a new shield and armor before plunging back into the battle after Patroklos' death. (A sturdy shoe would have been preferable.) For his part, Hector is a sensitive, thoughtful man, which makes him even more admirable when he is compared to many other superheroes.

Further, while both Achilles and Hector are described by Homer as tall, neither approached the monumental size of Gilgamesh or Rama, nor was either presented as a perfect man, as was Rama. They killed no *monsters* and had no particular *superweapons* (Achilles' armor and shield are defensive equipment, not offensive weapons). Achilles was not in love with any particular woman and so had to pass no *suitor's test*; Hector was happily married and deeply in love with his wife. Achilles did have a *sidekick* in Patroklos, but Hector was a loner.

While they did not meet all of Rank's criteria for the hero, however, they did satisfy a number of archetypes shared by their fellow heroes in other lands. As the son of the goddess Thetis, Achilles was *semidivine*. Both he and Hector are the victims of a *destructive female*[25] (more accurately, *destructive females*), and *divine intervention* abounds throughout the *Iliad*. That both were *chosen* to their roles is constantly repeated throughout the epic, and their comrades and opponents readily acknowledge their leadership. Achilles' ultimate demise in Troy was also preordained.[26]

Others, though not at a level of Achilles and Hector, also deserve inclusion in the superhero fraternity.

While Achilles was a superior military powerhouse, Odysseus was no slouch on the battlefield, and was certainly the more complicated individual. A super survivor unmatched in any mythology, the king of Ithaca was a man who did not know how to give up, not even when the odds against him seemed insurmountable. But he was much more than a survivor; he was, as one learns in Homer's second great epic tale,[27] the *Odyssey*, one of the most talented, versatile, and human heroes of them all.

The *Odyssey*

The action of the *Odyssey* begins some seven years after the fall of Troy. All of the other great heroes of the *Iliad* have either returned home to resume their former lives, or suffered a tragic fate. On the positive side, Menelaus and Helen are back in Sparta enjoying renewed marital bliss, while Agamemnon's return is a disaster. Who can fault him for acceding to Clytemnestra's suggestion that he take a hot bath before they became amorously reacquainted? He had, after all, just completed a long, sweaty trip home and did not suspect that Clytemnestra and her lover, her cousin Aegisthus, had other plans for him. Thus, after surviving ten years of war, Agamemnon is ignominiously hacked to death in his bathtub.[28] So much for cleanliness being next to godliness.

Ajax also meets a tragic end, although in his case this happens before he is able to return home. After Achilles is slain by Paris' arrow to his vulnerable heel, the defensive star of the Trojan War is convinced that he will finally receive his deserved recognition as the greatest remaining Greek warrior. But it was not to be. Once again his lack of charisma works against him; Agamemnon awards the fallen superhero's armor to Odysseus, thus proclaiming the latter the new number one hero.[29] Crushed by the injustice of this action, Ajax goes mad and commits suicide.

Diomedes proves to be the most sensible of the Greek heroes. Upon his return home after the difficult war in Troy, he is not greeted with a ticker tape parade or the happy embrace of a loving wife. Instead, he learns that his wife has found someone else to occupy her bed. While others in his place might have responded with sword or spear, Diomedes takes the news in stride and calmly goes off to Italy where he founds several cities and lives to a deep old age, honored by his subjects.

With Troy in flames and its greatest hero dead, the Trojans must either escape or fall under the Greek swords and spears. It is at this point that Aeneas becomes their leading superhero. Weaving his way through the conquered city, past many drunken Greek revelers, he leads a number of his people to their ships and sets sail. After an arduous journey, he becomes the father of a city that will later be Rome, and takes his place as a genuine superhero in the heroic epic that bears his name: the *Aeneid*. His exploits will be discussed at length in the following chapter. First, however, we will trace the perilous journey of Odysseus as Homer recounts it in the *Odyssey*.

Unlike his comrades, Odysseus is still struggling to get home some ten years after the fall of Troy. At the beginning of the *Odyssey*, he appears as a virtual love prisoner on the island of a beautiful nymph named Calypso, daughter of the Titan Atlas. The lovely goddess holds him captive "...in her hollow caves, longing to have him for her lord."[30] Try as she might, however, she cannot deter him from his determination to return to Ithaca, not even when she offers him immortality if he will agree to stay with her. The *Odyssey* is the story of his struggle to be reunited with his wife, Penelope, and their son, Telemachus. The Greek philosopher Aristotle summed up the *Odyssey* in the following way:

> The story of Odysseus is not long; a man is away from home for many years; Poseidon is constantly on the watch to destroy him, and he is alone. At home, his property is being wasted by suitors, and his son is the intended victim of a plot. He reaches home, tempest tossed; he makes himself known, attacks his enemies and destroys them, and is himself saved. This is the heart of the matter: the rest is episodes [Poetics, 17].

How far Aristotle's tongue was in his cheek when he wrote those lines we cannot know, but if we were to take them at face value we might be inclined to view this great epic as little more than an ancient Greek soap opera. Moreover, if we accept the phrase "...the rest is episodes" as a negative value judgment we would have to apply a similar yardstick to virtually every heroic epic ever written, for it is in "episodes" and the skill with which they are presented that we find the meaning of epic literature; their composite strength determines the ultimate greatness or mediocrity of the work in which they appear. In the *Odyssey*, we find some of the most fascinating and memorable episodes ever written. It is through these episodes that we gain the true portrait of Odysseus the human being and the hero.

To an ordinary man, the promise of immortality plus the companionship of a beautiful goddess would be an irresistible combination, an offer that cannot be refused. But Odysseus is neither superficial nor ordinary. The extent of his unhappiness at being a refugee is so great that it even arouses the sympathy of the gods on Mount Olympus. At last, Zeus answers his prayers and orders Calypso to allow her unhappy love-captive to leave her island and resume his journey home to Ithaca.

The unhappy nymph reacts with predictable anger when Hermes delivers the supreme directive, but she knows that it would be unwise to disobey Zeus. With a heavy heart she seeks out Odysseus. She finds him "...sitting on the shore, and his eyes were never dry of tears ... as he mourned for his return; for the nymph no more found favor in his sight" (75). It turns out that, in spite of his deep depression, Odysseus has not led the life of a monk on Calypso's island. As Homer tells it, "...by night he would sleep with her, unwilling lover by a willing lady" (75). Unwilling, perhaps, but one might sum up his philosophy in the following way: brood if you must, but when a beautiful goddess wants you to sleep with her, reject her at your own peril. Gilgamesh is a good example of what the consequences of such a rejection can be.

In the same episode, moreover, we begin to get a sense of Odysseus' exceptional versatility. Though primarily a cerebral man, he demonstrates very impressive practical skills. When Calypso gives him permission to leave her island, he does not hesitate in order to ponder a course of action, as one might expect an intellectually oriented individual to do. Instead, he immediately begins to build an escape vessel which is more like a yacht than a raft. Homer describes it in detail:

> And now he set to cutting timber, and the work went busily. Twenty trees in all he felled, and then trimmed them with the axe of bronze, and deftly smoothed them, and over them made straight the line.... He bored each piece and jointed them together, and then made all fast with treenails and dowels ... and set up the deckings, fitting them to the close-set uprights, and finished them off with long gunwales, and therein he set a mast, and a yard-arm fitted thereto, and moreover he made him a rudder to guide the craft. And he fenced it with wattled osier withies from stem to stern, to be a bulwark against the wave, and piled up wood to back them [*Odyssey* 78].

It is safe to say that few superheroes would know what "wattled osier withies" are, much less what to do with them. In addition, he cuts and sews his own sails and launches the finished vessel with handmade levers.

Odysseus the ladies' man was even more impressive than Odysseus the shipbuilder. That he was very appealing to the fair sex is indisputable. How many wives would wait twenty years, as Penelope did, for a husband to come home for supper? How many a man is so desirable that a goddess would grant him immortality, hoping to keep him by her side forever? Moreover, Penelope and Calypso were not the only females whom the alluring king of Ithaca dazzled.

Shortly after sailing away from Calypso's island equipped with a supply of wine, water and some quick-energy snacks that the beautiful nymph provided for him, the intrepid Odysseus runs into serious trouble. Poseidon, the angry sea god, unleashes a terrible storm. Needless to say, the situation is desperate, but just when it looks like the end of our hero, along comes the cavalry in the form of a beautiful young sea goddess named Ino.[31] Rising from the ocean depths, she gives Odysseus the following instructions for survival: "Cast off these garments, and leave the raft to drift before the winds, but do thou swim with thine own hands and strive to win footing on the coast of the Phaeacians...." As Odysseus strips, Ino holds something out to him: "Here, take this veil imperishable and wind it about thy breast; so is there no fear that thou suffer aught or perish..." (*Odyssey* 81). Thus, with an early version of a Mae West, Odysseus successfully swims to the safety of the shore, temporarily out of Poseidon's reach.

Though a great swimmer and equipped with Ino's marvelous life preserver, Odysseus is totally exhausted by the time he washes up on the beach of Phaeacia. With his remaining strength he is barely able to crawl over to a large pile of leaves; burrowing into it, he immediately falls asleep.

It is no coincidence that the Phaeacian princess Nausicaa chose that particular day and that specific area of the beach to do her wash, for during the previous night Athena sent her a dream, indicating that she would be getting married very soon, and therefore she should make sure that her best clothes and linens were clean for the occasion. As a footnote, the goddess added that it would be a good idea to take along some garments for her future husband.

Athena's purpose soon becomes clear. After Nausicaa and her attendants finish their washing and settle down to eat the picnic lunch they have packed, they begin to play a game of catch. Their playful voices fill the air as one of them inadvertently throws the ball into the water, waking the exhausted Odysseus from his slumber. He slowly climbs out from beneath his cover of leaves, modestly holding a leafy branch in front of himself to cover his private parts. Caked as his body was with dry sea salt and brine, he must have looked like a beached sea monster. Terrified, the women flee for their lives; but due to the courage given her by Athena, Princess Nausicaa remains. As Odysseus approaches her, he turns on his matchless charm:

> I supplicate thee, O queen, whether thou are a goddess or a mortal.... to Artemis, then, the daughter of great Zeus, I mainly liken thee, for beauty and stature and stateliness.... Never have mine eyes beheld such an one among mortals, neither man nor woman; a great awe comes upon me as I look on thee [*Odyssey* 91].

What young girl could have resisted such flattery? The enraptured Phaeacian princess immediately provides him with a sparkling clean outfit and allows him to go off to bathe in private.

If he was irresistible before his bath, one can imagine the effect a freshly washed, fragrantly scented Odysseus had on Nausicaa. (He had rubbed himself from head to toe with olive oil, the deodorant of choice in ancient Greece.) When she beholds the stylishly dressed spic and span hero whom Athena has made "...greater and more mighty to behold, and from his head caused deep curling locks to flow, like the hyacinth flower..." (93), she falls completely under his spell. The extent of her desire to become better acquainted with Odysseus is apparent in the words she later utters to a handmaiden: "Would that such a one might be called my husband, dwelling here, and that it might please him here to abide!" (95). She does not know, of course, that this cannot happen.

In addition to Calypso, Ino, and Nausicaa, the enchantress Circe belongs on Odysseus' list of female conquests. His short stay on her enchanted island, however, can hardly be considered romantic. In this particular "episode," Odysseus' men have ignored his warnings and strayed from their leader in order to explore. When he finally locates them, he discovers to his horror that Circe has given them a magic potion which has turned them into swine.

Unknown to Circe, Odysseus is prepared for his encounter with her: Hermes, the messenger of the gods, has given him a powerful antidote to counteract any drug she might secretly put into his food or drink.[32] Thus, when she serves him up one of her powerful swine-cocktails, instead of obediently following her to the pigpen to join his comrades, he draws his sword. She realizes at once that he is no ordinary vagrant, and eschewing small talk, she makes the following proposal: "Nay, come, put thy sword into the sheath, and thereafter let us go up into my bed, that meeting in love and sleep we may trust each the other" (*Odyssey* 154).

To his credit, Odysseus demands that she first return his men to their normal state.

She willingly agrees. Odysseus succinctly relates how he kept his part of the agreement: "I went up into the beautiful bed of Circe" (155). By his own account, he remained with her for one year. So much for Odysseus the faithful husband.

Odysseus' prowess as a world-class survivor, lover, boat builder, and swimmer only begins to scratch the surface of his wide ranging abilities. Above all, he is a thinking hero, one who is constantly put to the test. There is no better example of Odysseus' brilliance than the episode in which he plans and executes one of the most famous and clever jail-breaks of all time.

Odysseus and his men have landed on a strange island. Seeking shelter, they enter a cave, unaware that it is the dwelling place of the Cyclopes, Polyphemus. This fierce son of Poseidon, one of a race of giants with a single eye in the center of their foreheads is not a gracious host. Instead of extending the strangers hospitality in Greek fashion, he holds them captive by placing an enormous boulder before the opening of the cave and calmly proceeds to make a snack of a number of them. It is clear that it is only a matter of time before Odysseus and his remaining men become the main course.

In spite of the extremely stressful circumstances, Odysseus is able to devise a workable escape plan. He tells Polyphemus that his name is Noman, and gives the gigantic cannibal a great deal of wine. While Polyphemus sleeps off the effects of the alcohol, Odysseus has his men sharpen a wooden stake. Next, he instructs them to heat the tip of the stake until it is glowing red and then plunge it into the drunken monster's eye. It is a nasty plan, but it works.

When the other Cyclopes inquire why he is screaming so loudly, Polyphemus repeatedly shouts, "Noman has blinded me!" Just as Odysseus expected, Polyphemus' cohorts surmise that he has had too much sun and go back about their business, thus allowing Odysseus to carry out the next phase of his plan. He has each of his men tie himself under one of Polyphemus' sheep and wait for the giant to remove the boulder from the cave entrance when he takes his flock out to graze. Fortunately, Polyphemus does not pat down the animals thoroughly as they exit, and so the great escape is successful.

Like all intelligent people, Odysseus is very curious. The best example of his curiosity is the famed episode in which his ship approaches the domain of the Sirens, twin virgin daughters of the sea god, Phorcys. Circe had warned him about them as he prepared to depart from her island: "Whoso draws nigh them unwittingly and hears the sound of the Sirens' voice, never doth he see wife or babes stand by him on his return, nor have they the joy at his coming..." (*Odyssey* 182). Undaunted by the warning, Odysseus has members of his crew stuff their ears with wax so that they cannot be lured to their deaths by the Sirens' song. This done, he orders them to lash him to the ship's mast and not to untie him until they are out of hearing distance. In this way he becomes the first to hear the enchanting Siren song and survive.

Odysseus' intelligence was matched only by his courage. To say that he was a brave and daring hero would be an understatement. Time and time again he demonstrated his valor on the battlefield of Troy and during his ten-year struggle to return to his wife and son, but never more so than when he made a perilous journey to the realm of the dead. In Book XI of the *Odyssey*, Homer gives the details of this journey to the Underworld, and in so doing provides us with one of the earliest accounts of the Ancient Greek concept of the afterlife. Unsurprisingly, he portrays the realm of death as a dark, gloomy place, ruled by the god Hades and his wife, Persephone, and populated by the shades[33] of the departed. Odysseus perceives the incorporeal essence of the shades soon after his arrival

there, when he sees his mother and tries to embrace her. She explains to him why this is impossible:

> For the sinews no more bind together the flesh and the bones, but the great force of burning fire abolishes these, so soon as the life hath left the white bones, and the spirit like a dream flies forth and hovers near [*Odyssey* 168].

Saddened by his inability to make physical contact with his mother, he moves on.

In the course of his journey, he encounters the shades of Greek heroes from the past and present: among others, those of Heracles, Ajax, Agamemnon and Achilles.[34] Homer's attitude toward death is clear in the exchange between Odysseus and the shade of Achilles. Odysseus praises his former comrade in arms as a "...great prince among the dead," to which the latter responds: "Rather would I live on the ground as the hireling of another, with a landless man who had no great livelihood, than bear sway among all the dead that be departed" (*Odyssey* 176).

When he returns to the world of the living, Odysseus is able to count himself among a very small number of heroes who can boast that they have been to the world of death and returned.

In addition to intelligence and courage, Odysseus demonstrates a capacity for extreme cruelty, a quality that is not uncommon among superheroes. The best example of this can be found in the well-known concluding episode of the *Odyssey*.

Odysseus has finally managed to reach Ithaca and, disguised as a beggar, is in the dining hall of his home watching Penelope's suitors gorge themselves on his food. Believing that he will never return, the princes of Athens have been courting his wife, using his home as a social club. In spite of their obnoxious behavior, however, not to mention the fact that they have plotted to assassinate his son, Telemachus, most modern readers would consider his ensuing actions excessive. Stringing his bow, Odysseus begins a bloodbath. Not satisfied with killing the ringleader with a well-placed arrow, he continues the slaughter until the room is littered with the suitors' corpses.[35]

Even if we were to justify the massacre of the suitors, though, it would be difficult to deny that Odysseus was responsible for setting the example for his son's cruelty during this episode. To show his father that he is made from the right stuff, Telemachus has those maids who have fraternized with the suitors separated from the rest and orders them to clean the blood and gore from the room. One can imagine Odysseus proudly watching as his son dispenses justice after the maids have completed their housecleaning assignment:

> ... he [Telemachus] tied the cable of a dark-prowed ship to a great pillar and flung it round the vaulted room, and fastened it aloft, that none might touch the ground with his feet.... the women held their heads all in a row, and about all their necks nooses were cast, that they might die by the most pitiful death. And they writhed with their feet for a little space, but for no long while [*Odyssey* 352].

All in all, Odysseus is a more modern version of the archetypal superhero than those we have seen so far. His birth, as far as we know, was not spectacular, let alone miraculous; he was not abandoned as a child, nor was there ever any conflict with his father, to whom he was thoroughly devoted. He performed remarkable feats although he could not claim divine parentage, was thoroughly vulnerable and had no superior means of transportation.

Opposite: **Circe and the crew of Odysseus on the enchantress' island. (Woodcut by R. Brend' Amour.)**

Odysseus slays Penelope's Suitors. Song 22 from the translation of the *Odyssey* by Simon Schaidenreisser.

He traveled countless miles over raging seas, overcame unbelievable obstacles and, against all the odds, returned home unscathed. What he did have was superior intelligence and unflagging determination. Using these gifts, he emerged victorious over the powerful elements of nature, won over enchanted goddesses and princesses, defeated a ferocious giant, and returned home to resume his rightful place as king of Ithaca. He was an absolute loner, uninterested in glory or fame, and yet was well loved by many and universally acclaimed. A sentimental man who could weep openly,[36] he was capable of extreme brutality to those he considered his enemies. The women in his life were just the opposite of destructive; without their devotion and aid he would certainly have perished.

A variation of one familiar archetype that Odysseus satisfied is the *suitor's test archetype*. When he finally returned to his home, disguised so well as a beggar that not even Penelope recognized him, he had to perform two tasks in order to regain his place at the head of his family. First, in a scene reminiscent of the one in which Rama won the hand of Sita in the *Ramayana*, he had to string his mighty bow after all of the suitors had failed in their attempts to do so. Odysseus accomplishes this task with little effort. This is parallel to Rustam wielding the mace of Sam when no one else could manage to do so, King Arthur effort-

***Opposite:* Odysseus, tied to the mast of his ship, listens to the seductive song of the Sirens. (Woodcut by R. Brend' Amour.)**

lessly removing Excalibur from the stone in which it was embedded after many knights had failed to do so, and Rama snapping the huge bow of Raja Janaka after countless others proved unable to bend it.

Odysseus also passes a second test once he has eliminated all of his wife's suitors. Penelope requires him to provide the details explaining the unusual construction of their marriage bed, something only Odysseus could know since he built it. He passes this test unhesitatingly, and goes on to live a long life, unlike many other superheroes whose brawn far overshadowed their brains.

Heracles

No discussion of Greek superheroes would be complete without inclusion of the greatest of them all, the man-god Heracles. If ever there was a model archetypal representative of the genre, it is this incomparable son of Zeus, better known to the western world by his Roman name, Hercules.

The son of Zeus and the Thebean queen Alcmene, from his very conception Heracles was destined one day to become a deity in his own right, a destiny he fulfilled after his death. In some locales, he was worshipped as fervently as his Olympian relatives.[37] The story of his life is one of the most fascinating in superhero literature.

Young King Amphitryon has just taken the beautiful princess Alcmene as his bride, but because of an agreement he struck with his father-in-law, he agrees he will not consummate their marriage until he completes an important military mission. To Amphitryon's misfortune, Zeus, ever on the lookout for fertile ground in which to sow his endless supply of wild oats, has taken a liking to Alcmene. His seduction of the unknowing queen, while one of countless such extramarital escapades, is different in that it presents an interesting moral and psychological question: how can one make love to a married woman without using force and yet allow her to remain faithful to her husband? Zeus, never at a loss to find a solution to a problem that involved satisfying his Olympian libido, comes up with a unique plan: he transforms himself, at least in appearance, into the husband, Amphitryon. Whereas others in his place might have needed to enlist the skills of a professional makeup artist to succeed with such a ruse, the father of the gods is a master of metamorphosis. In the wink of the eye, a duplicate Amphitryon appears before the blushing bride.

It is said that time passes very quickly when one is having fun, but such rules do not apply to Zeus. Using his divine power, he slows down time to make his night of lovemaking with Alcmene last three times as long as a normal one. By the time his passions are satiated, Heracles has been conceived. But the plot thickens at this point.

Alcmene scarcely has time to recuperate from her extended nocturnal exertions with the Thunderer when Amphitryon returns from his successful military venture, eager to become better acquainted with his new bride. We can only guess how he felt, though, when Alcmene greets him with something less than ardor. Wondering, perhaps, whether he should change his brand of olive oil or toothpaste, the disappointed Amphitryon consults a blind soothsayer named Tiresias,[38] who proceeds to give him a detailed account of what has happened in his absence. As upset as he must have been by the news, Amphitryon still insists on claiming his marital bedroom rights that night, and as a result of his first union with Alcmene, Iphicles, the twin brother of Heracles, is conceived.[39]

Predictably, Hera is not overjoyed to learn that her husband has strayed again. Zeus

The Greek superhero Heracles (Roman: Hercules).

does not attempt to conceal the fact that he has fornicated with Alcmene, but because Hera is aware that she is powerless to punish him directly for it, she decides to bide her time and take out her anger and frustration on Zeus' soon-to-appear extramarital offspring.

Hera's anger has risen to the boiling point by the time Alcmene goes into labor. Zeus, on the other hand, is happily playing the role of expectant father, bragging to all and sundry on Mount Olympus that another child he has fathered is about to be born. It has been prophesied, he adds smugly, that a child of his blood will be the first child born that day and will one day become a famous king. But Hera has other plans. Using her authority as the goddess of procreation, she manages to delay Heracles' birth just long enough for the future king of Mycenae, Eurystheus, to be born prematurely.[40] By doing this, the prophecy can be fulfilled, though not in the way Zeus expected. Eurystheus, it turns out, is the son of the king of Mycenae, Sthenelus, who is a grandson of Zeus. This is a mild preview of Hera's ongoing hostility toward this latest stepchild, whom Zeus named after her in a vain attempt to diminish her hatred.

From the very outset it is evident that Heracles has supernatural strength. One night, as his terrified twin brother looks on from their common cradle, he easily strangles two huge serpents that Hera has sent to destroy him. By the time Heracles reaches manhood, he is skilled at every aspect of warfare, and has become famous for his remarkable feats of strength and valor. Had there been tabloids in ancient Greece, Heracles would have provided them with abundant heroic and salacious grist for their daily pulp mills.

One particular set of adventures from that early time firmly establishes Heracles' reputation as a superhero and a superlover, and earns him a place in the Greek version of the *Guinness Book of Records*.

A killer lion is rampaging through a particular city, eluding capture by the terrified locals. Enter Heracles. With his bare hands, he dispatches the lion and in so doing wins the undying gratitude of the indigenous king. As a reward, the king offers Heracles the services of his fifty daughters, hoping that the latter will produce some outstanding grandsons for him when their genes mingle with those of the great superhero. His hope is not misplaced; Heracles impregnates all fifty of them in a single night of lovemaking![41] Undoubtedly, Zeus was very proud of his energetic, fertile son.

Hera, on the other hand, is more determined than ever to destroy Heracles as the tales of his exploits reach her ears. The years pass. In addition to a growing number of spectacular adventures, Heracles marries and begins a family. Distraught to see her hated stepson doing so well, Hera induces a state of temporary insanity to come over him, and it is during this lapse into madness that the hapless superhero kills his children and two of his nephews.

Having regained his senses after the atrocity, Heracles is shattered. Seeking guidance, he consults the Delphic Oracle. The latter advises him that the only way to atone for his crime is to offer his services to King Eurystheus for a period of twelve years. It is in this context that Heracles performs the twelve labors that have earned him everlasting fame and immortality. Though all of these labors are extraordinary, several deserve special attention, as they involve easily recognizable archetypal material.

It must be pointed out here that King Eurystheus, under the influence of Hera, has assigned Heracles tasks that he considers impossible for anyone to accomplish, an ancient Greek version of *Mission Impossible*. The first labor is an example of this: Heracles is ordered to kill the Nemean Lion, a monster with skin that cannot be pierced by any weapon. A lesser hero would have been stumped, but not Heracles. Using a combination of brain and muscle power, he rips out the lion's claws and uses them to kill and flay the beast. The lion's skin becomes his unique outfit, thus paving the way for the costumed superheroes of a later era.[42]

The second labor is no less a challenge to his mental and physical abilities than the first. King Eurystheus orders him to destroy the Lernean Hydra, a terrifying creature with nine heads, one of which is immortal. The difficulty involved in killing this monstrosity is compounded by the fact that each time Heracles knocks off one of its heads with his war club, two new ones grow in its place. Undaunted, Heracles enlists the aid of a faithful *side-kick*, his nephew Iolaus. Their battle plan is simple but effective: as Heracles knocks off one of the heads, Iolaus quickly cauterizes the stump before the two replacements can arise. When he has killed the Hydra by eliminating all of the heads, Heracles dips his arrows into its poisonous blood, thus acquiring a potent *superweapon* for the future.

The third and fourth labors involve the capture of a sacred stag and a rampaging bear, and are not overly exciting. The fifth labor, however, is noteworthy, since it not only demonstrates Heracles' ingenuity, but also has peripheral consequences. The task is to clean the Augean Stables, huge, filthy pens containing the numerous sheep, bulls and the other farm animals of a king named Augeas. Since these stables have not been cleaned for thirty years, the stench from the great sea of manure makes them virtually unapproachable. But Heracles has confidence that he can move mountains, even those composed of manure; he easily solves the problem by diverting a nearby river so that it flows directly through the stables. The filth is washed away immediately. This done, he sets off to report his success to an increasingly frustrated Eurystheus, who undoubtedly relished the idea of Heracles sinking into the deep mounds of dung. On the way back, the triumphant superhero decides that some diversion is in order and so he stops at a vacant field and paces off the dimensions that will serve for the activity he envisions: a sporting contest that will later have international participation and be called the Olympic Games.

The next significant labor is number eight of the twelve. His assignment this time is to capture and tame a herd of flesh eating horses.[43] The owner of the herd, a certain Diomedes (not to be confused with his namesake of *Iliad* fame), is known for his nasty habit of feeding visitors to his horses. (One can only wonder why anyone other than those intent on suicide by horse would visit such a man.) Again, Heracles easily carries out his assignment. With the skill of an experienced cowboy, he corrals the equine carnivores and succeeds in taming them by feeding them their former master.

As impressive as it was, however, the successful completion of the assignment was not the most significant event connected with the eighth labor; rather it was what took place on his journey to Diomedes' kingdom of Thrace. It was during this episode that Heracles took time out to do a favor for King Admetus of Pherae. At the latter's request, the great superhero descends to the kingdom of the dead in order to see if he can bring back the king's wife, Queen Alcestis. The difficulty of such a task is compounded by the fact that in order to do this favor Heracles must defeat Thanatos (Death) in a wrestling match. Even Death, however, proves to be no match for Zeus' mighty son. A grateful King Admetus must have hailed Heracles as the greatest superhero of all time when his wife was returned to him.

Labor nine is a deadly variation of an American college panty raid. Together with a select crew, Heracles sets out to steal the magic girdle of the Amazon queen, Hippolyte, as ordered by King Eurystheus. There are several versions of what happens as he reaches the land of the ferocious female warriors.[44] Whichever version one accepts, however, the result is the same: Heracles strips Hippolyte not only of her girdle, but of her life as well. However, that is not the end of the story for the Amazon queen. As we shall see, Hippolyte is resurrected in modern times as a bit player in the American comic book, *Wonder Woman*.

During the course of his tenth labor, Heracles performs a number of sensational feats. His primary mission is to bring back the Cattle of Geryon, a seemingly simple task when compared with the ones he has already completed. The catch is that Geryon is no ordinary fellow: he has three heads, six hands and three bodies. In view of this, it is easy to understand why he is heralded as the strongest man alive. When one also considers the fact that Geryon has employed a son of the god Ares and a two-headed dog to guard the herd, it is understandable why Heracles does not consider it a milk run. But he is not discouraged. On the way to Geryon's pasture, perhaps to get his muscles in shape for the main event, Heracles kills a large number of wild beasts and digs a long channel out of the land. In so doing, he creates two continents: Africa and Europe.

Finally, he reaches Geryon's territory. In a series of lightning maneuvers he batters down the two-headed watchdog, Orthrus, and the son of Ares, Eurytion. Then, without so much as a pause to refresh himself, he proceeds to drill an arrow through all three of Geryon's bodies, instantly killing the monster. To top it off, he sends another arrow sailing into Hera's breast as the enraged goddess attempts to intervene against him. By any standards, it was a good day's work for a superhero.

Labor eleven once again challenges Heracles' strength and intelligence. He is ordered to retrieve the golden apples of the Hesperides. These apples, given to Hera by her mother as a wedding present, hang at the top of a huge tree around whose trunk the deadly serpent, Ladon, is coiled.[45] When Heracles arrives at the tree and sees how far he will have to climb, he decides on another course of action. He approaches the Titan Atlas, and makes the latter an offer he cannot refuse. He will, he says, take the burden of the earth onto his own shoulders for a while if Atlas will pick the apples for him. (How he could have thought such a feat easier than climbing the tree only Zeus knows.) It is not very difficult to imagine how quickly the sore-shouldered Titan accepted the offer. After all, he has been shouldering his heavy load without so much as a coffee break ever since he and the other Titans were defeated in the Great War with the Olympians.

After Heracles does away with Ladon by means of a well placed poisoned arrow, he flexes his muscles and takes the burden of the earth onto his back while Atlas saunters over to the tree and casually picks the golden fruit. Zeus' son is fortunate that Atlas does not have a brain to match his gigantic body, for if it were otherwise, he would still be out there holding up our world. Instead, Atlas fulfills the first part of the deal with the best of intentions, but quickly begins to have second thoughts. He is not anxious to take back his burden because his back has not felt so good in eons.

By the time he returns to Heracles he has made a decision which he relates to Heracles: he will bring the golden apples to Eurystheus and return in a few months to resume his former post. Meanwhile, he says, he will enjoy his freedom. Heracles must really have begun to sweat when he heard that unpleasant piece of news. But he is a quick thinker. He pretends to acquiesce to Atlas' new plan, but he has one of his own. As Atlas is about to leave, he asks Atlas to take back the world for just a few moments so that he can put a pad on his shoulder. Poor empathetic fool that he is, Atlas falls for the ruse. He must have felt quite depressed as he watched Heracles wave goodbye and walk off into the sunset with the golden apples. In this instance, however, one Titan's misfortune is another's salvation. So it was for Prometheus; on his way back to report another successful mission to Eurystheus, Heracles takes the time out to set the suffering Titan free.

For his twelfth and final labor, Heracles must travel to the realm of death and capture Cerberus, the three-headed canine guardian of Hades' realm. He accomplishes this and more. Along with Cerberus, he brings the Athenian hero Theseus back to the world of the living. In so doing, Heracles is the first to make two successful round-trips to the other world.

The myth of Heracles does not end with the successful completion of his labors for King Eurystheus. The list of his subsequent military victories and remarkable accomplishments include aiding the gods in their battle against the giants, and at another point wounding Hades himself. His feats provide enough material to fill a volume.[46] If anything, however, each of his victories makes Hera increasingly determined to destroy him. Finally, she is able to achieve her goal.

The fact that Heracles was not inclined to lead a celibate life has already been noted. That he was also unsuited for a monogamous relationship also becomes quite clear very quickly to his second wife, Deianira, who is unable to accept his infidelities.[47] Indirectly, this penchant for straying is the undoing of the great superhero. The tragedy begins to unfold, ironically enough, when he rescues Deianira from a sexual assault by the Centaur Nessus. Heracles quickly incapacitates the would-be rapist by shooting him with a few poisoned arrows. It is a costly victory. As Nessus takes his final breaths, he secretly offers Deianira some of his blood, telling her that she will be able to ensure her husband's fidelity by dipping one of his garments into it. She accepts Nessus' deadly offer, her judgment clouded by her desire to keep Heracles on the straight and narrow path. Predictably, soon thereafter Heracles becomes involved in another affair, this time with a young woman named Iole. When Deianira learns of this latest infidelity, she decides to test the efficacy of Nessus' serum. She sends her husband a hand-woven robe onto which she has sprinkled the Centaur's tainted blood.

What is more natural for a tired superhero to do after a hard day on the battlefield than to take off his lionskin uniform, enjoy a nice hot bath, put on a comfortable robe and unwind? This is what Heracles is probably thinking as his servant helps him on with the stylish garment his wife has so painstakingly made for him. As soon as he puts the robe on, however, he realizes that something is terribly wrong. His skin begins to burn excruciatingly as a napalm-like substance enters his pores. His pain is so great that he tears wildly at the robe, ripping off huge pieces of his skin instead. Within minutes, he has literally torn himself apart. This is how Graves describes the gruesome incident: "He tried to rip off the shirt, but it clung to him so fast that his flesh came away with it, laying bare the bones. His blood hissed and bubbled like spring water when red-hot metal is being tempered" (Graves 201). No doubt Hera was smiling on Mount Olympus as she watched the painful demise of her archenemy. But she does not have the last laugh. Through the intervention of Zeus, Heracles is resurrected, and after a time Hera not only accepts this, but buries her former anger and looks upon him as a son whom she loved "...next only to Zeus" (Graves 203).

Heracles possessed all of the requisites for superherodom and then some. The archetypes of the hero abound in the myths dealing with his life: *miraculous birth, archenemies, sidekicks, destructive females, superweapons, resurrection*— they are all present. He was Gilgamesh, Osiris, Rustam and many other superheroes rolled up into one. No other superhero was more valorous or any craftier; none fought more battles against seemingly impossible odds, killed more monsters, performed more incredible feats of strength, or was either more deeply loved or hated by gods. His last triumph was the attainment of immortality; he conquered physical death and became an equal of the Olympians after his resurrection.

The Flash

Greek mythology, like that of Egypt, provided rich material for the American comic book and television industries. Two prominent superheroes in the New World can trace their origin to the land of Achilles and Heracles.

The Flash first made his appearance in January 1940, in National Comics' *Flash #1*. While he wore the winged shoes and helmet of his mythic ancestor, unlike Hermes the American speed demon was human, the product of a scientific experiment gone awry. A typical American superhero, the Flash devoted his life to fighting evil.

The Flash, conceived by the writer Gardner Fox, continued to enjoy star status until February 1949, when sagging comic book sales forced National to discontinue publication. Before he was temporarily relegated to comic book heaven, the speedy superhero had appeared in thirty-two issues of *All-Flash*, as well as in many issues of *All-Star*, and *Comic Cavalcade*. Like many other forties comic book superheroes, the Flash was resurrected in the 1950s. In 1956, he appeared in *Showcase #4*, this time with a new persona. The original Flash had been the alter ego of a young college science student, Jay Garrick, who was accidentally exposed to heavy water fumes during an experiment in the science lab. As a result of the mishap, he attained an unusual ability: he was able to run so fast that he could not be seen. Using this miraculous speed, he could outrun and catch bullets in flight. This proved valuable when he battled armed foes. His transformation from a nerd to a superhero also enabled him to become a football star, which attracts the attention and later the affection of Joan Williams, his future wife.

The revamped version of the speedy superhero has a police scientist, Barry Allen, as the Flash's alter ego. In this later series, Allen obtained his Hermes-like speed as the result of accidental exposure to dangerous chemicals. (By then it was known that heavy water does not emit toxic fumes.) In March 1959, National revived the comic bearing the Flash's name, becoming what Maurice Horn calls "The quintessential superhero strip of the 1960s."[48] Along with Hawkman, Sandman, the Atom, the Specter, Doctor Fate, the Hourman and the Green Lantern, the Flash was one of the founding members of a superhero fraternity labeled the Justice Society of America.

In the course of his adventures, the Flash confronted many colorful archenemies; the most notable of these was the Fiddler, a wicked musician who used a magic Stradivarius to bend others to his evil will. Some other super villains he battled were the super gorilla Grodd, the illusive Mirror Master, and the chilling Captain Cold.

By the late sixties, the Flash comic book had declined in popularity, but the character lived on in a short-lived weekly television series, which was aired between 1990 and 1991.

There are many hero archetypes evident in the origin story and later adventures of the Flash. As the literary reincarnation of the Greek god Hermes, the Flash is a modern *man/god*; his origin (both the original and later version) represents variations of two archetypes: the *conquest of death* (in that Jay Garrick survived the deadly chemicals) and the *miraculous birth* (in that the Flash was born as a result). His *super weapon* is the unbelievable speed he possesses; he defeats many *archenemies*, some of whom would qualify as *monsters*, and when he dons his uniform and sheds his alter ego (Jay Garrick in the original, Barry Allen in the later version), we see a variation of the *transformation* archetype. Finally, as can be seen in the illustrations, the Flash was eventually resurrected, and will probably appear again one day in an HBO movie.

Opposite: **The Flash, January 1940. (DC Comics.)**

The Flash (a later appearance).

Wonder Woman

The greatest female hero of them all, Wonder Woman, also has roots in the mythology of Ancient Greece. Her unlikely creator was not a feminist, but an American attorney/psychologist with no experience in the field of comic book writing. His name was William Moulton Marston, the man who gained a degree of fame as the inventor (although this is disputed) of the polygraph. Using the pen name Charles Moulton, he produced the first episode of Wonder Woman for National Comics' *All-Star #8* in December 1941, a time when the Allied cause desperately needed superheroes to combat Nazi Germany and the other evil Axis powers. By the summer of 1942, the colorful Amazon had become popular enough to earn herself a comic book bearing her own name, and later a place in the Justice League of America. In addition to her place in comic book lore, Wonder Woman has also been the subject of a full-length feature film and a popular 1970s television series.

Marston's stated reason for introducing Wonder Woman was to create a superhero who would serve as a "...counter to the 'bloodcurdling masculinity' of most comic books."[49] As was the case with other popular American superheroes of her time, Wonder Woman was a staunch patriot who devoted her life to eliminating evil. She differed from her male counterparts, however, in that she preferred not to employ violence to achieve this goal. Rather, she battled her nemesis with "force bound by love." Phyllis Chesler says the following in a critical essay on the Wonder Woman series:

> The stories stress the need for women to be "strong"—physically, morally, and scientifically—in order to counteract and subdue the "evil" use of force by men. Wonder Woman was conceived as a counter to the bloody "masculinity" of most American comic books.... As Wonder Woman says: "The better you can fight, the less you'll have to."[50]

Another noted feminist, Gloria Steinem, was one of a number of famous women who praised the early strip. Marston, she said in an introduction to a volume dedicated to the Amazon princess, had shown that "...women are full human beings," who could be as brave as men without being as cruel.[51]

Wonder Woman's origin story takes place on an uncharted mythic location called Paradise Island. The future American superheroine is presented as Princess Diana, daughter of the Amazon queen Hippolyte. The time is World War II.

One day, a plane carrying the American intelligence agent, Steve Trevor, crashes on the island. By means of the miraculous "Purple Ray," Diana nurses the injured man back to health and in the process falls in love with him. At this point, the goddess Aphrodite declares that it is time for an Amazon to accompany the American back to his country in order to help him battle the Nazis. Hippolyte announces a contest to determine which of the young Amazons will have that honor. Against her mother's prohibition, Diana dons a mask and becomes one of the contestants. Naturally, she emerges as the winner. When she divulges her identity to her mother, the latter reluctantly gives her permission to take Steve Trevor back to America. She also provides her daughter with a suitable costume for her new role.

How could Hippolyte have been Wonder Woman's mother, one might ask, remembering that Heracles killed her during his mission to steal her girdle. Moreover, how could she not have recognized her daughter, disguised as the latter was with nothing more than a tiny mask? Marston would have replied that the beauty of mythology is its lack of logical restrictions. When in need, be creative! He needed Hippolyte, so he resurrected her,

gave her a daughter and sent the daughter to the United States to defend democracy and promote women's rights. This is the stuff of myths.

Over the years, Wonder Woman has proved herself to be a superhero equal to any male worthy of the title. As is the case with the males, moreover, she satisfies a good number of hero(ine) archetypes. Originally a princess on Paradise Island, she undergoes a miraculous *rebirth* to become America's Wonder Woman, appropriately clad in a costume that resembles an American flag. She passes a stringent *suitor's test* to win the man she loves, and once in the land of the free and the home of the brave, she is born again as her superhero's spectacled alter-ego, Diane Prince. Like Superman, she transforms herself from one identity to the other with the speed of light when the situation demands (without the need of a telephone booth).

In her early years, Wonder Woman battled many *archenemies* in addition to the hated Nazis. One such nemesis was the evil genius Dr. Psycho, a misogynist who vainly used his occult powers in an attempt to "...change the independent status of modern American women back to the days of the sultans and slave markets, clanking chains and abject captivity." Another of her opponents was the ultra right wing, foreigner hating Dr. Frenzi. Wonder Woman ultimately exposed him to his green-shirted cult followers as the despicable, freedom-destroying villain he was. Yet a third classic *archenemy* was another woman hater, Thomas Tighe, a man determined to destroy anything of benefit to the fair sex. In an episode reminiscent of the labors of Heracles, Wonder Woman had to race around the world within twenty-four hours and perform five seemingly impossible tasks for him in order to save the financially troubled Holliday College for Women.

Changes in the later Wonder Woman comic books were not limited to her costume and makeup.[52] Increasingly, the stress was placed on adventure rather than lofty ideals. The *superweapons* she wields to defeat her enemies are defensive ones, but no less impressive than those of the male heroes. On each wrist she wears a bullet-deflecting bracelet forged from Athena's shield, the Aegus. In addition, she possesses a golden lasso, reworked by the god Hephaestos from the girdle of Aphrodite. This fabulous lasso has the power to force anyone she snares with it to tell the truth and obey her unconditionally (a precursor of the polygraph). Her *transportation* is an invisible plane, a *super vehicle* that travels more than three thousand miles per hour. As is the case with many superheroes, she often performed her feats aided by a number of *sidekicks*: Wonder Queen, Wonder Sister, Wonder Tot and even Wonder Dog, all appropriately costumed. In spite of these market-driven changes, Wonder Woman remains the archetypal female superhero, an equal to any of her Greek ancestors.[53]

Opposite: **Wonder Woman. December 1941. (DC Comics.)**

6

Rome

To the ancient Romans, the origin of the world was not nearly as important as the origin of their great city. Even their gods were, to a great extent, idealized Romans whose primary duty was to uphold and further the well-being of the state. Since they realized that they could not compete with their Greek cousins in the area of metaphysics, the pragmatic Romans "borrowed" the Greek pantheon, making a number of minor changes and a few local additions.[1] Thus, Zeus was worshiped in Rome as the god Jupiter, Hera as Juno, Athena as Minerva, Aphrodite as Venus, Poseidon as Neptune, Artemis as Diana, Hades as Pluto, Hephaestos as Vulcan, Hermes as Mercury, Ares as Mars and Hestia as Vesta. Only Apollo retained his original name, although he did not enjoy the degree of importance or popularity that he had in his Greek homeland.[2] The fact is that the Roman clones were not nearly as substantial as their Greek models. They were more abstractions than dynamic personalities; the accounts of their most interesting adventures are undisguised translations of Greek myths.

The few noteworthy gods who were indigenous to Italy are even more abstract. One example of this is the ancient god, Janus, after whom the first month of the present calendar year was named.[3] Although an important deity, Janus was more a concept than a living being. As the god of beginnings, water boundaries, and crossings (bridges, etc.), he was in charge of entrances and exits. This dual role made it necessary for him to have two faces, so that he could see the comings and goings of important and powerful Romans. His significance is attested to by the fact that in Rome alone there were five major shrines devoted to him. But in spite of this adulation, there are no Roman myths depicting his exploits, and so he remains unknown as an individual.

While they may have lacked originality in their mythological base, the Romans did have their superheroes. Moreover, as in many other cultures, the greatest of these were the offspring of unions between humans and divinities. Romulus and Remus, the mythical twin brothers who vied with each other to found a great new city, were leading examples of this archetype. Their sibling rivalry is one of the best known of all time.

It begins in Alba Longa,[4] a city in the vicinity of present-day Rome ruled by a king named Numitor. His place on the throne is insecure, however, due to the ambition of his brother, Prince Amulius. Finally, the latter stages a coup and sends Numitor into exile. To make certain that no legal heir to the throne will appear one day to squeeze him or his descendants out of power, Amulius sees to it that Numitor's daughter, Rhea Silva, is appointed to the post of Vestal Virgin. Since serving in the temple of Vesta was one of the most prestigious positions a woman could hold in Ancient Rome, Amulius was confident that his niece would not attempt to avenge her father. The added fact that as a Vestal Virgin she would not procreate meant that there would be no child to act against him in the future.

Rhea Silva was fortunate. A more uncivilized uncle might have used other means to ascertain that there would be no attempts to reinstate the true king on the throne.

The goddess Vesta was an official component of the Roman state religion, the deity who presided over the family and state hearth. Since family and home were sacred to the Romans, homage to Vesta was an important part of every worship service and her temple was one of the most sacred shrines in Rome. A perpetual flame burned there, tended by the six young maidens selected to be the priestesses. Those who were chosen for the role began their studies between the ages of six and ten, and only after a rigorous ten-year training period were they officially appointed Vestal Virgins. For the next ten years they performed their duties in the temple of Vesta, thereafter becoming teachers of the next group of novices. A priestess who broke the vow of celibacy was severely punished, either whipped to death or buried alive.

One would think that such a position would have had very few applicants, demanding as it was, but nothing could be further from the truth. Since the Vestal Virgins wielded enormous moral as well as political power, the richest and most influential families in Rome vigorously competed to have their daughters chosen for service. The prestige of a Vestal Virgin was enormous, so great that a chance meeting with one could often mean the difference between life and death. For example, if a condemned man happened to cross paths with one of Vesta's priestesses on the way to the execution place, he was immediately pardoned regardless of the crime he had committed.

As far as the vow of celibacy was concerned, moreover, in eleven centuries only twenty priestesses were punished for breaking it. Either the Vestal Virgins were extremely loyal to their vows or extremely clever at concealing their indiscretions.

Prince Amulius' thought process was not difficult to follow: without sex there could be no babies and without babies there could be no heirs to claim the throne. What he could not anticipate, however, was the rampant libido of the god Mars. According to one myth, the dreaded god of war comes across the sleeping Rhea Silva and decides that for a change he will make love instead of war. Needless to say, when the unsuspecting Rhea Silva wakes up she is an ex–Vestal Virgin (or a Vestal ex–Virgin). This becomes increasingly visible to everyone as the months pass. Finally, she gives birth to twin sons: Romulus and Remus.

Amulius is neither impressed nor pleased by the arrival of his new twin grand nephews. He orders Rhea Silva to be thrown into the Tiber, and then has Romulus and Remus placed in a box and floated after her. The result is a double failure for Amulius. The river god, Tiberinus, saves Rhea Silva's life, falls in love with her, and makes her his wife. Meanwhile, the box containing the twins washes up at the foot of the Palatine Hill. Luckily, a passing she-wolf with strong maternal instincts hears the babies' cries, rescues them, and nurses them as if they were her own offspring. Once they are old enough to be weaned, a neighboring woodpecker brings solid food to them every day.[5] Eventually, a herdsman and his wife adopt the twins.

The brothers grow up as happily as any Walt Disney characters, but unlike Mickey Mouse and Donald Duck, they are not destined to continue their tranquil existence. One day, after an altercation, a group of neighboring shepherds takes Remus prisoner and brings him to the major landowner for punishment. Romulus immediately goes to his brother's aid, but as it turns out that was unnecessary. Fortunately, the landowner is none other than their grandfather, ex-king Numitor. He reveals their true identities to them and enlists them to help him overthrow their evil grand uncle so that he can regain his crown. The counter coup is a success.

With Numitor back on the throne, Romulus and Remus decide to found a city on the spot where they washed ashore years before. The seven hills in the area seem ideal to them, but their problems begin when it comes time to decide who will be the ruler of the city. Since they have no coin to flip, they look skyward for a sign from the gods. Romulus stands on the Palatine Hill, Remus on the Aventine. For a while they gaze up into an empty sky. Straining his eyes, Remus sees six huge buzzards and runs to report the sighting to his brother, who is still scanning the heavens. It is worth the wait. Suddenly, a flock of twelve buzzards glides over the Palatine. Romulus declares himself the winner and informs his unhappy brother that he has decided to name the new city after himself: Roma. One has to admit that it does have a much nicer ring to it than Rema, which might have been the case had Remus seen the twelve buzzards first. Somehow it just would not sound right to say "When in Reme do as the Remans do."

Remus is not a gracious loser; he seethes with anger as Romulus and his followers work feverishly on the blossoming city. Finally, unable to restrain himself, he leaps over the newly built walls. Romulus is so angered by this hostile act that he slays his brother. However, unlike Cain, after his act of fratricide Romulus does not become a marked man who must flee in shame. According to the customs of his time, he has acted honorably in that he was protecting the sanctity of Rome's border. Thereafter, he remains in the city as its ruler for more than forty years, helping to make it one of the greatest cities of all time.

The ultimate end of Rome's founder is rather mysterious. As an old man, he one day goes out to review his troops during the height of a thunderstorm and simply disappears. However, after a time, he is resurrected and worshiped under the name of the Sabine war god, Quirinus.[6]

It is immediately apparent that Romulus and Remus do not have heroic stature equal to those already discussed. They slew no *monsters*, had no *superweapons* with which to annihilate their enemies, were opposed by no significant *archenemies*, had no *sidekicks*, were required to pass no *suitor's tests*, were opposed by no *destructive female*, did not possess *supernatural powers* and were not *invulnerable*. The problem is that there is woefully insufficient anecdotal material to enable us to become well acquainted with them as individuals. However, there are archetypal elements connected to their myth that earn them inclusion in the superhero club.

The story of their birth fits the classic Rankean superhero pattern very well.[7] They are sons of most distinguished parents (a god and a princess); their origin was preceded by difficulties and was threatening to their father's usurper; they were surrendered to the water, in a box, and rescued by an animal; they located their (grand)father when they had grown up, exacted revenge not on, but with, him, and one of them achieved rank and honors. We do hear of Romulus' later military successes, but these were unspectacular. For the Romans, the Romulus/Remus myth is important because it is connected to the foundation of their illustrious city. Even the deification of Romulus is contrived and unclear. In a sense, Rome is the superstar and the twins no more than supporting actors. This deviation from the standard superhero myth of that time anticipated more modern myths in which the human hero plays a secondary role to an inanimate one.[8]

While Romulus and Remus are upstaged by a city, there is one Roman hero of super-heroic stature who stands alone, one who had earned his fame fighting on the battlefield of Troy before the Eternal City came into existence.

Aeneas

Homer's Fifth Hymn provides information about Aeneas' origins. It tells of Zeus' decision to turn the tables on Aphrodite, the mischievous goddess of love who had so often caused him to be led astray:

> ... in Aphrodite's soul Zeus placed sweet longing/ to mate with a mortal man; his purpose was that even she/ might not be kept away from a mortal's bed for long/ and that some day the smile-loving goddess might not/ laugh sweetly and boast among all the gods/ of how she had joined in love gods to mortal women/ who bore mortal sons to the deathless gods/ and of how she had paired goddesses with mortal men [*Apostolos* 48].

Apparently, Zeus knows a few tricks of Aphrodite's trade. Thus it is not long before he causes the goddess of love to become infatuated with a handsome Trojan cowboy named Anchises. One day, while the latter is tending to his cattle, Aphrodite suddenly appears before him, freshly bathed in ambrosia and decked out in her most suggestive outfit. It would be an understatement to say that Anchises was interested. Suspecting that the beautiful female standing before him is more than mortal, he asks her to identify herself. Never a slave to the truth, Aphrodite tells the thunderstruck Anchises that she is a princess who has been abducted from her homeland, brought up in Troy and destined by Hermes to be Anchises' wife. Anchises does not need much convincing. He declares, "...neither god nor mortal man will restrain me/ till I have mingled with you in love..." (Apostolos 51). Those Trojan cowboys certainly did have a way with words.

After he "mingles" with the love goddess for as long as his strength allows (poor Anchises falls asleep from sheer exhaustion), Aphrodite awakens him, this time appearing in her divine splendor. He is now certain that she is a goddess and expresses fear of the consequences he will suffer for having made love to her. He is afraid, with good reason, that after her no mortal woman will ever be able to satisfy him. To calm him, Aphrodite informs him that he is going to be the father of a great hero, one who will eventually build a new Troy and become its leader. Then, after warning him to keep their romantic interlude a secret, she departs.

There are several versions of what happened next, one more unpleasant than the other for poor Anchises. However, all agree on one thing: he was unable to keep the secret of what transpired that memorable sunny afternoon on Mount Ida. In fact, in view of human nature, one might conclude that his tryst with Aphrodite became the primary, if not sole, topic of his thoughts and conversation for many days. After all, how often does a mortal get to "mingle" with the goddess of love? However understandable his behavior might have been, it did not mitigate the punishment exacted on him for his locker-room bragging.

According to one myth, he was paralyzed; others have him either killed or struck blind by Zeus' thunderbolt. Whichever version of his fate one accepts, it is clear that Anchises learned an important lesson: when you sleep with a goddess, keep your mouth shut about it. That there was a divine double standard which allowed the gods to gossip about such occurrences is not surprising. After all, Zeus never said that life was fair. Fortunately for

Anchises, though, the father of the gods was kind enough to erase his memory of the hours he had spent with Aphrodite.

When Anchises appears in the *Aeneid*, he is neither blind nor paralyzed, but simply old and lame. We first see him carried on his son's back as the latter leads the remnant of his people in an exodus from the defeated city of Troy. Before many chapters have passed, moreover, Aphrodite's one-time lover has shuffled off his mortal coil.

The *Aeneid*

The Roman author Virgil, alias Publius Vergilus Maro (70–19 B.C.), was fortunate to have lived during the golden age of Roman literature.[9] His father, a politically connected self-made man of means, saw to it that he received the best education available at the time. In the great city of Rome, young Virgil studied with the leading teachers and rubbed elbows with some of the most important political leaders of his day, including the emperor, Augustus. He was also fortunate in that he grew up during one of the rare lulls in the series of civil conflicts that continually plagued the imperial city. But peace did not last for very long. When he was in his twenties, he experienced firsthand the confrontation between the forces of his emperor and those of Marc Anthony. History is unclear about whether or not Virgil served in Augustus' army, but one thing is certain: he was extremely happy when Anthony and Cleopatra were defeated in the battle of Actium in 31 B.C. Two years later, he began work on his monumental epic with the dual aim of glorifying Rome and Augustus and of fusing Roman and Italian ideas. But it was by no means a dull piece of propaganda. For more than ten years Virgil worked on the *Aeneid*, refining and reshaping it into the masterpiece it ultimately became. A perfectionist, he was never satisfied with the final product; he declared on his deathbed that the *Aeneid* was a failure. It was the good fortune of Rome and the literary world that his request to have the manuscript destroyed was not granted. Today, Virgil is considered to be one of the two greatest poets that Italy has ever produced (Dante being the other), and is looked upon by many as a Roman Nostradamus because of the many prophetic statements he made in the *Aeneid*. Whether we consider him a great poet or a prophet, however, we must credit him with having created, in Aeneas, an impressive archetypal superhero.

The *Aeneid* is divided into two major parts, the first parallel to Homer's *Odyssey*, and the second to the *Iliad*. Virgil portrays Aeneas as Achilles and Odysseus rolled up into one — a clever, resourceful superhero who virtually single-handedly saved his entire people from annihilation and laid the foundations for a future Roman state.

One can summarize the plot of the *Aeneid* almost as succinctly as Aristotle summarized the *Odyssey*:

Pretending to have given up their siege of Troy, a number of Greeks hide within a huge, hollowed out wooden horse that they have left behind as a "gift" to their opponents. In spite of several warnings not to trust any gift given by the Greeks, the Trojans take the horse into their city and begin to celebrate their seeming victory. That night, as the Trojans sleep off the effects of their victory celebration, a heavily armed party of Greeks emerges from the hollow wooden horse and opens the city gates to admit the remainder of their army. The bloodthirsty invaders immediately unleash the fury that has built up during the previous ten years of warfare, and they kill, loot and burn indiscriminately. Amidst the bloody chaos, the Trojan hero, Aeneas, is able to lead a group of his countrymen to their ships. Thus begins a long journey in search of a new homeland, a journey that takes him and twenty shiploads of followers to Carthage, Thrace, Crete and Sicily. Finally, they land on the coast of Italy in the vicinity of present-day Rome and decide to settle there. But there is a problem: they cannot build their new city until they have defeated the forces of the mighty Rutulian king, Turnus, who views Aeneas as a threat to his leadership in the region. Turnus also knows that he will lose the beautiful princess Lavinia to Aphrodite's son if the latter is permitted to remain. The *Aeneid* ends with an archetypal showdown between Aeneas and Turnus in which the Trojan hero makes short work of his opponent. As Aristotle said of the *Odyssey*, all the rest is episodes.

The colorful adventures experienced by the hero(es) of a heroic epic provide the key attraction of the genre. For the most part, this is the case with the *Aeneid*, although Virgil was not nearly as gifted a storyteller as Homer. Despite this shortcoming, plus the fact that Virgil's work is essentially derivative, openly propagandistic, and the action often mechanical, the *Aeneid* remains one of the most powerful epic poems of all time. The explanation for this is that the weaknesses in the work are more than compensated for by a sensitivity to the human condition that is rarely seen in the genre. Thus, the adventures Aeneas experiences during his travels are less important in themselves than they are for what they say about our complicated, often tragic, and sometimes triumphant species. The *Aeneid* is not merely the story of a superhero performing extraordinary deeds; it is a stark depiction of the price in suffering that we pay for war, and it is as well one of the greatest love tragedies in world literature.

From the very beginning of Virgil's work the gods are very much involved in the action. Juno continues to plague the Trojans in retaliation for the Judgment of Paris, but the terrible storm she unleashes cannot destroy them because they are under the protection of Neptune. When Neptune sees the plight of Aeneas and his followers, the god of the sea commands the winds and waves to become calm. Meanwhile, Jupiter dispels Venus' fears by giving her the assurance that her son, Aeneas, will live to become the father of a great race that will include such luminaries as Romulus, Remus and Julius Caesar.

Although Virgil's inclusion of the gods in the *Aeneid* emulates his Greek model, the divine Roman clones he depicts seem to be tedious propagandists when compared to the gods in Homer's works. Unlike the Olympians, whose robust, charismatic personalities and exploits keep the reader in a constant state of awe and fascination, the Roman counterparts seem insipid. It is not until we come to the human interaction that the strengths of the work begin to emerge.

The first stop of the battered Trojan fleet (only seven ships have survived at that point) is Carthage, an African nation under the rule of Queen Dido, a beautiful, capable leader who had to take over the reigns of government when her husband was assassinated. The picture we are given of Carthage is one of a robust, exciting, quickly developing nation:

> The eager men of Tyre [Carthage] work steadily/ some build the city walls or citadel/ they roll up stones by hand; and some select/ the place for a new dwelling, marking out/ its limits with a furrow; some make laws/ establish judges and a sacred senate;/ some excavate a harbor; others lay/ the deep foundations for a theater/ hewing tremendous pillars from the rocks/ high decorations for the stage to come....[10]

Dido receives the visitors magnanimously, offering them not only hospitality, but also treating them as equals. Moreover, while Carthage is not a world power at that point in history, Dido's greeting to Aeneas' people demonstrates that she and her people are highly

civilized and well informed. She declares: "But who is ignorant of Aeneas' men?/ Who has not heard of Troy, its acts and heroes/ the flames of that tremendous war? We Tyrians/ do not have minds so dull, and we are not/ beyond the circuit of the sun's yoked horses ... (Virgil, Book I, lines 796–800). She graciously offers them safe escort if they choose to leave, giving them this option: "...should you want to settle in this kingdom/ on equal terms with me, then all the city/ I am building now is yours" (I, 805–807).

The gods are still watching. For differing reasons, Venus and Juno agree to make Dido and Aeneas fall in love.[11] Dido cannot be faulted for letting her emotions overpower her intellect; she is a recent widow, and in need of someone with experience to assist her as she attempts to develop her country. What chance does she have to resist a handsome, dashing, seemingly available superhero? Add to this the intervention of Cupid and it is clear that the ensuing course of events is inevitable. The *Aeneid* describes the effect of Cupid's arrows: "...the supple flame devours her marrow/ ....Across the city/ she wanders in her frenzy" (IV lines 88, 90). Love immobilizes Dido, halting the wheels of progress in her developing nation:

> Her towers rise no more; the young of Carthage/ no longer exercise at arms or build/ their harbors or sure battlements for wars/ the works are idle, broken off; the massive/ menacing rampart walls, even the crane/ defier of the sky, now lie neglected [IV, lines 113–118].

Finally, in a deserted cave where they have taken shelter from a Juno-induced storm, Aeneas and Dido make love.

Although the gods appear to control the action, Virgil recognizes that fate is in command, that as powerful as Jupiter is, in the last analysis he is merely the administrator of fate's decrees. Aeneas is destined to found a new nation in Italy and not even the gods can change that.

When he sees that Aeneas has extended his stay in Carthage, Jupiter sends Mercury to command Aeneas to get moving. It is an order Aeneas cannot disobey.

Dido becomes aware that Aeneas and his people are getting ready to depart when she sees the Trojan ships being loaded. She is crushed. In a scene as modern as it is ancient, she confronts Aeneas and accuses him of deceiving her. Initially, she appeals to his sense of decency, and when that does not work she attempts to evoke his pity. Still unsuccessful with that approach, she hints that she will commit suicide if he leaves her. Aeneas is not moved. He responds cooly: "I am not furtive. I have never held the wedding torches as a husband; I/ have never entered into such agreements" (IV, lines 457–459). Dido loses control; she curses him soundly, and a moment later begs him to stay with her for a short while to enable her to gradually accustom herself to the idea of losing him. But Aeneas is adamant: "(his) ... mind cannot be moved; the tears fall, useless" (IV, line 619). Realizing at last that it is a lost cause, Dido orders a huge funeral pyre to be built, and as the Trojan ships sail away she curses Aeneas and his followers.[12] Then, before her assembled people, she mounts the funeral pyre and falls on the sword Aeneas has left behind.

Aeneas' desertion of Dido is not a unique act for a superhero in ancient times. After all, women were considered possessions that could be discarded guiltlessly once their usefulness had been exhausted. His treatment of Dido is parallel to the way Rustam treats Tahmina, nor was Rama's cruelty toward Sita any less shameful. Of course, none of those superheroes was as bestial with women as the serial rapist Gilgamesh.

Opposite: **The Roman god Jupiter. (From a statue in the Vatican.)**

In Book II of the *Aeneid*, Virgil presents a more positive side of the Roman superhero. In one of the most sensitive and tragic episodes of the work, Aeneas demonstrates the deep love and devotion he has for his wife, Creusa.

As the triumphant Greek army sacks and burns everything in sight, Aeneas stealthily leads a group of survivors to the Trojan ships. When they reach the ships, he discovers that Creusa is missing. Virgil's description of the incident is so powerful that the reader shares the anguish Aeneas feels as he vainly attempts to find her. With little thought for his own safety, he returns to the scene of carnage. Virgil has Aeneas himself recount the episode: "...And I retrace/ my footsteps; through the night I make them out/ My spirit is filled with horror everywhere" (II, lines 1015–1017). He scours the occupied city, desperately calling out his wife's name. Finally, a ghostly image of Creusa appears to tell him that he must go on without her, that it is his destiny to found a new nation. Virgil has Aeneas give this account of the apparition:

> When she was done with words — I weeping and/ wanting to say so many things — she left/ and vanished in transparent air. Three times/ I tried to throw my arms around her neck; three times the Shade I grasped in vain escaped/ my hands — like fleet winds, most like a winged dream [II, 1065–1070].

Tears flowing from his eyes, Aeneas makes his way back to the other survivors and leads them away from the tragic scene.

The above episode is not the only one in the *Aeneid* to depict the chaotic nature of war and the tragic human consequences that result from it. The death of Priam, which Aeneas recounts in excruciating detail to Dido and her followers, is another such example. Aeneas describes the gruesome scene that he personally witnessed in Priam's palace when Achilles' son, Neoptolemus (alias Pyrrhus), broke through the main gates and began to slaughter everyone in his path. The Carthaginians listen in horror as he describes how King Priam, old and feeble, donned his armor and prepared to fight despite Hekuba's attempt to dissuade him. She implores him to "Come near and pray: this altar shall yet save us all, or you shall die together with us" (II, lines 703–704). Just when she has convinced Priam not to go on with his suicidal mission, Neoptolemus breaks into the shrine and slaughters one of his sons before his and Hekuba's horrified eyes. Unable to restrain himself any longer, the old Trojan king throws his spear feebly at Achilles' son, who simply laughs as he blocks it with his shield and then, "...with his left hand clutched tight the hair of Priam/ his right hand drew his glistening blade, and then/ he buried it hilt-high in the king's side/ This was the end of Priam's destinies..." (II, lines 741–744).

The fate of Aeneas' father is another tragic consequence of the strife. Virgil clearly understood that not only those who fight on the battlefield suffer and die in war. The fact that noncombatants also fall victim is generally underplayed or completely overlooked in traditional heroic epics.

Old and lame, Anchises' first inclination is to commit suicide as the Greeks pour through the walls of Troy in a murderous frenzy. Finally, however, he heeds the supplications of Aeneas and the rest of his household, and agrees to accompany them, convinced by an omen that it is the will of the gods that he not end his life.[13] Model son and father that he is, Aeneas lifts his father onto his shoulders, takes his son, Ascanius, into his arms, and carries them to the ships. Unfortunately, Anchises does not live to see his son overcome adversity and triumphantly found a mighty new nation. Exhausted by the grueling journey, the old man dies en route and is buried in Sicily. A grieving Aeneas describes his great loss: "...It is here [in Sicily] that — after all the tempests of the sea — I lose my father/ Anchises, stay in every care and crisis./ For here, O best of fathers, you first left/ me to my weariness, alone..." (III, lines 915–920).

A number of other Trojans in Aeneas' company also succumb to the hardships of exile in Sicily. At one point, a group of the women set fire to the fleet in an attempt to halt the torturous journey, but Jupiter saves the ships by causing a heavy downpour. Aeneas is dispirited and briefly considers remaining in Sicily, but fate has not left this option open to him. In the end, he chooses a middle course, leaving behind the old, the infirm, and those who for one reason or another simply do not want to go on. With the remainder of his people, he sets sail again in search of their future homeland.

In Book VI, Aeneas demonstrates beyond dispute that he is a world-class superhero. Joining the elite ranks of Odysseus and Heracles (Roman: Ulysses and Hercules), he descends to the realm of the dead. Ever the cautious adventurer, however, before he sets out he makes certain that he will be able to return.

In Aeneas' time, if one had an unusually difficult problem, one paid a visit to an accredited oracle for a solution. As a mighty leader, Aeneas chooses the best one available, the Roman counterpart of the Delphic Oracle: the Sibyl of Cumae.[14]

The oracle is undaunted when Aeneas tells her of his plan to visit the other world to see his father. A true professional, she calmly explains that in order to descend to the realm of the dead and return, he must first find the legendary Golden Bough. This is how she describes the miraculous object: "...its leaves and pliant stem are golden, set/ aside as sacred to Prosperina"[15] (VI, lines 191–192). She goes on to explain that anyone who desires to visit the Underworld must pluck the golden fruit, and that only a chosen one can accomplish this feat. In her words:

> So let your eyes search overhead; and when/ the bough is found, then pluck it down by hand/ as due: for if the Fates have summoned you/ the bough will break off freely, easily/ but otherwise no power can overcome it/ hard iron cannot help to tear it off [VI, lines 202–206].

Directed by two doves sent to him by his mother, Venus, Aeneas quickly and easily finds the golden bough. He immediately plucks the fruit from it as directed and sets off for the land of the dead, accompanied by the Sibyl.

Virgil's depiction of the afterlife is as fascinating as it is confused. In essence, what he describes is a combination of the Christian afterlife (heaven, hell, purgatory and limbo), the Germanic Valhalla, and the Greek Underworld. It is a foreboding journey, but Aeneas is unafraid. As they wander through the darkness and shadows, the young Trojan superhero and the Sibyl see the most horrible demons of mythology: the Gorgons, Harpies, and Scyllas. He views the five great rivers of the Underworld: the infamous Styx; dreadful Cocytus, the river of wailing; Lethe, the river of forgetfulness; Acheron, the river of woe; and Phlegethon, the river of fire. They see great numbers of shades (spirits of the dead) swarming on the near shore of the Styx vainly supplicating the ancient ferryman of the dead, Charon, to take them across.[16] Unlike the hapless shades, Aeneas and the Syble are admitted immediately when they show Charon the Golden Bough. Once on the other side of the Styx, it is a simple matter of drugging the three-headed guard dog, Cerberus, and moving on.

The next shades they encounter are those of dead babies, followed by those of men who have been unjustly executed, and those of suicides. All of these, Aeneas learns, have undergone the last judgment of the magistrate, Minos.

Soon they come to the so-called Fields of Mourning, where they encounter the shades of those who have died because of love. In a scene "borrowed" from Homer's *Odyssey*,[17] Aeneas instantly recognizes the shade of Dido, her gaping, self-inflicted wound still fresh; but, although he pleads with her to speak to him, "She turned away, eyes to the ground,/ her face/ no more moved by his speech than if she stood/ as stubborn flint..." (VI lines 617–619). Even death has not lessened her resentment over the way Aeneas had treated her. With tears in his eyes, Aeneas watches her walk off with Sychaeus, the man who was "...once her husband."

Next, they come upon a scene of fire and brimstone, an ancient counterpart of a fundamentalist preacher's vision of hell. Aeneas is in awe when he sees "...a broad/ fortress encircled by a triple wall/ and girdled by a rapid flood of flames/ that rage: Tartarean Phlegethon whirling/ resounding rocks..." (VI, lines 726–730). Undeterred, he sees writhing Titans, buried there by Zeus' thunderbolt, and suffering sinners who include in their number those who hated their brothers or struck their fathers, as well as those who deceived a client without sharing the spoils with family or friends. He passes sinners who rebelled against the state, and those who were killed because of adultery. The punishments vary. Some, like Sisyphus, repeatedly roll a giant boulder up a hill only to have it come crashing down again; some are stretched on giant, burning wheels; some have their livers pecked out by giant birds. It is fairly safe to assume that Aeneas was holding onto the Golden Bough very tightly as he went through this section of the Underworld.

Having seen the worst of Pluto's offerings, the two finally arrive at their destination, the Groves of Blessedness, a combination of heaven and Valhalla: "...a gracious place. The air is generous/ the plains wear dazzling light; they have their very/ own sun and their own stars" (VI, lines 848–850).

Aeneas and the Sibyl are overwhelmed by the beauty of this paradise. They watch as the shades of former athletes perform their exercises on verdant plains to the accompaniment of the beautiful music of Orpheus. They marvel as departed heroes pursue those same activities that made them famous in life, while "pious poets" and "pure priests" feast amidst the beautiful flowers. Then, in a deep green valley, Aeneas sees his father, Anchises. His efforts to embrace the latter fail: "...Three times/ he tried to throw his arms around Anchises'/ neck; and three times the Shade escaped from that/ vain clasp — like light winds, or most like swift dreams" (VI, lines 924–927).[18]

Anchises' explanation of why crowds are gathered at the shore of the river Lethe would delight a Buddhist monk. They were the shades, he informs Aeneas, of those who would one day take on another body and live again on earth. Naturally, Aeneas is puzzled. He cannot understand why anyone who has been in a place like the Groves of Blessedness would want to return to the trials and tribulations of the world above, why anyone who has experienced the freedom of weightlessness would want to drag around another ponderous body. Like a patient schoolteacher, Anchises explains to his son that only a few persons have led pure enough lives on earth to earn a direct trip to the Fields of Gladness (equivalent to nirvana); therefore, most will have to experience many incarnations before reaching that level. Needless to say, Aeneas is impressed by his father's lecture on reincarnation. But Anchises has much more to say. In a speech rivaling the best of the great Greek orator Cicero, he details the future glory of the Roman state Aeneas will found in the near future. Finally, having finished his oration, Anchises accompanies his son and the Sibyl to the exit and bids them an emotional farewell.

Once back on terra firma, and armed with the promise of future glory, Aeneas proceeds on his mission, one that earns him his place alongside the likes of Gilgamesh, Rustam, Rama, Achilles and the other superstars of mythology.

With the end of Book VI, the Virgilian *Odyssey* ends, giving way in Book VII to the Roman equivalent of the *Iliad*. While the final outcome is never in doubt, there is still much for Aeneas to overcome before he achieves his ultimate goal. And although his military adventures in Italy contain familiar archetypal material, the human factors continue to predominate.

If it had been up to King Latinus, the ageing monarch of Latium (a province in what is present-day Italy), Aeneas would not have had to fight a war to establish his supremacy in the region. Years before, Latinus had heard a prophecy that his daughter, Lavinia, was destined to marry a foreigner and produce a great race of future world rulers. For that reason, he unhesitatingly offers Aeneas both a military alliance and Lavinia's hand in marriage; but there is a major problem: Juno's hatred of the Trojans.

The queen of the gods still strives to exact revenge, in spite of the fact that she knows that ultimately she must give in to fate. As she puts it, "I cannot keep him from the Latin kingdoms/ so be it, let Lavinia be his wife,/ as fates have fixed. But I can still hold off/ that moment and delay these great events..." (VII, lines 414–417). With this in mind, she summons Allecto, one of the dreaded Furies from the worst part of the Underworld. Her instructions to Allecto are simple: to make things as miserable as possible for Aeneas. Allecto is up to the task. Virgil describes her as a demon "...in whose heart are gruesome wars/ and violence and fraud and injuries/ a monster, hated even by her own father/ Pluto..." (VII, lines 431–434). Eager to get to work, Allecto makes a beeline for Latium.

The malevolent Fury focuses her attention on Lavinia's mother, Amata. She is aware that this is fertile ground in which to plant her seeds of hatred, since Amata is determined to have her daughter marry the Rutulian hero Turnus. At Allecto's urging, Amata hides her daughter outside of the city so that Aeneas cannot get at her and proceeds to arouse all of the women into a state of orgiastic abandon. Allecto watches with glee as they:

> ... deserted their houses, bared their necks/ and hair before the wind. Still others crowded/ the skies with quivering cries; dressed in fawn hides/ they carried vine-bound spears. And at the center/ Amata lifts a blazing firebrand/ of pine and, raging, sings the wedding song/ of Turnus and her daughter as she rolls/ her bloodshot eyes [VII, lines 524–531].

Satisfied that Amata is doing a first class job of rabble-rousing, Allecto next stops off to visit Turnus, who is receptive to her anti–Aeneas diatribe. Very quickly, his Mediterranean temper rises to a fever pitch as Allecto works on his wounded vanity: "...Insane he raves/ for arms, he searches bed and halls for weapons/ Lust for the sword and war's damnable madness/ are raging in him and — above all — anger" (VII, lines 607–610). Thus, with the women of Latium debauching in the hills and Turnus ranting and raving below, the wheels of war begin to turn.

Meanwhile, Venus has not been idle. In a display of divine one-upmanship, she has her husband, Vulcan,[19] produce a sword, spear, shield and suit of armor for her son. These implements of war make those fashioned for Achilles by his Greek Doppelgänger, Hephaestus, look like they came from a bargain basement. The shield is so magnificent that Virgil takes three full pages to describe it. That is not surprising since the entire future history (up to Virgil's time) of Rome is inscribed on it.

Armed with his super weapons, Aeneas begins to recruit warriors from among the neighboring tribes. The most noteworthy assistance comes from Evander, king of the city of Pallanteum. Along with his army, Evander entrusts his son, Pallas, to the generalship of Aeneas after the latter promises to personally look after the untested youngster. Evander weeps as he watches Pallas ride off to war. The prayer he utters demonstrates that his own life is second-ary to him: "...If I still live to see him, still to meet him/ again, then I do pray for life and I/ can stand all trials. But ... if you threaten my son with the unspeakable, then now/ oh now let me break off this cruel life" (VIII, 750–754). Unfortunately, Aeneas is unable to fulfill his vow to keep Pallas safe; during the battle Pallas is killed by the stronger, more experienced Turnus. This sets the stage for the final showdown between Aeneas and the Rutulian leader.

Before the main event is discussed, however, there is one more superhero in the *Aeneid* worthy of mention: the Amazon princess, Camilla. An archetypal female warrior, Camilla is a super virgin, a devotee of Diana (Artemis) who performs spectacular feats on the battlefield. Any who might have thought that a woman was out of place in such a setting soon changed their minds when they saw Camilla. This is how Virgil describes her in the battle against Aeneas' forces: "...one breast laid bare for battle/ Camilla with her quiver charges, wild/ and now she showers stout spearheads, and now/ untiring, she takes up a two-edged ax/ the golden bow and arrows of Diana/ clang, loud upon her shoulders..." (XI, lines 855–860). Together with her virgin comrades she cuts her way through the allied lines, littering the field with corpses until she is finally ambushed, and killed by a thrown spear. A warrior to the end, her last words are a plea to Turnus to finish the job she has begun: to kill all of the remaining Trojans. But fate has decreed otherwise.

The long awaited battle is, as is often the case in heroic epics, a gross mismatch. Dur-ing the course of Virgil's epic poem, Aeneas has evolved to superhuman status. By Book II he is "Father Aeneas," sire of a future nation, a superhero whose feats in battle are prodi-gious. Apparently, however, Turnus was more courageous than intelligent. Unlike Hector in his confrontation with Achilles, the Rutulian warrior stands his ground as Aeneas charges at him waving over his head a spear "as huge as a tree." He even has the temerity to pick up a huge stone and throw it at the Trojan superhero; but his aim is as bad as his judgment and the stone misses its mark. Aeneas counters by unleasing his spear, which speeds toward its target like a guided missile, hits Turnus' shield dead center and pierces all seven layers of it before entering the Rutulian's huge thigh. The wound is severe, but not life threaten-ing. Turnus still has enough strength to plead for mercy. Displaying as much dignity as one can with a spear protruding from one's thigh, he concedes victory to Aeneas and relinquishes any claim on Lavinia. His humility almost saves him: "Aeneas stood, ferocious in his armor/ his eyes were restless and he stayed his hand/ and as he hesitated, Turnus' words/ began to move him more and more..." (XII, lines 1252–1255). However, just as it seems he will spare Turnus' life, Aeneas recognizes the belt that Turnus had taken from the corpse of Pallas. The *Aeneid* ends as a furious Aeneas sinks his sword into the chest of Turnus, whose "...limbs fell slack with chill; and with a moan/ his life, resentful, fled to Shades below" (XII, lines 1270–1271). Fate, no respecter of fair play, had turned thumbs down.

* * *

Virgil's *Aeneid* adds another great representative to the superhero genre, a warrior prince whose life story is replete with many familiar archetypes. Like Achilles, Aeneas was the son of a mixed union between a human and a divinity. However, while Achilles' mother, Thetis, was a minor sea nymph, the goddess who gave birth to the Trojan superhero was the Olympian Venus, the powerful goddess of love.

Aeneas was not an *abandoned* baby, as were Gilgamesh and Romulus, but he was certainly one of the *chosen ones*. In that respect, he can be compared to Rama or King Arthur. When Troy finally fell to the Greek invaders, he and he alone was able to lead his people to the Promised Land (unlike Moses, however, he was able to enter). In order to fulfill his fate, he was often aided by the *divine intervention* of his mother.

Though he is not described as *invulnerable*, as the *Aeneid* progresses that becomes Aeneas' de facto condition. And while he has no partner equal in stature to a Tonto or Enkidu, his young friend, Achates, is a bona fide *sidekick*. On the negative side, Turnus fills the role of *archenemy*.

In the persons of Allecto and Amata we have the almost mandatory *destructive females*, and in Dido the *deserted lover*. The war in Italy is a variation of the *suitor's test*, with Lavinia as the prize. Aeneas' successful round-trip to the Underworld fulfills the *triumph over death* archetype.

Aeneas is a genuine representative of the superhero genre, not only due to his extraordinary strength and valor, but also because he represents the values of his time and origins. To Aeneas, family and country are the primary driving forces; one could find no more loyal son or father. In his world, women are used as the means to a higher end (Dido), or are simply "prizes" (Lavinia) to be allotted to the winner of a given contest. Once they become wives (Creusa), however, they earn the rank of "family" and are treated accordingly.

Virgil is more ambivalent on the subject of war than Homer; he places more emphasis than his Greek models on the inevitable pain and suffering that result from human conflict. At the same time, he acknowledges that war is the route to unparalleled glory.

Because Virgil was primarily an intellectual rather than a spontaneous writer, and more of a scholar than an epic writer, Aeneas is more psychologically complex but less charismatic than Homer's heroic figures. To a greater extent, then, the form and the message in the *Aeneid* are in competition with the content, and demand the reader's careful attention. Those who take the time to understand the multifaceted Trojan superhero will find that it is time well spent.

7

Scandinavia and Germany

The frozen North is the home of many gods, a number of whom can rightly be called superheroes. The exploits of these Norse divinities have been detailed by the Icelandic scholar Snorri Sturleson, in a work titled the *Prose Edda*,[1] a witty, energetic little volume written in approximately 1220. Snorri's work stands today as the primary source of Norse and Germanic mythology.

Unlike a contemporary work by Saxo, who served as the archbishop of Lund from 1178 to 1201,[2] the *Edda* is an objective presentation, relatively free from proselytizing. Since the pagan Norsemen recorded practically nothing in writing, it is difficult to obtain a comprehensive, unbiased depiction of their belief system. Sturleson's work becomes even more impressive when one considers the fact that by the twelfth century, the period during which the mythic material was finally recorded, a militant Christianity determined to suppress the heathen past had gained a firm foothold in the region.

The *Prose Edda* consists of a prologue and four major sections. Since the work was intended to be a treatise on the poetry of the region rather than a study of mythology, only the first and second sections deal with the latter field. It is during his explanations of various "kennings," a term used to explain the ubiquitous metaphors in the Germanic poems,[3] that Snorri often recounts the myths of his ancestors. The following is a brief review of the major elements of Norse (Germanic) mythology.

Norse Creation Myth

It is hardly surprising that ice and snow play a prominent role in the origin myth of the Norsemen. Before creation, they believed, there was nothing but an empty space called the Ginungagap, consisting of mist, ice and snow and divided into two major geographical sections: north and south. (How an empty space can consist of anything, much less be divided into sections, is no problem for mythologists, who thrive on contradiction.)[4]

While no area of the Ginungagap could be considered an attractive site for a vacation

126

home, the north side, Niflheim, was the drearier region, viewed by some as the realm of the dead. Muspellsheim, the southern area, was no tropical island, but it did have light and a certain measure of warmth.

For eons nothing changed. At one point, however, the ice began to melt and as it did it formed matter. The result of this spontaneous generation was the ancestor of the frost giants,[5] the giant Ymir. Nursed by the cosmic cow, Zendavesta (in some versions of the myth she is named Adumla), Ymir was able to survive. Where Zendavesta came from remains a cosmic question.

Zendavesta was also in need of sustenance, but since there were no grassy meadows in the neighborhood, nor any farmers with handy bales of hay, she had to make do with what was at hand: nothing but salty blocks of ice. As she licked the ice, something very remarkable happened: a living being named Bori (Buri) was formed, destined to become the father of the earliest gods and the ancestor of our world's creators.

Bori in time produced a son named Bor (the reproductive mechanics involved are unexplained), who in turn mated with one of the Frost Giants and fathered the three brothers Vili, Ve, and, last but certainly not least, the future number one deity in the Teutonic pantheon, Odin (alias Woden or Wotan).

What followed was an archetypal generational coup d'etat. The three brothers challenged and killed the ageing colossus, Ymir, as well as the fierce Frost Giants, thus becoming the supreme powers in the young universe. Dracula would have envied the Frost Giants their way of dying, for with the exception of one couple they all drowned in the gushing blood of Ymir.[6]

In other mythologies, the defeated old guard usually disappear or, like the Titans, they are buried somewhere and forgotten unless they happen to shift their position and cause an earthquake. Not so with Ymir. He was the earliest example of recycling on a giant scale. From his flesh the victors created Midgard (the earth), from his blood the oceans, from his bones the mountains, from his teeth the cliffs and crags, from his skull the heavens, and from his brains the clouds. Nor was his remaining torso wasted; it became the giant ash tree Ygdrasill, the Norse equivalent of Atlas, only in plant form. The function of the great tree was to hold up the world. As an encore, Odin took Ymir's eyebrows and from them fashioned a fence that he placed around the entire earth.

The three busy brothers continued their work. When they were satisfied that Ymir had been fully recycled, they took some of the sparks from Muspellsheim and used them to create the sun, the moon and the stars. Finally, while out on a walk along the shore one day, Odin, Vili and Ve found two pieces of driftwood and began to whittle on them. Before long they had carved out the first two human beings (shades of Pinocchio), whom they named Ash and Embla. To complete the job, Odin gave each a soul, Vili gave them reason and motion, and Ve, not to be outdone, provided them with senses and speech. Homo sapiens had arrived.

The next beings to appear were the gods, although it has never been clear where they came from. In fact, they were often viewed more as human beings than as divinities. In his fine work *Myth and Religion of the North*, Turville-Petre emphasizes the fact that the ancient Icelanders considered the gods nothing more than crafty men who had deluded people into believing in their divinity.[7] The Norse gods, like those in Egypt, are mortal and have many human characteristics, both positive and negative.

A unique characteristic of the Norse gods was their division into two quite different factions: the Aesir and the Vanir.

The Aesir lived on Asgard, a mountain in the center of the earth (comparable to Mount Olympus), while the less important Vanir occupied a place named Vanaheim, which is never described in the existing myths. Petre describes the war that the two sets of gods waged against each other:

> The significance of the divine war remains obscure. Many have seen in it the record of some incident in history, even as a religious war between the fertility gods, the Vanir, and the more warlike Aesir.... The historical events said to be reflected in the myth have been assigned to very different ages [Petre, 159].

In any event, the Aesir, consisting of Odin, Thor and eleven others,[8] were the primary gods of Scandinavian and Germanic mythology. Two of the Aesir, Odin and Thor, eventually competed for the leadership of Asgard.[9] Both of these man-gods easily qualify for inclusion in the superhero pantheon.

Odin

Various versions of Odin's origin exist. One belief was that he began his career as a minor god and gradually worked his way to the top of the divine pecking order. This version prevailed among those peoples who were the ancestors of present day Germans.[10]

A number of sources specify that he was always the leader of the gods, the CEO at birth. In the *Prose Edda*, he is described as "...the highest and the oldest of the gods. He rules all things and, no matter how mighty the other gods may be, they all serve him as children do their father" (Snorri 48). According to this account, Odin was the creator of the world and man; however, he was credited with these accomplishments much later by those who zealously worshiped him.[11] Whether he was a remarkable overachiever or simply born to his high status, the fact remains that Odin's fingers were deeply immersed in the universal pie. His specialties included warfare, magic and poetry.

As the god of poetry, Odin was understandably the uncontested favorite of poets. In accordance with his dual nature, when he was not involved with poetry Odin was busy fulfilling his responsibilities as the god of war. In that role, he was often identified with the Roman war-god, Mars.[12] The ancient Germanic warriors called the Berserkers worshiped him in this capacity. In the *Ynglinga Saga*, Snorri describes these fierce followers of Odin: "...as frantic as dogs or wolves; they bit their shields and were as strong as bears or boars; they slew men, but neither fire nor iron could hurt them. This is known as running Beserk."

Though he did not personally fight in wars, Odin decided who was to be victorious and who was to fall in battle. Military leaders would offer him human sacrifices to ensure their entry into Valhalla, the great hall of heroes where slain heroes spent eternity.

Only those who were worthy of Odin were brought to Valhalla. The trip to that fantastic domain was taken in style. When a warrior fell in battle he was immediately snatched up by one of the armor-clad maidens called Valkyries and taken to the Great Hall.[13] Valhalla was gigantic. Its framework of spears boasted no less than 540 doors to admit the fallen warriors, doors so wide that eight hundred of them could enter abreast.

Opposite: The Norse god Odin. (From a statue by B. E. Fogelberg.)

A Valkyrie, feared female warrior in Norse mythology. (From a statue by Stephan Sinding.)

Light in Valhalla was provided by the reflection on the heroes' swords of huge, continually burning bonfires. This light was amplified by the massive roof, constructed in its entirety of gleaming shields. Although they had no television to entertain them, the fallen heroes were not bored in Valhalla. They spent their days doing the thing they loved best: hacking each other to pieces. At night, tired out by the exertions of the day, they were made miraculously whole again so that they could renew their fighting on the next morning.

Although he did not personally participate in the heavy fighting, as the god of war and heroes Odin often commenced hostilities. He began the military action by hurling his deadly spear into the midst of the combatants, as he had done at the onset of the war between the Aesir and the Vanir. And what a spear it was! The importance that the ancient Norse and Germanic peoples placed on their weapons is evidenced by the fact that each had a unique name. Odin's spear was called Gungnir. Forged by dwarves, Gungnir was more reliable than a heat-seeking missile. Once unleashed, it never missed its intended target, whether it was a moving or a stationary one. In addition to this super-spear, Odin sported a golden helmet and beautiful armor, and was often accompanied by two ferocious wolves. His means of transportation was also very impressive. The Lone Ranger and Silver, as well as Rustam and Rakhsh would have been left in the dust by the thundering hoofbeats of Odin's swift steed, Sleipnir. No wonder, since Sleipnir had eight powerful legs and was able to propel his rider across any terrain, be it the earth, the sky, or the ocean. Odin simply shouted the Norse equivalent of a "heigh-ho, Sleipnir," and eight powerful legs began to move more swiftly than an ice storm over a fjord.

Odin's sphere of influence was not limited to poetry and war; he also could control the wind, an aptitude that earned him the worship of sailors.[14] Moreover, he was a master magician with a ready stock of powerful incantations at his disposal. If one wanted a lame horse cured or an enemy's chains removed, one called on Odin for the proper words.[15]

The ability to metamorphose was another powerful weapon in Odin's arsenal. He could transform himself at will, into a serpent, an eagle, or any other form needed at a given moment. This particular aptitude was often very useful, but never more so than during the following adventure.

Odin's objective was to obtain the formula for mead, the beverage that was to become the official drink of the gods. The problem was, however, that the giant who possessed the formula had no intention of sharing it. Undaunted, Odin transformed himself into a serpent and bored his way through the solid rock wall of the giant's castle. Then, he became "friendly" with the giant's sister, and as a reward for sleeping with her for three nights she allowed him to take three gulps of the precious drink. This done, he became an eagle and soared off toward Asgard with his prize.

But victory was not to be gained so easily, since the giant from whom he had stolen the mead shared the ability to change shape. No sooner had Odin become airborne than he noticed another eagle right on his tail. It was the Norse version of a modern chase scene. Suffice it to say that Odin's eagle was a swifter model, a fact that was particularly appreciated by the other Aesir on those quiet evenings when they had the urge for a little swig or two of the delicious, divinely intoxicating beverage their leader had secured for them. How eagerly the gods must have shouted encouragement as Eagle-Odin approached Asgard. How fervently they must have cheered when Odin regurgitated the mead into the three jars they had placed on the divine wall.

As a result of Odin's successful venture, the Norse gods gained a beverage delicious enough to challenge Olympian nectar. But the gods were not the only ones to benefit from the theft of mead. The spoils of Odin's bravery have been passed down to mankind in slightly weakened but still divine form. We call it beer. This contribution alone would be enough to earn Odin first place in the hallowed hero hierarchy of many lands.

Odin derived another of his titles, "Lord of the Gallows," the hard way. According to one of the better-known Eddic poems, during one adventure he was wounded in the side by a spear and hanged from a tree where he remained for nine days.[16] Thereafter he had the power to resurrect those who had been hanged.

In yet another myth, Odin is described as omniscient. According to one version, he obtained this power after drinking from the Well of Knowledge. But he paid a high price for the acquisition. Mimir, the giant who guarded the Well, allowed Odin to drink from it only after Odin agreed to give up one of his eyes in return. Odin agreed to the deal, and so his eye was placed under the fountain. (Another version of the myth places the eye under the great tree of life, Ygdrasill.)

There is yet another version of how Odin attained knowledge. In this account, when Mimir died Odin had the old fellow's head embalmed and thereafter carried it with him wherever he went. By using magic, he could get the head to answer the most complex questions. But Mimir's head was not his only source of information gathering. To complement the talking head of Mimir, he had an effective, if rather primitive, intelligence apparatus in the form of two ravens, Huginn and Muninn. The feathered duo would fly to all corners of the earth each day, and in the evening return to Odin. Then, perched on his shoulders, they would tell him what they had seen and heard during their flight. Were they alive today, these forerunners of the loquacious American cartoon magpies, Heckle and Jeckle, would command astronomical salaries as coanchors on any major television network.

Like his fellow Greek father-god, Zeus, from time to time Odin engaged in extramarital affairs, often utilizing powerful love potions he had personally formulated and manufactured to seduce his targeted prey. Unlike Zeus, however, Odin did not have to listen to his wife's constant complaints about his infidelities. Frigg, the goddess of marriage and childbirth, was similar to Hera in that she enjoyed defeating her husband's will, but she did not expend undue energy in an attempt to keep him on the straight and narrow marital path. Instead, she adopted the philosophy that what was good for the gander was good for the goose, and, as a result of her frequent extramarital escapades, she was often compared to Venus. Due perhaps to this relatively open marriage, the first couple of Norse mythology did not bicker a fraction as much as their Greek counterparts.

Thor

The only serious competition Odin had for leadership among the Norse gods came from the mightiest warrior in Asgard, the strapping, red-bearded god of thunder, Thor (known in the Germanic world as Donar[17]). Snorri writes the following about him: "He is strongest of all gods and men" (Edda 50). In fact, in a large area of Scandinavia it was Thor and not Odin who was considered the leader of the gods: "In Norway and in Iceland after its colonization, and to some extent in Sweden, Thor appears as the chief god...."[18]

The contrast between the two mighty gods is striking. While Odin relied primarily on his brain to accomplish his goals, Thor employed brute force. For Odin, a glass of wine or mead during a meal usually sufficed to quell his thirst; Thor, on the other hand, was an insatiable glutton. Odin was the champion of the aristocracy, while Thor was the favorite of the common people, who felt a kinship with him because "He guarded not only the halls of Asgard, but the humbler homesteads of Norway and Iceland..." (Davidson 91). Later, as Christianity began to gain a foothold in the North, it was Thor who became the chief rival of Jesus in the battle for the people's devotion. Unlike Jesus, who advocated turning the other cheek in response to mistreatment, anyone who wronged Thor did so at his extreme peril. The Thunder God's philosophy might well be summed up in a slogan: "Make war, not love."

Whether or not Thor was the official chairman of the gods, it is clear that he was their greatest superhero. It was he who defended Asgard against the giants and other enemies and "...maintained the order of the universe" (Petre 75). To accomplish these formidable tasks, Thor had some impressive superweapons at his disposal.

As already discussed, Odin's spear was a formidable weapon; but to compare it to Thor's mighty hammer, aptly named Mjöllnir (translation: "the Destroyer"), would be like comparing a firecracker to a bomb. Forged by the same dwarves who had fashioned Gungnir,[19] Mjöllnir was the ultimate offensive superweapon. When Thor hurled it, whether at a giant or a mountain, the target was invariably shattered. Its mission accomplished, Mjöllnir flew back to Thor's hand more accurately than the best Australian boomerang and shrank to pocket size. Replicas of Mjöllnir were used by the Scandinavians to consecrate treaties and marriages, and since it was viewed as a potent phallic symbol, it was often placed on a woman's lap during the wedding ceremony to ensure fertility. And in the same way that gravestones of Christians bear a cross, those of many ancient Norsemen had Thor's hammer etched into their surfaces. As time passed, the Aesir grew more and more dependent on Thor and his hammer for their very survival.

Mjöllnir was not the only noteworthy weapon wielded by Thor in his numerous adventures. In battle, he wore impenetrable iron gloves, wielded a battle-axe, and had a magic belt that doubled his normally incredible strength.

Unlike Odin, Thor did not have an eight legged horse to transport him, but he was not housebound by any means. Whenever he desired to leave his 640 room mansion, he simply got into his chariot and was whisked away by the two marvelous he-goats harnessed to it. His goats, who could travel at speeds that would earn them speeding citations on most major highways of the world today, had one other interesting characteristic that worked to Thor's benefit: they were a constant source of food. He could cook and eat them at any time and then restore them to life with a touch of his hammer. For someone with an insatiable appetite like his, they were the perfect companions.

As might be predicted of a superhero/god of his stature, Thor had powerful enemies, including the entire population of Giantland. Numerous myths tell how he destroyed this or that giant or giantess with his hammer, whether for the noble purpose of protecting Asgard from attack, or for personal, at times petty, reasons. Put very simply, Thor hated giants; he regarded them as his and his fellow Aesir's natural enemies. While he was always victorious in his clashes with them, Thor knew from experience that the giants were no pushovers. This is evident in the myth detailing his confrontation with the ferocious behemoth, Hrungnir, as told by Snorri in the *Prose Edda*. It is a fascinating story.

Odin taunted Hrungnir one day by boasting that his horse was faster than any that the giants could put into the field. Incensed by the boast, Hrungnir mounted his prized horse, Gold-mane, and set out after Odin in yet another archetypal chase scene. As the Shah of Persia often did, Odin had bitten off more than he could chew. While eight-legged Sleipnir was faster than Gold-mane, the giant was relentless; he chased Odin all the way into Asgard, becoming more enraged every second. Frightened, Odin and the other gods who were at home that day managed to quiet Hrungnir down by offering him a drink of mead. One drink led to another, however, and before long the giant was drunkenly boasting that he was going to "...pick up Valhalla and carry it into Giantland, sink Asgard in the sea and kill all of the gods except Freyja and Sif whom he would carry home with him" (*Edda* 103). As the situation deteriorated, the SOS went out for Thor. The Thunder God dropped what he was doing, hitched up his goats and sped to the rescue. He quickly located

the angry giant and began to taunt him. Hrungnir responded by challenging Thor to a duel, to be held in Giantland on a given date. The Thunderer accepted the terms without hesitation, and Hrungnir rode home to make preparations for the fight of the century.

When the other giants heard what was going to happen they were both proud and frightened. Because of Thor's unmatched strength, it was the first time that any of them had ever dared to meet him willingly in single combat. To even the odds, they constructed a huge clay figure, implanted a horse's heart in it, and waited for the arrival of the bearded superhero-god.

No doubt it was a sellout crowd. Thor, always the showman, appeared on the day of the fight to the accompaniment of loud peals of thunder and bright flashes of lightning. The clay goliath was so frightened that "It is said that it made water when it saw Thor" (*Edda* 104). Finally, Hrungnir appeared. Thor charged his adversary at a dazzling speed and unleashed a mighty hammer throw. At the same time, Hrungnir hurled an enormous whetstone at his opponent. Crash! Thor's Hammer and the whetstone collided in mid-air with a deafening sound. The latter was smashed to bits. Undeterred after the collision, Mjöllnir continued its murderous flight, smashing into Hrungnir's head and blasting it to smithereens. Hungrir fell like an oak tree hit by a bolt of lightning. But Thor did not come through unscathed; a fragment of the stone ricocheted and pierced his skull. To the added dismay of the Aesir, one of the dead giant's legs landed on Thor and pinned him to the ground.

Try as they might, the gods were unable to lift the gigantic leg from their immobilized champion, who now had a major migraine headache from the rock fragment lodged in his head. Finally, Thor's three-year-old son, Magni, stepped over and nonchalantly lifted Hrungnir's leg to allow his father to scramble out. As a reward for this, Thor gave his superson Hrungnir's horse, Gold-mane, this in spite of the fact that Odin asserted that it should be given to him.[20] As the crowd dispersed, Thor made his way to the sibyl Groa, who specialized in incantations designed to remove rocks from the heads of superheroes. Unfortunately, she was distracted during the procedure and forgot her lines, and so Thor probably had to take quite a few aspirins until the final curtain came down for him during Ragnarök, or as the German's call it, Götterdämmerung: the Twilight of the Gods.

Another myth centered on Thor recounts the unorthodox way he recovered Mjöllnir after a giant named Thrym stole it from him and buried it deep in the earth.[21] When Thor requested the hammer's return, Thrym agreed to comply only if he were given the chief Valkyrie, Freyja, as his bride. Since the gods felt that they needed the hammer more than they needed Freyja, a delegation of Aesir went to her to ask if she would be a good sport and accept the giant's offer. Freyja, however, was no martyr. She was so angered at this proposal that the veins in her neck swelled up like balloons and popped the necklace she was wearing.[22]

Just when all seemed lost, one of the Aesir came up with an original idea: Thor could impersonate Freyja. After getting Thor to agree to the plan, they gave him women's clothing, put Freija's hastily repaired necklace around his neck, and sent him and the god Loki to Thrym's castle.

Thrym was enchanted when he saw whom he thought was the desired Valkyrie. His ardor grew as he watched Thor hungrily devour "...one entire ox, eight large salmon, and numerous side dishes" (Larousse 262). By the time Thor had gulped down three barrels of mead, the giant's passion was almost out of control, fueled by Loki's explanation that "Freyja"

Opposite: **The Norse god Thor slays the Giants, powerful enemies of the Aesir. (From a painting by M. E. Winge.)**

had not eaten in eight days because "she" had been so eager to become a bride. Unable to restrain himself any longer, Thrym lifted Thor's veil and was about to kiss him, but when he saw the fire in the Thunder God's eyes he hesitated. (We must assume that Thor had shaved off his beard for his transvestite role.) Loki calmed Thrym down by explaining that "she" had not slept for the past eight nights due to the passion she felt when she envisioned her wedding night. That did it! Thrym immediately sent for the purloined hammer, and when it arrived, placed it on what he thought were his future bride's knees. It was the last thought he ever had. Thor grasped Mjöllnir: "Then throwing off his veil he ... joyfully struck down Thrymn and all Thrym's band of giants" (Larousse 263). Thus, thanks to Thor and Mjöllnir, Giantland had to attend a funeral instead of a wedding.

Although the giants could be considered a collective archenemy of Thor, he had another rival who was more dangerous than all of the others put together. Like his distant cousin in Genesis, the world serpent, Midgardsörm, was a symbol for evil in the world of the ancient Norsemen. According to myth, it lay beneath the sea with its body coiled around the earth, waiting for the day when it would arise and destroy mankind. The following encounter between Thor and Midgardsörm appears in the *Prose Edda*.

One day, Thor disguised himself as a young man and asked the giant, Hrym, if he could accompany him on his boat for a day of fishing. At first the giant refused, but when Thor promised to supply his own bait and assured him that he would be able to assist with the rowing, Hrym agreed to take him on as a passenger. Then, good to his word, Thor located the biggest ox in the vicinity, knocked its head off with his hammer, brought the huge piece of bait into the boat and began to row. Hrym was impressed by Thor's strength and endurance, but when the latter insisted on rowing far out into the ocean he became nervous and angry. They had entered Midgardsörm's territory.

They hadn't been fishing for very long when Thor got a bite on his line. He did not know it at first, but he had hooked the world serpent itself: "The Midgard Serpent snapped at the ox-head, but the hook stuck fast in the roof of its mouth..." (*Edda* 80). Midgardsörm pulled so hard on the line that Thor's legs went right through the bottom of the boat and he had to dig his heels into the ocean floor to stop the serpent from dragging him away. Finally, the God of Thunder managed to hoist Midgardsörm into the boat and was about to deliver the coup de grace when the terrified Hrym cut the line.

There are conflicting accounts of what happened next. One version claims that Thor finished his archenemy off with a hammer throw; but Snorri expressed his doubt about this. He wrote, "...I think the truth is that the Midgard Serpent is still alive and is lying in the ocean" (80). In view of the fact that the two met again during the final battle called Ragnarök, Snorri's belief was well founded.

Thor in America

One can disagree with Petre's claim that "Thor stands in contrast to Odin, a chaotic, amoral figure, as the upholder of order; he is the chief god of our world..." (Petre 86). But it is impossible to deny that the Thunder God was the more colorful, more heroic of the two. Stan Lee, the founder of Marvel Comics, recognized this when he introduced Thor in the 1960s publication, *Journey into Mystery*. The mighty, red-bearded god became a

Opposite: **The Norse god Thor. (From a statue by B. E. Fogelberg.)**

popular star in the Marvel pantheon and in 1966 earned a comic book bearing his own name.

Stan Lee himself devised the plot for the *Thor* comic book, and for eight years was the primary writer, assisted by his brother, Larry Lieber. The artist who first drew *Thor* was Jack Kirby, the dean of comic book art. No longer a redhead, the American version of Thor has flowing golden locks.

Lee exercised a great deal of poetic license in his depiction of the Thunder God. In his version, Odin is Thor's father, not his rival for supremacy in Asgard. In the ongoing plotline, Lee utilized the standard American comic book device of the superhero alter-ego. His Thor does not exist on his own, but must be summoned up through the medium of an American doctor (specialty undisclosed) named Don Blake. The episodes in the *Thor* publication are standard superhero fare: epic battles with various monsters loosely based on Norse mythology, divine intervention by Odin and others of the Asgard entourage, and a stalwart archenemy in the form of Loki (whom Lee transforms into Thor's stepbrother), the leading troublemaker of the Aesir. Many elements from Norse mythology are included in the various episodes, although often these only vaguely resemble the original material. A good example is the origin story of Marvel Comics' Thor, as written by Stan Lee:

Don Blake, a lame American doctor is on a European vacation when an alien spaceship lands in his vicinity. He is awestruck at what he witnesses when he goes to investigate: he sees a group of huge stone creatures performing incredible feats of strength. Fearing what they will do if they discover him, he flees, but in his haste he makes a noise that attracts their attention. He barely escapes, taking refuge in a large cave. To his horror, he discovers that a gigantic boulder blocks the only way out of the cave. Just when he is about to give up, the wall of the cave opens, revealing a secret chamber. Once inside the chamber he finds what appears to be a gnarled wooden stick. When he unsuccessfully attempts to move the boulder with the stick he loses his temper and strikes it against the boulder. There is a flash of lightning and miraculously Dr. Don Blake is metamorphosed into the Norse Thunder God, Thor. The object that he thought was a stick also undergoes a transformation; it becomes the famous hammer of Thor. Armed with his trusty Mjöllnir, Thor defeats the stone giants, causing them to beat a hasty retreat back to their own planet, Saturn.

A number of other Norse gods deserve at least a brief introduction at this point. One of these is Tyr (Tiw), an important bit player who was originally the god of legality and government, the closest thing to a super lawyer that Asgard produced. As the Germanic world became more militarized, he specialized in the laws governing war, taking on a role somewhat similar to that which Athena filled in Greek mythology. While Tyr's parentage is uncertain, some myths call him the son of Odin. All agree, however, that he was extremely brave. His courage was proven during an incident involving one of the leading archenemies of the gods, Fenrir, the demonic, monster wolf. Snorri recounts the story in his *Edda*:

The gods fashion a fetter out of unbreakable material, and attempt to trick Fenrir into allowing himself to be bound with it. First they challenge his renowned strength, and when they see that he is skeptical, they promise that "...if you don't succeed in snapping this cord ... we will set you free again" (*Edda* 58). Finally, Fenrir agrees to submit to the test. He has only one stipulation: one of the gods has to place his hand in Fenrir's mouth as a pledge of good faith. Tyr volunteers, bravely placing his right hand between the wolf's huge, jagged teeth. Fenrir is then tied securely with the fragile cord.

He struggles to free himself, but no matter how hard he tries he cannot break the fetter. Finally, he requests that they free him as promised, but the gods do not keep their part

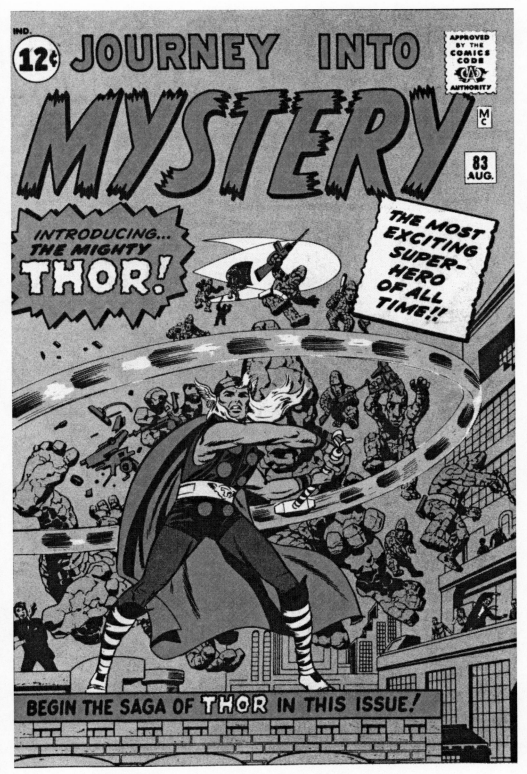

Thor, *Journey into Mystery* #83, August, 1962. (™ and ©2007 Marvel Entertainment Group,
Inc. All rights reserved.)

of the bargain. Instead of setting him loose, they chain him to a huge boulder deep beneath the earth, where he can do them no harm. Unfortunately, Tyr pays the price for this defensive action. Needless to say, he was known thereafter as the one-handed god.

The Norse gods were not all noble, positive figures. Loki is quite the opposite. One of the oldest Germanic gods, he was the son of giants. Gradually, he evolved from a mischievous trickster into a super-demon whose favorite pastime was causing trouble for the other gods. He is often credited with being Fenrir's father and in at least one myth he sired Midgardsörm and the death-goddess, Hel. In spite of his negative reputation (well earned), he was a companion of both Thor and Odin during various adventures. They invited him along from time to time because they knew that he was cunning enough to get them out of tight spots. Perhaps it did not occur to them that he was often responsible for getting them into those tight spots in the first place.

Odin respected Loki's all-encompassing knowledge. As a result, "He became Odin's serving man. Odin always had a good word for him, though he often laid heavy tasks upon him, all of which he performed. Loki knew almost everything that happened and told it to Odin" (MacCulloch 140). It was Loki, for example, who angrily predicted Ragnarök. He made this prophesy when Thor threatened to annihilate him for insinuating that he had slept with Sif (Thor's wife). While Loki's claim may not have been true, it was open knowledge that Loki did very well with the goddesses. Moreover, like Odin, he did not limit his erotic escapades to females, and also had the ability to change himself into other forms. He was a thief, a liar, foul-mouthed, slanderous, cruel, and ultimately a traitor. In short, he was a devil in Norse clothing.

Although very little is known about the god Heimdall, the miraculous nature of his birth is unparalleled in world myth. Snorri describes it in the following way: "Nine maidens gave birth to him, and all of them sisters" (*Edda* 54). One's imagination boggles at the attempt to picture this spectacular entry into the world, or to guess how many midwives were necessary to assist it. At any rate, Heimdall's job was to guard the Rainbow Bridge, Bifröst, which separated Asgard from Giantland. Everyone agreed that he was perfectly suited for this kind of work because he needed hardly any sleep, could see many miles in front of himself, and had such acute hearing that he could hear the grass growing. With his trusty trumpet, Gjöll (Gjallarhorn), at his side, the Norse Gabriel stood ready to warn the gods when an enemy approached. That his hearing was so keen is even more remarkable given the fact that one of his ears was hidden beneath Mimir's fountain, sharing that space with Odin's eye.

The best looking and most popular of the gods was Odin's son, Baldr: "...there is nothing but good to be told of him. He is the best of them and everyone sings his praises.... He is the wisest of the gods and the sweetest-spoken, and the most merciful" (*Edda* 51). Unfortunately, Baldr met an untimely end because of Loki's evil doing. The following myth details his death:

One night, Baldr dreams that he is going to die. When he discloses this dream to the other gods, they are upset enough to send the goddess Frigg on a mission to avert the tragedy. Working tirelessly, Frigg extracts an oath from all living things on earth that they will do no harm to Baldr. Unfortunately, she has failed to have mistletoe take the oath, thinking the bush too young to be of any consequence. It is a fatal error.

The gods, believing that Baldr is invincible as a result of Frigg's mission, indulge in a strange pastime during their leisure hours: they hurl sticks, stones, darts, and whatever else they can get their hands on at Baldr and marvel at the fact that he remains unhurt. Enter the demon Loki.

Like Eris, his counterpart in Greek mythology, Loki hates to see anyone happy. For this reason, he is determined to get rid of Baldr. Using his charm, he tricks Frigg into revealing that she has not extracted a protective oath from mistletoe. Soon thereafter, he suggests that the gods play the game of "Hit Baldr." This time, however, the game has a tragic ending. Baldr's blind brother, Höd, is encouraged by Loki to take a turn. When the latter agrees, Loki gives him a sharpened twig from a mistletoe bush. Then, telling Höd where to hurl the deadly spear, he watches the latter score a direct hit. Baldr is instantly killed.

With the exception of Loki, the Aesir sink into a profound state of grief when they realize what has happened. Finally, Frigg suggests that one of them go to the realm of death to persuade Hel, the goddess who reigns there, to allow Baldr to return to life. Hermod, another son of Odin, volunteers to carry out this mission.

After an arduous journey, Hermod enters Hel's kingdom and secures an interview with its busy potentate. The goddess of death listens with interest as Hermod describes how grief stricken everyone in Asgard is over Baldr's death. She is moved by his heartfelt request that she allow the popular god to return to life; finally, she agrees to do it on one condition: "If everything in the world, both dead or alive, weeps for him, then he shall go back to the Aesir, but he shall remain with Hel if anyone objects or will not weep" (*Edda* 83).

The gods get to work immediately. Messengers are sent out with weepmeters and return with the news that the tears are flowing in torrents for the beloved god. Men, beasts, the earth, stones, trees, and even metals are weeping. But, alas, there is always one spoilsport in a group; the giantess Thökk refuses to shed a tear for the dead god. She declares bluntly that Baldr "...was no use to me/ alive or dead/ let Hel hold what she has" (84). Later, the sorrowful gods learn that it was Loki, disguised as the giantess, who kept Baldr from returning to Asgard. This, however, is not the end of the popular god. As we shall see, he is resurrected after Ragnarök.

Special mention must be given to the only god of the Vanir who was able to achieve status equal to the Aesir: the god Frey.

Frey had an impressive arsenal. In addition to a horse that was as fast as the wind, a sword that slashed and stabbed without assistance, and a chariot drawn by a swift golden boar, he also had a magic ship. The ship, named Skibladnir, was not only the swiftest ship in the world, but also large enough to accommodate all of the gods plus their military gear. Like Frey's sword, moreover, it was completely automatic. A further feature of Skibladnir was that when Frey reached his destination, he could fold it up and put it into a small travel pouch.

With all of his state-of-the-art hardware, Frey was certainly a formidable deity; however, he never used his power for negative purposes. On the contrary, he was heralded as the god who gave sunshine, rain, peace and prosperity. If Baldr was the best loved, Frey was by far the most generous, and for that reason he was worshiped by fertility cults and antiwar advocates.

Unlike their Greek counterparts, almost all of the Norse and Germanic goddesses derived their identity primarily from their association with their husbands. Thor's beautiful, blonde haired wife, Sif, appears in a few myths, but it is always Thor who is central in the action.[23]

Hel, the goddess of death, is not a major figure in Norse mythology. She is described as having half of her face human and half blank. She is ugly, but not evil and has no significant myths in which she is the major player.

Idun, the wife of the scribe god, Bragi, guards the apples of immortality. Since the gods were mortal, however, one questions her success at this occupation.

Of all the Norse goddesses, Frigg alone stands out as an individual. The Romans recognized her importance, equating her with their goddess of love, Venus. According to at least one account, she and Odin shared the responsibility of choosing the warriors who were to fall in battle. She is often confused with Freyja, the leader of the Valkyries; this is understandable, since Frigg has at least thirty names with which she was identified.

Ragnarök

The most powerful myth in Norse mythology is the myth of *Ragnarök*. In English, it is translated as the *Twilight of the Gods*, The equivalent for this event in modern German is *Götterdämmerung*.

As previously indicated, the ancient Norsemen did not believe that their gods were immortal. In their mythological framework, whoever and whatever had life was fated to eventually die. This included the human race, the gods, indeed, the world itself. The tragic death of Baldr was the single event that set the wheels of the Norse Apocalypse into motion.

When the Aesir learned that Loki was behind their beloved Baldr's demise, they swore an oath to avenge him. Before long, they captured the demon-god and chained him up like a common criminal. But there was nothing common about Loki; he broke his bonds with relative ease and fled to join Fenrir, the giants, and the other enemies of the gods. The momentum for a cataclysm was building.

The situation grew steadily graver; omens were everywhere. One day, a member of a brood fathered by the demon-wolf, Fenrir, attacked the sun and extinguished it. The earth was enveloped in a terrible, uninterrupted winter, punctuated by bloody wars in which brother killed brother. Everyone mobilized for the approaching Armageddon, even those in the realm of death where the hound, Garm (a counterpart of the three headed Greek guardian of Hades, Cerberus), began to howl incessantly. Loki was very busy. He made a stealthy journey to the Rainbow Bridge and stole Heimdall's sword. When the latter realized what was happening he sounded the warning on his horn. It was too late; the giants were poised to attack, joined by Fenrir, who had broken loose from his bonds. The cosmic tree, Ygdrassil, swayed dangerously and was in danger of toppling over; mountains collapsed, trapping the dwarves in their underground workshops. The World Serpent, Midgardsörm, hastened toward Asgard, leaving incredibly destructive tidal waves in its wake. Besieged on one side by the fire giants, on the other by Loki and Fenrir, Asgard was in mortal peril. The sky split in half from the terrible fires; the Rainbow Bridge went up in flames and collapsed.

The opposing armies finally collided on the fields before Valhalla, resulting in a massive ocean of blood and gore. There were no victors. Death was everywhere. Nothing survived. Ragnarök. Götterdämmerung. The Twilight of the Gods.

Odin was the first of the Aesir to be killed in the action. Neither his lightning fast eight-legged horse, Sleipnir, nor his trusty spear, Gungnir, nor the surrounding army of furiously fighting Valkyries could stop the fire-breathing wolf, Fenrir, from swallowing the king of the gods. With the aid of a special shoe made from impenetrable leather, Odin's son, Vidar, avenged his father's death. He put his foot on Fenrir's lower jaw, opened Fenrir's mouth with one hand and with the other, plunged his sword into the wolf's mouth all the way down to the heart.

Thor fell soon after Odin, but not before dispatching his archenemy, Midgardsörm. The red-bearded God of Thunder shattered the huge serpent's head with his mighty hammer, but in so doing breathed in a fatal dose of the latter's venom and toppled over, dead. In yet another encounter, Heimdall and Loki killed each other. One by one, all of the gods fell, until only Tyr remained. Not for long. After a furious battle, he and the death dog, Garm, slew each other.

Without the protection of Thor and the other gods, the human race was quickly extinguished. The earth went up in flames, leading to the destruction of all plant and animal life. The end. Finis. Das Ende. Everything was kaput. Or was it?

The answer, of course, is that there would be no one to read about Ragnarök if it had truly been the final curtain. Certainly, for Odin, Thor, Fenrir, Midgardsörm, Loki and so many others there was to be no encore before Marvel Comics; but there were a few survivors, and even one resurrection. Somehow, Höd, two of Odin's sons (Vidar and Vali), and two of Thor's sons (Magni and Modi) survived the holocaust, to be joined by a new generation of peace-loving gods.

Where these new gods came from is unknown; it has been said that they were always there, waiting for the opportunity to assume power. Their leader was none other than the resurrected Baldr. Thus, the ancient Norsemen gave their mythology an old-fashioned Hollywood ending. Peace. Unfortunately, though, their descendants did not follow the pacific script. The new race of humans soon reverted to the destructive ways of the past. A new age of superheroes was approaching.

* * *

The ancient Norsemen produced more than their share of world-class heroic figures. It is irrelevant whether Odin, Thor and the other "gods" were actually deities, or simply cunning old men who could fool the people into viewing them as such. In the last analysis, they were traditional superheroes, sharing the archetypal richness of their counterparts in many other lands. *Superweapons* such as Thor's hammer and Odin's spear are equal to those wielded by any of the superheroes already discussed. The same could be said of their marvelous means of *transportation*. As excellent as the Lone Ranger's Silver and Rustam's Rakhsh were in transporting their riders, they pale beside Odin's steed, Sleipnir, or Thor's recyclable goats, not to mention Frey's automatic, shrinkable ship. And where is it possible to find more formidable *archenemies* than the evil serpent Midgardsörm, the cosmic wolf Fenrir, or the super demon Loki? Has there ever been a more *miraculous birth* than that of Heimdall, or any *final battle* as fierce as Ragnarök? Odin's ability to *transform* himself into other beings, Baldr's *resurrection* and near-perfect *invulnerability*, the great hall Valhalla, where heroes could battle with death on a daily basis — all of these and more archetypes are prominent in the world of the Norse superhero-gods. The names and places have changed, but the players beneath the masks are all cut from the same timber. Gilgamesh, Rama, Rustam, Achilles, and the all-too-human Egyptian and Greek gods — they are all members of the same exclusive club.

Germany

Between the years 375 and 500, one of the greatest folk migrations in world history took place. The fierce Huns swept down from the north, joined by a number of Germanic

tribes seeking new habitable and arable land to settle. Packing up all their worldly possessions, entire villages from the Danish isles and the coastal areas between the North and Baltic
seas joined the southward trek that was to change the face of Europe for all time. When
the dust had settled, the Roman Empire was gone. A number of the northern tribes chose
Scandinavia as their new home, while others, including the Huns, Goths, Vandals, and
Burgundians, dispersed and eventually disappeared from the world scene. Yet others settled in what are today Italy, Spain, France, England, the Netherlands, Germany and the
North of Africa. It was a time of extremes, a time of adventure, a time that was ripe for
superheroes. The German national epic, *Das Nibelungenlied* (*The Song of the Nibelungen*),
presents a fascinating picture of this violent, heroic era.

The basic subject matter in the *Nibelungenlied* is well known to many through Richard
Wagner's famous opera *Das Rheingold*. There are, however, a number of striking differences
between Wagner's work and the medieval epic poem. This is due to the fact that the anonymous twelfth century author had to blend two independent legends in order to produce a
cohesive work: the legend of Siegfried (Norse=Sigurd) and that of Brünhild (Norse=Bryn-
hild). The Icelandic version, which was written somewhere between the mid-ninth and
mid-eleventh centuries, is pieced together from various poems found in the *Poetic Edda*,
alternately called the *Elder Edda*. This is a collection of thirty-four mythical and heroic
poems, compiled by an anonymous author during the thirteenth century. The heroic poems
recount the story of the great superhero Sigurd (Siegfried in the *Nibelungenlied*), a member of a mythical race called the Völsungs.

Brought up by a dwarf named Alberich, Sigurd does not know who his true parents
are. In traditional hero fashion, when he comes of age he sets out to seek adventure. Before
very long, he encounters a sleeping dragon. Undaunted, Sigurd kills the dragon and becomes
the owner of the huge store of riches that it had been guarding, the famed Nibelungen Treasure.

Now a very wealthy hero, Sigurd continues to build his reputation as a superhero. One
day he comes across a sleeping Valkyrie, Brynhild (Brünhild), on a remote mountaintop,
surrounded by a ring of fire that Odin has placed there. Sigurd manages to free her and
becomes her lover. But adventure calls again, and soon he is off to King Gunnar's
(Gunnar=Gunther) land. After drinking a magic potion that erases his memory, Sigurd marries Gunnar's sister, Gudrun (Gudrun=Kriemhild). To complicate the plot even more, he
later helps Gunnar to win Brynhild as a bride.

The problem is that while Sigurd does not recall their previous relationship, Brynhild's memory has not been erased. When she learns of her former lover's deceit, she longs
for revenge and eventually goads Gunnar into murdering Sigurd. But in spite of herself, she
is still in love with the fallen Völsungen hero; when his body is about to be cremated she
throws herself on his funeral pyre. But that is not the end of the story.

The young widow, Gudrun, eventually marries the notorious Hun Atli (Atli=Etzel=
Attila), who is much more interested in Sigurd's treasure than in his widow. With the treasure in mind, he invites all of his in-laws for an old-fashioned heathen feast. Instead of win-
ing and dining them like a good in-law, however, he has them all slaughtered. To their
credit, Gunnar and his people do not reveal the location in the Rhine where they have sunk
the Nibelungen treasure.

Now it was Gudrun's turn to prove her mettle as an avenger. First, she kills Atli's children, then she tricks him into drinking their blood. Finally, with a few well-placed dagger
thrusts, she puts an end to the legendary Hun. The Icelandic version of the story ends at

that point, only to appear again, with some major changes, in the twelfth century German epic, the *Nibelungenlied*.

Siegfried

The *Nibelungenlied* has the veneer of a Christian epic, but when one peels away this thin layer the ancient Germanic values dominate: courage, honor, loyalty and a deep sense of fatalism. First and foremost, though, the epic tells the story of Siegfried, the greatest Germanic superhero of all time. The story begins with a dream.

One night, the lovely young Burgundian princess, Kriemhild, dreams that the wild falcon she has raised is torn apart by two eagles. When her mother explains that the falcon represents a husband, Kriemhild asserts that she will never marry. What she does not know is that young prince Siegfried of the Netherlands, having heard the reports of her great beauty, has already made up his mind to marry her. He announces this one day to a group of his vassals: "I shall take fair Kriemhild the fair maiden of Burgundy ... on account of her very great beauty..." (*Nibelungenlied* 23). Accompanied by a mere eleven vassals, Siegfried boldly sets out for Burgundy, the land ruled by Kriemhild's brother, King Gunther.

When Siegfried and his retinue arrive in Burgundy, Hagen,[24] the wise, loyal vassal and chief advisor to King Gunther, immediately recognizes the prince from the Netherlands and introduces him to his sovereign. Siegfried is given a royal welcome, and before long becomes a favorite in Burgundy. King Gunther and the other Burgundians are particularly impressed by Siegfried's battlefield prowess. At Gunther's request, he fights alongside Gunther and the Burgundian army and is instrumental in a stunning victory over the Danes and Saxons.

A whole year passes before Siegfried and Kriemhild meet. When they do, however, it is a magic moment. Each is in awe of the other's beauty. The author of the *Nibelungenlied* describes this momentous meeting in the following way: "Leave was granted to her to bestow a kiss on the handsome man, and never in all his life had anything so pleasant befallen him."[25] For the next twelve days the two are seen together almost constantly, although they never have the opportunity to be alone.

Gunther, in the meantime, has been told of a beautiful Icelandic princess named Brünhild, and decides that she will be his bride. There is, however, one problem: Brünhild, a militant feminist, is not anxious to become subordinate to any man.[26] She has stipulated that in order to marry her a suitor would have to defeat her in three physical contests: spear throwing, rock throwing and jumping. Now that would seem to be a minor obstacle for a great king. After all, one might assume, Brünhild is just a weak woman, while Gunther is a battle-tested warrior. What Gunther doesn't know, however, is that Brünhild is a Valkyrie. Nor is he aware that many an aspiring bridegroom has had to limp home empty-handed after the contest, that is, if they were still able to limp. No one has come close to defeating her. Clearly, Gunther is no match for the powerful Valkyrie; it is time for him to make a deal with Siegfried.

Not only is Siegfried the greatest warrior of the time, but he also has in his possession an extraordinary item of apparel: the mythical "Tarnkappe," a magical cape that makes the one who wears it invisible. Gunther approaches Siegfried and requests his assistance in the three contests. In return, he says, he will give Siegfried his sister Kriemhild as a bride.[27] It is an offer the prince from the Netherlands cannot refuse. Together with Hagen and an

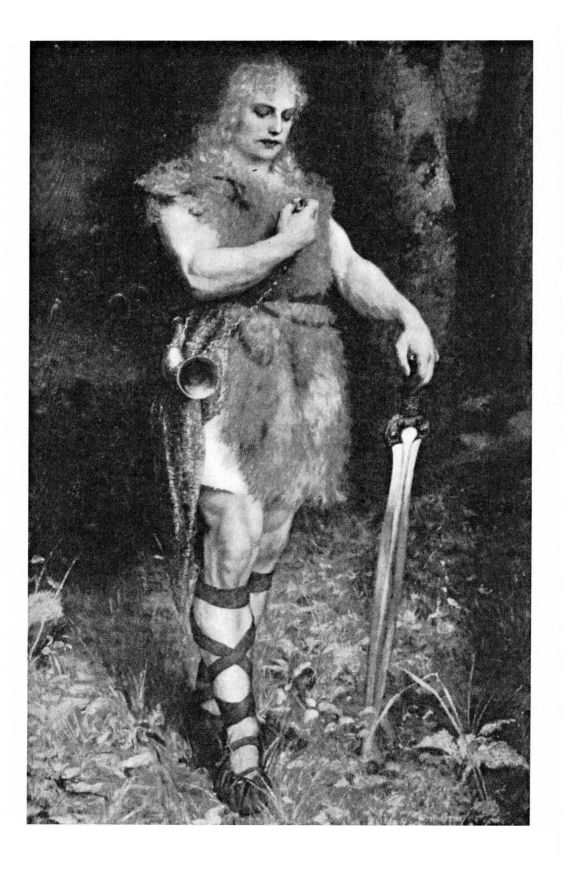

impressive group of followers, Gunther and Siegfried travel to Iceland to declare Gunther's intention to enter the contest.

Brünhild accepts the challenge, confident that Gunther poses no threat to her perfect record. The word is spread throughout the land and the crowds gather to witness the slaughter of the bold foreigner. To everyone's astonishment, however, the contest does not turn out the way they expect: Brünhild is soundly beaten in all three events.

The mighty Valkyrie cannot believe that the puny foreigner has beaten her. Something, she thinks, is rotten in Iceland. What she does not know is that Siegfried, not Gunther, is the true victor. Made invisible by the tarnkappe, the mighty superhero literally carried his future brother-in-law on his shoulders and performed the feats, the latter feigning the motions. Very shortly thereafter, the announcements for a double royal wedding are sent out. Siegfried and Gunther look forward excitedly to their wedding nights. Unfortunately, only one of them has his expectations fulfilled.

Siegfried's wedding night is all he has expected and then some: "...for as he lay with the young lady and inured her so tenderly to his noble loves, she became as dear to him as life, and he would not have exchanged her for a thousand others" (*Nib.* 87). Gunther's first night with his new bride, on the other hand, is a dreadful nightmare. As the author so succinctly understates it, "...he had lain more pleasantly with other women many a time" (87).

Although she cannot figure out how she lost the contests, Brünhild continues to be very suspicious. This suspicion quickly turns to rage when Gunther enters the bridal suite that evening, dims the lights, and attempts to embrace her. Instead of reciprocating, the furious Valkyrie announces in no uncertain terms that she will have none of it. She declares, "Take note of this: I intend to stay a maiden till I have learned the truth about Siegfried" (88).

Were Gunther a scholar living a few centuries later, he would have realized that the author of the *Nibelungenlied* had difficulty with this particular episode because he was caught between two myths. As already discussed, in the old Norse version of the story Siegfried and Brünhild not only knew each other, but had also been lovers at one time. This accounts, perhaps, for her undue interest in the hero from the Netherlands on her wedding night, even though this motivation does not appear anywhere in the text of the *Nibelungenlied*. On the other hand, it was undoubtedly obvious to her that the only person capable of besting her in the three contests was Siegfried, which made her suspect that he had played a role in the deception. Of course, poor Gunther could not have known any of this; all he knew was that he was being denied something that he wanted very much, and kings are used to having their way. What he did next was a catastrophic mistake. He tried to subdue Brünhild by force.

Anyone with even a modicum of knowledge about Valkyries knows that they are very dangerous ladies. Alas, though, runaway hormones can cloud a man's judgment and cause him to act without considering the consequences of his actions. As it turns out, Gunther has a whole night to think about this, for, when he attempts to "tumble her shift," Brünhild overpowers him, takes the silk girdle (more a sash) from her waist, and ties him up with it. Then, still not satisfied that he has been properly punished for his audacity, she hangs him on the wall. On the wall! Who would have thought such a thing possible — a mighty king beaten black and blue and hanged on his bedroom wall by his irate bride? "He had to stay hanging there the whole night through till dawn, when the bright morning shone

Opposite: **Siegfried. (From a painting by F. Leeke.)**

The Burgundian King Gunther and his wife, Queen Brunhild. (From a painting by Schnorr von Carolsfeld.)

through the windows" (88). And he might still be hanging there today had he not promised never to touch her again. Only after he had made such a promise did she literally let him off the hook, thus sparing him the further humiliation of being found in that condition by the servants.

At breakfast, Siegfried notes his brother-in-law's dejection and asks him what is wrong.

The Germanic hero Siegfried and his wife, Kriemhild. (From a painting by Schnorr von Carolsfeld.)

Swearing Siegfried to secrecy, Gunther blurts out the details of his disastrous wedding night. His depression lifts, however, when Siegfried volunteers to help him one more time.

That evening, Siegfried secretly dons his magic cape and, according to the plan he and Gunther had agreed upon, waits in the master bedroom for the mismatched couple to appear. At last they arrive. Gunther dismisses the servants, douses the lights and hides in a far corner of the room. Then "Siegfried laid himself close by the young lady's side ... as if he were the great King Gunther and clasped the illustrious maiden in his arms..." (91). Brünhild warns him to keep away, but Siegfried continues to make advances, confident that she is no match for him. He is almost wrong. Dead wrong. In spite of Siegfried's remarkable strength, Brünhild lifts him up and throws him out of bed as if he were nothing more than an oversized frisbee.

Siegfried is astounded by what has happened, but he is not about to give up so easily. He returns to the bed and attempts to caress her again, only to be lifted bodily this time and carried to the wall. The unthinkable is about to happen. The greatest Germanic superhero of all time is about to be hanged on a bedroom wall by a woman. What will happen to his reputation? Siegfried feels a rising panic; he realizes that a lot more than his personal honor is at stake. This is reflected in his thoughts: "...if I now lose my life to a girl, the whole sex will grow uppish with their husbands for ever after..." (92). With a new outburst of strength, derived from the responsibility he feels to defend the honor of the entire male sex, Siegfried fights back mightily. Gunther cowers in his dark corner, terrified, as his wife and brother-in-law bounce each other around the room like enormous ping pong balls. Finally, almost exhausted, a bruised and battered Siegfried manages to gain the upper hand, and with a mighty effort he "...crushed her on the bed so violently that she shrieked aloud, such pain did his might inflict on her" (92). With her remaining strength, Brünhild tries to get her sash off in order to tie her tormentor up with it, but Siegfried is no Gunther. Finally, she stops struggling and agrees to submit. Then, while Siegfried pretends to undress, Gunther sneaks over from his hiding place and takes Siegfried's place in the rumpled bed, where he quickly consummates his marriage. In so doing, he reduces the once powerful Valkyrie's strength to that of "any other woman."

If Siegfried had not acted foolishly after his epic battle, the episode might not have had tragic consequences. But he could not leave the royal bedchamber without taking a couple of souvenirs, namely Brünhild's sash and one of her rings. Even at that point disaster could have been avoided had he kept the theft to himself. Instead, he compounded his folly by giving the two purloined items to his wife.

Twelve happy years pass. Siegfried's father, Sigmund, has retired, leaving the reins of leadership to his mighty son. The good relations between the great Germanic hero and his wife's relatives in Burgundy are illustrated by the fact that he and Kriemhild name their son Gunther. Brünhild, however, continues to brood about her puzzling situation. Having gotten to know her husband's limitations, she is more certain than ever that he would never have been able to overpower her in that grueling bedroom battle. Her suspicions are increased, moreover, by the fact that although Siegfried is supposed to be Gunther's vassal he is never required to pay any tribute. Finally, under the pretense that she misses them very much, Brünhild convinces her husband to invite Siegfried and Kriemhild for a visit. The unsuspecting couple happily accepts the invitation.

As far as family visits go, Siegfried's and Kriemhild's visit to Burgundy is one of the most unpleasant ever recorded. What starts out as a gala event eventually deteriorates as the two queens have a terrible argument. Brünhild starts the fireworks off by asking her sister-in-law why Siegfried has not fulfilled his obligations by paying proper tribute to Gunther. Kriehmild sharply responds that her husband is not Gunther's vassal, setting off a childish exchange in which each claims her husband to be the better man. Finally, Kriemhild loses her patience and publicly calls Brünhild a harlot, asserting that Siegfried, not Gunther, was the one who deflowered her on her wedding night. Then, to prove that her claim is true, she produces Brünhild's ring and sash. The ex–Valkyrie bursts into tears and rushes to her husband with the demand that Kriemhild be punished for the terrible insult.

Gunther is placed on the horns of a dilemma. He knows that it would be suicidal to make an enemy of Siegfried. On the other hand, he cannot ignore the matter if he wants to retain his honor. Reluctantly, he questions Siegfried. To Gunther's relief, Siegfried not only swears that he never claimed to have been Brünhild's first lover but also assures his brother-in-law that he will punish Kriemhild for her loose tongue. He puts it in the following way: "If my wife were to go unpunished for having distressed Brünhild I should be extremely sorry.... Women should be trained to avoid irresponsible chatter.... I am truly ashamed at her unseemly behavior" (116). While Gunther is satisfied with Siegfried's response, however, the matter does not end there.

Gunther's right-hand man, Hagen, is the embodiment of the Germanic code of honor. A highly intelligent advisor as well as a brave and fierce warrior, his strongest quality is absolute loyalty, not so much to Gunther the person, as to Gunther the king. Thus, while Gunther is willing to let the insult to his wife pass, Hagen is determined to avenge the slur on the crown. The only way he can do this is to kill Siegfried.[28]

Killing a superhero is much easier said than done. Hagen knows full well that Siegfried is virtually invincible as a result of having bathed himself in the blood of the dragon he had slain to obtain the Nibelungen treasure. He is also aware, however, that there is one spot on Siegfried's body that is vulnerable. The problem is that he does not know the location of that spot. Never at a loss for a plan, Hagen is determined to gain the necessary information.

After convincing Gunther that it would be very profitable to eliminate Siegfried (using the Nibelungen treasure as an incentive), he cunningly tricks Kriemhild into divulging her husband's guarded secret, pretending that this knowledge will help him to protect Siegfried in the upcoming battle.[29] With the skill of a master salesman, he persuades her to sew a cross on Siegfried's tunic, on the spot between the shoulder blades where a clinging leaf had prevented the dragon's blood from making contact with Siegfried's skin.

The rest is relatively easy. During a hunt, Hagen tricks Siegfried into laying down his arms to take part in a footrace to a nearby spring. With childish fervor, Siegfried agrees. It is no contest; swift Siegfried reaches the fountain far ahead of Hagen. When he bends over to take a drink, Hagen drives a spear deep into his back, through the mark that Kriemhild has made on the tunic. In a death scene worthy of any Italian opera, the dying superhero expresses his final wish to Gunther:

> May God have mercy on me for ever having got a son who in years to come will suffer the reproach that his kinsmen were murderers.... But if you feel at all inclined to do a good deed for anyone, noble King ... let me commend my dear sweetheart to your mercy. Let her profit from being your sister.... As to my father and his vassals, they will have to wait long for me [132].

Thus, it is with concern for his family in mind that Siegfried dies. The first part of the *Nibelungenlied* ends with Siegfried's burial and the arrival of the Nibelungen treasure in Burgundy.

Although the major hero of the work is absent, Part II of the *Nibelungenlied* is an excellent example of the superhero genre. As the work unfolds, the prime focus is shifted from that of an individual, Siegfried, to an entire race. The central figure is now Kriemhild, who has been called "...the most grandiosely conceived of all the heroines of medieval poetry...."[30] It is in essence the story of Kriemhild's quest for revenge, a quest that results in a bloody war punctuated by a blend of chivalrous heroism and barbaric cruelty. The Christian veneer has totally disappeared by the conclusion of the epic.

As heir to the Nibelungen treasure, Kriemhild has become a very wealthy widow. However, she is interested in this wealth only insofar as its use can enable her to exact revenge on her husband's assassin.

Hagen is unafraid; he makes no attempt to conceal the fact that it is he who has done away with Siegfried. On the contrary, he taunts her with this admission. As far as he is concerned, he has merely done his duty. Moreover, he realizes that Kriemhild is a danger to the kingdom, and tries vainly to obtain Gunther's permission to kill her.

Hagen watches with growing alarm as Siegfried's widow begins to build herself a power base in Burgundy. She does this by using her enormous wealth to buy an army. The author describes her fortune in the following way: "It was as much as a dozen wagons fully loaded could carry away from the mountain in four days and nights coming and going thrice in a day!" (147). Before she can consolidate her power, however, Hagen has the remaining Nibelungen treasure seized and sinks it in the Rhine.

This is the last straw for Kriemhild. For thirteen years, the only thing that has sustained her is the desire for revenge. "Kriemhild's heart was burdened with sorrow that was ever fresh for the passing of her lord and the loss of her treasure, and her laments never ceased until the day she died" (*Nib.* 149).

Finally, the opportunity to avenge Siegfried's murder presents itself in the form of a wedding proposal from Etzel (Attila), the king of the Huns. Hagen is against the match. He warns Gunther not to permit it, saying, "If Etzel marries her and she lives long enough she will do us some great harm.... When all is said, she will have many fine men at her command" (157). But Gunther and his brothers, Gernot and Giselher, see no danger in a marriage between their sister and Etzel. Tragically, at least for them, Hagen was right. After being assured by Etzel's envoy that she will have the support of Etzel's armies to address any wrongs that have been done to her, Kriemhild marries the elderly Hun and spends the next twelve years preparing for the day of reckoning.

It should have been obvious to Gunther and his brothers that Kriemhild's invitation to visit her and Etzel after all those years had an ulterior purpose, particularly since the messengers emphasize that Hagen must accompany them. Hagen is the only one to realize that it is a trap, but he is unable to convince Gunther to reject the invitation. Even though he knows such a journey will result in death, Hagen agrees to accompany his king, proof that he values his allegiance more than life itself. And once they set out, he never looks back, not even when the omens indicate that his premonition of impending doom is justified.[31]

From the moment the Burgundians arrive in Etzel's kingdom, Hagen and Kriemhild make no attempt to conceal their mutual hatred. Hagen goes so far as to insult her publicly when she asks him if he has brought her treasure with him. He spits out the following reply: "I have brought you nothing and be damned to you!" (217). He continues to show his disdain by refusing to stand up in her presence, and then boldly blurts out that it is he who killed Siegfried: "There is no denying it, mighty Queen.... I bear the entire guilt for your ruinous loss. Now let anyone who likes avenge it, be he man or woman" (222). From that point on, Hagen tries to goad the Huns into attacking him.

The first hostile act is committed by Hagen's sidekick, a daring musician/warrior named Volker. Without justification, he kills one of Etzel's men during a tournament which was arranged by the unsuspecting king of the Huns to entertain his guests. While Etzel is able to prevent open warfare at that point, it is not long before Hagen's continued provocations achieve the desired result: the Huns attack, inflicting heavy casualties on Gunther's men. The bloodbath has begun.

Hagen and Volker fight like true heroes, cutting down their enemies by the score.[32] But they are greatly outnumbered. At one point, the Burgundians are trapped in a burning hall, and they would have perished of thirst had Hagen not convinced them to drink the blood of their fallen comrades. But it is a hopeless cause. Their army slaughtered, one by one the leaders of the Burgundian forces are killed, until at the end only Gunther and Hagen remain. Exhausted, they are finally overpowered and taken prisoner by the legendary king, Dietrich of Bern, who has reluctantly allied himself with Etzel. It is a costly alliance for Dietrich: in the course of the ferocious battle he suffers the loss of all his men but one, his loyal vassal, Hildebrand. The final scene of the *Nibelungenlied* is as grotesque as any to be found in all of epic literature.

In a heroic epic, the fitting end for a hero is to die fighting on the battlefield. Heroes are not expected to have ordinary deaths. Even the seemingly unheroic death of Siegfried cannot be considered disgraceful, in that his killer, Hagen, is a nobleman and has no way to kill him other than to stab him in the back. No stretch of logic, however, can validate a claim that Gunther or Hagen die nobly. Kriemhild gives the order for her brother's execution after Hagen declares that he will tell her where the Nibelungen treasure is only when Gunther is dead. Of course, he has no intention of keeping his word.

But, one may ask, how can Hagen, the epitome of the loyal vassal, purposely cause his king to be beheaded? The explanation lies in the nature of Hagen's loyalty, not in his lack of it. As has already been pointed out, Hagen was not loyal to Gunther the person, but to the ideal of kingship that Gunther embodied. In fact, it is clear that he had a fairly low opinion of Gunther the man or he would not have acted as he did. His reasoning must have led him to conclude that Gunther's weakness would eventually cause him to divulge the secret place in the Rhine where the treasure was sunk. Such an action would dishonor the crown, something Hagen could not permit. By having Gunther killed, he was making certain that the crown remained unsullied.

That Hagen is a brave man cannot be disputed, since he knows that his actions will cost him his life. When Kriemhild realizes that he has tricked her, she picks up Siegfried's old sword and cuts off his head. Revenge has its price; in Kriemhild's case it is her life. When Dietrich's vassal, Hildebrand, sees what has happened, he draws his sword and hacks Kriemhild into little pieces. Although Hildebrand was Hagen's opponent in the recently concluded battle,[33] by killing Kriemhild he adheres to the hero's code that forbids a woman from killing a warrior. Such an unspeakable act demands swift, ruthless vengeance, which is exactly what Hildebrand exacts. The *Nibelungenlied* ends on a sad, pessimistic note:

> There lay the bodies of all that were doomed to die. The noble lady was hewn in pieces. Dietrich and Etzel began to weep, and deeply they lamented both kinsmen and vassals.... The King's high festival had ended in sorrow, as joy must ever turn to sorrow in the end ... [291].

* * *

Siegfried satisfies a number of the archetypal criteria and is therefore an excellent representative of the superhero genre. He had no peers on the battlefield, fell in love with a woman he had never seen, underwent a *suitor's test* to win her (albeit he passed the test for another), was *invulnerable* except, like Achilles, for one flawed spot, had a most intelligent

The battle between the Burgundians and Huns in King Etzel's palace. (From a painting by Schnorr von Carolsfeld.)

and ferocious *archenemy,* sported a *superweapon* in the form of the magic cape of invisibility, and met his end because of a (in his case, two) *destructive female(s)*. Siegfried also had a quality which many of the other champions lacked: he was a good family man and a genuinely "nice guy." Compared to the serial rapist Gilgamesh, the "love them and leave them" supercads Rustam and Aeneas, the mendacious cynic Odysseus, the ill-tempered, brooding Achilles and the ultra self-righteous Rama, he was a four star mensch as well as a sterling superhero. Such a combination is very rare in the world of superheroes. That is, of course, until we come to the United States, where being a good guy is as American as apple pie.

8

The United States

Very few Americans would know the name Hugo Danner. And yet, without him the greatest American superhero of all time would not have seen the light of day, for while the Kryptonian couple, Jor-El and Lara, were the biological parents of the man of steel,[1] his true progenitor is the hero of Philip Wylie's now almost forgotten novel, *Gladiator*. Maurice Horn gives credit where credit is due, acknowledging that the concept for Superman was "Based heavily on Philip Wylie's science-fiction novel..." (642). James Steranko also emphasizes the significance of *Gladiator* in the creation of Superman. He writes: "The source for the essence of Superman and his development was influenced by Philip Wylie's striking novel, *Gladiator*" (I, 37). Sam Moskowitz, in a foreword to Wylie's novel, goes even further, declaring openly that the authors of *Superman* had not only borrowed the central theme from Wylie, but had even paraphrased some of the dialogue of *Gladiator* in their initial submissions. In his words, "...no one would dream the idea had once been the basis of a popular novel by a renowned American author."[2] It is therefore important to examine the literary ancestor of Superman, known on his native planet as Kal-El, before moving this discussion to the mythic city of Metropolis.

Gladiator

Unlike the majority of superheroes already discussed in this study, Hugo Danner had no exalted ancestry. His parents were neither divine nor possessed any royal blood in either of their family trees. His father, Abednego, was a meek, nondescript biology professor in a small college somewhere in the heartland of America. His mother, Matilda, on the other hand, was a religious zealot whose Christian humility was contradicted by her heavy-handed domination of her husband. The mismatched couple sat unhappily together in church each week, she praying while he meditated "...on the structure of chromosomes."[3] No clear thinking person could ever have guessed that such an ordinary couple would eventually produce an offspring whose abilities and exploits were as phenomenal as those of any superhero in world history. It is even more startling considering their relationship. Procreation was not an item on their marital agenda. As Wylie describes it:

> They had, in fact, avoided its mechanics except on those rare evenings when tranquility and the reproductive urge conspired to imbue him with courage and her with sinfulness. Nothing came of that infrequent union. They never expected anything [*Gladiator* 13].

155

As a biology professor, Abednego Danner undoubtedly realized that even an "infrequent union" could result in conception, but he was nevertheless rendered speechless the day Matilda announced that she was pregnant. It was the news he had been hoping against hope for all along, although he did not realize it until that time. Becoming a father was his opportunity to make his mark, to prove that he was not a nonentity after all. But it is necessary to backtrack a bit in order to understand why he was so elated.

The many hours that Professor Danner spent in church immersed in thought about chromosomes had not yielded any startling results in his modest home laboratory. For fourteen years he had vainly attempted to prove that an organism's muscular strength could be increased almost limitlessly if one were able to discover the elusive "determinant." Then, one spring day, he came home from school and found that he had done it. A frog fed on a serum he developed had produced a brood of tadpoles so strong that they smashed through the glass of the fish tank and proceeded to leap about the laboratory eight feet at a time before suffocating in the hostile environment. Elated by this initial success, Abednego injected a pregnant cat with his serum and waited. The newborn kittens were even more extraordinary than expected. Fearing that he would not be able to control them once they began to grow stronger, he drowned all but one. Aptly named Samson, the ferocious kitten swiftly grew to cathood and began to wreak havoc. It wrecked the Danner living room, killed a number of dogs, and tore a neighbor's cow to pieces. Reluctantly, the professor ended its short reign of terror with a potent poison cocktail. Samson died an epic death. As Wylie describes it, "The dying agonies of Samson, aged seven weeks, were Homeric" (12). The next step was to test the formula on a human being.

Clearly, Abednego could not divulge his secret to his fundamentalist wife, who was violently opposed to any tampering with "God's creatures." Indeed, the idea of asking her to take part in an experiment such as the one he planned was unthinkable, and the risks so great that he hesitated to go ahead with it at all. He was afraid that the entire male sex might suffer terrible consequences if a girl with super strength were to be born, a fear reminiscent of the one Siegfried had while battling Brünhild in her dark bedroom:

> If the child was female and became a woman like his wife, then the effect of such strength would be awful indeed. He envisioned a militant reformer, an iron-bound Calvinist, remodeling the world single-handed. A Scotch Lilith, a matronly Gabriel, a she–Hercules. He shuddered [14].

Ultimately, however, the scientist in him won out, and so one evening he secretly put a dose of his serum into some blackberry brandy and watched nervously as his wife drank two full glasses of the mixture. Months later, on Christmas day to be exact, Matilda Danner gave birth to a healthy baby, described by a neighbor as "...A beautiful boy. And husky. You never saw such a husky baby" (16). They named him Hugo.

Abednego Danner watched happily as his surreptitious experiment yielded a great personal, as well as an unparalleled scientific, triumph. His wife, who had reluctantly tolerated his theories, realized immediately that the super baby she had given birth to was the result of his "wicked" work. For the first time in their marriage, though, the henpecked professor stood his ground when she angrily confronted him with her accusations: "Yes ... I did it!" he shouted. "You can knock me down. You can knock me down a thousand times. I have given you a son whose little finger you cannot bend with a crow-bar.... You cannot bend him to your will. He is all I might have been" (18). Matilda was impressed by her husband's sudden outburst of self-assertion, even though he reverted to form by ending with a plea for forgiveness and then collapsed from the strain of having defied her. She never forgave her husband for what he had done; nonetheless, unlike Hera, she did not hate Hugo.

... While Matilda's maternal instincts enabled her to love and accept her unusual child, the outside world was not as broad minded. By the time Hugo reached his fifth birthday, his abnormal strength had become known to the neighbors; they forbade their children to play with him for fear he would do them harm. A very sensitive boy, Hugo attempted to gain acceptance by pretending that he was no stronger than anyone else, but his efforts were unsuccessful and he became increasingly isolated [20].

Outwardly, Hugo's life seemed to go along fairly normally. Fortunately for those around him, he was by nature a very decent, gentle person. This, coupled with Abednego's moral guidance, restrained him from misusing his remarkable "gift." However, while he confided the extent of his physical abilities to his doting father, he did not divulge the negative aspects of his super strength. For he learned very young that superiority bears a steep price tag.

The first time Hugo used his great strength against another person was a bitter experience for all concerned. He was only six years old, too young to keep his emotions in check when the school bully began to torment him. Needless to say, he soundly whipped the other boy. However, instead of pride and satisfaction, "...it made him ashamed. He thought he had killed the other boy. Sickening dread filled him" (25). His tormentor recovered from the broken arm and numerous bruises Hugo had inflicted, but Hugo never forgot what followed: he was whipped by the town blacksmith, prayed over by the minister, examined by the doctor and "enveloped in hate" by everyone else. Unlike the superheroes of old who gained respect for their prowess, Hugo had earned only contempt from those around him. In Wylie's words, "And Hugo, suffering bitterly, saw that if he had beaten the farmer's boy in fair combat, he would have been a hero. It was the scale of the triumph that made it dreadful" (25).

At the age of seven, Hugo had another occasion to put his super strength to a test, this time to save a life. He was walking along the road when he saw a man pinned under the weight of a wagon. In spite of the efforts of seven full grown men to lift it, the wagon could not be budged, not, that is, until Hugo stepped over and applied his super strength to the task. Immediately, the two ton burden jerked up into the air and the man was pulled out. Instead of proclaiming him a hero, however, the would-be rescuers became abusive and ordered him to "beat it or get smacked." They could not admit to themselves that a small boy was able to succeed where they had failed.

His defense against the unwanted gift of strength was to ignore it, which he did successfully until he was ten years old. At that age, while roaming in the woods one day, he discovered just how great his physical powers were:

There in the forest, beyond the eye of man, he learned that he was superhuman.... He ran. He shot up the steep trail like an express train, at a rate that would have been measured in miles to the hour rather than yards to the minute.... He sped like a shadow across a pine-carpeted knoll. He gained the bare rocks of the first mountain, and in the open, where the horror of no eye would tether his strength, he moved in flying bounds to the summit [28].

Hugo's negative childhood experiences were dwarfed by those that followed. Repeatedly, his "gift" proved to be a curse, separating him from others and preventing him from forming normal relationships. One of the lowest points in his life occurred as a result of the winning touchdown he scored in a crucial college football game. The victory celebration was more like a wake, however, because it was won at the cost of a human life: when an opposing player tried to block him as he sped toward the goal line, he broke the opposing player's neck with a flick of his arm. His remorse was agonizing: "He knew that he was guilty of a sort of murder. In his own eyes it was murder. He had given away for one red moment to the leaping, lusting urge to smash the world. And killed a man" (86–87). He dropped out of school after that incident and began the archetypal proving period which all superheroes must go through. But Hugo was an unusual hero in that his goal was neither adventure nor glory, but rather the expiation of a terrible "sin." Nonetheless, his ensuing experiences were textbook superhero fare.

As a crew member on a trawler, he defeated his first monster during one voyage, not a sea serpent but a huge shark that was about to attack a sailor who had fallen overboard. In a flash, Hugo was in the water and, with very little effort, "He snatched the lower jaw in one hand, and the upper in the other. He exerted strength. The mouth gaped wider, a tail twelve feet behind it lashed, the thing died with fingers like steel claws tearing at its brain" (90). While this incident helped him to atone for his action on the football field, he continued to suffer. "Driving a truck. Working on a farm. Digging in a road. His mind a bitter blank, his valiant dreams all dead" (91).

Philosophers may thrive in tranquil, bucolic surroundings, spinning out their ideas far from the madding crowd, but a superhero needs a different setting to best utilize his gifts. And what better place than war? Give a superhero a good military conflict and he will take to it like a hawk to an uplifting thermal. How would Achilles or Odysseus have earned the world's adulation had there been no Trojan War? Rustam in peacetime might have been just another unskilled laborer, Rama one more macho husband, Siegfried an overgrown teenager. Hugo Danner was no exception. When he heard that war had broken out in Europe his blood began to race: "All the ferocity of him, all the unleashed wish to rend and kill, was blazing in his soul.... A war. In a war what would hold him, what would be superior to him, who could resist him?" (95). With these thoughts in mind, he joined the French Foreign Legion and became a combatant in the First World War, the "war to end all wars."

Suffice it to say that Hugo lived up to his potential on the battlefield, astounding those around him with his Herculean performance. The war had given him a raison d'etre, a niche in a world which had previously rejected him. In addition, he had acquired a true friend. Tom Shayne was Hugo's Patroklos, Enkidu and Tonto all rolled up into one. It is not surprising then, that he went completely berserk when he saw his beloved sidekick blown apart by a German artillery shell. The resultant slaughter made Achilles' rampage through the Trojan ranks after the death of Patroklos seem like child's play:

> He ran into the bubbling, doom-ridden chaos, waving his arms and shouting maniacal profanities. A dozen times he was knocked down.... He was like a man of steel. Bullets sprayed him.... His hands went out, snatching and squeezing. That was all. No weapons, no defense. Just-hands. Whatever they caught they crushed flat, and heads fell into those dreadful fingers, sides, legs, arms, bellies.... His fingers had made a hundred bunches of clotted pulp and then a thousand as he walked swiftly forward in that trench [112].

Single-handedly, Hugo turned back a major German assault, killing thousands of the enemy in the process.

As great as his abilities in battle were, however, he was not able to bring an end to the hostilities. He planned to force peace on the Germans and their allies,[4] but at the same time he realized that "He could not wrap his arms around a continent and squeeze it into submission. There were too many people and they were too stupid to do more than fear him and hate him" (123). The war ended before he could put his plan into effect.

Returning to a world no longer at war did not bring peace to the sensitive superhero. As he wandered from place to place in search of a goal he could not define, he became increasingly disgusted with humanity. Time and again he was made to suffer simply because he refused to feign mediocrity. He was fired from a steel mill because he worked too hard and too well, an experience that soured him on the working class. With the help of Thomas Shayne's father, he found a position in a bank, but here, too, he was made to suffer for doing what was right: as a reward for saving a fellow worker who had accidentally locked himself inside the time vault and was quickly running out of oxygen (he broke the huge lock with his hands), he was not only fired, but arrested and given a brutal third degree by the police, who demanded to know how he had done it:

> They beat his face with fists that shot from the blackness. They threw him to the floor and kicked him. When his skin did not burst and he did not bleed, they beat and kicked him more viciously. They lashed him with rubber hoses. They twisted his arms as far as they could — until the bones of an ordinary man would have been dislocated.... They tried to drive a splinter under his nails ... [143].

Finally, when he could take no more, Hugo flexed his powerful muscles and easily broke free. Shrugging off the bullets from six police revolvers as if they were no more than annoying gnats, he punched a giant hole through the prison wall, knocked the startled policemen guarding him senseless, grabbed hold of the officer who had begun the abuse and calmly hailed a cab to make his escape. He later released his terrified hostage, but not before giving him a demonstration of his super strength: "Still holding the policeman's arm, he walked to the taxi and, to the astonishment of the driver, gripped the axle in one hand, lifted up the front end like a derrick, and turned the entire car around" (145).

By this time, Hugo had gotten fed up with urban civilization. His next stop was at a farm in Upstate New York, where he was hired to do menial labor by a stingy farmer named, appropriately enough, Cayne. But even country life proved to be calamitous for the unlucky superhero.

One day, the farmer he worked for went off to New York City to display his cattle at a show. Now this would not have been significant had Mrs. Cayne gone with her husband; but she remained home, ostensibly because of a bad cold. The true reason why she did not accompany her husband, however, was the strong, sensitive farmhand in whom she had taken more than a casual interest.

Given the circumstances, one would expect an archetypal love scene to follow. For a while, moreover, that was the way the scenario unfolded: a superhero and a lovely, unhappily married young woman lying side by side in a field, speaking softly to each other. They lean toward each other, lips pursed, when suddenly "The rhythmic thunder bore upon them like the wind. A few yards away, head down, tail straight, the big bull charged over the ground like an avalanche" (154). Talk about bad timing! For anyone other than a superhero that would have been not only a very frustrating but also life-threatening situation. For Hugo and Mrs. Cayne it was undoubtedly the former — for the bull, the latter. Nonchalantly, as if flicking away a large fly, Hugo unleashed a wicked punch that sent the enraged beast to animal heaven with a broken neck.

All right, one is inclined to think, the love scene was delayed a bit, but all's well that ends well. Unfortunately, however, this particular episode did not end well. While Hugo might have been a true superman, Mrs. Cayne was no Lois Lane. Instead of flinging herself into her hero's arms, the terrified farmer's wife "...gathered her legs under herself and ran" (155). More dejected than ever, Hugo made his way back to the big city, having learned that farm life was not the solution to his problem.

Back in the city, Hugo learned that he had become a rich man. The relatively modest sum of money he had left with Thomas Shayne's father before setting out on his odyssey had been wisely invested for him. An astute financier, Mr. Shayne was happy to inform Hugo that he had become a millionaire. When Hugo learned the details of the investments, though, the seemingly good news turned sour. Shayne, it turned out, had invested his money in the armaments industry, the very establishment responsible for his friend's death. Utterly depressed and disillusioned, Hugo sent all of the money to his parents, preferring to live like a semi-derelict rather than benefit from what he considered to be an industry of murder.

Disillusioned with capitalism, Hugo next tried to find a place for himself with the political left wing. He approached a leading communist official and offered to use his strength to free a pair of fellow travelers who had been condemned to death on trumped up charges. But the offer was turned down; the Party leaders had decided that the two would serve their cause better as martyrs. This cynical attitude was the final stroke. Completely repulsed by the world around him, Hugo decided to leave the "civilized" world. To this end, he signed up with an archaeological expedition that was headed for the Yucatan: "Hugo realized at last that there was no place in the world for him. Tides and tempest, volcanoes and lightning, all other majestic vehemences of the universe had a purpose, but he had none" (177). To his credit, however, Hugo had kept these feelings to himself when, just a short time earlier, his dying father asked him how his "gift" affected his life. To comfort the old biologist, Hugo lied that he was happy, hinting that he had been able to use his super strength to end the war. Elated by the well-intentioned falsehood, Abednego Danner handed over all of his laboratory notes to Hugo, assigning him the task of creating others with his extraordinary capabilities. His final words were joyful: "...I shall die.... But I shall not be dead because of you" (163). Unfortunately, Hugo could not share his bliss.

The final scene in *Gladiator* would have been more fitting had the entire work been more a mythologically centered heroic epic than a socio-philosophical study. Hugo and the leader of the archeological expedition, Dr. Harding, were out together studying the remains of an ancient temple when a four-ton stone in the roof of the temple dislodged and would have crushed the professor like an eggshell had Hugo not caught it as effortlessly as if it were made of paper. Since he was first and foremost a scientist, Dr. Harding was more interested than shocked by the experience. Finally, in answer to the professor's persistent questioning, Hugo divulged the truth. For the first time in his life, someone did not condemn him for what he was, but viewed him as the potential sire of a perfect race. Hugo listened carefully as Dr. Harding explained what he had in mind:

> Don't you see it, Hugo? You are not the reformer of the old world. You are the beginning of the new. We begin with a thousand of you. Living by yourselves and multiplying, you produce your own arts and industries and ideas. The New Titans! Then — slowly — you dominate the world. Conquer and stamp out all these things to which you and I and all men of intelligence object. In the end — you alone are supreme [188].

Fortunately for the world, Hugo was no Adolf Hitler. While his initial reaction to Harding's proposal was euphoric, his intellect quickly began to rebel against the plan. He realized that there were grave dangers:

> Conscience was bickering inside him. Humanity was content; it would hate his new race. And the new race, being itself human, might grow top-heavy with power.... If his Titans disagreed and made war on each other — surely that would end the earth [189].

Unable to decide on his course of action, Hugo gathered up his father's notebooks and made his way to the mountains to seek a resolution to his dilemma. Suddenly, a savage storm broke. Leaning against a bare rock, Hugo shouted his pent up doubts into the raging elements: "Now-God-oh, God — if there be a God — tell me! Can I defy You? Can I defy Your world? Is this Your will? Or are You, like all mankind, impotent?" His answer came in the form of a lightning bolt: "It struck Hugo, outlining him in fire. His hand slipped from his mouth. His voice was quenched. He fell to the ground" (191).

The professor found his remains several days later blackened by the fatal lightning bolt. His father's notes were at his side, reduced to a pile of ashes.

Although the ending has been justly criticized by literary critics as contrived and superficial, it is, archetypally speaking, a fitting end for a Titan. And while *Gladiator* certainly cannot be considered one of the ageless works of literature, Hugo Danner is nonetheless worthy of inclusion in our select group of world-class superheroes, one who deserves to be remembered in his own right and not merely as the literary precursor of America's universally popular Superman.

Hugo Danner's birth was hardly a classic demonstration of the Rankean pattern for the birth of a hero. His parents were not "most distinguished," his father far from regal. There were no prophecies warning against his birth, unless one considers mother Matilda's distrust of her husband's scientific work such an omen, nor was Hugo abandoned to the elements as a baby, to be saved and nursed by an animal. There was no father-son conflict, and no final glory, at least not in the traditional sense. In spite of these seeming deficiencies, however, there is no doubt that Hugo is an archetypal superhero.

For one thing, Hugo's conception was certainly extraordinary, if not miraculous. Unlike ancient mythology, moreover, which customarily credits a particular divinity with effecting such miracle births, Philip Wylie adhered to the standards of his own time, substituting the modern equivalent of the gods: science. It is the secret formula that is responsible for the super baby who, without it, would probably have been just one more milquetoast in the Danner household, to be ordered about and abused by the reigning matriarch. But this *magic* conception and birth are not the only evidence that Hugo Danner was essentially a twentieth century model of an ageless archetype.

Hugo had no *superweapons* for one very good reason: he simply had no need for them. Due to his extreme strength, he himself was a superweapon, equal in destructive power to Thor's hammer, Odin's spear, or Indra's dart. This is made evident in Wylie's mythological description of Hugo's first experience of combat in the war: "So he walked through the trench, a machine that killed quickly and remorselessly — a black warrior from a distant realm of the universe where the gods had bred another kind of man" (101).

Other familiar archetypes are also present. The archetypal nature of Hugo's relationship with Thomas Shayne is clear and has already been pointed out. While this *sidekick* archetype is easily identified, however, the search for a traditional *archenemy* does not yield such apparent results. The fearful neighbors, the German army, the abusive policemen, the pathetic communist leader — none of these qualify as bona fide archenemies, since none comes close to approximating Hugo in strength or stature. The fact that Hugo had no Hector, Ravan or Turnus on whom to direct his personal wrath, however, does not mean that he lacked an archenemy of colossal proportions; indeed, there was only one who was powerful enough to defeat him in the archetypal showdown — Hugo himself. It was Hugo Danner whom he battled continually, and it was Hugo Danner who brought him to his melodramatic death on a mountaintop in the Yucatan. The thunderbolt can be seen on the one hand as *divine intervention*, and as such it was convenient. On the other hand, it was an unnecessary intervention, since Hugo had already made a decision not to inflict himself and his kind on the world any longer.

The archetypes of *flawed invulnerability* and *monster slaying* can also be found in *Gladiator*, although they are not as clearly delineated here as they are in the ancient heroic works. Once again, we must search internally. Hugo Danner's vulnerability was not located in a spot on his heel or back, but rather in his fragile, tortured psyche. Moreover, that is also the place where the monsters he had to defeat dwelled. While he was easily able to shrug off machine gun bullets and bayonets, rip apart a killer shark or a steel vault with his bare hands, he was unable to conquer the psychic pain induced by his super sensitivity. His vulnerable spot was finally pierced, not by an arrow or a spear, but by the unbearable pain of separation. Hugo could not live with his species, having seen it in its most negative light, and as a result he could not live with himself. His final journey to the mountaintop was a prayer, not for answers, but for release. He desired peace, not progeny. Little did he suspect that death would not be able to prevent him from producing an heir, not another Hugo, but an alien being from a distant, doomed planet. Hugo was dead, but his replacement would soon streak toward earth. A caped, costumed superhero was about to burst onto the American scene.

Superman

The year 1933 was an ominous one for the world. On January 30 of that year Adolf Hitler became the chancellor of Germany. Influenced by the mustached miscreant in Berlin, two young Americans created a malevolent, ugly character who was the antithesis of a superhero. They called their character Superman; his origin story appeared under the title *Reign of the Superman* in their high school publication, *Science Fiction;* but it was very obvious that it would go no further. The world had no need for another super villain.

By 1938, as the Nazis gained strength, there was a critical need for some counter force to battle them. The threatened democracies needed superheroes. In the movie theaters, Tarzan was at the height of his popularity, but as great as the remarkable vine-swinger was in his jungle setting, he could not be expected to defeat the Luftwaffe and Panzers alone.

In the pulp magazines Doc Savage and the Spider performed exceptional feats for their enthralled readers, while in the realm of comic strips, Dick Tracy, Buck Rogers, Flash Gordon, and Terry and the Pirates, among others, did the same. Before long, many of these were drafted to fight for democracy against the demonic Axis powers, often appearing on the radio, in film, and in a burgeoning new medium: the comic book. No longer limited to reprinting newspaper strips, the publishers of comic books, DC Comics at the forefront, had begun to develop their own stable of superheroes. Among these champions of freedom was the greatest superhero of all, a mighty Kryptonean transplant, the one and only Man of Steel: Superman.

In reality, the greatest American superhero was not born far out in space on the dying planet Krypton, but in Cleveland, Ohio. The creators of the Man of Steel were just as unlikely. They were neither epic poets with the talent of Homer or Firdowsi nor scholars of ancient mythology with stature equal to that of Joseph Campbell or Lorre Goodrich. Rather, they were two seventeen-year-old high school students with vivid imaginations and little more than a modicum of artistic talent; their names were Jerry Siegel and Joseph Shuster. Their rudimentary tale was to become the basis for a world-wide enterprise that continues to this day.

It was Siegel who came up with the idea on a steamy summer evening in 1933, an idea which he eagerly shared with his friend the following morning. Together they developed their hero as a "genius in intellect," a "Hercules in strength," and a "Nemesis to wrongdoers." It mattered little that Shuster's early sketches of this champion of justice were strikingly similar to the popular pulp hero, Doc Savage. No one seemed to care that the idea of an alien from somewhere in outer space had already been introduced by Voltaire as early as 1752,[5] and exploited by numerous other authors from that time on. Was it really significant that the theme of dual identity had been fully explored in virtually every major mythology as well as in countless literary works, ranging from Goethe's *Faust* to Dostoevsky's *Double?*[6] In spite of everything, however, the brainchild of the two teenagers was unique, and would make a mark on the superhero genre as none had ever done before. The forces of evil now had a most imposing archenemy.[7]

An avid science fiction devotee, Jerry Siegel readily admitted that his major source for the idea of Superman had come from one of his favorite literary works, Philip Wylie's *Gladiator*. But his superhero would be no social outcast like Hugo Danner. In the guise of a mild-mannered reporter, Clark Kent, the Kryptonian colossus would be able to lead a relatively normal life when not cruising the skies of Metropolis in search of wrongdoers. This was one of the touches that distinguished Superman from all of his predecessors. As Steranko states, "The business of being a reporter and having an alter ego had been done dozens of times before. The only difference was that Superman was playing the role of Kent. Siegel's mythical blending of the three themes[8] was inspirational" (37). In any event, this dual identity, combined with the remarkable attributes he was given by his creators, made Superman arguably the greatest superhero of all. He is not only one of the ten most recognizable "people" on this planet, but has even been compared by some of his zealous fans to Jesus Christ.

Throughout the years, the Man of Steel has undergone an evolutionary process that has significantly increased his powers. Following the model of Heracles, the first superhero to dress for the part, Superman discarded his ordinary street clothes for the familiar skin-tight blue and yellow leotard with accompanying red cape. And like Heracles' costume, the material used for Superman's was no ordinary cotton blend. Indestructible,[9] it came from the lining of the passenger compartment in the space ship that had brought him from Krypton.

While Superman was originally limited to leaping long distances, he soon acquired the ability to fly. (Why leap over tall buildings with a single bound when you can fly over an entire city?) Gradually, this ability improved so greatly that he could fly faster than the speed of light. Moreover, somewhere along the way he developed X-ray vision,[10] a talent that would make any voyeur's mouth water. This was followed by microscopic-, telescopic-, heat-cold-, and every other kind of super-vision imaginable.

The list of Superman's growing superpowers presented a new difficulty for the successors of Siegel and Shuster. (In one of the worst business deals in history, the two had sold the rights to *Superman* in 1938 for $130.) Ironically, the ultimate superhero was becoming too powerful. How could the reader's interest in his adventures be maintained if the outcome of his encounters was always certain? Therefore, when it seemed that Superman's invulnerability was so complete as to admit no believable challenge by an adversary, green kryptonite was introduced, fragments of Superman's home planet whose effect on Superman was life threatening.[11]

It must be noted that the idea for the greatest American superhero was not snatched up by the publishing industry at once. For six years virtually every comic syndicate rejected the concept, declaring it immature, unimaginative or crudely drawn. At last, however, Harry Donenfeld, the publisher of DC (Detective Comics), decided to publish it on a trial basis in the first issue of a new comic book, this in spite of the fear that the publishers of *Gladiator* might sue for plagiarism. They did not, and the rest is history.

The Superman epic continues to the present day. By 1940, the Kryptonian immigrant formerly known as Kal-El was fighting for "truth, justice and the American way." And he was fighting on many fronts: in the comic books that came to bear his name, in a daily newspaper strip, in a number of animated cartoons[12] and on the radio. By the time America entered the war, moreover, an increasingly better equipped and mightier Superman was defeating the evil "Japanazis" in one battle after another.

As great as he was, though, Superman was no more able to end World War II than Achilles could the Trojan War, or Hugo Danner World War I. But end it did, and with the cessation of hostilities the world changed. So did Superman.

The key to Superman's survival has not been his ability to fly or to see through walls, but his great versatility. For example, in the immediate postwar period, America's great champion of justice adjusted to the lighter spirit of the times by temporarily becoming a comic figure. Instead of U-boats and panzer divisions, Superman battled mischievous arch-enemies such as the Prankster, the Toyman, the Puzzler and Mr. Mxyztplk.[13] Most super-heroes would not have survived this transition to slapstick in the macho world of their genre, but the brainchild of Siegel and Shuster demonstrated that he was a super-survivor. While many other members of the club declined or failed during the postwar calm, Superman's new pratfall, pie-in-the-face image made him even more popular. Nor did he limit his popularity to the comic books and newspapers; during this time he starred in two Columbia serials: *Superman* (1948) and *Superman and the Mole Men* (1950). Only Batman came close to matching his success, and the Caped Crusader occupied a distant second place.[14] Competitors watched with envy as the Man of Steel defeated time and logic in 1949 by appearing simultaneously in his own book as an adult, and in the offshoot *Superboy* series, which depicted him as an adolescent boy of steel. Six years later, he moved from America's newsstands to its living rooms in a syndicated television series,[15] and in 1959, *Action Comics #252* brought forth his female counterpart, Supergirl, a cousin who had also survived the dangerous journey from the exploding planet Krypton.[16] Since then, he has appeared in several full-length motion pictures (with at least one more in the planning stage at this writing), and in a number of television series, i.e., *Superboy, Lois and Clark,* and, more recently, *Smallville.* After a three month "vacation" in 1986, moreover, during which he once more adjusted to changing times,[17] Superman reemerged. Even death in 1993 could not defeat him. As befits a superhero of his stature, he has been resurrected and continues to perform mind boggling feats of strength and courage.

Despite all of the obvious advantages, being Superman on the planet Earth has had its drawbacks. For one thing, his dual identity resulted in an extremely complex love-triangle, one in which he had to compete with himself for the affection of a woman. It is hardly surprising that Lois Lane's hormones were aroused even at the thought of Superman, while Clark Kent, her mild-mannered, bumbling colleague on the *Daily Planet,* rarely aroused more than annoyance.[18] Why, one might ask, would Superman care if she did not love his

Opposite: Superman, *Action Comics* #1, June 1938. (DC Comics.)

wimpish Döppelgänger? After all, Clark was merely his disguise, not his true identity. It is at best a psychological web, one which even Freud would have been unable to untangle.

It would seem that even had he been able to resolve this bizarre ménage à trois, there would still have remained insoluble problems.[19] Larry Niven, in his essay entitled "Man of Steel: Woman of Kleenex,"[20] pointed this out very graphically. After an initial discussion on the mating habits of Kryptonians, he speculates on what would happen if Lois Lane and Superman were ever to become lovers. He points out the fact that our virgin superhero has waited a long time to satisfy his sexual needs, emphasizing how difficult it must have been, since "He has x-ray vision and knows exactly what he's been missing" (Niven 76). His frustration must have been as colossal as his strength, considering the fact that he lived in the huge city of Metropolis, no doubt teeming with large numbers of females who are better physically endowed and more sensuous than Lois.

Niven indicates what would happen if Superman were to let his X-ray vision cause him to succumb to the temptations of the flesh. Rather than ecstasy, he writes, there would be disaster.

> The problem is this. Electroencephalograms taken of men and women during sexual intercourse show that orgasm resembles a "kind of pleasurable epileptic attack." One loses control over one's muscles.

Rather than let us draw our own conclusions, he adds:

> ... Superman would literally crush LL's body in his arms, while simultaneously ripping her open from crotch to sternum.... Kal-El's semen would emerge with the muzzle velocity of a machine gun bullet [76–77].

Clearly then, one is inclined to agree with Niven that normal sex between Superman and an earth woman is impossible, whether she be Lois Lane or Lana Lang, the girlfriend of his Superboy days.

On the other hand, for a superhero who can fly faster than the speed of light, nothing is impossible. At the present time, he and Lois are married once again, and she seems to be none the worse for wear. It is obvious that in the world of the superhero, logic is a rare visitor. One can be thankful that literary critics like Leslie Fiedler were premature in ringing the death knell of the American superhero.[21] More than twenty-five years have passed since Fiedler expressed this judgment, and yet the Man of Steel is still with us. He has been battered somewhat, even temporarily destroyed, but he always comes back to continue his unending fight for truth, justice and the American way.

Just as a rose remains a rose no matter what one calls it, Superman by any other name would still be an archetypal superhero. At first glance, one might conclude that he does not satisfy the Rankean criteria for the birth of a hero; however, a more careful examination of his origins yields evidence to the contrary. His parents were certainly "most distinguished." Although not a king, his father, Jor-El, was an elite member of Krypton's Science Council, and his mother, Lara, was also a gifted scientist.

Since we are not told anything of Superman's physical birth, one must assume that there were no great difficulties preceding the event, nor was there ever a prophecy warning that his birth would endanger his father or anyone else. Nevertheless, and because of the great danger that threatened his entire planet, baby Kal-El was surrendered to the alien element of space, a rocket ship taking the place of a box or basket.

Jonathan and Martha Kent,[22] the couple who discovered him in the safely landed rocket ship, were simple farm people who lived on the fringe of the town called Smallville.

That the town's name is apt is evident in a second origin story. In this version, Jonathan Kent parks his pickup truck outside of the orphanage with the uncovered rocket in it and no one even notices. (How they managed to get the rocket into the truck is another unanswered question.)

The adult Kal-El is not physically reunited with his distinguished parents,[23] but he certainly does achieve rank and honors on his new planet. While the origin story of Superman created by the two youngsters from Cleveland does not meet all of the criteria for a hero's birth set forth by Otto Rank, as the epic tale of America's greatest superhero developed during the ensuing decades, a wealth of archetypal material is apparent.

Clearly, Kal-El is one of the *chosen* and was originally presented as the sole survivor from a doomed planet. (Supergirl and the three outlaws from Krypton who appear in the 1980 movie *Superman II* are offshoots of his commercial success.) On earth as Superman, he is even more a *man/god* figure than Heracles or Osiris were in their lands, with many abilities that they could only have dreamed of possessing. His *superweapons* are part of his being rather than external: super strength, supersonic speed, X-ray vision and skin so tough that the most destructive weapons cannot penetrate it. His *invulnerability* is archetypally flawed by his inability to withstand the effects of Kryptonite. He has no *sidekick* per se, unless one considers Clark Kent, the other half of his dual identity, as such. *Divine intervention* takes the form of science in the modern heroic epic, and this holds true for Superman; it is only because of the scientific know-how of his father that baby Kal-El survived the cataclysm on Krypton, and throughout his adventures science plays a dominant role. The number of *monsters* he battles in the course of his illustrious career is astronomical, his *archenemies,* led by the diabolical scientist Luthor, are legion. He *defeats death* more than once,[24] and undergoes several important *transformations.* Until recent years, the question of a *suitor's test* did not arise, since Larry Niven's stance that no woman could survive as his mate was an unspoken fact.[25] Presently, however, he is married to Lois Lane, indicating that he has managed to overcome this obstacle and pass the most difficult test of his life.

In conclusion, no discussion of the Superhero would be complete without the inclusion of America's Superman. Like Gilgamesh, Achilles, Rustam, and Rama, he exists beyond time and place, and will most likely continue to excite us for as long as we allow our imaginations to soar with him.

Captain Marvel

In February 1942, Fawcett Publications invaded Superman's airspace with their own flying, bullet-deflecting, Nazi-bashing superhero. With a face modeled after that of the American actor Fred MacMurray, the red-suited Captain Marvel quickly became Superman's greatest competitor, eventually aided by a growing family of Marvels. No flash in the pan, before he made his first exit from the world of superheroes some thirteen years later, Captain Marvel had starred in more than six hundred adventures in *Whiz Comics* and *Captain Marvel Comics*, and made scores of appearances in later publications such as the *Captain Marvel Jr.*, *Mary Marvel*, and *Marvel Family* series, as well as in the books of a number of other superheroes. While his demise was credited by some to be the result of the plagiarism suit instituted by Superman's publisher, DC Comics, against Fawcett, in fact Fawcett had decided to withdraw from the comic book business as early as 1953 because of the declining market.[26] At any rate, Captain Marvel was no more plagiarized from Superman than was Aeneas from Achilles. That they shared characteristics is attributable to the fact that they are archetypal superheroes, children of the human collective unconscious.[27]

While Siegel and Shuster looked to science fiction for their model hero, the creators of Captain Marvel focused on mythology for theirs. And while Superman took several years to display more than a modicum of humor, the "Big Red Cheese" (as he was affectionately labeled by his creators) evoked the reader's smile from his inception. His most common facial expression was one of complete befuddlement, usually accompanied by the phrase, "Holy Moley," which has since become part of the American vernacular. The satirical penchant of Captain Marvel's originator, Bill Parker, and the work of the illustrator Clarence Charles Beck combined to produce a superhero who was able to poke fun not only at the world, but at himself as well. There are even episodes where a character in a Captain Marvel story learns Captain Marvel's secret identity by reading about it in a *Captain Marvel* comic book. While this type of playfulness may or may not prod one to indulge in deep metaphysical speculation, the adventure lines and artwork of the early issues of *Whiz* were simple in the extreme, leading James Steranko to comment: "Compared to Captain Marvel, headliners like Superman ... read like King Lear" (Steranko II 8).

Unlike his blue-suited rival from Metropolis, Captain Marvel was not conceived by a teenager in the middle of a hot summer's night. The assignment to enter Fawcett into the world of superheroes was given to Bill Parker, who was moved from his position as supervising editor of Fawcett's movie publications. Parker's first plan was to create a comic book stable of six major characters, superheroes whose extraordinary abilities were derived from biblical and mythological figures. He intended to imbue one with **Solomon's** wisdom, another with **Heracles'** strength, a third with **Atlas'** stamina, a fourth with **Zeus'** power, a fifth with **Achilles'** courage and the a sixth with **Mercury's** speed. The acronym formed from these powers was SHAZAM, a word that was to become the name of the old wizard who passed on his super powers to Captain Marvel.

When the idea of a group of heroes was overruled, Parker combined the six into one mighty mortal whom he first called Captain Thunder, adding an alter ego in the form of a young boy named Billy Batson. Before the exploits of this new hero came to press, however, his name went through a metamorphosis: first he became Captain Marvelous and then, ultimately, Captain Marvel.

As was the case with Superman, it took Captain Marvel a few issues (five to be exact) before he developed the ability to fly, but unlike the Kryptonian transplant he never did develop the power to see what he was missing. Even without X-ray vision, however, he was billed as "The World's Mightiest Mortal," and fortunately for democracy he was as much in tune with the "American Way" as Superman, although the two superheroes have quite different beginnings. Captain Marvel's origin story follows:

Cheated out of his inheritance by an evil uncle with whom he lived after his parents died, teenaged Billy Batson is barely able to sustain himself on the few dollars he earns selling newspapers in the gloomy subway station where he spends his nights. One night, a mysterious stranger appears and asks Billy to follow him, leading him to the deserted underground station. A strange, driverless train suddenly appears; he boards it with the stranger and is taken to the hidden abode of the wizard Shazam, a godlike figure with the requisite white flowing beard. The latter greets Billy and proceeds to tell him that he has been chosen to be Captain Marvel, the "strongest and mightiest man in the world...." The perplexed young newsboy listens in disbelief as the wizard explains that in order to change into the champion of good, he merely has to say his (Shazam's) name. Billy does as instructed;

Captain Marvel and Billy Batson, *Whiz* **#22, October 3, 1941. (DC Comics.)**

a lightning bolt immediately strikes him, transforming him into Captain Marvel. (The old wizard's name acts like a toggle switch, changing Billy back to himself when he utters it as Captain Marvel.)

Although Billy Batson is unharmed by the transformation into the red-suited super-hero, Shazam is not so fortunate. A thin rope that had been holding a huge granite block over his head snaps when the lightning bolt flashes, crushing him. It is not a total tragedy, however, since Billy is able to summon Shazam's spirit in times of need.

With the entrance of the Big Red Cheese onto the scene, the Allies have a new champion. Superman continues to battle the Nazis and "Japanazis" in his comic books, while Captain Marvel carries on an incessant struggle with such Axis villains as Captain Nazi and Nippo the Nipponese, winning victory after victory for the forces of democracy. When he is not defeating his country's foes, the worlds "Mightiest Mortal" is engaged in combat with his number one archenemy, the ultra sinister scientist, Dr. Sivana. Among other colorful villains that he confronts are the deadly Mr. Mind, a super worm (shades of Midgardsörm) with a propensity for evil; Mr. Ibac,[28] a diabolical fiend with the harmless alter ego named Stinky Printwhistle; Oggar, the world's mightiest immortal; Mr. Atom, a super robot; the Red Crusher, an Asian communist; and a host of assorted monsters from this and other galaxies.

As Captain Marvel became more popular, he expanded his field of combat to the movie theaters.[29] But while the forces of evil could not defeat him, the realities of the market place and the growing cost of litigation compelled his early (though temporary) retirement in 1954. Like the mythical Phoenix, however, Captain Marvel refused to stay dead. His name was unsuccessfully used in a short-lived strip by an obscure publisher some twelve years later.[30] In 1967, *Marvel Comics* introduced their version of a superhero named Captain Marvel; one who, in spite of the fitting name of the publishing company, did not soar to the heights of the original. In the 1970s, however, DC Comics resurrected the World's Mightiest Mortal under the title *SHAZAM*, and from there he moved to television. Holy Moley!

It was not long after the debut of Captain Marvel that the Marvel superfamily began to form. The first additions were three young men from different parts of the country, all named Billy Batson. By shouting out the magic word, SHAZAM, they, too, became super-heroes; not captains, to be sure, but Lieutenant Marvels, outranked by the illustrious leader who formed them into a "Squadron of Justice." Never as popular as the bungling swash-buckler who led them, they only appeared in a half dozen or so episodes. But there were other Marvels on the horizon.

Captain Marvel Junior

In December 1941, Captain Marvel, Jr., made his debut in Whiz Comics #45, a teenaged chip off the old Red Cheese block who soon became a popular superhero in his own right. His origin story is the following:

Freddy Freeman and his grandfather are out fishing when they see someone drowning. Unknown to them, it is the evil Captain Nazi, who has landed in the lake after being punched by Captain Marvel. The two unsuspecting fishermen take the unconscious victim into their boat. When he awakes, Hitler's henchman repays their kindness by killing the

Opposite: **Captain Marvel Debut, *Whiz* #2, February 1940. (DC Comics.)**

old man and seriously injuring Freddy with a blow from an oar. Fortunately, Captain Marvel rescues the injured teenager and flies him to Shazam's throne room, where he summons the ancient wizard's spirit and begs him to restore Freddy's health. Shazam replies that while he can save the youngster's life, the injury is so severe that Freddy will never walk again without the aid of crutches. On the bright side, though, he tells Captain Marvel that, if he is willing, he can share some of his remarkable powers with the youngster. Captain Marvel selflessly agrees. Later, when Freddy awakens and sees his hero, he whispers the latter's name. There is a flash of lightning, and Freddy is magically transformed into Captain Marvel, Jr., the world's mightiest boy. Unlike Captain Marvel's red costume, Junior's is blue. From then on, whenever he utters the name *Captain Marvel*, he is transformed from one to the other of his identities. He refers to himself from then on as CM3, lest by speaking his name he be changed into Freddy.

Captain Marvel, Jr., was a commercial success for several years, appearing in his own book and those of Captain Marvel and the Marvel Family until the year 1953. This was the year that Fawcett Publications went out of business. In 1972, the rights to the Marvel characters were bought by DC Comics and new adventures began to appear under the title *SHAZAM*. In this series, there is a revised origin story, somewhat similar to the original.

In the new version, Freddy Freeman spends his formative years in New England. Freddy is sent to live with his grandfather after his parents are killed in an auto accident. Freddy and his grandfather move to the Midwest, where Freddy becomes a star athlete and befriends Billy Batson.

During the course of a radio spelling bee hosted by Billy, the two boys meet Mary Bromfield, a beautiful young girl who turns out to be Billy's twin sister. Shortly thereafter, Freddy is on a fishing trip with his grandfather at the same time Captain Marvel and Captain Nazi are engaged in a brutal battle. (The latter had recently awakened after spending fifty years in suspended animation.) The remainder of the second origin story is virtually identical to the original.

Like the Senior Captain, Captain Marvel Junior collected a number of archenemies, including such unspeakable villains as Mr. Macabre, the Acrobat, Sabbac, Captain Nippon, Dr. Eternity, etc.

Mary Marvel

During the Second World War, women proved themselves increasingly capable of performing tasks in areas that were previously considered the exclusive domain of the male. As a result, in December 1942, Fawcett introduced a new female hero, Mary Marvel, the third member of the mighty Marvel triumvirate.[31]

As previously mentioned, Billy Batson and Freddy Freeman meet the girl who turns out to be Billy's long-lost twin sister at a radio spelling bee. At one point in the activity, Billy notices that Mary is wearing a broken locket. During an intermission, Billy receives a message requesting him to visit a dying woman named Sarah Primm. He immediately becomes Captain Marvel and flies to see her. To his surprise and delight, she tells him (he has transformed back into Billy) that Mary is his twin sister, and that she knows this because she served as their nurse after the death of their parents. Sara explains that when she could no longer care for them, she was forced to place them in an orphanage. At the same time that she was a nurse for the Batsons, Primm was also the nurse of a very wealthy lady whose

Captain Marvel, Jr., *Master Comics* #27, June 1942. (DC Comics.)

child was stillborn. With the intention of providing a good home for at least one of the Batson twins, she substituted Mary for the dead baby. In order to enable Billy to locate his sister in the future, she gave him half of a locket, explaining that Mary had the other half. Having told Billy the story, she shuffles off her mortal coil.

After the spelling bee, Billy and Freddy discover that Mary has been kidnapped. They say the magic words, become the two Marvel superheroes and rescue her. Later, the two heroes revert to their teenage forms and inform Mary that she and Billy are twins; they reveal to her how they become Captain Marvel and Captain Marvel Junior. Meanwhile, the kidnappers have recovered from the beating inflicted on them by Captain Marvels Sr. and Jr. and are able to seize Billy and Freddy and gag them before they can utter their transforming words. Not knowing what else to do, Mary utters the word SHAZAM. To everyone's astonishment, there is a flash of lightning that transforms her into the superheroine, Mary Marvel, complete with a costume that matches Captain Marvel's.[32] She quickly demolishes the kidnappers and removes the gags from the two boys' mouths so that they can transform back into their super alter-egos. The three then fly to Shazam's lair to receive his spirit's blessing.

Mary Marvel comics were discontinued in 1948, but Mary continued to appear in the *Marvel Family* until 1953. She was resurrected by *National Publications* in 1973 and canceled again in 1978. From 1979 to 1982 she and other *SHAZAM* characters appeared in *Adventure Comics*. In recent years, Mary Marvel has appeared briefly in a miniseries entitled "*The New Beginnings*," was given a new origin story and a change of uniform (to white), had an interlude with Captain Marvel Junior, and from time to time can be seen in *Supergirl* and *Superwoman* comics.

* * *

At first glance it might seem extremely problematic, if not impossible, to discuss the three Marvel superheroes in Rankean terms. After all, they are fully grown superheroes from the very first moment we encounter them.[33] An additional complication exists in that we cannot fill in the gaps by viewing the origins of their three "hosts": Billy and Mary Batson, and Freddy Freeman. This is so because the latter three are not the alter egos of the superhero Marvels in quite the same way that Clark Kent is of Superman. Technically, the Marvels do not have dual identities; they are separate from the three youngsters who become them when the proper words are spoken. Nevertheless, they are not independent entities since they do not have independent existences, at least not in the material world. They can only be summoned into being through the efforts of the three specially gifted young mediums. Thus, while Clark Kent is actually Superman at any given moment, Billy Batson and Captain Marvel are unable to exist simultaneously in the same dimension. The same holds true for Mary Batson and Mary Marvel[34] as well as for Freddy Freeman and Captain Marvel Junior. In the case of the Batsons, the vocalization of the name *SHAZAM* is akin to pressing a toggle key on some metaphysical computer, serving to suspend the one personality in limbo while releasing the other to our physical reality. A second vocalization of the magic word reverses the process. In the case of Captain Marvel, Jr., calling out the name of Captain Marvel toggles him and his host, Freddy Freeman, back and forth from that very same never-never land to the here and now. Fortunately, the Marvel line of succession stopped with the teenaged Junior Marvel; for if we were to follow through logically, the next super Marvel would have had to call out the name Captain Marvel Junior to become Captain Marvel Junior Junior and so forth and so on.

Since the births and later histories of the three "hosts" have nothing whatsoever to do

Mary Marvel Debut, *Captain Marvel Adventures* **#18, December 1940. (DC Comics.)**

with the origins and development of the mighty Marvel triad, their humble origins and ensuing unheroic lives do not violate, indeed they are not applicable to, Rank's criteria for the origins of the hero. The origins and lives of the Marvels, however, do conform significantly to the archetypal pattern.

While the parentage and circumstances of birth of the Mighty Marvels is not explicitly stated, an examination of the three origin stories provides us with important clues. It would not be unreasonable to conclude that Shazam parented the three mighty Marvels without the aid of a female, delivered from the wizard by the flashing lightning. Thus, their "births" are archetypically *miraculous*, even more so in that they are *resurrected* every other time the magic words are spoken. Shazam, then, is an extraordinary individual, the archetypal parent of a hero. One might even identify him as an archetypal divinity: not only has he lived three thousand years, but, like the Norse god, Odin, he sees and knows everything that happens in the world. He differs from Odin in that he does not derive this knowledge via the reports of a pair of tireless ravens, but by means of a giant television screen which has but one channel: The Historama Network.[35]

Two other hero archetypes that appear most frequently in the tale of the three Marvels are the *archenemy* and the *sidekick* archetypes. In addition to the numerous colorful villains already mentioned, the Marvel family as a whole also battled a collective *archenemy* in many of their adventures. To keep pace with the expanding family of superheroes, Captain Marvel's number one antagonist also gained two allies: a son, Sivana, Jr., and a daughter, Georgia. Eventually it became routine for Captain Marvel and his two *sidekicks* (at times accompanied by the Lieutenants Marvel and the comic Uncle Marvel[36]) to do battle with the sinister Sivanas.

The *man/god* archetype is also present, as well as the frequent motif of *divine intervention*. Since the all-knowing, all-seeing Shazam is a classic divinity, his children would have to be at least semidivine. Therefore, each flash of lightning that calls forth or temporarily retires one of the magnificent Marvels can be viewed as an act of the gods whose initials comprise the name of the divine father of the superheroes.

When it comes to *monster slaying*, the Marvels are second to none. The number of such beings who are defeated by the three either individually or as a group is literally astronomical, since the intrepid trio often carry on their fight against evil in other galaxies. They are able to do this because they, like others of their genre, have *super transportation* (the ability to fly) and built-in *super weapons* (strength, speed), and are almost *invulnerable*. In keeping with the flawed invulnerability of Achilles, Siegfried, and Superman, it is indicated that the Marvels can be destroyed while they are in the suspended state, locked in the very vulnerable teenage beings of their three hosts, Billy, Freddy and Mary. Fortunately, the latter always manage to wiggle out of tight spots, many times ripping off a gag just in the nick of time to shout *SHAZAM* or *CAPTAIN MARVEL* and avert disaster. When it comes to superheroes, it is clear that the three children of Shazam are Marvelous representatives of the superhero genre.

Captain America

In addition to Captain Marvel, the arsenal of democracy produced another superheroic captain in those early years of World War II. He appeared in his own comic book in March 1941, clad in patriotic red, white and blue, a personification of Old Glory, born to do battle with Hitler's hordes (see illustration). He was aptly named *Captain America*. Steranko describes the debut of this mighty chauvinist: "...Captain America ... is an archetype of opposing forces locked in a death struggle, almost mythical in its simplicity" (Steranko II 52). In the very first issue he demonstrated how well he fit into the genre. He came onto the scene full grown and with a faithful *sidekick*, Bucky, a villainous Nazi *archenemy*, The Red Skull, *super strength*, and a *superweapon* in the form of a red, white and blue shield complete with stars.[37] It was just what the country needed: an American Aeneas, created in an American laboratory by the *divine intervention* of science. The Axis powers had reason to shudder as this *chosen* champion of freedom battered his way into American mythology. Captain America's origin story, which follows, is typical of the American Superhero genre.

Steve Rogers, a young American who is unfit for military service because of his frail physical condition, longs to fight against the Axis powers. An American general becomes aware of his patriotic fervor and presents him with an unusual opportunity to become a warrior for democracy. Aware of the risks involved, Steve unhesitatingly agrees to become a test subject for a revolutionary "Super Soldier" serum. To his and the general's delight the experiment is an unqualified success. After taking the serum, Steve acquires bulging muscles and super strength. The government provides him with a costume modeled after the American flag, a bulletproof shield,[38] a .45 sidearm and the code name "Captain America."

Assuming a cover identity as an inept private in an army camp in Virginia, Steve meets a teenager named James Buchanan "Bucky" Barnes. Bucky accidentally learns that Steve is Captain America and pleads with the latter to make him his sidekick. After a rigorous training regimen, Bucky is ready to join the Captain in a relentless battle with Hitler and Tojo.

The one mistake Timely Publications made was to identify their daring new superhero too closely with the war. During the hostilities, there was no greater champion of democracy, but when the hostilities ceased, Captain America became archaic. Nothing seemed to halt his decline into superhero limbo, neither the introduction of a female *sidekick* in 1948, Golden Girl, to replace the Robin-like Bucky, nor the retitling of the magazine to *Captain America's Weird Tales* one year later. The public was as fickle as ever. Hadn't Odysseus faded from the spotlight once he killed Pene-

Captain America, circa 1950s. (™ and ©2007 Marvel Entertainment Group, Inc. All rights reserved.)

lope's suitors? And who sang the praises of Rustam and Rama once they had become old and were unable to defeat entire armies singlehandedly? Steranko wrote a terse eulogy for the wartime superhero: "Captain America became an artifact of an era past" (Steranko II 55).

Superheroes do not die easily, however, and in May, 1954, *Atlas Comics resurrected* Captain America. Before very long, he faded away once more, but like the mythical Phoenix, in March 1964, he began to appear periodically in a new publication called *Tales of Suspense*, and in 1968 he was given a book bearing his own name once more. Over the years he has changed from a super warrior to a spy, to a policeman, to a homeless drifter. He has been a neurotic recluse, a ghetto crime fighter, has had substitute Captain Americas take his place periodically, and at one point was exposed as a reactionary fraud (Horn 156). He has endured, even though he has never reached the heights that he occupied when scripted by Stan Lee and drawn by Jack Kirby. Captain America has appeared on film, in paperback form, in animated cartoons, on television, and from time to time he will make a guest appearance in another superhero's comic book. As Horn so aptly puts it, "...Captain America has always mirrored the American psyche: in the 1940s he was the super-patriot, in the 1950s he was the reactionary, today he is the unsure giant. He is America" (156).

9

Finland

To those who live beyond the confines of Scandinavia, the Baltic States and northern Siberia, the names Väinämöinen, Ilmarinen and Leminkäinen may sound as if they belong to visitors from a planet in a distant solar system. To a Finn, however, they are synonymous with greatness. These are the names of their national superheroes, equal to any, past or present, who ever trod the earth. The story of their remarkable adventures can be found in the great epic poem *Kalevala*, first published in 1849 by Dr. Elias Lönnrot.[1] While these adventures may seem quite different from those of any other superheroes discussed to this point, their archetypal essence is clear. The fifty runes (cantos) that make up the *Kalevala* do not have a cohesive plot as do, for instance, Homer's two great epics, but they do tell a story well worth recounting.

The *Kalevala*

The work begins with an exposition of the Finnish creation myth, a prelude to the birth of Väinämöinen, the greatest Finnish superhero. As was the case in many ancient cultures, the Finns did not see the creation of the world as an exclusively male endeavor. In their version, creation began when the virgin of the air descended into the formless sea (chaos) and was impregnated by the winds and the waves. A seabird appeared, built a nest on the virgin's knee, and proceeded to lay six golden eggs and a seventh made of iron. Whether because the sea was very choppy or the virgin's knee an unsteady platform for such a heavy load, the eggs toppled from the nest and broke into pieces. While this has all the earmarks of a tragedy, things worked out quite well. Unlike Humpty Dumpty, for whom falling and breaking meant the end, the broken eggs in the Finnish myth marked the beginning: the shattered eggs formed the earth, sky, clouds, sun, moon, and stars.

Years passed, and still the virgin mother had not delivered her offspring. During her extended pregnancy, she tried to keep as busy as possible, creating all the capes, bays, seashores and the various depths and shallows of the oceans. Thirty years passed, but still no baby appeared.

Finally, the unborn baby decided that enough was enough and began to pray to the sun and moon to get him out; but they did not cooperate. He finally decided that the best way to get anything done was to do it himself and so he began to force his way out of his mother's recalcitrant womb: "...he moved the portal/ With his finger, fourth in number/ Opened quick the bony gateway/ With the toes upon his left foot/ With his nails beyond the threshold/ With his knees beyond the gateway" (Kirby rune I, 319–324). If Väinämöinen thought that birth was the only obstacle to overcome in life, he learned otherwise as soon as he hit the water.

Since he was neither fish nor amphibian, he had to get to land, no easy task for a newborn baby without a boat. So he began to swim. And swim. And swim. By the time he climbed up onto shore he was eight years old. He must have looked a lot older, though, because even at this early point in his life the *Kalevala* says, "Thus was *ancient* Väinämöinen/ He, the ever famous minstrel/ Born of the divine Creatrix/ Born of Ilmatar, his mother" (Kirby I, 341–344). Clearly, eight years in saltwater can really age a person.

After Väinämöinen dried himself off, he went about the business of taming nature. First he planted an oak tree which grew so well that the sun and moon were hidden by it. Thanks, however, to a diminutive stranger who miraculously emerged from the sea armed with an axe, a tragedy was averted. The latter quickly cut down the monstrous oak and Väinämöinen cleared the land for planting. The latter was then given fire by a passing eagle,[2] and with the help of the god, Ukko,[3] raised a bumper barley crop. Finally, he was ready to perform some superheroics.

Väinämöinen's first adventure was to engage in a poetry contest with Joukahainen, a young upstart from Lapland. It was a rout. The poetically unequaled Väinämöinen won the contest without effort, only to be challenged to a duel by the youth. The wise hero refused to be baited by the younger man, however, and, by means of his magic songs, sang Joukahainen into a swamp: "Then indeed young Joukahainen/ Knew at last and comprehended/ And he knew his course was finished,/ ... For in singing he was beaten/ By the aged Väinämöinen" (Kirby III, 331–336).

In order to save himself, Joukahainen promised to give Väinämöinen his sister, Aino, as a wife. Väinämöinen could not resist the offer, especially when Joukahainen explained the benefits of marriage: "She [Aino] shall dust your chamber for you/ Sweep the flooring with her besom/ Keep the milk-pots all in order/ and shall wash your garments for you/ Golden fabrics she shall weave you/ And shall bake you cakes of honey" (Kirby III, 461–466).

But Aino was not ready to become an obedient housewife, nor did she like the idea of marrying an old man. Thus, she wandered into the forest and drowned herself in a lake. Väinämöinen became depressed when his attempts to recover her were unsuccessful, but his mother reminded him that there were other fish in the sea, and told him to go out and catch one. Taking her pragmatic advice, the grieving superhero decided to woo the famed Maiden of Pohja (Lapland).

It should have been a relatively easy journey, but there was a fly in the ointment: Väinämöinen had a relentless enemy: "...the youthful Joukahainen/ He, the puny son of Lapland/ Long had cherished his resentment/ And had long indeed been envious/ Of the aged Väinämöinen (Kirby VI, 23–27). Waiting in ambush, Joukahainen shot an arrow at his rival that missed the intended target but killed Väinämöinen's horse.

Väinämöinen fell into the water and was taken far out to sea by a storm. Things looked very grim, but Joukahainen's victory party proved to be premature. After all, the old superhero had been swimming since the day he was born, and he did have some powerful friends. Thus, after several days at sea, the very same eagle who had given him fire not only saved him but carried him in first-class comfort to Lapland so that he could win the hand of the Maiden of Pohja. Once again, though, an unexpected difficulty arose.

The aged Mistress of Pohja greeted Väinämöinen amiably and declared that, while she was not against a marriage between him and her daughter, there was one condition: she would not give her consent until he produced a *Sampo* for her. Unfortunately, a *Sampo* is as rare as snow in the Sahara. Perhaps rarer.

But what exactly is a *Sampo*, might ask one who is unschooled in Finnish lore, and what is its function? The answer to these questions is not certain, for like the Holy Grail a *Sampo* is as much an idea as a concrete object. What is known is that it is a magic mill that not only produces food staples like corn and salt, but coins as well. The *Kalevala* never does give a detailed physical description of this wondrous object.

Obviously, not everyone is able to create a *Sampo*, not even the old hero Väinämöinen. However, thinking fast, he proves the validity of the adage "It's not what you know, but who(m) you know." Fortunately, Väinämöinen just happened to know a master blacksmith. Therefore, he confidently replied, "Only bring me to my country/ And I'll send you Ilmarinen/ Who shall forge a Sampo for you..../ He's a smith without an equal..." (Kirby VII, 328–329, 333). Satisfied that her daughter's suitor would keep his end of the bargain, Louhi gave her blessings and provided him with a horse and sledge for his journey home. Alas, though, wedded bliss was not the old hero's fate.

On the way back to Finland, Väinämöinen met the Maiden of Pohja and immediately began to make advances. To his dismay, the young beauty made it clear that she was not interested in settling down in the role of housewife. The fact was, she viewed marriage as an unhappy lot for women. Claiming that she was given the information by a little bird, she put it in this way:

... the frost makes cold the iron/ Yet the new bride's lot is colder/ In her father's house a maiden/ Lives like berry in the garden/ But a bride in house of husband/ Lives like house-dog tightly fettered/ To a slave comes rarely pleasure/ To a wedded damsel never [Kirby VIII 70–80].

After a while, she became more compliant, but agreed to accede to his wishes only if he could perform a series of difficult tasks. Confident in his skills as a master magician, Väinämöinen unhesitatingly accepted the challenge.

One has to admire Väinämöinen's ensuing performance. Without undue difficulty he successfully passed the tests the Maiden of Pohja had devised for him: he split a horsehair with a dull, pointless knife-blade, tied an egg in invisible knots, peeled a stone, and hewed a pile of ice without having a single splinter scatter from it or the slightest fragment loosen. But the marriage-shy Maiden set one final task: Väinämöinen had to make a boat from the splinters of a spindle and move it into the water without touching it. Undaunted by the seemingly impossible assignment, Väinämöinen began to work. Everything was going fairly well for a while, but before he could complete his task he had an accident: he cut his knee severely with his axe and was unable to stop the bleeding.

Then his magic spells he uttered/ And himself began to speak them/ Spells of origin, for healing/ And to close the wound completely..../ But the blood gushed forth in torrents/ Rushing like a foaming river ... [Kirby VIII 177–180, 187–188].

Before long, the wounded hero had lost enough blood to fill seven large boats and eight oversized tubs. Fortunately, just as his supply of the precious red fluid was about to run out, unexpected help arrived. An old man mysteriously appeared and, with the help of his son, declared that he could stem the flow of blood with a magic salve. Before he performed this much-needed first aid, however, he demanded that Väinämöinen tell him the

The Finnish hero Ilmarinen forges the Sampo.

story of the origin of iron, a tale which also included an account of the superhero-blacksmith Ilmarinen's birth. This is the story the old hero told:

After Ukko had separated the air and the continents from the water, he rubbed his hands together and placed them onto his left knee. Three well-endowed maidens were created, from whose breasts gushed various-colored milk: black, white and red. From the black milk came the softest iron; from the white, the hardest steel; and from the red, undeveloped iron. When Iron went to visit its eldest brother, Fire, it was attacked by the latter and had to flee to the marshes. For three years it hid there, emerging finally to return to Fire so that it could be forged into weapons. At this point, a miraculous birth took place: "Then was born smith Ilmarinen/ Thus was born, and thus was nurtured/ Born upon a hill of charcoal.../ In his hands a copper hammer/ And his little pincers likewise" (Kirby IX 107–109, 111–112). Ilmarinen immediately set up his forge and convinced Iron that Fire was a positive force. But Iron was skeptical. Finally, Ilmarinen explained to Iron that Fire could shape him into useful objects such as "...men's keen sword-blades/ Or as clasps for women's girdles" (IX 151–152). Satisfied with this reassurance, Iron agreed to accompany Ilmarinen back to his workshop.

Once in the fire, however, Iron could not stand the pain and begged to be removed. The super smith agreed to do this only after the latter had sworn an oath never to do harm to its brothers. This done, Ilmarinen swiftly forged a number of weapons and tools and experimented with various substances until he found the proper smelting medium to produce steel. The first arms race had begun. Immediately, Iron and Steel battled each other, a portent of the nature of future warfare.

When Väinämöinen finished his account of Iron's origin, the old man kept his part of the bargain, stemming the flow of blood from the suffering hero's leg with a powerful, homemade ointment and a silk bandage. As good as new, Väinämöinen returned home, eager to fulfill Louhi's request and thereby win the latter's daughter. But the road to love was still a very rocky one for the Finnish super magician.

The first obstacle arose when Ilmarinen refused Väinämöinen's request to go to Pohja to produce a *Sampo*. Clearly, he was not overjoyed over the prospect of a trip to Pohja: "Not in course of all my lifetime/ While the golden moon is shining/ Hence to Pohjola I'll journey..." (X 107–109). Aware that it would be futile to use reason on his stubborn friend, Väinämöinen tricked Ilmarinen into climbing a high spruce tree and then used his magic to sing up a storm. The mighty winds uprooted the tree and carried the unwilling smith to Pohja.[4]

After several unsuccessful attempts, Ilmarinen finally managed to forge a working *Sampo* for Louhi. Now it was time for her to keep her promise and give her daughter to Väinämöinen. The Maiden of Pohja had other ideas. She did not, she said, intend to give up her "...delightful life as maiden" (X 456). Thoroughly depressed, Ilmarinen returned home to report his failure to Väinämöinen. The Finnish heroes, it seems, were very good at their specialties, but when it came to women they simply did not have what it takes. At least not all of them. There was one notable exception.

The next few episodes in the *Kalevala* deal with the escapades of Leminkäinen, the third member of the Finnish triumvirate of superheroes. Unlike the others, he was a handsome ladies' man whose primary talent was seduction. To that end he set out for the island of Saari to win the affections of the beautiful maiden, Kyllikki. That she would be no pushover, however, was indicated by the fact that the sun, the moon and a star had failed to win her over as a bride for their sons, not to mention the hordes of suitors from various regions of the north whose advances she had repulsed. She was simply not interested. Undaunted by this, and undeterred by his mother's warning that the people of Saari would never accept him because of his lower station, Leminkäinen declared: "If my house is not as noble/ Nor my race esteemed so mighty/ For my handsome shape they'll choose me/ For my noble form will take me" (XI 75–78). Exuding such confidence, he reached Saari.

At first, the Finnish Casanova was discouraged. The maidens of Saari greeted him with unexpected ridicule, a reception that would have caused most men to slink away ignominiously. But Leminkäinen was a professional lover; he turned on the charm and very soon had won them over: "Not a maid, however modest/ But he did not soon embrace her/ And remain awhile beside her" (XI 154–156). The one exception was the one he wanted most of all — Kyllikki. She remained unimpressed. Leminkäinen was simply not her type, and she let him know it in no uncertain terms: "Nought I care for such a milksop/ Such a milksop, such a humbug/ I must have a graceful husband..." (XI 179–80). Rather than accept the fact that his goal was unrealistic, Leminkäinen acted in a fashion that would have made Gilgamesh proud of him: he carried Kyllikki off in his sledge. She screamed and pleaded, but he refused to let her go.

Finally, at the end of her strength to resist, Kylikki gave in, but not before she had worked out a most unusual prenuptial agreement with her would-be husband. He vowed never to go to war again in return for her oath not to attend another village dance.

Leminkäinen kept his part of the agreement, but the lure of the dance floor was too strong for the footloose Saari, and soon her husband received reports that she was dancing the nights away with all of the neighborhood Lotharios. Leminkäinen was upset, but not so much so that it caused him to crawl into a corner and waste away. The fact was that he had recently become rich as a result of a buried treasure he discovered on his land. Whether or not this convinced him that he could afford a good divorce lawyer or not is not mentioned in the *Kalevala*, but whatever the case might have been, he made an immediate decision to divorce Saari and go to Pohja so that he could marry the Merry Maiden who had already rebuffed his two countrymen. Anticipating opposition from the Laplanders, he donned his war-shirt and coat of mail and set out to conquer the entire country, by force if need be. And he almost succeeded. Using the magic of his song, he disposed of all opposition, leaving the way to total victory clear. But he made one fatal mistake: he left a survivor.

The ancient Greeks would have known better. Experience had taught them that survivors have the nasty habit of returning to fight another day. But Leminkäinen was young and naive, and so he had no inkling that when he spared the life of the blind cowherd Märkähattu, he was opening himself up to future peril. He could not conceive the possibility that such a lowly person would be any threat to him. This is evident in his response to Märkähattu, when the latter asked him why he had been spared: "Therefore 'tis that I have spared thee/ That thou dost appear so wretched/ Pitiful without my magic" (XII 484–486). After adding some more disparaging remarks about the cowherd's life and character, the young hero dismissed the whole matter from his mind and resumed his mission.

The old Mistress of Pohja was unimpressed when Leminkäinen demanded that her daughter marry him. First she reminded him that he was a married man, and when he assured her that he was about to cut the bond with his unfaithful wife, Kyllikki, she told him that she would agree to his demand only if he could successfully perform an assignment. She phrased it this way: "Never will I give my daughter/ To a vain and worthless fellow/ To a hero good for nothing/ Therefore you may woo my daughter/ Win the flower-crowned maiden/ If you hunt the elk on snowshoes/ In the distant field of Hiisi" (XIII 24–30). Like a true superhero, Leminkäinen confidently accepted the challenge. He packed his bag, fitted himself with state-of-the-art snowshoes and poles, dusted off his trusty spear and set out for Hiisi. But it was not to be a milk run. The elk of Hiisi apparently had been hunted by many other aspiring bridegrooms and had never been caught.

Before long, Leminkäinen was in trouble. He had broken his snowshoes, his poles and his spear point, and was forced to call on the forest deities for assistance. Finally, with their aid, he captured the elusive elk. When he proudly delivered the elk to the Mistress of Pohja, however, she simply assigned him another task: to capture the fire-breathing steed of Hiisi. Once again, he set out to do as commanded, and when he accomplished that she added yet another difficult task. Shades of Heracles!

Leminkäinen should have known by then that he was being led on a wild goose chase by the wily old woman, even though no actual goose was involved. But his overactive hormones obscured his judgment. Whatever the reason, he agreed to shoot a swan on the river Tuonela, the river that flowed through the realm of the dead. What he was unaware of was that he was being led into an ambush. Lying in wait by the river was none other than Märkähattu, eager to avenge the insults Leminkäinen had leveled at him. To make things worse, he had a formidable, though unconventional, weapon with him: a sea serpent that could be thrown like a spear.

When Märkähattu heard Leminkäinen approach, the blind cowherd flung the serpent in the direction of his footsteps. It was as deadly as any modern guided missile: "Through the hero's heart he hurled it/ And through Lemminkäinen's liver/ Through the arm-pit left it smote him/ Through the shoulder right it struck him" (XIV 409–412). To add insult to fatal injury, Märkähattu then threw the young hero's body into the river, where the son of Tuoni cut it into eight pieces with his sword: "Thus did Leminkäinen perish/ Perished thus the dauntless suitor/ Down in Tuoni's murky river..." (XIV 457–459). To put it mildly, it was an unsettling turn of events for the would-be groom.

Leminkäinen's mother quickly learned from the sun that her son had been killed, and his body thrown into Tuoni. A lesser woman would have thrown up her hands and shrieked, or fallen into a dead faint upon hearing such tragic news, but not she. Instead, as if she were accustomed to hearing that her son had been cut into pieces and flung into a river, she hastened to Ilmarinen's workshop and placed an order for a giant rake: "...O forge me,/ Forge a rake with copper handle/ Let the teeth of steel be fashioned/ Teeth in length a thousand fathoms/ And of fathoms five the handle!" (XV 199–203). Ilmarinen lived up to his reputation as the best smith in the world by producing the requested rake in record time. Then, armed with this grappling tool, Ilmarinen's mother began combing the bottom of Tuoni for her son's remains.

One can imagine the poor lady's horror when she began to find little pieces of her son: "Half his head, a hand was wanting/ Many other little fragments/ And his very life was wanting" (XV 277–280). But the hero's loving mother would not quit; she continued to grapple with her giant rake and little by little she located the missing pieces. All of them. Osiris would have turned green with envy. Dr. Frankenstein would have turned even greener had he seen what followed. Working with the skill of a team of microsurgeons, she meticulously joined all the pieces, down to the smallest vein. Finally, using a magic potion and a series of incantations, she brought Leminkäinen back to life, as good as new.

Meanwhile, back on the homefront, Väinämöinen was busily building himself a boat. The project was almost complete when, to his frustration, he found that he lacked the three magic words necessary to complete it. After a long search that failed to uncover the sought-after words, he decided to journey to Tuonela, the land of the dead, believing that he would find them there. He was undeterred by the warning issued by Tuoni's daughter: "O thou fool, of all most foolish/ Man devoid of understanding..../ Many truly wander hither/ Few return to where they came from!" (XVI 265–266, 271–272).

Väinämöinen learned quickly enough that her warning had not been an empty one. Soon after his arrival in Tuonela, the old hero was locked in an intricate prison by Tuoni's son. For anyone else this might have been the end of the story, but not for someone with the capabilities of Väinämöinen. As the *Kalevala* tells us, "Väinämöinen, old and steadfast/ Uttered then the words which follow: 'May not ruin overtake me/ And an evil fate await me,/ Here in Tuonela's dark dwellings...'" (XVI 363–368). He then transformed himself into a snake and wriggled through the nets that were supposed to imprison him forever. Free again, he issued the following advice to anyone who might try to duplicate his journey to the land of the dead: "Sons of men, O never venture/ In the course of all your lifetime/ Wrong to work against the guiltless/ Guilt to work against the sinless/ Lest your just reward is paid you/ In the dismal realms of Tuoni!" (XVI 401–406).

In spite of his sojourn in the Finnish equivalent of hell, Väinämöinen was still determined to learn the three magic words so that he could finish work on his boat. To this end he went to his friend, Ilmarinen, and ordered a pair of shoes, gauntlets, a shirt and a mighty stake, all to be forged of iron. He would need these, he explained, for his visit to the sleeping giant named Antero Vipunen. Once again Ilmarinen rose to the task, filling his old friend's order immediately.

Even with his custom-made armor and weaponry, however, Väinämöinen did not have an easy time of it. After awakening Vipunen by thrusting the iron stake into the giant's mouth, he lost his footing and was swallowed. Again, for anyone else (except perhaps Pinocchio) this would have been the final act. The indefatigable old superhero was undaunted; he calmly took out his knife and carved himself a boat from a piece of birchwood he happened to have with him. This done, he then began to sail up and down Vipunen's entrails, giving the latter a major stomach ache. To compound the latter's discomfort, Väinämöinen built a fire. When Vipunen could not relieve his heartburn by means of every magic spell at his disposal, he finally conceded defeat and supplied Väinämöinen not only with the desired magic words but with every magic spell he knew. Armed with this new knowledge, Väinämöinen sailed out of Vipunen's mouth and returned home, where he quickly completed his boat and embarked on his quest to win the hand of the Maiden of Pohja. What he did not know, however, was that he had a young rival: Ilmarinen.

To their credit, the two heroes behaved in a civilized manner as the love triangle developed. Each made a vow to the other not to attempt to take the young lady by force, and agreed that the choice of husband was hers alone to make. Poor old Väinämöinen never had a chance. Even though the Mistress of Pohja favored him, her daughter rejected him outright: "Him from Väinölä I choose not/ Nor an aged man will care for/ For an old man is a nuisance/ And an aged man would vex me" (XVIII 657–660). Her mind was made up. She wanted the younger man.

If Ilmarinen thought he was going to have a cakewalk, he soon learned otherwise. In a now familiar scenario, the Mistress of Pohjola informed him that he would have to perform some tasks if he wanted to be her son-in-law. These tasks were so difficult that they would have been impossible to accomplish had not Ilmarinen found an ally — the Maiden herself. With her assistance, Ilmarinen easily plowed a field of serpents, captured the ferocious Bear of Tuoni, the Wolf of Manala (a cousin, no doubt, of Cerberus) and then created an iron eagle that snared a ferocious pike from the river of Tuonela. Louhi was impressed. When she saw how well he had performed, she conceded that he would be a fit mate for her daughter. And so the two young lovers were betrothed, leaving poor old Väinämöinen to lament the fact that he had not married at a young age:

> Woe is me, a wretched creature/ That I did not learn it sooner/ That in youthful days one weddeth/ And must choose a life-companion!/ All thing else a man must grieve for/ Save indeed an early marriage/ When in youth already children/ And a household he must care for [XIX 503–510].

He further cautioned older men not to compete with young men for a woman. He knew from experience the inevitable outcome of such contests.

A magnificent wedding celebration was prepared. Everyone who was anyone received an invitation to the gala affair, everyone, that is, except the hot-headed hero Leminkäinen, who had earned a reputation as a troublemaker.[5] As it turned out, it was to be a momentous occasion not only for the bride and bridegroom but also for all future generations in many lands. For it was at Ilmarinen's wedding that a young brewmistress named Osmotar brewed the very first ale. The *Kalevala* praises this wonderous new drink: "For the ale is of the finest/ Best of drinks for prudent people/ Women soon it brings to laughter/ Men it warms into good humor/ And it makes the prudent merry/ But it brings the fools to raving" (XX 420–424).

The reception was a great success. All in attendance ate, drank, sang and danced to their hearts' content. The bride's happiness was short-lived, however, for no sooner had the festivities ended than she was given the details on what her new life as Mrs. Ilmarinen would entail. The picture of a woman's lot in marriage presented to her by Osmotar was so bleak that it is a wonder she did not run away. In an impassioned speech, Osmotar listed the disadvantages of marriage for a woman: she would be leaving behind the love of her family to become a servant in her in-laws' house; she would have to start the fire every morning, feed the animals, clean the house, feed and wash the children, dress and act in such a way as never to displease her husband, take no naps, care for the other males in the house, cook, fetch water, do the bidding of her mother-in-law at all times, etc., etc. Moreover, she would have to do all of this without so much as the slightest complaint.

As if the scenario described by Osmotar were not bad enough, an old woman who happened to be there related the story of her own dismal marriage, a marriage that was marked by mental and physical abuse and, finally, homelessness. The old woman completed her tale of woe with the following words:

> In my youthful days I never/ I could never have believed it/ Though a hundred told me of it/ And a thousand tongues repeated/ Such distress would fall upon me/ Such distress should overwhelm me/ As upon my head has fallen [XXIII 843–849].

By this time, the poor Maiden was probably looking for an escape route.

Ilmarinen, too, received some final instructions on marriage. He must, he was told, never beat his wife with a whip, but at the same time he must not prevent his father and mother from beating her. He must be her teacher, but if she should fail to heed his teaching, he would then have the right to whip her lightly, not with a leather whip, but with a reed, so long as he did it silently so that no one else heard. He was even given directions on where to strike her: "Always strike her on the shoulders/ On her buttocks do thou strike her/ On her eyes forbear to strike her/ On her ears forbear to touch her/ Lumps would rise upon her temples/ And her eyes with blue be bordered..." (XXIV 249–254). Armed with this sage advice, Ilmarinen took his new wife home.

Meanwhile, Leminkäinen, greatly offended at not having been invited to Ilmarinen's wedding, armed himself and set out for Pohjola to exact revenge. Using magic, he eventually overcame all of the dangers and reached his destination. Once there, he proved his prowess by cutting off the Lord of Pohjola's head during a duel. His victory was short-lived. The Mistress of Pohjola was understandably enraged by the death of her Lord and immediately raised a force of one thousand swordsmen to fight against Leminkäinen. Terrified, the Finnish hero fled for his life. When he finally reached home territory with the posse in hot pursuit, his mother advised him to go into hiding for a few years. She gave him the directions to a distant, secret island that his father had once used as a refuge from battle.

Leminkäinen could not have been happier during the initial stages of his exile. No wonder, since all of the island's male inhabitants were off on a military expedition, leaving the entire female population at his disposal: "Thus a thousand brides he found there/ Rested by a hundred widows/ Two in half-a-score remained not/ Three in a completed hundred/ Whom he left untouched as maidens/ Or as widows unmolested" (XXIX 241–246). Leminkäinen's amorous island interlude came to an abrupt end when the local menfolk returned from battle. The disappointed super-lover was forced to make a quick retreat to his boat, much to the sadness of many weeping young ladies. Then, after an arduous sea journey during which he survived a shipwreck, he returned to his homeland, ready to do battle against the forces of Pohjola.

Home, however, was not so sweet for the returning hero. He soon learned from his old mother, whom he found hiding in the forest, that the Pohjolans had burned down his house and laid waste to the entire countryside. Determined to exact revenge, Leminkäinen set sail for Pohjola with an old sidekick named Tiera. What followed was a clash of magic during the course of which Leminkäinen barely escaped with his life. Once again, he was forced to retreat to his homeland.

At this point, the focus of the *Kalevala* shifts, this time to the adventures of a new set of characters: the chieftain-brothers Untamoinen and Kalervo. As is often the case with brothers in mythology, the two had become bitter enemies. Ultimately, Untamoinen defeated his brother and committed fratricide. But he made the same mistake that Leminkäinen had once made: he spared the life of a pregnant young woman who eventually gave birth to a strapping baby boy. What Untamoinen did not know was that the baby, named Kullervo, was his dead brother's son.

Kullervo was a true super baby. At the age of three months he was already speaking fluently and threatening to punish his father's slayer: "Presently when I am bigger/ And my body shall be stronger/ I'll avenge my father's slaughter/ And my mother's tears atone for" (XXXI 109–112). When Untamoinen heard about this he led his men on a mission to kill the bragging baby. He found out, however, that this was easier said than done. First the would-be assassins put Kullervo in a barrel and pushed it out into the ocean. After three nights they went to see if he had drowned and, to their surprise, found him sitting calmly on the barrel, fishing. Next, they built a huge fire and threw the child onto it. Three days later they saw Kullervo sitting in the embers without a single singed hair. Finally, they put a noose around his neck and hanged him. Three days later they went to see his dead body. Instead of a corpse, however, they saw a very much alive son of Kalervo happily carving heroic pictures on the tree from which he had been hanged. A frustrated Untamoinen finally gave up trying to kill his seemingly invulnerable nephew and settled for keeping him as a slave.

Kullervo was undoubtedly the worst slave that Finland had ever seen. First he was given the relatively easy assignment of babysitting an infant, but instead of rocking the cradle and seeing to it that the baby was safe, Kullervo "Broke his [the baby's] hand, and gouged his eyes out/ And at length upon the third day/ Let the infant die of sickness..." (XXXI 223–225). Needless to say, he was not asked to babysit again.

Next, he was assigned the task of clearing the forest, but again, he failed miserably. In the course of his bungling he managed to destroy the best timber, rendering the forest useless. Untamoinen was totally frustrated by such ineptitude, but tried again to find a project suited to Kullervo. He ordered the youngster to build a fence. The finished product was enough to give the distraught slave master an ulcer. Kullervo had "...made the fence continuous/ And he made no gateway through it/ ....Up among the clouds it towered" (XXXI 317–318, 332).

Untamoinen should have quit before any further damage was done, but he decided to give Kullervo one more chance to prove that he could make himself useful: he assigned the youngster the simple task of threshing the grain. Instead of threshing the rye as instructed, however, the youngster pounded it to useless chaff. That was enough for the distraught uncle. He packed the boy's things and sold him to Ilmarinen for two worn-out kettles, three broken hooks, five worn-out scythes and six worn-out rakes.

As it happened, Ilmarinen got the worst of the deal. At least part of the blame for what followed, however, must be placed on his wife, who mistreated her new slave right from the outset. For no obvious reason, she baked the young man a cake with a large stone in it and sent him off to tend the cattle. During his lunch break, Kullervo made himself comfortable on a hillock, took out his knife and tried to cut himself a piece of cake. To his great sorrow, the knife blade broke in two as it hit the stone. Weeping, the youngster said, "Save this knife I'd no companion/ Nought to love except this iron/ Twas an heirloom from my father..." (XXXIII 91–93).

Kullervo's sorrow immediately changed to a desire for revenge. First he drove Ilmarinen's entire herd of cattle into the marshes, where they were devoured by wild animals. Next, he gathered a herd of wolves and bears, used magic to make them appear to be cattle, and brought them back to Ilmarinen's homestead. When the unsuspecting smith's wife went out to milk the cows, she got the shock of her life. It was the last one she would ever get: "So she stooped her down to milk them/ And she sat her down for milking/ Pulled a first time and a second/ And attempted it a third time/ Then a wolf sprang fiercely at her/ And a bear came fiercely after" (XXXIII 209–214). She begged Kullervo to save her, but he refused. Thus, Ilmarinen became a widower.

Kullervo knew that Ilmarinen would not allow his wife's death to go unavenged and so he fled for his life. (He must have concluded that a man who could produce a Sampo would certainly know how to overcome invulnerability.) While wandering in the forest, he chanced upon a fairy-tale type figure: the blue-robed Lady of the Forest. To his great joy, she informed him that his mother, father, brothers and sisters were not dead, but living on the border of Lapland. He happily made his way to the area the Lady had described.

Kullervo's reunion with his mother was dampened somewhat by the news that his oldest sister had disappeared while picking berries. Nevertheless, the young man moved in with his parents and attempted to help with the domestic chores. He did not succeed: "For his rearing had been crooked/ And the child was rocked all wrongly/ By perversest foster-father/ And a foolish foster mother" (XXXV 7–10).

Everything he did, he did wrong, whether it was fishing, rowing a boat, or something as simple as threshing the water. His father, Kalervo, became increasingly frustrated. Finally, he decided that a trip would do his son (and them) some good, and so he sent the lad off to pay the taxes. For once, it seemed as if the youngster had succeeded in carrying out an assigned chore, but on the way home catastrophe struck. When a beautiful, blonde-haired maiden whom he met along the road rejected his advances, he resorted to force: "Kullervo, Kalervo's offspring/ Dragged into his sledge the maiden/ And into his sledge he pulled her/ And upon the furs he laid her/ Underneath the rug he rolled her" (XXXV 153–156). She continued to demand her release, so he bribed her with fancy clothes and silver. Finally, her head turned by the beautiful material things, she allowed him to make love to her.

On the following morning, the young woman asked Kullervo who he was, and when he identified himself she suddenly became despondent; for she was none other than his missing sister. Her anguish is described in the following lines: "Quickly from the sledge she darted/ And she rushed into the river/ In the furious foaming cataract/ And amid the raging whirlpool/ There she found the death she sought for..." (XXXV 259–263).

Kullervo made his way back to his parents' house in a suicidal frame of mind and told his mother what had happened. The old woman dissuaded him from taking his own life, urging him to do penance instead. But such a suggestion was not to his liking. Instead of doing penance, he vowed to see to it that his uncle, Untamoinen, would suffer for all the harm he had done:

> To the mouth of Death I wander/ To the gate of Kalma's courtyard/ To the place of furious fighting/ To the battle-field of heroes/ Upright still is standing Unto/ And the wicked man unfallen/ Unavenged my father's sufferings/ Unavenged my mother's tear-drops/ Counting not my bitter sufferings/ Wrongs that I myself have suffered [XXXV, 363–372].

What followed has the earmarks of a mythological soap opera. Kullervo armed himself and set out to do battle with his evil uncle. His father and brother were relieved that they would be rid of him, and let him know it in no uncertain terms. He had, they said, brought them nothing but trouble. Only his mother was sad.

Once on the road, he was overtaken by a messenger who informed him that his father had died. Kullervo felt no sadness at the news and kept going. Then another messenger overtook him with the news that his brother had died. Again, Kullervo was unmoved. A little while later yet another messenger brought him the tidings that his sister had also shuffled off the mortal coil. He couldn't have cared less. Finally, a messenger brought the sad news that his mother was also dead. This time, he was moved, but not enough to return to arrange her funeral. He was more determined than ever to kill his uncle. And the god, Ukko, was on his side. In answer to Kullervo's prayer, the god provided him with a magnificent sword.

Within a short time he arrived at his uncle's territory and proceeded to slaughter everyone in sight. Then, his desire for revenge satisfied, he burned all of the houses to the ground, went back to the spot where he had seduced his sister and committed hara-kiri: "Thus died Kullervo the hero/ Thus the hero's life was ended/ Perished thus the hapless hero" (XXXVI 344–346).

Meanwhile, back at the homestead, Ilmarinen was still weeping over the untimely death of his wife. Finally, unwilling to spend the rest of his life as a bachelor, the lonesome super-smith took matters into his own hands. Painstakingly, he forged himself a young maiden from gold and silver. But as good at his craft as he was, and as beautiful as his finished product was to the eye, there was a major problem — she was frigid. When Ilmarinen slept next to her that night, the side of his body that leaned against the metal maiden became frozen. Obviously, there was a major flaw in his design. Unable to overcome this flaw, the disappointed would-be lover decided to give her to Väinämöinen, no doubt thinking that the latter was too old to be particular about his female conquests. But the ancient hero, who was becoming more and more of a philosopher/preacher as the decades slipped by, was not interested. He responded to Ilmarinen's offer in the following way: "...it suits not my position/ Nor to me myself is suited/ Thus to woo a bride all golden/ Or distress myself for silver/ ... For the gleam of gold is freezing/ Only frost is breathed by silver" (XXXVII 229–232, 247–250). The *Kalevala* leaves it to the reader's imagination to decide whether Ilmarinen took Väinämöinen's advice and recommitted his icy metal maiden to the fires of his forge, or gave her away to the Saxons.

Ilmarinen's quest to find a wife was not over. He decided that he would take another journey to Pohjola in order to win the hand of his dead wife's younger sister. It was a practical idea; it would eliminate the difficulty involved in getting to know a whole new set of in-laws, and he assumed that he would be given preferential treatment because of his former place in the Pohjolan family. Unfortunately, that was not the scenario that unfolded when he reached the home of the Mistress of Pohjola. Without preamble, he told his former mother-in-law that her daughter had departed this life, and almost without pausing to let the shock set in, requested that he be given the younger sister in wedlock. Louhi's response was anything but the favorable one he expected. She said, "No more daughters will I give you/ Sooner would I give my daughter/ And would give my tender daughter/ To the fiercely-foaming cataract/ To the ever-seething whirlpool/ As a prey to worms of Mana/ To the teeth of pike of Tuoni" (XXXVIII 55, 59–64).

Ilmarinen was stung by this negative reaction, but superheroes do not give up that easily. Angrily, he burst into the young maiden's chamber and demanded that she take her sister's place as his wife. Her response, however, was even more upsetting than her mother's had been. After calling him a scoundrel and a murderer, she informed him that she would never go "...unto a smith's black coalhouse/ To a stupid husband's homestead" (XXXVIII 109–110). Ilmarinen reacted the way any good scoundrel would: he dragged her out to his sledge kicking and screaming, and set out for home. But it was not a pleasant journey for either of them. After a constant barrage of verbal abuse from his captive, Ilmarinen finally lost his patience and used his magic to turn her into a seagull.

Once more, the scene shifts. In the next adventure the three superheroes from Kalevala, Väinämöinen, Ilmarinen and Leminkäinen, joined forces to steal the Sampo from the kingdom of Pohjola. Before they set out, however, Väinämöinen had Ilmarinen forge him a super weapon: a sword unequaled by any other. This is how the *Kalevala* describes the finished product, which was made from silver and gold: "On its point the moon was shining/ On its side the sun was shining/ On the haft the stars were gleaming/ On the tip a horse was neighing/ On the knob a cat was mewing/ On the sheath a dog was barking" (XXXIX 103–108). Ilmarinen then donned a suit of steel armor and they set out for Pohjola.

Shortly after that they attained an unexpected means of transportation: an abandoned, wooden boat that was weeping copious tears because it had never been used in a glorious war. The two heroes were only too happy to grant the boat's wish for action. With Väinämöinen at the helm and Ilmarinen rowing, they set out to sea. As they moved swiftly along, they were met by another boat, this one captained by none other than Leminkäinen, who offered to join them in their quest of the Sampo.

It was a perilous journey, past dangerous rocks, deadly whirlpools and huge waterfalls, but the intrepid heroes refused to be stopped, not even when their boat was "beached" on the back of a giant pike. It was during that episode that Väinämöinen proved himself to be the number one warrior. When both of his companions attempted and failed to kill the monster-fish with their swords, the old hero drew his weapon and thrust it into the pike's mouth: "In the fish's jaws fixed firmly/ Then the aged Väinämöinen/ Presently the fish uplifted/ Dragged it up from out the water/ And the pike in twain he severed" (XL 166–170). After they had eaten their fill of pike, Väinämöinen suggested that they put the teeth and bones to use as well. And so he constructed a beautiful kantele, a magic harp. There was only one problem: try as Ilmarinen and Leminkäinen might, they could not get the kantele to produce any music.

When they reached Pohjola, the Mistress and all the other people there also tried their hands at the kantele, with just as little success. Finally, the harp began to speak, explaining that it would only allow its creator to play it. Hearing this, Väinämöinen flexed his fingers and began to strum the strings. If there was ever any doubt about who the greatest musician in the world was, it was dispelled as he played. The music he produced charmed all of the creatures on earth and caused them to weep from sheer joy. Even Väinämöinen could not hold back his tears, tears which "Overflowed the blue sea's margin/ Down below the sparkling water/ To the black ooze at the bottom" (XLI 214–216). The old wizard's tears were ultimately transformed into beautiful blue pearls.

After he had finished playing, Väinämöinen announced to the Mistress of Pohjola the reason he and the others had come there, warning her that if she did not give up the Sampo willingly they would take it by force. As one might expect, Louhi did not take kindly to such threats. In response she "Summoned all her youthful swordsmen/ Bade them all to aim their weapons/ At the head of Väinämöinen" (XLII 62–64). The crafty old hero was not about to lose his head, however, and so he began to play the kantele, lulling all of the Pohjolans to sleep with his seductive melodies: "Into sleep he plunged the heroes/ And they sank in lasting slumber/ And he plunged in languid slumber/ All the host of Pohja's people/ All the people of the village" (XLII 90–94). With the enemy dozing away, the Finnish heroes were ready to seize the Sampo and carry it back to their homeland.

Gaining entrance to the copper mountain vault where the Sampo was kept was no problem for Väinämöinen; he simply sang his way into the chamber. Then, with the aid of a giant bull, they managed to uproot the magical mill[6] and secure it on their boat.

They might have succeeded in carrying out their plan to completion without incident had it not been for Leminkäinen's cockiness. Refusing to heed Väinämöinen's warning that it was too early to claim victory, the headstrong young hero began to sing a victory song. And what a voice he had! He sang so loudly that his voice frightened a crane far away in the vicinity of Pohjola. The crane was so shaken up that it flew wildly toward the Mistress of Pohjola's estate, screeching at the top of its lungs. It was enough noise to wake everyone, including Mistress Louhi, who immediately sized up the situation. Aware that the theft of the Sampo had diminished her magical powers greatly, she prayed to the gods to stop the three Finnish bandits before they could reach their homeland with the purloined Sampo.

Louhi's prayers were answered. First the gods sent down a thick cloud, so thick that Väinämöinen's boat could not move through it. Undaunted, Väinämöinen took out his sword. "With his sword he clove the water/ In the sea his sword plunged deeply/ Mead along his blade was flowing/ Honey from his sword was dropping/ Then the fog to heaven

Opposite: **The greatest Finnish superhero, Väinämöinen, playing the kantele.**

ascended/ And the cloud in air rose upward..." (XLII 383–388). Before they could move on, however, a water giant emerged from the sea to threaten their boat. Again, Väinämöinen rose to the occasion. He grasped the giant, Iku-turso, by the ears, and made him beg for his life. But now Ukko, the number one god, was becoming impatient. He unleashed a furious storm, during the course of which Väinämöinen lost his beloved kantele; but although he was greatly upset by this loss, the old hero-poet rallied his despairing companions to action. By means of his magic song, he managed to calm the winds and sea while Lemminkäinen strengthened their listing boat with new and stronger bulwarks.

While the two Finnish heroes were battling for their very survival, Louhi gathered a military force to lead against them. Who could blame her? After all, Sampos don't grow on trees, not even in Finland. Together with a hundred skilled swordsmen and a thousand archers, she set out after her enemies.

The battle that followed was replete with magic. First, Väinämöinen conjured up a reef, against which Louhi's war vessel crashed and broke into pieces. Countering skillfully, the Pohjolan matriarch transformed herself into a giant eagle, taking her warriors beneath her wings and onto her tail: "Then she flew, her wings extending/ And she soared aloft as eagle/ And she poised herself and hovered/ To attack old Väinämöinen..." (XLIII 61–164). Ignoring Väinämöinen's offer to share the Sampo with her, Louhi swooped down on his boat, determined to destroy him and his cohorts. But victory was not to be hers: "Then the lively Lemminkäinen/ Drew his sword from out his swordbelt/ Firm he grasped the sharpened iron/ And from his left side he drew it/ Striking at the eagle's talons/ At the claws of eagle striking" (XLIII 219–224). Väinämöinen joined the battle, striking at eagle–Louhi with the boat's rudder and mast and sending all of the Pohjolan swordsmen and archers crashing into the sea.

While it was clear to her that she had suffered a military defeat, Louhi was not yet ready to throw in the towel. Grasping the Sampo with her remaining talon, she flung it into the sea where it broke into pieces: "Then the fragments all were scattered/ And the Sampo's larger pieces/ Sank beneath the peaceful waters/ To the black ooze at the bottom..." (XLIII 267–270). Väinämöinen, contrary to what one might have expected, was extremely pleased at this outcome and was unimpressed by Louhi's threats to destroy his land and all of his people. He calmly gathered what small fragments of the Sampo he could and declared that he would plant them once he reached his homeland, thus assuring Kalevala (Finland) good fortune forever. Once again, though, he had underestimated the wily old Mistress of Pohjola.

Things went smoothly for Väinämöinen and his people for a while. With a new kantele he had fashioned for himself, the old hero was the delight of the land. His beautiful melodies thoroughly charmed man and beast, not to mention the grass, trees and flowers. Meanwhile, however, Louhi incessantly prayed to the gods for the destruction of Kalevala. Her prayers were not unheard. In the depths of Tuonela was the hideous blind demoness named Loviatar: "...the worst of Tuoni's daughters/ And of Mana's maids most hideous/ She, the source of every evil/ Origin of woes a thousand..." (XLV 25–28). Loviater, it turned out, was the answer to Louhi's prayers. To make it worse for the Finns, she was pregnant.

Where does a hateful monster go to give birth? That was the problem confronting Loviatar as her pregnancy progressed. She had sought to have her offspring in the mountains, in the swamps, in the ocean, beneath waterfalls, underneath precipices — but nothing happened. Already long overdue and in extreme pain, she was finally directed by the god Jumala to go to Pohjola. She followed the creator god's advice and was taken by Louhi to a little deserted sauna. There, amidst the steaming stones, she gave birth not to one but to nine offspring, sons all, and all as repugnant as she:

> One as Pleurisy she destined/ One did she send forth as Colic/ And as Gout she reared another/ One as Scrofula she fashioned/ Boil, another designated/ And as Itch proclaimed another/ Thrust another forth as Cancer/ And as Plague she formed another [XLV 163–170].

The ninth offspring remained unnamed, though we are told that he, like his brothers, went forth to the land of Väinämöinen to spread his malice. Once again, however, the ancient hero was up to the challenge. Using all the magic at his command, he conjured up a salve to cure the diseases foisted upon his people: "And from death he saved his people/ Thus saved Kaleva's descendants" (XLV 361–362).

In spite of Väinämöinen's great power, Louhi still refused to give up. Her next effort to destroy Kalevala came in the form of a huge, ferocious bear. The old hero quickly dispatched the beast, turned its skin into a tapestry and its flesh into a feast for his people. But then he made a mistake. To celebrate his victory, he began to play his kantele and sing his incomparably beautiful songs. In fact, he sang and played too beautifully, for as he continued, both the sun and the moon were so enthralled that they descended from the sky in order to hear him better. This was just what Louhi was waiting for. As soon as they got within her reach, she snatched them up and carried them off to a mountain hideaway. Next, she stole fire from all of the homes in Kalevala, thus plunging the entire region into darkness. It seemed that at last she had conquered her old archenemy. That might very well have been the case, moreover, had it not been for the intervention of the god Ukko.

Even her enemies would have had to concede, albeit probably grudgingly, that the Mistress of Pohjola was world-class when it came to hiding things. When Ukko saw that the sun and the moon were missing, he immediately began to search for them. He came up empty. But a god, especially when he is the number one god, does not accept defeat, and so Ukko solved the dilemma as only he could have: "In the air a light struck Ukko/ And a flame did Ukko kindle/ From his flaming sword he struck it/ Sparks he struck from off his sword blade" (XLVII 67–70). With the fire that resulted from these divine sparks, Ukko created a new sun and moon.

Unfortunately, the maiden he left in charge of the newly created fire let it slip through her fingers and it was lost. Now it was up to Väinämöinen and Ilmarinen to find it. Painstakingly, they traced the errant fire to the primeval Lake Alue, only to learn that it had been swallowed there by a fish.

The fire-swallowing fish proved to be an extremely elusive prey. After many futile attempts to catch it with the gigantic net they had constructed, the two heroes were finally aided by a dwarf who mysteriously appeared from beneath the water. Together, they managed to snare the pike containing the fire. But they had yet another obstacle to overcome: they were unable to touch the fish without being badly burned. Again outside help was offered, this time by the son of the Sun, who expertly cut open the pike, only to learn that the pike was but the last in a series of fishes who had swallowed one another. Finally, the son of the Sun cut open the last fish to expose the purloined spark of fire within it: "But the fire flashed up most fiercely/ From the Sun's son's hands who held it/ Singed the beard of Väinämöinen/ Burned the smith much more severely" (XLVIII 243–246). The unleashed fire then continued to burn its way across Pohja and other regions until Väinämöinen finally captured it. After Ilmarinen tamed it, they brought it back to the homes of Kalevala.

The stage was set for the final victory over Pohjola. Once his burns had healed, Ilmarinen attempted to forge a new sun and moon. As was the case with his silver and gold maiden, the finished products were aesthetically pleasing, but they did not work. His silver sun and golden moon simply would not light up. As usual, it was up to Väinämöinen to save the day. Through his powers of divination, the old wizard learned where Louhi was hiding the priceless celestial bodies, armed himself and set out for Pohjola. The final showdown was approaching.

What followed had all of the drama of an early American western film. Väinämöinen reached his archenemy's kingdom and immediately issued his challenge to a large group of Louhi's warriors: "If the sun from rock ascends not/ Nor the moon from rocky mountain/ Let us join in closest conflict/ Let us grasp our trusty sword-blades!" (XLIX 207–210). The battle was brief and conclusive. With lightning swiftness, Väinämöinen cut off the heads of all of the Pohjolans. Then, without so much as a pause for refreshments, he hurried off to complete his task.

Presently he located Louhi's hiding place and killed the serpents who stood guard there; however, the old hero's spells were insufficient to gain him access to the chambers in which the sun and moon were locked. Uncharacteristically dejected, Väinämöinen made his way back home to report his failure to his sidekick, Leminkäinen. At first, the latter chided him, but then, at Väinämöinen's request, he forged a trident, a dozen hatchets and a number of keys and spears. Soon the two heroes were ready to return to Pohjola to complete the mission.

Coincidentally, Louhi decided to do a little reconnoitering at that very time. Assuming the form of a hawk, she flew to Ilmarinen's workshop and began to question him. When she asked him what he was presently forging, he replied: "'Tis a neck-ring I am forging/ For the aged crone of Pohja/ That she may be firmly fettered/ To the side of a great mountain" (XLIX 351–354). Realizing that she was doomed if she continued to resist, Louhi swiftly flew back to Pohjola and released the sun and moon. Kalevala had won at last.

The *Kalevala* ends on a strange note. It tells the story of a young woman named Marjatta, a paragon of virtue who was fanatically careful to avoid anything that was even remotely connected to sex. The extent to which she went to guard her virtue is described: "If her mother sent her milking/ Yet she did not go to milking/ And she spoke the words which follow/ 'Never such a maid as I am/ Udders of the cows should handle/ Which with bulls have been disporting...'" (L 27–32). She even refused to ride in a sledge drawn by any horse beyond the age of six months, since there was the possibility that a horse that old might have had communion with the opposite sex. But she did have one weakness: she liked cranberries. Why is that a weakness, one might ask. After all, cranberries can hardly be considered a threat to female virtue. While this may be true in the modern world, however, it seems that Kalevalan cranberries were a potent lot. At least, this was true of one particular cranberry that had grown to ripeness in the land of Väinämöinen.

One day, Marjatta was sitting on the slope of a hill when she suddenly heard a voice calling to her: "O thou maiden, come and pluck me.../ None ... yet has touched me/ None has gathered me, the wretched" (L 83, 93–94). Upon closer inspection, she discovered that the voice belonged to a cranberry. She could not resist. After all, this berry was as pure as she. But when she picked the berry, a totally unexpected scene followed:

Then from ground the berry mounted/ Upward to her shoes arose it/ Upward to her knees of whiteness/ Rising from her knees of whiteness/ Upward to her skirts that rustled/ To her buckled belt arose it/ To her breast from buckled girdle/ From her breast to chin arose it/ To her lips from chin arose it/ Then into her mouth it glided/ And it dropped into her stomach [L 109–122].

The next thing Marjatta knew she was pregnant. Despite her efforts to conceal her condition (she wore loose-fitting, beltless dresses), her parents discovered the secret. Needless to say, neither her mother nor her father believed the explanation she offered. One can just imagine the scene: Marjatta asserting, between tears, that she had been seduced by a cranberry, while her parents screamed at her to tell the truth. Indeed, instead of helping her, they called her some choice names and turned her out of their house.

Secure in her innocence, and with the aid of a faithful girl-servant, Marjatta managed to find a tiny stable where she gave birth to a baby boy. The young mother worked very hard to rear her newborn, and was doing rather well until one day when, as she held her son on her lap, he suddenly vanished into thin air. Poor Marjatta. First she was seduced by a cranberry and then her baby disappeared. She was understandably distraught. She began to search everywhere for him, sparing no effort. She asked the moon and the stars to tell her where he was and they refused. The sun, however, was more obliging: "Well, indeed I know your infant/ He it was who me created..." (L 410–411). Then he told her that the baby was in the swamp, sunk up to his armpits in the marsh. Marjatta immediately rushed there, found him, and brought him home in triumph. But there was a problem: no one would baptize him until Väinämöinen had given his approval.

The old hero was summoned and presented with the problem. After thinking it over, he made the following judgment:

> As the boy from marsh has risen/ From the ground, and from a berry/ On the ground they now shall lay him/ Where the hills are thick with berries/ Or shall to the swamps conduct him/ With a club his head to shatter! [449–455].

Before Marjatta could express her horror at Väinämöinen's cruel judgment, the baby made an eloquent speech in which he condemned the old wizard in no uncertain terms. Among other things he said:

> Wretched old man, void of insight/ O how stupid is your judgment/ How contemptible thy sentence!/ Thou hast grievous crimes committed/ Likewise deeds of greatest folly/ Yet to swamps they did not lead thee/ Shattered not thy head with wood clubs [458–464].

Apparently, this was enough to convince an old man who was there that this was a most worthy baby, and so he baptized him on the spot, declaring him to be the new king of Carelia (eastern Finland and part of the former Soviet Union). Infuriated by this disregard for his authority, Väinämöinen packed his bags and sailed away into the sunset, leaving the following prophesy:

> Men will look for me and miss me/ To construct another Sampo[7]/ And another harp to make me/ Make another moon for gleaming/ And another sun for shining/ When the sun and moon are absent/ In the air no joy remaineth [494–500].

Like Kronos and many others before him, Väinämöinen had learned that there comes a time when one must give way to the new generation.

*   *   *

The *Kalevala* is a veritable gold mine of archetypal material. In the course of the work we see not one but three *miraculous births*: those of Väinämöinen, Ilmarinen and, finally, the "virgin" birth of Marjatta's child. At the other end of the cycle there are two examples of the *resurrection archetype*. The first takes place when Ilmarinen's mother painstakingly reassembles her son and brings him back to life; the second involves the journey that Väinämöinen makes to the *realm of death* and back, a journey also made by Gilgamesh, Odysseus and Aeneas in the course of their adventures.

There is also a plethora of *superweapons* wielded by the superheroes of the *Kalevala*. These range from the powerful magic of Väinämöinen to the more conventional implements of war: swords, spears and the like, most of which were forged in the smithy of Ilmarinen, the Finnish answer to the Greek god, Hephaestos. Nor should one forget those provided to Kullervo by the god Ukko. In addition to *superweapons*, the heroes of the frigid north are frequently provided with *super transportation*, whether it be a magically constructed boat or one with the remarkable power of speech.

Very few heroes in all of world mythology, moreover, have a more awesome *archenemy* than Väinämöinen. Louhi's powers are second only to his, and she often uses them to outdo the great Finnish wizard at his own game. Time after time she demonstrates that she is not only the Mistress of Pohjola, but a mistress of magic as well, now *transforming* herself into an eagle or a hawk, now stealing the sun and the moon, a feat that would certainly make her the greatest thief of all time. It is clear that in addition to being an exemplary *archenemy* she is also the epitome of the *destructive female*, thus placing her in yet another archetypal configuration. Indeed, were there a super-villain(ess) Hall of Fame, she would gain entry on the first ballot.

In addition to a super *archenemy*, Väinämöinen has the ideal *sidekick* in the person of Leminkäinen, the second greatest superhero in the *Kalevala* and certainly the greatest creative genius of the work.

Another familiar element that can be found in the *Kalevala* to an unparalleled extent is the *suitor's test archetype*. All three superheroes, Väinämöinen, Ilmarinen and Leminkäinen, must pass seemingly impossible tests in order to win the ladies of their dreams, tests that make those which were assigned to Rama and Odysseus seem like child's play. Indeed, even Heracles would have had difficulty with many of them. It should be pointed out here that the Finnish work does differ from other heroic epics in that the women chosen by the superheroes to be their brides were unanimously opposed to the union, and had to be taken by force even after the tests were passed.

In the story of Kullervo, we see several archetypes. The Abel/Cain, Romulus/Remus *fratricide* motif is repeated when his uncle slays his father, and thereby Kullervo becomes an *abandoned baby*. That he is *semi-invulnerable* is evidenced by his ability to survive the numerous attempts on his life, his one weak spot being his conscience, which proves as fatal as Achilles' heel in that it ultimately does him in.

The *Kalevala* has all of the above archetypes and more: *evil serpents, a chosen one* (Väinämöinen alone is able to play the magic kantele), *divine intervention, monster slaying*—in short, a collection that would have made Carl Jung smile.

The Green Lantern

Väinämöinen's mastery of magic is not a unique ability for a superhero. On the contrary, from the Arthurian wizard Merlin to the American comic strip hero Mandrake,[8] superhero magicians have made their marks on world mythology. In chapter four of the present study we met with one such example in the person of Ibis the Invincible, although the feats he performed were not the result of practiced legerdemain. As we saw, with the

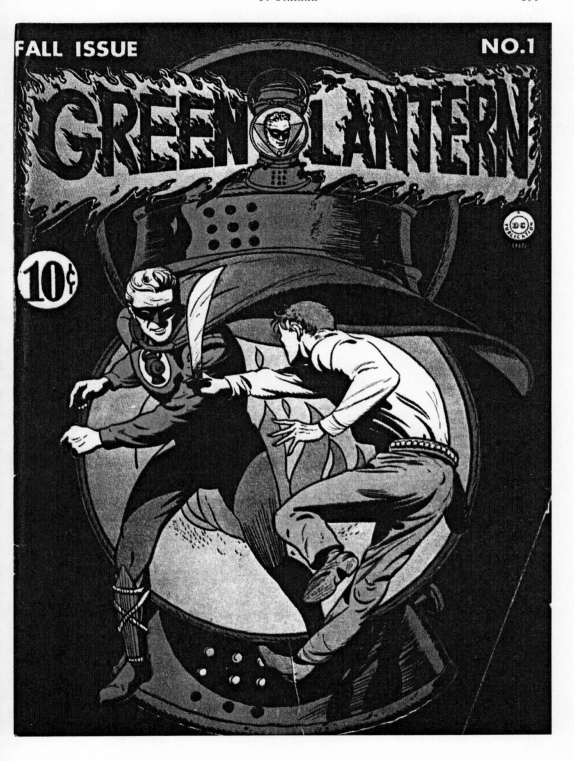

The Green Lantern, *Green Lantern* #1, Autumn 1941. (DC Comics.)

aid of his Ibisstick (a variation of the archetypal magic wand) the former Egyptian Prince was able to conquer the laws of nature and exceed the limits that are set for ordinary mortals. But Ibis was not a lone comic book super magician of America's golden age of heroes. Indeed, in the 1940s the shelves of corner candy stores in America were replete with colorful characters able to dazzle their readers with remarkable feats of magic. Among these was one who had made his debut some two years before Ibis, and who continues to perform today, albeit with more of a sci-fi persona than he originally boasted: The Green Lantern. His origin was announced in *ALL AMERICA #16* as follows:

Alan Scott, a railroad engineer, is the sole survivor of a terrible train wreck. No accident, the bloody wreck was caused by an explosive device planted on a bridge by a scoundrel whose company had lost the contract to build the bridge. Scott learns that he owes his miraculous survival to a magical green lantern with the power of speech. The lantern informs him that it was first made into an oriental lamp from a meteor that landed in Ancient China centuries before. Its creator, Chang by name, was later murdered by his fellow villagers who were in turn slain by the lantern.

As Scott listens in awe, the magic lantern goes on to describe how it was later reformed into a train lantern by a mental patient whose sanity it restored. It explains that it flames three times — once to bring death, once to bring life, and once to bring power. With these words, it flames for the third time to grant Scott power.

Following the lantern's instructions, Scott uses a piece of its metal to fashion a ring for himself. In order to maintain the power of the lantern, he must touch the ring to it every twenty-four hours.

As related above, the Green Lantern's magic wand came in the form of a ring forged from the metal of a magic lantern, much like the one Aladdin possessed many centuries before. Before long, Allan Scott attained a sidekick by the name of Doiby Dickles, as well as a series of archenemies. The most notable of the latter was the very sexy Harlequin, who, unknown to Scott, just happened to be Allan's secretary. Later, she became a government agent and battled on the side of law and order.

The Green Lantern last appeared in his own book, *All-American Comics*, in 1948, but continued to be seen in *All-Star* and *Comic Cavalcade* until 1951. He was revived by National in 1959, this time with a new alter-ego: the test pilot, Hal Jordan. But he still had his ring. In August 1960, the new Green Lantern was given his own book again, but the plot soon thickened to the point where there were hundreds of Green Lanterns from many planets. Before the book was shelved again, the superhero was teamed up with his like-colored stablemate, the Green Arrow. Together, the two dealt with some of the pressing social issues of the day: racism, cultism, drug abuse and the like. In May 1972, the book was canceled and the Green Lantern became a member of the Justice League of America, where he continues to fight evil along with Batman, Superman, Wonder Woman and other all–American superheroes.

10

The Super Antihero

It has been said that the more things change, the more they stay the same. When analyzed, it is evident that this well known aphorism is simply an affirmation of archetypes. It would seem only natural, then, to apply it to a discussion of the superhero. Certainly, the circumstances of the modern hero have changed, but as has been repeatedly shown in this study, in spite of the seeming differences among individuals, the essence of the superhero has remained constant. In the preceding chapters, we have seen indigenous representatives of the genre from various lands and eras. While the essence of the hero remains constant, however, in most cases the gods are no longer the source and sustenance of his or her power. In ancient times, as often as not the gods were given credit for parenting the extraordinary beings who captured the world's imagination: Gilgamesh, Achilles, Heracles, Aeneas — all were sons of divinities, imbued by their godly genes with powers far beyond those of ordinary mortals.[1] Moreover, even in those instances where the gods were not the biological parents, they were personally associated with the heroes' lives, extending special protection and assistance in times of need, or quite the opposite when a particular hero provoked their disfavor. Thus, Heracles was the son of Zeus, Achilles of Thetis, and Aeneas of Aphrodite. And while Odysseus was 100 percent human in origin, the goddess Athena virtually adopted him as her own and kept him free from serious harm. Similarly, Rama was able to prevail over his enemies because he was favored by Brahma and the other Indian gods, while Rustam literally owed his entry into the world to the obstetric know-how of a divine bird.

There are obvious reasons why the epic writers of the present hesitate to ascribe divine heritage to their superheroes. For one thing, the growth of scientific knowledge has resulted in the disinclination to explain the phenomena of the universe in supernatural terms.[2] This need not be the result of disbelief in the divine, indeed the very opposite is sometimes the case. Modern readers and viewers are well aware that the superheroes presented to them are not and never were real in a literal sense. Therefore, to give credit to God for having created a fictitious hero could call the authenticity of God into question; it could be seen as an attempt to relegate Him to the sphere of popular myth rather than that of reality. Such a course might be considered unacceptable by any who follow an orthodox belief pattern. Therefore, many epicists have offered a plausible, alternative source for their superheroes, one that rivals the divine and best appeals to the modern mind: science. Instead of springing from the head of Zeus or the womb of Aphrodite, our present day superheroes often attain life in the scientist's laboratory. With the aid of test tubes, chemicals and a growing understanding of the universe, man himself has begun to challenge the creative monopoly of God, if not always with success. From in vitro fertilization to cloning, scientists are increasingly in the business of creation.

As noted in previous chapters, science has played an important role in the origin stories of a number of modern superheroes. Hugo Danner was the result of a biological experiment, the Flash came into being because of a laboratory accident, Superman survived and was "reborn" on earth only because of his scientist-father's ability to build a space ship. While these were positive examples of the creative power of science, there are instances in which the results were disastrous. What was created in those failed experiments was not a superhero, but the very opposite; a being with extraordinary powers who, for one reason or another, became the archenemy of the human race. A leading example of such a super villain was the central figure in a work written by a nineteen-year-old English girl, Mary Wollstonecraft Shelley. The being she created had no name, even though today it is (incorrectly) known as Frankenstein.

Frankenstein

The idea of man creating life from inanimate material is hardly a new one. Medieval alchemists[3] crudely attempted to do so in their primitive laboratories, but even they were far from the first to interest themselves in such matters. Nor were they the last. From ancient mythology to modern science fiction, examples of this fascinating archetype abound in many cultures. The ancient Greeks told the story of King Pygmalion of Cyprus, who, disgusted by the licentious behavior of the women of his day, sculpted a beautiful young girl from ivory and proceeded to fall in love with his creation. He became increasingly frustrated when the lifeless maiden failed to reciprocate his love. The situation seemed hopeless, but thanks to divine intervention the story had a happy ending: his prayers to Aphrodite were finally answered. The goddess of love took pity on him and transformed the statue into a real woman, Galatea, who eventually became Pygmalion's wife.

A more recent example of this archetype can be found in the nineteenth century work *Pinocchio*, by Carlo Collodi. Virtually every child in the western world has heard the story of the kindly old shoemaker, Geppetto, who whittled a puppet from a piece of wood, a puppet that came to life and became a real boy of flesh and blood due to the intercession of a fairy godmother.

During the first decade of the nineteenth century, the German author E.T.A. Hoffmann also dealt with the theme of artificially created life. Unlike Collodi, however, Hoffmann used the archetype to expose the dark side of existence. His two short works, *Automatons* (1812) and *The Sandman* (1814), are classic examples. An unforgettable scene in *The Sandman* is the one in which the sinister lawyer Coppelius (alias Coppola) and his scientist cohort, Professor Spallanzani, argue over the beautiful female automaton that the professor has created. The reader winces as the automaton, ironically named Olympia, is eventually torn to pieces in a grotesque tug of war between Coppelius and Spallanzani.[4]

The literary setting for the creation of artificial life was not limited to the sculptor's studio or the carpenter's workshop. Even before our modern industrial age, the scientist's laboratory had been used as the setting for literary works and films. From Johann Wolfgang von Goethe's classic dramatic poem, *Faust*,[5] to the science fiction tales of today, there are countless examples in world literature and cinema depicting man as the creator of life.

The finished products in these works range from the human clones in the novel *The Boys from Brazil* to the mechanical robots in *Star Wars* and countless other such productions. In addition to the artificially created human and mechanical life forms, there is the intermediate android stage, the best known recent example being Mr. Data in the recent American television series *Star Trek: The Next Generation*.[6]

Clearly then, Mary Shelley had rich literary and mythological precedents when she began work on *Frankenstein* in June 1816. The setting was a cabin by Lake Leman, Switzerland. As a storm raged outside, Mary and a group of others including the famous English romantic poets Percy Bysshe Shelley (her husband) and Lord Byron, sat together in their rented cabin and listened as Byron read from a book of ghost stories. What happened after the reading is "...known to every English school-child, the reading of these stories led to Lord Byron's famous proposal at the end of the séance that 'We will each write a ghost story.'"[7] While the others eventually lost interest in the contest before producing anything worthy of mention, the nineteen-year-old daughter of a philosopher and an early feminist[8] was more than up to the task. Although early critics labeled it "disgusting," "a fabric of absurdities," the "dream of a madman," and devoid of "manners or morality" upon its anonymous publication (Florescu 154), Mary Shelley's novel eventually achieved worldwide acclaim. It has been translated into all major European languages, and into Japanese, Urdu, Arabic, and Malaysian, to name but a few others. Between 1910 and the present, moreover, the story of Frankenstein has been the subject of more than forty full-length films and at least one play, and has served as a model for the Hulk, a successful American comic-book and television character whose story will follow.

Much of the confusion about Mary Shelley's work stems from the fact that most people are familiar with the 1931 version of the story first offered by Universal USA, a production that significantly differs from the original novel. Moreover, even though there have been recent films truer to Mary Shelley's novel, the old image perseveres.

A further problem is that more often than not the artificially created being is referred to by the name of its scientist-creator or as a "monster" when, in fact, it was never given a name by the author, and was less a monster than a victim of its creator's megalomania. Whether or not one agrees that the obsessive scientist and his laboratory offspring were "...the antithetical halves of a single being ... the solipsistic and generous halves of the one self,"[9] one cannot help but conclude that Dr. Frankenstein was as mad as a hatter. It is clear, too, that the work is rich in familiar archetypes.

The full title of Mary Shelley's work is *Frankenstein, or the Modern Prometheus*. It is obvious from this choice of titles that the author was thinking along mythological lines, blurry as that thinking might have been. For, while Victor Frankenstein and Prometheus shared the compulsion to create life, a closer study of their basic natures leads one to conclude that they are about as alike as a zebra and a pair of striped pajamas.

Prometheus, as he appears in the trilogy of the great Greek dramatist Aeschylus, was not only the creator of the human race but its savior as well. Aeschylus tells us that when Zeus successfully concluded his war against the Titans, he decided to remove unworthy mankind and replace it with a higher species. Enter Prometheus. Although he had aided Zeus and the other Olympians in the struggle with his fellow Titans, Prometheus would not permit the destruction of his mortal children and so he stole fire from the god Hephaestos and brought it down to earth, providing humans with the tool necessary to conquer nature and challenge the gods. This, of course, did not sit well with Zeus, who disliked being challenged, especially by puny humans. To demonstrate his anger he punished

Prometheus: he had his former ally chained, first to a rock beside the sea and later to a mountain peak in the Caucasus. To top it all off, he commissioned an eagle to peck at his prisoner's liver continually. As we have seen in a previous chapter, had it not been for Heracles Prometheus might still be there today.

What a striking contrast between this loving, self-sacrificing creator and the megalomaniacal Dr. Frankenstein. In the latter's own words, the only motivation he had for creating a living being was so that "...a new species would bless me as its creator and source.... No father could claim the gratitude of his child so completely as I should deserve theirs" (Shelley 52). While his scientific knowledge and surgical skills were undeniable, it is very difficult to understand how any thinking person, let alone such a gifted scientist, could have failed to be aware that his work was not going as planned, that the being he was creating from the spare parts of pilfered corpses would win no beauty contests. The shock and dismay Dr. Frankenstein displayed when he saw his creation come to life on that dreary November evening is unrealistic. One can only conclude that he had worked all those months with his eyes closed. Mary Shelley has Dr. Frankenstein describe his creation in this way:

> His yellow skin scarcely covered the work of muscles and arteries beneath.... No mortal could support the horror of that countenance. A mummy again endued with animation could not be so hideous as that wretch. When those muscles and joints were rendered capable of motion, it became a thing such as even Dante could not have conceived [Shelley 56, 57].

What did the modern Prometheus do when confronted with this cosmetic failure? Did he hire a leading plastic surgeon to cover up his being's aesthetic shortcomings? Did he philosophically conclude that beauty is only skin deep and that one should not judge a book by its cover? Hardly. Like the true escapist he was, Dr. Frankenstein dashed out into the cold night and walked the streets for hours, and when he returned to find his "monster" gone, he breathed a sigh of relief and proceeded to put the whole unpleasant business out of his mind. Some Prometheus!

Compared to the way Victor Frankenstein behaved after his "monster" came to life, the latter's behavior pattern in the weeks and months that followed was very understandable. After all, although eight feet tall, chronologically he was a newborn baby, with no life experience and no loving parents to serve as guides in the thorny labyrinth of life. No wonder he was so bewildered and angry. No wonder he struck out savagely at the creator who had renounced him, murdering the latter's innocent young brother. This deed was monstrous to be sure, but not necessarily the deed of a monster. In light of the circumstances, one might say that it was an impulsive, childish expression of spite and frustration, a tragic act of revenge that was a masked cry for attention. Dr. Frankenstein's ensuing actions, however, are much more difficult to understand or forgive. Even though he knew full well who the guilty party was, he did not divulge it to the authorities. He remained silent to protect himself, and by so doing set the stage for further catastrophes.

In keeping with his pattern of running away from problems, Dr. Frankenstein's course of action after his brother's murder was to withdraw to an isolated, mist-covered mountain peak in the Swiss alps. As he wandered about the glacier, the rain "pouring in torrents," he unexpectedly saw "...the figure of a man, at some distance, advancing ... with superhuman speed" (Shelley 94).[10] For all his forgetfulness, he recognized the intruder at once as his own creation and greeted him with a shower of invective. Among other things he called him a "devil" and a "vile insect," and threatened to trample him to dust. (His sense of proportion apparently had been destroyed by his repeated bouts of madness. Either he thought that his "monster" had shrunk or that his foot had grown significantly.) To his and the reader's great surprise, however, the "monster" replied to this invective with the verbal skill of a practiced orator and the profundity of a philosopher/theologian. He reminded his enraged creator that such threats were foolish in view of their disparate size and strength, and followed that up with an accusation/plea: "Remember that I am thy creature; I ought to be thy Adam, but I am rather the fallen angel, whom they drivest from joy for no misdeed" (Shelley 95). When he saw that Dr. Frankenstein was listening, he added: "The guilty are allowed, by human laws ... to speak in their own defense before they are condemned.... I ask you not to spare me; listen to me, and then, if you can, and if you will, destroy the work of your hands" (96). Although still agitated, Dr. Frankenstein grudgingly agreed to listen to the creature's tale, which was as unrealistic as Dr. Frankenstein's lack of surprise when he heard his "monster" speaking as eloquently as an experienced attorney.[11]

Briefly summarized, the story the "monster" told was as follows: After fleeing from the doctor's laboratory, he wandered aimlessly, first through the forest and then through open country. Not surprisingly, the few people he encountered along the way reacted with fear and horror. Children ran for their lives, women fainted, and irate villagers hurled stones and other objects at him, not because he had done anything wrong, but because they were appalled by his frightening appearance. Escaping deeper into the forest, he finally found a kennel-like hovel attached to a small cottage and settled into it to escape the bitter cold and the "barbarity of man." By accident, he discovered that he was able to see into the cottage through a small chink in the wall of his hovel. In this way he was able to observe the activities of the impoverished family who lived there: an old blind man and his son and daughter. Soon, the "monster" was secretly clearing the snow from the road, leaving stacks of firewood that he had chopped by the cottage door, and performing other clandestine services for them. By listening to the daily conversations of his adopted "family," he quickly learned how to speak.

One day a stranger arrived at the cottage, a young Arabian woman who was none other than the son's long lost love. The "monster's" education was enhanced greatly by this turn of events. As Felix (the son) attempted to teach his Arabian beauty French by reading from the great works of world literature, the "monster" listened and absorbed the material. As a result, he was then able to teach himself to read when he stumbled upon a cache of books. Apparently, Dr. Frankenstein had given his baby a first class scholar's brain to go with his eight-foot body.

Unfortunately, though, familiarity with the works of Plutarch and Goethe did not teach the poor "monster" just how ungrateful and mean humans can be. He learned this the hard way when he revealed himself to the family he had grown to love, hoping for their acceptance. After all, he had chopped a lot of wood for them. While the old blind man received him with kindness, the scene instantly changed when the others arrived. One of the women fainted, the other ran for her life, and Felix attacked him with a stick. "I could have torn him limb from limb," the "monster" declared at this point in his narration, "...but my heart sank within me as with bitter sickness, and I refrained" (129). On the following day, the inhabitants of the cottage were gone.

The next experience he related was essentially similar. Totally frustrated, he burned down the hovel and cottage and again wandered aimlessly through the forest, scrupulously avoiding any contact with human beings. One day, however, he risked his life by emerging from the cover of the woods to save a child who was drowning in a river. He was rewarded for this heroic act with a bullet from the rifle of the child's father. The latter had not seen the rescue and automatically concluded that the ugly stranger was doing his daughter harm. At that point, wounded and in great despair, the "monster" declared war on humanity. "Inflamed by pain," he explained, "I vowed eternal hatred and vengeance to all mankind ... a deep and deadly revenge, such as would alone compensate me for the outrages and anguish I had endured" (135).

His vow notwithstanding, the "monster" had not yet become the evil being everyone who saw him assumed him to be. This is clear from his description of the next incident.

Having reached the outskirts of Geneva, he concealed himself in a field to catch up on lost sleep. Fate, however, soon intervened. He was awakened by the approach of a young boy. In spite of his reading and experience, he naively thought that he might be able to make a friend. Wrong again. Not only did the youngster react with fear and hatred, but he made the mistake of identifying himself as Victor Frankenstein's brother, William. This was too much for the "monster" to bear, and so William Frankenstein became the first casualty in the recently declared war. After killing the youngster, the "monster" placed a little picture he had taken from the corpse into the pocket of a sleeping young girl, thus throwing the blame for the murder onto her. He was able to do this, he explained, "Thanks to the lessons of Felix and the sanguinary laws of man..." (137). He was becoming more human every day.

The "monster" concludes his tale with an impassioned plea to Dr. Frankenstein. If the latter will provide him with a mate, he swears, he will take her away to some remote South American jungle and never be seen again by man. After great hesitation, Dr. Frankenstein agrees, and before long begins work in the laboratory he sets up in a remote and desolate area of Scotland. The work is proceeding very well until the manic-depressive scientist begins to have second thoughts. He is plagued by the fear that his odd couple might decide to have children: "...a race of devils ... who might make the very existence of the species of man a condition precarious and full of terror" (158). And so, while his "monster" watches, Dr. Frankenstein tears his nearly completed mate to pieces. It is a costly, incomprehensible act. How, one might ask, could someone who was so knowledgeable about human anatomy, someone who was able to build a living, functioning creature piece by piece — how could such a great scientist fail to know enough to omit those pieces that make reproduction possible? And how could he not realize that by denying his creature a mate he was asking for big trouble? As brilliant a scientist as he was, Dr. Frankenstein, it seems, was ignorant when it came to "monster" nature. He did not even stop to ponder what the "monster" meant by the parting words: "I shall be with you on your wedding-night" (161).

Unlike his creator, the creature kept his word. He demonstrated this on Dr. Frankenstein's wedding night by sneaking into the bridal chamber and strangling the bride, an unforgettable wedding present. His revenge complete, he then made his way to the furthest regions of the north in an effort to get as far away from human beings as possible. His war with humanity was over.

The work ends with the death of the unhinged scientist during the relentless pursual of his hated archenemy over the endless ice floes. (One wonders what he would have done had he caught up with him.) In the final scene, the "monster" stands over Dr. Frankenstein's body, overcome by grief, and declares that mankind need fear no further evil from him, that he will soon follow his creator into death. That's what he thought. What he didn't know was that the film industry had other plans. More than forty of them.

There are no superheroes in *Frankenstein*. Dr. Victor Frankenstein, for all of his scientific success, is a weak, indeed a despicable character, an egocentric, power-hungry fanatic who brought suffering onto others because he refused to accept responsibility for his actions.

The being that he created had the potential, perhaps, to become a superhero, but this potential was perverted by the cruelty of man. Herein lies the tragedy of *Frankenstein*, and also one of the great paradoxes of world literature. As Harold Bloom points out, the "monster" is "...more human than his creator" (215). In spite of this, however, in the minds of most he is considered just the opposite: a heinous, super villain. Yet, this maligned creature shares many of the archetypal characteristics of the superhero genre.

While not evident upon first glance, a more careful examination of the Frankenstein creature's "birth" reveals it to be surprisingly in line with Otto Rank's formula for the birth of a hero. For one thing, the parents are most distinguished: the respected Dr. Victor Frankenstein and his true mate, science. The origin of the creature was certainly preceded by extraordinary difficulties, including grave robbing, organ and brain transplants, and microsurgery. The "intercourse" between the parents took place in the scientist's secret laboratory, and although there was no literal prophecy cautioning against the "birth," Dr. Frankenstein knew that there were taboos involved. He indicates as much when he recounts the later stages of his work: "...often did my human nature turn with loathing from my occupation" (53). But he persevered until he succeeded in bringing his being to life. Then he abandoned it, not to water, but to a world for which it was not prepared. And ultimately, it took its revenge on him, the cruel father. Mary Shelley's original creature was uncommonly strong, and as the film industry delivered sequel after sequel it seemed to develop *invulnerability*. It had an *archenemy* in the person of its creator, with whom it engaged in a prolonged *final battle*. But for all of this, it is still no hero. For want of a better designation, and taking into account the metamorphosis it underwent in the film studios, we might say that Dr. Frankenstein's progeny is one of the most popular super antiheroes of all time. Looked at from another standpoint, though, the original Shelley creation is also a super victim.

One cannot help but see some parallels between the nature of the "monster's" experiences and those which Hugo Danner underwent during his short life. Both were products of scientific experiment and both were ostracized by society because they were different, Hugo for his uncommon strength, the "monster" for his aesthetically jarring appearance. Both tried to do good deeds for others and both were punished for their efforts, and both, for one reason or another, became killers. Ultimately, moreover, both served as models for American popular superheroes. The Kryptonian descendant of Hugo Danner has already been discussed; now let us look at the modern offspring of the Frankenstein "monster."

The Hulk

Using Mary Shelley's *Frankenstein* as a primary source for the idea, *Marvel Comics* introduced a new character in May 1962. As was the case with Dr. Frankenstein's creation, the Hulk[12] was a product of science gone awry, and like the former "...he was never understood, always mistaken for evil..." (Horn 324).

Although he never achieved the success of his fellow Marvel super antihero, Spider-Man (who will be discussed later), the Hulk has survived in the competitive field of comic books and was the star of a prime-time television series in the 1980s. He has also been the subject of two full-length television movies and a cartoon series. Below is the origin story of this "American son of Frankenstein."

A teenager named Rick Jones carelessly parks his car in a prohibited nuclear test site in the Southwestern desert minutes before a prototype of a gamma ray bomb is to be det-

onated. Bruce Banner, the scientist who is the inventor of the new weapon, sees the boy and rushes to save him. Unfortunately, while he is able to push the young hotrodder to safety in a nearby ditch, Banner is caught in the blast. The gamma radiation he absorbs does not kill him, but it does have a remarkable effect: when he becomes angry, Dr. Banner is transformed into a huge, powerful being that becomes known as the Incredible Hulk.

The Hulk has undergone several metamorphoses since his inception. He has changed from gray to green,[13] has had his alter egos fused by Dr. Strange, only to be reseparated by Thunderbolt Ross and fused again by means of gamma radiation and the psychotherapy of Doctor Leonard Sampson. Eventually, Bruce Banner became a unified personality, seven feet tall, articulate, and prone to acerbic sarcasm.

Whether Stan Lee wished his creation to be a symbol for existential man, an example of the Freudian theory of a bifurcated psyche (ego/id), or was offering the reader "...a mythic narrative identifying the technology of mass destruction with the psychopathology of modern life ... ,"[14] he provided his rugged green giant with many of the superhero archetypes: *a fantastic birth*, *near invulnerability*, *super strength*, an *alter ego* (Bruce Banner), a *sidekick* (Rick Jones), an *archenemy* (Thunderbolt Ross), and a large supporting cast.

Dracula

The Frankenstein "monster's" costar in the world of modern super antiheroes is a denizen of the night, a dreaded super villain whose very name sends involuntary shivers down the spines of the bravest among us: Count Dracula. At least one perceptive researcher in the field recognized that the sinister count, immortalized by the Irish author Bram Stoker, deserves a place among some of the greatest modern super beings. According to Anthony Haden-Guest, "Dracula is part of that small pantheon of twentieth-century myths, ranking way up there alongside such diverse idols as Tarzan, Sherlock Holmes, the Frankenstein monster, the slightly faded James Bond and Mickey Mouse" (Radio Times, August 1974). Comparing the infamous Transylvanian bloodsucker to the king of the jungle; the pride of Scotland Yard, the suave lover/killer, 007; and the world's most famous rodent may arouse indignation in some of the fans of these famed characters, but there is no doubt that he and the not-so-jolly greenish giant operate on a psychological wavelength shared by a host of mythological monsters: that of sheer terror.

While some would like to believe differently, the fact of the matter is that the inspiration for a book on Count Dracula was not merely the product of a writer's overactive imagination or a shellfish-induced nightmare.[15] Nor was the world's greatest vampire purely of mythological origin. The fact is that there was a real-life character who was far more terrifying than his mythical descendant.

The Historical Dracula

Proof that the mythical Dracula still lives, at least in American living rooms, can be established by a reading of television program listings for a period of several months. It will be the exception to the rule if there is no Dracula or Dracula-related offering listed during a given month. In one four month period of 1990, for example, the following programs were offered to the viewing public: *A Polish Vampire in Burbank; Blacula; Vampires on Bikini Beach; Dracula vs. Frankenstein; The Bat; Love at First Bite; The Vampire Lovers; Captain Kronos: Vampire Hunter; Taste the Blood of Dracula; Dracula's Dog; Vampire at Midnight; Dracula A.D. 1972.* There is no doubt that we love to be frightened by Dracula and his vampire kin. In a survey taken between 1970 and 1978 in Madame Tussaud's Wax Museum in London, the fictional Dracula was judged to be the fifth most hated person in world history.[16] As hated and terrifying as the mythical Dracula is, however, he is a lightweight in the field of horror compared to the historical figure after whom he was modeled. In fact, while the latter had no obvious redeeming characteristics, the Transylvanian Bat/Man had a positive side, at least for those of his victims who were females.

Chelsea Quinn Yarbro, who has authored a number of vampire novels, put it in the following way: "What is it that a vampire really does? He bestows conditional immortality. How does he do it? By a very pleasurable, erotic experience.... What's so bad about that?" (Riccardo 4). Although Bram Stoker did not express it as openly in his Gothic tale as did some of the writers and filmmakers who followed, Dracula would have been able to teach such heralded lovers as Don Juan and Casanova a thing or two about the fair sex. The orgasmic effect he had on his "victims" indicates that he was at least as erotic as he was terrifying,[17] and it should also be pointed out that he was not the type to indulge in one-night stands. In fact, as Stoker's work shows, the irresistible Count took pains to develop a lasting, indeed an eternal relationship with those who became "flesh of his flesh and blood of his blood." The historical Dracula, on the other hand, did not balance the agony he inflicted on his many victims with even a modicum of pleasure, nor did he bother with them once he had done his dirty work.

In the vicinity of Innsbruck, Austria, there is a castle named Castle Ambras that sports an unusual art collection. Hanging there are representations of some of the most infamous human fiends in history, including a portrait of Count Dracula.

In the portrait one sees no sharp teeth, no black cape, no hypnotic eyes — just a rather unspectacular looking fellow with long, curly hair, a bushy moustache, large green eyes, and a rather long, thin, beaklike nose. The fact that he was a member of the upper class can be deduced from the regal headdress (almost a crown) and the ermine cape. Contrary to appearances, however, this was no ordinary fifteenth-century nobleman. During his life, the son of Dracul[18] was better known to the people of his area as Vlad Tepes, or *Vlad the Impaler*, a nickname which he more than earned. In the course of his short life (1431–1476), Vlad Tepes assumed a leading place in the gallery of world-class mass murderers by chalking up a tally of more than 100,000 victims. Before the gruesome details of his bloody handiwork are presented, however, it is helpful to understand the milieu in which he existed.

No one who is even casually familiar with the Dracula myth can help but feel at least a modicum of unease upon hearing the name *Transylvania*. The word conjures up visions of dark dank castles, baying wolves, full moons and, of course, the shadows of huge bats outlined in the pale moonlight. And not without reason. This area, now part of western Romania, is a land of "...innumerable caverns, whose mysterious depths seem made to harbor whole legions of evil spirits...."[19] In addition to indigenous superstitions, Transylvanians adopted those they heard from the early German colonists and numerous gypsy clans that often camped there. Witches, werewolves and monsters of all sizes and shapes aroused the imaginations and fears of the population. It is no wonder that the most dreaded vampire of all would eventually find a home there, for this was a land obsessed with death, a land where frightening omens abounded.

Many Transylvanians believed, for instance, that death was near if one heard the crowing of a black hen or the unprovoked bark of a dog. (How one could tell the color of a hen by the sound of its crowing, or know if a barking dog had been provoked are questions best left unasked.) Moreover, death was not the end of one's difficulties. Numerous rituals were performed after the grim reaper claimed a victim. Needles, pins and thread were placed in a coffin with a corpse so that the departed could repair any damage incurred to his or her clothing during the difficult journey to the next world. Nor did Transylvanians neglect to place some money under the deceased's tongue for any tolls that were demanded along the way. If these and other rituals were not performed, the spirit of the dead person was doomed to wander the earth forever as a portent of disease and misfortune. Such was Transylvania, the land the infamous Impaler called home. And there was no place like home when it came to torture and mass murder.

Dracula's father was, ironically enough, a champion of Christianity. His position as a charter member of the *Societas Draconis* (Order of Dragons) gave him a great deal of prestige. The order consisted of twenty-four princes, each handpicked by King Sigismund of Hungary to protect Catholicism from the infidel Turks.[20] Due to his membership in such an exclusive club, he was given the nickname "Dracul" by his contemporaries.

In 1431, the same year that his infamous son was born, Dracul became the Prince of Wallachia (part of Romania). Rank has its privileges. As the leader, he was able to provide young Dracula with the finest education available at the time. In addition to his training for knighthood, the precocious young nobleman learned German, Hungarian, Italian, French, Romanian, Church Slavonic and Latin. But as he soon discovered, life has its downside, even for the son of a prince, for, while little Dracula impressed his tutors with his superior mental prowess, his father was getting himself into deep trouble as a result of his Machiavellian machinations. Switching sides almost as easily as a chameleon changes color, Dracul proceeded to make an alliance with his former enemies, the Turks. It was a bad move. In 1442, the forces of Hungary defeated the Turks, an event which cost Dracul his seat of power in Wallachia and sent him scampering off to Turkey for asylum.

Dracula was down but not out. One year later, aided by his Turkish friends, he was back on the Wallachian throne. But there was a catch. Understandably, the Turks did not fully trust a person whose loyalties were as changeable as the weather, and so to insure themselves against any possible future betrayal they kept his two sons, Dracula and his brother, as hostages. For four years, Dracula remained a prisoner/guest of the Turks in a fortress in western Antolia.

Another youngster might have wasted this time or brooded about the injustice of the world, but not Dracula. The indomitable Transylvanian transplant used every free minute to develop his burgeoning talents. Under the able tutorage of his "hosts," Dracula added Turkish to his linguistic repertoire, mastered military tactics, and became an expert at what was soon to become his forte: the use of terror. The Turks had never had a better student in this field.

The situation changed very quickly in 1445,[21] as Dracul continued to play the opposing Christian and Turkish powers against each other. In so doing, he placed his sons in grave danger. Unlike his brother, Radu, who survived by submitting to the amorous advances of the Turkish prince Mehmed, Dracula thrived under the pressure: "Whatever he had to suffer toughened his character to a diamondlike hardness" (Florescu 60). This hardness, combined with his innate intelligence, molded him into a super survivor. When his father was assassinated in 1447, it is a safe bet to say that the future Impaler did not shed many tears. He undoubtedly realized that he had been used as a pawn by the former, and accepted that as the normal way of the world.

By 1448, Dracula was ready to make his own mark. With the support of the Turks, who recognized him as a kindred spirit, the seventeen-year-old led an expeditionary force into Wallachia and carried out a successful military coup, only to be overthrown within a year by the forces of Hungary.

For the next eight years, Dracula was a count of no-account, wandering from Moldavia to Transylvania and then back and forth again, dependent on the good offices of others to protect him as the political alignments continued to shift like desert sands in a windstorm.

In 1456, Dracula got his big break when the ruler of Wallachia, Janos Hunyadi, died of the plague. Dracula was reinstated as prince of Wallachia, a position he retained for the next six years. It was during this time that he made his reputation as one of the most bloodthirsty despots of all time.

Dracula's objective when he assumed the throne of Wallachia for the second time was to centralize his power at home. To this end, he carried out a bloody purge of the hostile elements within the Wallachian nobility. His favorite form of punishment was impalement, an excruciating procedure in which a long, sharpened stake was inserted into the rectum of the victim. These stakes were "...rounded and oiled so that the victims would writhe in agony for a while before succumbing to the mercies of death" (Glut 4). But it would be wrong to think that he was an overly specialized torturer and murderer. When he felt the need for a change, he would impale his victims through the head, the navel, the heart, or the stomach, and when impalement grew tiresome, he would have them buried alive, crushed by carts, drawn and quartered, hanged, decapitated, roasted alive, boiled in kettles, skinned, or hacked to pieces. When in a rare, merciful mood, he would limit the punishment to blinding an offender, or cutting off his or her limbs, ears, nose, or sexual organs.

Dracula was equally comfortable ordering mass or individual executions, and to demonstrate that he had no gender or age biases, he often had women and children impaled alongside the menfolk. Nor can anyone say that Dracula was not an imaginative murderer, or without a sense of humor. He showed the latter when a delegation of ambassadors from Turkey came to visit him in his castle and refused to remove their hats (saying that it was their custom to keep their heads covered). In response, Dracula saw to it that their custom was maintained by ordering the hats nailed to their heads.

Dracula loved to entertain company. During some of his outdoor dinner parties, he would have a group of impaled victims in various stages of dying ring the table. Dinner guests who expressed revulsion were immediately hoisted onto their own stakes to join the others.

In addition to his lack of age and gender bias, Dracula also demonstrated that he was not bigoted against any nationality, religion or social class. The proof of this is that among his 100,000 victims there were Moldavians, Wallachians, Transylvanians, Bulgarians, Hungarians, Germans and Gypsies. Impaled alongside Catholics were Protestants, Muslims, Jews and members of the Greek Orthodox Church. Peasants were not denied the right to be impaled either, although the nobility did have disproportionate representation on the stakes.

One should not conclude from the above that Dracula was a totally immoral man.

There are recorded instances in which he showed himself to be a diligent guardian of marital fidelity, an unstinting believer that a woman must be a virgin before marriage, an active champion of law and order, and a determined enemy of poverty and homelessness. Let us look at a few examples of his social conscience in action.

There is more than one account of how Dracula dealt with women who engaged in extramarital affairs. When he learned of such behavior, he would order the guilty woman's sexual organs cut out, after which she was skinned alive and left to die in a public square. Young girls who failed to remain pure were impaled through the vagina with a red-hot iron stake. In all probability, there were many faithful wives and virgins in Wallachia during the reign of Dracula. The fact that Dracula did not punish men as severely when it came to sexual misconduct is but an indication of his understanding nature. No doubt, he realized that "boys will be boys."

Dracula's great love for law and order provided his Wallachian subjects with a degree of security they had never known before, at least with regard to their material possessions. No wonder, since the penalty for stealing even the smallest item was immediate impalement on one of the stakes that always stood ready for use in public squares and other accessible locations throughout the kingdom. The public, following the example of their prince, also joined the struggle to stamp out crime. Criminals were quickly apprehended by the citizens. Motivation was provided by the prince's threat to burn down their villages and impale them if they failed to turn in the culprits.

Politicians today must envy the unique manner in which Dracula solved the problem of poverty and homelessness. On one occasion, he invited all of the beggars in his land to a sumptuous meal in a large house he had chosen for the gala occasion. After they had eaten and drunk their fill, the generous host ordered the doors of the house locked and the house burned down with them in it.

For those who still remain unconvinced that Vlad Tepes had any civic conscience, it must be noted that he is often given credit for founding the city of Bucharest. Romulus has gotten far more recognition for the founding of Rome, but one must credit the Wallachian prince for getting a great deal done in spite of a very busy impalement schedule. In fact, some Romanians consider him a national hero, a defender of his nation's independence. This was evidenced in 1976, the five hundredth anniversary of his death, when Romania declared a "Dracula Year." During that year, he was the main subject of many magazine articles, as well as radio, television and film presentations. In addition, a commemorative stamp was issued to the newly discovered "George Washington of the Romanian people" (Florescu 220).

It is very clear from the above that the historical Dracula was at least as frightening as his mythical clone. One can come to this conclusion even if one discounts the reports that he often chopped off his victims' hands and drank their blood, and from time to time killed women by severing their jugulars with his teeth. When the Great Impaler died in 1476, whether heroically or as an assassination victim, there must have been many sighs of relief in Wallachia and the vicinity. Little did they know that he would be back one day as a vampire.

Vampires

Although the designation *vampire* has become synonymous with Bram Stoker's Dracula, there have been many related figures in world myth and literature in such diverse lands as Assyria, Greece, Mexico, China, India, Malaya, Arabia, Japan, etc. These dreaded beings go under different names and appear in different forms, but their essence is the same. In much of Eastern Europe the term *nosferatu* (undead) is applied to the vampire, a name that was particularly dreaded by children whose parents often used it to frighten them into being good.[22] In Servia (present day Bosnia) and Wallachia (a province of Romania) they appeared as bloodsucking ghosts and were respectively called *Vukodlak* and *Murony*. In ancient Greece they were labeled *Lamias*, beautiful phantom women who feasted on the flesh and blood of young men.

In Greece, the belief in vampires did not end with the advent of Christianity. Early Greek Christians believed that excommunicated persons were kept alive by the devil and that they roamed the countryside at night in the form of dogs, toads, spiders, fleas and other creatures, destroying innocent people. These were referred to as *Burkolakkä* or *Tympanitä*. The Arabs and Persians spoke of malevolent beings called *ghouls*, who maintained their existence by drinking the blood of their victims. In India, there is a divine counterpart to the human vampire, the evil god *Kali*, who delights in drinking the blood of his sacrificial victims. Japan, for its part, sports a monster cat that feasts on the blood of sleeping women and young girls. Obviously, then, vampires are equal-opportunity bloodsuckers; they never turn down a good drink of blood regardless of the religion, race or sex of the donor.

A first cousin of the vampire, whose legend is as old as time and as wide as the world..."[23] is the werewolf. Werewolves are generally depicted as men or women who have the ability to metamorphose into wolves in order to satisfy their craving for human flesh and blood. This frightening phenomenon of transformation has been given the name *lycanthropy*, and has been the subject of intense study by serious scholars of mythology, folklore and literature. Summers cites the widespread belief in the Slavic countries: "...the man who has during his life been a werewolf almost necessarily becomes a vampire after his death" (15). Nevertheless, he cautions, "...the two must be carefully distinguished. They are entirely different, separate and apart" (15). The major difference between the two is that while the werewolf is a living person the vampire exists in a limbo-like state somewhere between life and death, and is often referred to as "undead." Despite their close relationship, however, the werewolf does not approach the frightening stature of the Transylvanian Terror.

The Mythical Count Dracula

Unlike famed authors of horror stories such as the German Romanticist E.T.A. Hoffmann and the American Edgar Allan Poe, Bram Stoker was not a tormented man who performed his literary labors while tottering on the edge of madness. The son of a country clergyman and a graduate of the prestigious Trinity College, Stoker combined the manners of an English gentleman, a natural Irish wit and the physique of a professional athlete (the latter despite the fact that he was scarcely expected to survive childhood). That for twenty-seven years he was employed as the business manager of the famous Victorian actor Sir Henry Irving and later became a professor of English are also not outward indications of the talent or temperament to create "...one of the three most invoked characters in English literature" (Copper 74). Nevertheless, it was Stoker who produced, in *Dracula*, the definitive tale of terror.

The primary plot of Stoker's work is not very complicated: Jonathan Harker, an English real estate broker, travels to Transylvania to close a deal with a local Count. Harker describes Count Dracula in the following way:

His face was strong — a very strong — aquiline, with high bridge of the thin nose and peculiarly arched nostrils; with lofty domed forehead, and hair growing scantily round the temples but profusely elsewhere. His eyebrows were very massive.... The mouth, so far as I could see it under the heavy moustache, was fixed and rather cruel-looking, with particularly sharp white teeth.... The general effect was one of extraordinary pallor.[24]

Harker further notes that the Count had hairs in the palms of his hands and that his breath was "dank." One knowledgeable in the lore of *Nosferatu* would have immediately been put on alert by his appearance. The emaciated look, the canine teeth, the hair in the palms of the hands, the extreme halitosis — these are definitely vampire warning signals. But Harker was a simple entrepreneur, and so, in spite of his unease, it did not dawn on him at first that he was dealing with a most unusual client. Perhaps if Dracula had possessed red hair, blue eyes and a single nostril, as do the Undead in the myths of certain countries, his true identity would have been more apparent.

Harker's suspicion that the situation is more than a little unusual grows when he hears strange sounds during the night and sees three "terrible women" hovering about. No doubt he knew he was in deep trouble when he discovered Dracula sleeping in an earth-filled coffin, and with "...fresh blood which trickled from the corners of the mouth and ran down over his chin and neck" (Stoker 60).

The scene switches to London, hometown of the two beautiful young women Lucy Westenra and Mina Murray. (Mina married Jonathan Harker after his escape from Castle Dracula.) Although not mentioned at first, Dracula's sinister presence pervades the action. An incident is reported in the newspapers, of a mysterious Russian ship that has appeared in Whitby harbor with no crew. Only the captain's corpse was onboard, his hands lashed to the wheel, a crucifix tied around his wrists. An examination of the ship's log reveals that the crew disappeared one by one and that the captain attributed these disappearances to an unknown, evil force, in some way related to the earth-filled, coffin-like boxes below deck.

Before very long, Lucy begins to show signs of acute anemia, which no one initially associated with the two puncture marks on her throat, or the "great bat" (104) that has been seen flapping at her window. Despite the intervention of the famous Dutch professor of the occult, Dr. van Helsing, Lucy cannot be saved. But contrary to appearances, she does not die. Her fiancé, Arthur Holmwood, is horrified to learn from Professor van Helsing that Lucy has been the victim of a vampire and that they will have to perform a most unpleasant procedure in order to save her from joining the ranks of the undead. Reluctantly, Arthur agrees.

Accompanied by Dr. Seward, the director of the local insane asylum, and the Texan Quincy Morris (the two other men who had proposed marriage to Lucy), van Helsing and Arthur go to the mausoleum that houses Lucy's body. When they open her coffin, the professor's theory is confirmed: "She seemed like a nightmare of Lucy ... the pointed teeth, the bloodstained, voluptuous mouth..." (220). Then, like a stage director discussing an upcoming scene to an actor, Professor van Helsing explains to Arthur how to drive the pointed wooden stake into Lucy's heart. To his credit, the young man rises to the challenge. Although "The Thing in the coffin" writhes and screams at the first blow, "Arthur never faltered. He looked like a figure of Thor as his untrembling arm rose and fell, driving deeper and deeper the mercy-bearing stake..." (222). Finally, the body is still and the professor is able to complete the ceremony by cutting off Lucy's head, filling her mouth with garlic and soldering up the lead coffin. One would think that the stalwart crew had earned a few pints of bitters at the local pub after all that work, but there was still a great deal to do.

No one can blame the professor and his posse of vampire hunters for having become upset when they note two puncture marks on the increasingly ill Mina Harker's throat. And when they burst into her room and found Dracula with her, "...forcing her face down on his bosom..." (288) as blood streamed down his bare chest, they realize that they have to act fast. After chasing him off with a powerful combination of holy wafers and crucifixes, they are faced with a two-fold task: to save Mina and to find and destroy Dracula.

Stoker's work ends with an archetypal chase scene and showdown. Mina, who had agreed to undergo hypnosis in order to help locate Dracula, is able to locate him through ESP. He is on a ship heading toward his homeland. Professor van Helsing and his intrepid vampire-removal squad immediately engage in a harrowing race with time in the hope that they will be able to find the Prince of Darkness before the setting sun restores his powers. They make it with only seconds to spare. In a melodramatic finale, just as the sun begins to set, Jonathan Harker and Quincy Morris give him the old one-two in the heart with their knives, causing his body to crumble into dust. (It was fortunate for them that Stoker temporarily suspended the rule that called for a wooden stake.) Although Quincy Morris is a casualty of that final battle between the forces of good and evil, the story has a relatively happy ending. Mina recovers completely, van Helsing goes back to Amsterdam, and the others live happily ever after. As for Dracula, he is still with us in one medium or the other, and he undoubtedly will be for a long, long time to come.[25]

Although Stoker based his novel on traditional sources, he did make some additions of his own that have become an integral part of the vampire myth. The most striking of these are Dracula's lack of reflection (and shadow), his vulnerability to sunlight, his ability to transform himself into a bat, and his need to sleep in a coffin containing his native soil. These characteristics are shared by the vast majority of vampires who appear in the hundreds of print, film, television, and theatrical works inspired by Bram Stoker's novel.[26]

Another effective touch that Stoker added was to make Dracula dependent on drinking human blood for his survival. While folklore did tell of the vampire's love for blood, it was not a staple in his diet. The Romanians believed that the vampire could (and often did) eat anything, including manure. When one combines this with their touted talent as master cooks, one can only imagine what interesting gourmet meals vampires may have concocted for unsuspecting guests.

* * *

While we know nothing of Dracula's origins and therefore cannot apply the familiar Rankean birth criteria, there is no doubt that he is a super antihero of the highest order. As a full grown Nosferatu, the Carpathian Count is an archetype hunter's dream, albeit the archetypes he embodies are at times distorted and not always readily apparent.

One clear archetype found in the Dracula myth is that of flawed *invulnerability*. Like Achilles, Siegfried and Superman, he could be defeated if one knew his weak spots. However, although time and again we see him repulsed by crucifixes, holy water and/or garlic, pierced by wooden stakes, decapitated or reduced to ashes by exposure to the rising sun, one always suspects that he will continue to win his *battle with death* and be *resurrected* for yet another film or video. Assuredly, when the moon is full Dracula will rise from his coffin in order to secure a pint or two of his favorite red liquid.

In spite of the fact that Dracula converted each one of his dinner companions into a disciple (flesh of his flesh and blood of his blood), he was essentially a loner. Thus, one cannot accurately speak of a *sidekick* in his case (unless we deem his female followers as such). But he did have two formidable *archenemies,* one human and one divine. Professor van Helsing filled this role very well on the human level, doggedly battling the supernatural Count with his intellectual powers. Dracula's divine archenemy was much more powerful, none other than Jesus Christ himself. Theologically viewed, Dracula can be seen as the traditional devil-figure, an evil counterpart of the Christian God, in a constant battle with the latter for human souls. Unlike the superheroes we have previously discussed, however, in virtually all of the literary works and films dealing with him, Dracula is the loser in the inevitable *final battle.* On the other hand, while he is always defeated, he is never completely destroyed. Armed with his superpowers (a variation of *superweapons*), which include fantastic strength, the ability to *transform* himself into anything from a huge bat to a thin mist, and an indomitable, mesmerizing will, Count Dracula will undoubtedly continue to be the *chosen one* when the need arises to find a subject with which to terrify succeeding generations of puny mortals.

Dracula's Descendants

In addition to the numerous fictional sequels and spin-offs, from time to time there have been real-life practitioners of vampirism who would have made Bram Stoker's bloodthirsty super vampire proud. A number of such recorded instances of this so-called medical vampirism were so bizarre that they merit mention.

The first "reliably reported" (Haining 68) instance of medical vampirism fittingly took place in the Carpathian mountains, the home territory of Vlad Tepes. It was there during the first years of the seventeenth century that a grisly serial killer terrorized the region, brutally murdering and draining the blood of several hundred young girls. One can imagine the shock of the people when the official investigations determined that the killer was not a depraved sex maniac, but a noblewoman: Countess Elisabeth Bathroy, the wife of a Transylvanian general. The shock undoubtedly turned to disgust when it was revealed that the countess had committed the terrible crimes for cosmetic reasons: she believed that bathing in virgins' blood would keep her from ageing. While she was not executed along with the three servants who had assisted her with her "blood-baths," she was sentenced in 1611 to be walled up in her castle for life. Whether or not she was provided with a mirror to watch her hair gray and her face wrinkle is unknown, but if that was the case she had to suffer for only three years. In 1614, the Countess was found dead, "...her face down — the position of the 'undead,' facing Hell, not Heaven...."[27]

There are some who believe that it was Countess Bathroy and not Vlad Tepes who inspired the legend of Dracula. These scholars reason that while the latter was a brutal murderer he was not particularly obsessed by blood. In any event, the countess has earned her place as one of the greatest super villainesses in recorded history.

Another case of medical vampirism, one which was publicized throughout Europe and beyond, took place in Hanover, Germany, during the years immediately following the end of World War I.

It would be an understatement to say that the situation in Germany during the years following the war was desperate. The cost of the armed conflict in human life and materials had not only severely crippled the German economy, but also had done incalculable damage to the psyche of its people. The chaos and despair were greatly compounded, moreover, by the impossible demands made on the beaten country by the Treaty of Versailles.[28] It was in this milieu that a pederastic petty criminal by the name of Fritz Haarman, assisted by a fellow pervert named Hans Grans, whose list of crimes ranged from theft to murder, earned his place among the most infamous mass murderers of history. Some sources credit the "Hanover Vampire," as the press labeled him, with more than fifty murders. His method of killing his victims, all young boys, was to hold them down and administer a "strong bite on the throat." But he did not stop there. When the mood struck them, he and Grans would dissect the dead body and cook those parts that were most appetizing to them. A firm believer in the adage *waste not, want not*, Haarman would then prepare the remaining portion in the form of sausages and sell them in the little butcher shop he owned. The good Hausfrauen of Hanover happily formed long lines to purchase the well-seasoned meat, since there was a meat shortage at the time. An added attraction was the price: due to his low overhead costs, Haarman was able to undersell his competitors. To this day, there are many in northern Germany who recall the lines of the poem that they learned as children about Hanover's horribly hungry Herr Haarman:

> Warte, warte noch ein Weilchen,
> Dann kommt Haarman auch zu Dir;
> Mit dem kleinen Hackebeilchen
> Macht er Hackefleisch aus Dir.
> (Wait, wait but a little while,
> Harmann will come visit you,
> With his tiny little hatchet
> He'll make mincemeat out of you.)

Unlike his mythical predecessor, the Hanover Vampire did not turn to ashes when the sun rose on one morning in April 1925. Instead, he was led to the official chopping block where his head was deftly removed by the executioner's sword. Whether or not his mouth was stuffed with garlic to prevent him from returning for a sequel is not certain, but the fact that his sidekick, Hans Grans, was released on parole after having served twelve years of a life sentence must have made many German shoppers a lot more wary when they went out to buy their wurst.

John George Haigh, the third contender for entrance into the Medical Vampire Hall of Fame, carried out his nefarious activities during the last years of World War II. It is only fitting that he did so in England, the same country that Bram Stoker's Dracula had terrorized decades earlier. Unlike Fritz Haarman, however, whose appetite for human flesh identified him more with a werewolf than a vampire, Haigh was a chip off the Transylvanian bloodsucker's block. Between September 9, 1944, when he committed his first murder, and August 6, 1949, when he was executed, the former choir boy did away with nine human beings, drank their blood, and dissolved their remains in vats of sulphuric acid.

Why did Haigh become a super villain? Perhaps it was his parents' fault. After all, they were members of a cult called Peculiar People, whose primary belief seemed to be that anything enjoyable was sinful. Perhaps he became obsessed with blood because of the constant reminders that Christ had bled for him on the cross, an image that haunted his dreams. Perhaps he developed a taste for the precious red liquid as a result of sucking it from the wounds his mother inflicted on his knuckles with her hairbrush whenever he misbehaved. Or perhaps, as the investigators and prosecutor at his trial claimed, he was not interested in the blood at all, but merely sought to escape execution by pretending to be insane. His only interest, they claimed, was in monetary gain, a charge he denied. As he wrote in his diary, "It was not their money but their blood that I was after.... I made a small cut, usually in the right side of the neck, and drank the blood for three to five minutes..." (Copper 180). Count Dracula would have been proud of him.

The Batman

In addition to the flesh-and-blood "descendants" of the world's most famous vampire, it is very possible that a DNA test might indicate that one of the most famous and successful modern American heroes carries at least a few Transylvanian genes. One expert in the field of comic books has noted The Batman's resemblance to Dracula: "Dressed like a wealthy count by day, he would emerge Dracula-like at night for fantastic nocturnal forays amidst moonlit settings..." (Steranko I, 44). Unlike Superman, his invulnerable stablemate in National Publications, The Batman (the definite article was later dropped) has had to struggle along without the aid of super powers since his first appearance in *Detective Comics* in May 1939. And while in the end he is invariably triumphant, he has gotten his share of bumps and bruises along the way. In fact, he has been pummeled so often that one writer asserted: "Though a good deal was made of his extraordinary stamina, much of it, as it turns out, was for punishment ... there was some reason to believe he had a glass jaw" (Feiffer 27). Nor has Gotham City's Caped Crusader ever been mistaken for a clean-cut, all–American hero as has the Metropolis-based Man of Steel. In fact, in his early years he was presented as a fearful creature of the night, an early example of a new breed of superheroes who performed their exploits on the fringe of conventional society, at best only grudgingly accepted by the forces of law and order.

Another basic difference between Batman and other comic book superheroes of his time has to do with motivation. Batman's ongoing war against the criminal element was based on neither moral conviction nor altruism but on a personal vendetta: an old-fashioned quest for revenge. As Maurice Horn writes, "The Batman was an avenging vigilante ... a slightly unsavory character" (Horn 101).

Batman further differed from other American superheroes who were born during the war in that he did not battle incessantly against the minions of Tojo and Hitler as did Superman, Wonder Woman, Captain America and other super patriots. Batman's confrontations with the Axis were relatively infrequent during the forties because he simply did not have the time for such diversion. In keeping with the pledge he had made to avenge his murdered parents, he devoted his energies almost exclusively to the destruction of criminals.

In April 1940, Batman gained an assistant in this ongoing struggle, a "Boy Wonder," Robin, who was named after the famed altruistic hero of Sherwood Forest. Together, the *dynamic duo*, as they came to be known, shared a common basis for their hatred of the underworld: the parents of both had been murder victims.

Not everyone regarded the relationship between the two colorful crimefighters as a healthy one. In a book condemning the comic book industry as a threat to the morals of American youth, a moral crusader by the name of Dr. Fredric Wertham viewed the relationship between Batman and Robin rather negatively.[29] He wrote, "...the Batman type of story helps to fixate homoerotic tendencies by suggesting the form of adolescent-with-adult or Ganymede-Zeus type of love relationship" (Wertham 190). Dr. Wertham attempts to prove his contention by pointing out the fact that the wealthy socialite, Bruce Wayne (Batman's secret identity) and young Dick Grayson (Robin's civilian alter-ego) live together,

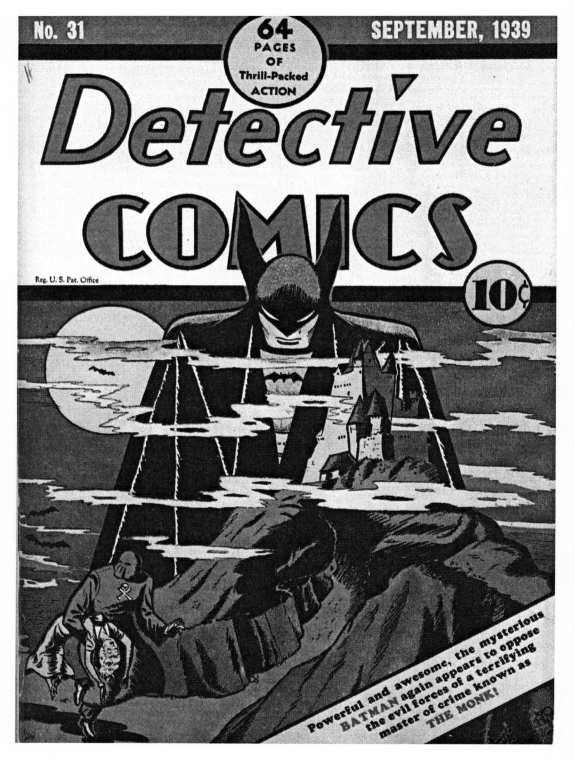

The Batman, *Detective* #31, September 1939. (DC Comics.)

worry about each other, and that, as a result, "The Batman type of story may stimulate children to homosexual fantasies..." (191). One wonders what the homophobic psychiatrist would have written about the Achilles-Patroklos or the Gilgamesh-Enkidu relationships had he been familiar with them. At any rate, Batman's reputation was defended by the editor of the later Batman newspaper comic strip. E. Nelson Bridwill called Dr. Wertham's charge "...one of the most irresponsible slurs ever cast upon our heroes."[30] Mr. Bridwell then provided a list of the female love interests in Bruce Wayne's life, including Julie Madison, Linda Page and Vicki Vale, all of whom satisfy the comic book maxim that characters' names must be short and Anglo-Saxon. Even those who wanted to believe that the dynamic duo were more than fighting partners could not bring themselves to do so. In his humorous article on the subject, Jules Feiffer makes the following observation:

> For ... personal reasons ... I'd be delighted to think Wertham right ... but conscience dictates otherwise: Batman and Robin were no more or less queer than were their youngish readers, many of whom palled around together, didn't trust girls, played games that had lots of bodily contact ... [Feiffer 43].

Macho Batman fans must have breathed a collective sigh of relief when they read those reassuring words.

Returning to the comparison between Dracula and Batman, one discovers that in his own way Batman is proving to be as hardy a survivor as his Transylvanian ancestor. Over the years he has built up a most respectable set of credits, and continues to add to it. One reason he has been able to do this is that, just as the Count had the capacity to transform himself into many other forms, the bat and wolf being the most frequently chosen, Batman has shown the ability to change with the times. After a long interlude during which he had discarded his frightening image and become more societally acceptable, he has once again become a fearsome creature of the dark. At present, he is still waging his war against crime. Dick Grayson (Robin) departed in 1982 to head his own comic book (*Teen Titans*), was replaced by another Robin who has since died, only to be succeeded by yet a third Robin in the film *Batman Forever* (1995). The latest Batman movie, *Batman Begins* (2005), is absent a Robin. In this version, Batman is depicted as a complex representative of the superhero genre.

The essence of Batman's origin has been embellished and altered over the years, but the basic elements have been retained: Young Bruce Wayne, a millionaire socialite, watches in horror as a hoodlum guns down his parents on a deserted city street. Thereafter, thanks to his great wealth, he is able to devote himself to a quest for revenge. Training relentlessly with state-of-the-art paraphernalia that he has gathered in the huge cave beneath his estate, at last he is ready to spring into action. In order to strike fear into the hearts of the criminals he intends to confront, he dons an eerie bat costume.

In the period of superhero decline following World War II, Superman was the only major American comic book superhero to enjoy more success than Batman.[31] But that balance has tipped, at least temporarily, in favor of the latter. The Batman movies have done very well at the box office and as releases on video. In addition, his legend has been strengthened by the countless comic books bearing his name, his many appearances with Superman in his own and the latter's comic magazines, his exploits as a member of the Justice League of America, the two movie serials put out by Columbia in the 1940s (*Batman; Batman and Robin*), the syndicated Batman newspaper comic strips, the television series of the late 1960s (the first superhero to command prime time television), the Saturday morning

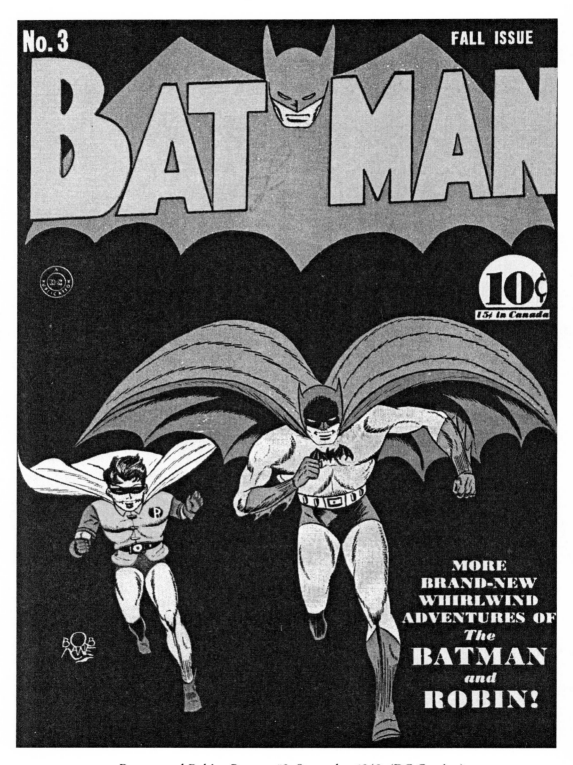

Batman and Robin, *Batman* #3, September 1940. (DC Comics.)

television Batman cartoon, four paperback novels in the 1960s, a graphic novel that was published in 1986,[32] and the countless Batman figurines, toys, clothing, etc. In short, the Gotham City superhero is as much an industry as his Transylvanian precursor and he shows no signs of slowing down. What Maurice Horn said in 1976 still holds true today: in the realm of superheroes, Batman "...remains one of the strongest and most secure..." (Horn 102).

* * *

From the archetypal standpoint, Batman's superhero status is indisputable. An athlete, acrobat and super-sleuth, "Batman is the Scarlet Pimpernel, Zorro, Fairbanks, the Shadow, the Bat, Sherlock Holmes, and Houdini all rolled up into one" (Bridwell 11). And while his birth did not meet the Rankean criteria for the birth of a hero, it was certainly not the norm. Like Athena, who emerged fully grown from Zeus' head, the Batman was born in adult form after the murder of his parents. Years later, his body honed to peak form through ceaseless exercise, he began to fulfill his oath to exact revenge. The Batman emerged, in great part, from Bruce Wayne's dark side, an avenger strangely reminiscent of the Egyptian god Horus, whose mission in life was similar. But while Batman is as much a mythic figure as Horus, he is certainly no god. He is a twentieth-century superhero, and whatever considerable powers he does possess come from human rather than divine sources, primarily from the realm of technology. While his excellent physical condition is very important when it comes to the frequent hand-to-hand clashes he engages in with the bad guys of Gotham City, brawn and athleticism alone are not effective against the arsenals of modern criminals. That is where his cache of *superweapons* come into play.

Initially, Batman had only a .45 caliber-type handgun to aid him in his war against crime, and although it was frowned upon by the authorities, he did not hesitate to use it. But as he gained respectability, his armory became more sophisticated. In addition to a utility belt containing exotic weapons such as miniature smoke bombs, explosive pills and sleep producing gas pellets, the Caped Crusader gradually acquired a large assortment of Batphernalia, ranging from a Bat-arang, to an assortment of Batropes, on which he is able to swing into action with a skill equal to Tarzan's. Added to all of these is the rich assortment of electronic and other gadgets hidden away in the secret Batcave, where the state-of-the-art equipped Bat-mobile, Bat-plane and Bat-copter are stored until needed. Even James Bond, who in many respects is a non-costumed version of Batman (though Batman is no match for 007 when it comes to romantic conquests), would have to be impressed by such a technological treasure chest.

One archetype which on first glance seems to be clearly lacking in Batman's makeup is that of *invulnerability*. A closer examination, however, yields a different conclusion, for, although one would be hard put to find a superhero who has been beaten and injured as frequently as Batman, the fact is that he always returns to fight another day. That he has no single point of vulnerability, as did Achilles, Siegfried and even Superman, makes him more survivable than they. At any rate, this has been the case until now.

When it comes to archetypal *archenemies*, Batman is second to none. Not even Dick Tracy's colorful adversaries can match those of Batman. Where in all of mythology is there a scoundrel more cleverly conceived than the perpetually smiling Joker? He is "...the perfect blend of clownish humor and malevolent evil" (Bridwell 13).[33] And has there ever been a more loveable/hateable rogue than the Penguin, with an umbrella for every criminal occasion? Or are there two more psychologically compelling villains than Two-Face and the Rid-dler?[34] Also opposed to Batman is the first lady of crime, the Catwoman, whose love for Batman could not keep her on the straight and narrow path for long. Added to all of those already mentioned are lesser known villains such as Tweedledum and Tweedledee, Punch and Judy, the Cavalier, the Scarecrow, the Crime Doctor, Dr. Death, Hugo Strange, etc. With so many enemies, it is no wonder that eventually Batman gathered some friends around him: Batwoman, Bat-Hound, Bat-Mite, and of course, the ultra-reliable Alfred, Batgirl and Aunt Harriet.

At the present time, Batman has reassumed his fearsome visage. Will this new-old Bat-man continue to woo audiences as the twenty-first century progresses? Not even his writ-ers know that. The only thing that is certain is that when the Bat-signal appears in the sky or the Bat-hotline rings, unlike Rustam who often dallied when the Shah sent for him, Bat-man will drop whatever he is doing, climb into his Batmobile or his Batcopter and speed off to answer the call. And one can wager with some confidence that there will be a Robin at his side.

Spider-Man

In August 1962, Marvel Comics introduced a character who soon became the super-star of its star-studded pantheon: the indomitable Spider-Man.[35] The quintessential out-sider, Spider-Man's popularity quickly soared, earning him three cartoon series, a feature film and his own newspaper strip. As early as May 1963 he had not only earned his own comic magazine but in the process gained a loyal following, particularly on college and uni-versity campuses. He was the perfect hero for the times, or more correctly "the embodi-ment of the ... anti hero" (Horn 630). The extent of his favored status among political radicals was discussed in the September 1965 issue of *Esquire Magazine*, where it was noted that he was as popular as the Cuban revolutionary Che Guevera. Certainly, one college stu-dent was indulging in hyperbole when he asserted that Spider-Man's creator, Stan Lee, was "...this generation's Homer," but there is no doubt that Spider-Man has become as much a part of America's mythology as either Superman or Batman.

In keeping with the traditional American comic book superhero, Spider-Man has an alter ego. In his case it is Peter Parker, a maladroit, impoverished, paranoid, part-time pho-tographer who barely ekes out a living by selling photographs of Spider-Man. With the exception of his heart-attack prone Aunt May (his Uncle Ben, like Bruce Wayne's and Dick Grayson's parents, was a murder victim), no one wanted to have much to do with Peter. In all probability, had it not been for a laboratory accident in which he was bitten by a radioac-tive spider, he would have gone through life unnoticed. But bitten he was, and as a result he acquired spider-sense, explained by Stan Lee as a blend of "...great strength and agility and a sixth sense which warned of approaching danger" (Daniels 138).

The origin story of Spider-Man first appeared in *Amazing Fantasy #15*, in August 1962.

Orphaned when his parents are killed in a plane crash, Peter Parker, an introverted bookworm at Midtown High School lives with his doting Aunt May and Uncle Ben. On a whim, one day he attends a science exhibit on radioactivity. During the course of his visit,

he is bitten by a spider that has been exposed to high doses of radioactive rays. As a result of the spider bite, Peter's strength and agility are greatly increased and he develops the ability to sense danger. In short, his abilities become proportionate to those of a spider.

Garbed in a self-designed costume and employing devices he calls "web shooters," Peter uses his newly acquired abilities to create an act that he performs in carnivals and on television. He calls himself *Spider-Man.*

One night, Peter returns home after a television appearance to learn that his beloved Uncle Ben has been murdered. With the aid of his super powers, Peter/Spider-Man apprehends the murderer and vows that from then on he will devote his powers to fight against crime. Shades of Batman.

For all of his skill at capturing lawbreakers, however, Spider-Man is generally mistrusted by the press and the law enforcement establishment. This is not surprising given the poor image that spiders have been given over the years in fable, folklore and film. (In the competition for the most hated and feared creature, the spider is challenged only by the wolf and the bat.)

In recent issues of his comic book, however, Peter has fared better. He has graduated from college, attended graduate school, and become a professional man. He married a young lady named Mary Jane, who apparently had nothing in common with Little Miss Muffet of nursery rhyme fame. Certainly, she would have thought twice about becoming Mrs. Peter Parker had she seen the horror film *Arachnophobia.*

Since his first appearance on the superhero stage, Spider-Man has appeared in a number of media other than the comic book. There have been several animated series bearing his name, as well as a daily and Sunday comic strip, and in three full length films. In spite of his seeming conversion to the comfortable bourgeois lifestyle, however, Spider-Man will always remain an outsider, a troubled, super antihero. His human-all-too human character may well explain why Spider-Man is considered by many to be the world's most popular superhero.[36]

* * *

Because science rather than divine intervention is responsible for Spider-Man's origin, his "birth" falls into the modern archetype for the birth of a super (anti)hero. Like Jay Garrick (the Flash) and Bruce Banner (the Incredible Hulk), Peter Parker derived his super powers from a laboratory miscue, not a planned scientific procedure as was the case with the Frankenstein being and Hugo Danner. Moreover, Spider-Man is similar to other super antiheroes: unwilling to play by the "rules" of the existing establishment. (The Batman is often labeled an antihero for this same reason.)

In keeping with his arachnid nature, Spider-Man is a loner. He has no *sidekick* to aid him in his fight against crime, or lend him money for carfare when his economic situation is critical (as it usually is). But while he lacks a *sidekick*, he has had no dearth of *archenemies.* Among the latter are such colorful characters as Kraven, the Hunter, the Vulture, the Gnome, the Slasher, Tarantula, and the Lizard.

Spider-Man, like Batman, is far from invulnerable and is often on the receiving end of physical punishment; but his spider power gives him the decisive edge over his criminal adversaries. With the aid of such *superweapons* as the web-creating devices he wears on his wrists, he is able to propel himself up the highest buildings to wait for his prey, and then conquer it with his super spider-strength. In recent years, he has also acquired a suit of armor equipped with mechanical spider arms that allow him to see around corners, built-in fire, police and emergency scanners, and a short range GPS system, to name just a few technological extras. There is no doubt about it, Spider-Man is a full-fledged member of the club. Move over Gilgamesh, Achilles, Rama, Rustam and you other senior superheroes; make way, Frankenstein and Dracula,[37] the "web slinger" is here, the superhero of the present.

Epilogue

Many writers and scholars have expressed their awareness that the study of mythology is a vital means of achieving at least a partial understanding of our past. Myths have been variously characterized as the vehicle of man's profoundest metaphysical insights, as God's revelation, and as "...the secret opening through which the inexhaustible energies of the cosmos pour into human cultural manifestation."[1] The German philosopher Friedrich Nietzsche likened the myth to a dream which carries us back into earlier states of human development and thereby gives us a means of understanding it better.[2] Mircea Eliade echoed this thought when he wrote: "The myth relates a history, that is, a primordial event that took place at the beginning of time...."[3] Joseph Campbell agreed, declaring that "Dream is the personalized myth, myth the depersonalized dream" (Campbell 19). The preceding study of the archetypal superhero, which is one of the most significant universal myths, clearly demonstrates that the superhero has a common origin, whether he appears in ancient Babylonia or Gotham City. Arguably, he is the ultimate product of the human psyche. Just as certain animals who have been reared in isolation will behave in a manner unique to their species, whether in the way they mate, build nests, or secure their food, homo sapiens formulates universal myths that seek to explain existence. The noted Swiss psychologist Carl Jung pointed to the plethora of archetypal mythological material that can be found in varied cultures and eras and concluded that their wellspring was a *racial unconscious,* a bridge extending between the human psyche of prehistoric times to that of the present. He saw myths as "...original revelations of the pre-conscious psyche...." But when asked how we might explain any given archetype he replied, "Not for a moment dare we succumb to the illusion that an archetype can be fully explained and disposed of.... The most we can do is *dream the myth onwards* and give it a modern dress."[4] As we have seen in the previous pages, we have done this throughout our history.

Perhaps the reason that we in modern times have more trouble equating mythology with reality is that we tend to demand a kinematic formulation of existence. Our modern minds are tuned to see life as a series of connected episodes which, like a piece of literature or film, have discernible beginnings, middles and ends. The ancients were not bound by such limitations. To them, antecedents were not necessarily related or significant. They viewed events as momentary intrusions in a timeless, boundless universe, a universe controlled by gods and demons who intervened continuously to see to it that their will was done. This view of existence made it possible for the ancients to believe in the heroes they created without undue concern for logic or physical realism. Their heroes could be gigantic in stature and possess superhuman strength. They had powers that violated the laws of nature, were often almost invincible, could transform themselves into eagles or serpents, shrink or grow at will, become invisible, wield super weapons with unimagined destructive capabilities, be transported by flying horses or recyclable goats, slay terrible monsters, cohabit with divinities and return from the dead, so long as the gods were with them.

We of the twenty-first century, although unable to believe in the literal reality of such heroes, nevertheless still dream our myths onward, clothing them in modern dress. Science and outer space provide us with our modern superheroes who fly as fast, are as strong, and undoubtedly fascinate us as much as Gilgamesh, Rustam, Rama, Achilles, Siegfried, and all of the other greats of long ago fascinated their audiences. We dream them onward, give them colorful costumes and pseudoscientific origins, but we no longer consider them real. Or do we? Perhaps we, too, secretly believe that one day we may look up into the sky and see the Man of Steel soaring above our Metropolis, or the signal calling for Batman to save the day. Perhaps we, too, long for the Lone Ranger to return to fight the growing forces of evil. Will they and the other heroes of our youth be up to the task? Will they be able to return us to the days of yore, when justice ruled, goodness was rewarded and evil punished? Who can say? Only the Shadow knows.

Chapter Notes

Chapter 1

1. Three men, Austen H. Layard, Hormuzd Rassam, and George Smith, found the bulk of the material in the ruins of two ancient libraries: the temple library of the god Nabu and the palace library of the king Ashurbanipal (668–633 B.C.). The location was Nineveh, the later capital of the Assyrian empire.

2. See Alexander Heidel, *The Gilgamesh Epic and Old Testament Parallels* (Chicago: The University of Chicago Press, 1946), 2–3.

3. An archetypal nature myth, which is not fully consistent from culture to culture. The Egyptians, for example, have deities for earth and sky, but in their mythology the earth deity is masculine, the god Geb, while the sky is represented by the goddess Nut.

4. This is the archetype of the "uroboros," or the "round," which is credited with being the source of all life. The uroboros often appears mythologically as the maternal womb or the union of male and female, the world parents in perpetual cohabitation.

5. Tablet I, column i.

6. Tablet I, column ii, lines 36, 39, 40, 41.

7. Tablet II, column iii, lines 15–18, 23–27.

8. In the Assyrian version, they met at a communal house. Enkidu blocked the door with his feet so that Gilgamesh could not enter.

9. We will see this archetype often, e.g., Achilles and Patroklos, Batman and Robin.

10. Tablet V, column IV, lines 15–19.

11. In the course of this work it will become very clear that the writers of the time had a negative attitude toward the female of the species. To women (goddesses are included under this rubric) are ascribed most of the evils of the world. The myth of Pandora is a graphic example: she of the box of evils, created by Zeus as a punishment for man.

12. Tablet 6.

13. Enkidu holds the bull by the nape of its neck and Gilgamesh delivers the coup de grace.

14. Tablet VIII, column ii, lines 18–22.

15. Homer, *The Iliad* (Chicago: University of Chicago Press, 1959), Book 18, 375–376.

16. Tablet X, column ii, lines 4–5.

17. Alexander Heidel's book, *The Gilgamesh Epic and Old Testament Parallels*, contains a thorough discussion of the Babylonian concept of death, 137–223.

18. Joseph Campbell, *The Hero with a Thousand Faces* (Cleveland, Ohio: Meridian Books), 381–391.

19. The ancients had a static, not a kinetic concept of history. Unlike moderns, who see life almost as a connected series of filmstrips, they saw no relationship between, or significance to, events of their past. They believed that all phenomena were simply momentary interventions of the gods, beyond their abilities to alter. Such a belief removed any responsibility man might have to seek an impersonal causation in the past or to take exceptional measures for the future. Time did not exist per se; the whole always was and always would be.

20. Carl Jung, *Psyche and Symbol* (New York: Doubleday), 129.

21. Tablet I, column i.

22. Otto Rank, *The Myth of the Birth of The Hero*, trans. F. Robbins and S.E. Jellife (New York: Vintage Books, 1964), 65. A strikingly similar archetypal pattern has been found to exist in American Native hero mythology. Katherine Spencer writes about this in her work *Mythology and Values,* Memoir 48 (Philadelphia: American Folklore Society, 1957), 2.

23. Moses, Romulus and Remus, Paris, Zal, and even Zeus himself are but a few others who were abandoned at birth for one reason or another.

24. Henry A. Murray, *Myth and Mythmaking* (New York: George Braziller, 1960), 51.

25. This archetype is also used in nonheroic literature. A case in point is Franz Kafka's *The Metamorphosis*. Of course, many fables and fairy tales are replete with examples of transformation from human to animal form and vice versa.

26. In Genesis the flood is the result of human sin, but in the case of the Gilgamesh myth the reason for the deluge seems frivolous. The two reasons we find in the tablets are (1) divine caprice and (2) Enlil's desire to eliminate human beings because they were making too much noise and disturbing his sleep. The serpent who steals the flower of immortality from Gilgamesh is not presented as evil, as is his cousin in Genesis, but is equally responsible for depriving humanity of enjoying eternal life on earth.

27. Enkidu is not alone in being unable to follow the rules for a safe return. In the Greek myth, Orpheus loses Eurydice because he cannot keep himself from looking back at her as they ascend, the one stipulation made by the goddess Persephone.

Chapter 2

1. The poem consists of 60,000 couplets, an astounding accomplishment. There are two beautiful copies of the work in New York City's Columbia University.

2. J.C.E. Bowen, ed., *Poems from the Persian* (Philadelphia: Richard Clay), 1964, 41.

3. Firdowsi, *The Epic of the Kings*, trans. Reuben Levy (Chicago: University of Chicago Press, 1967), 35.

4. An example of the questions posed to him: "What is the meadow where a fierce reaper cuts ripe and withered grass alike, and hears no cry of despair?" The answer: "Time."

5. Julian Hawthorne, ed., *The World's Great Classics: Persian Literature: The Shah Nameh* (London and New York: Colonial Press, 1900), 80.

6. That is to say, Batmobile, Black Beauty (Green Hornet), Kitt (the television series *Knight Rider*), Wonder Woman's invisible plane, Airwolf (TV series), etc.

7. See chapter I, p. 15.

8. See note 4, Chapter II.

9. See Thomas Bullfinch, *Mythology* (New York: Dell, 1964), 295.

10. In Greek mythology, Cronus was assisted by his mother, Gaea, who was upset because her husband/son, Uranus, buried her children back within her after their births to keep them from seeing the light of day (so they wouldn't challenge his authority). In fact, it was she who provided the sickle with which Cronus unmanned his father. The time symbolism here is obvious. Similarly, Zeus' mother, Rhea, aided him in defeating her husband/brother, who swallowed all of her children as they were born in order to nullify the prophecy that a son would supplant him as the leader of the gods. While these archetypes are applied to the gods in these instances, the fact is that the Greek gods (and others) were humanized to the extent that they greatly resemble the superheroes; one may even think of them as the super-superheroes of mythology.

11. The Simurgh saved him from being defeated by Sohrab; the "Creator" renewed his strength to enable him to defeat Esfandiyar; the king of Kabul relented when he saw Rustam dying. He called for a magic elixir to be administered to the hero's wounds, but Rustam rejected the offer with scorn.

Chapter 3

1. The literal translation of Bhagavadgita is "The Lord's Song." There have been those who look at the work as a permit for murder, while others see it as a blueprint for the good. Krishna is attempting to convince Arjuna that he must fight his relatives and friends to restore order, since that is not only the responsibility of a prince and a warrior but also that of a righteous man.

2 *Bhagavad-Gita as It Is*, trans. A.C. Bhaktivedanta Swami Prabhupada (Los Angeles: Bhaktivedanta Book Trust, 1976), 172–173.

3. Indian and Persian mythology are closely connected. Rustam was said to have ruled India in 1072 B.C., Darius from 521 to 485 B.C.

4. Ravana had earned Brahma's consideration by doing penance for thousands of years. During this period, he sacrificed one of his ten heads every thousand years. This seems to have impressed Brahma so much that he granted him the gift of indestructibility. Ravana had requested immortality, but Brahma reminded him that the law of existence was that whoever is born must die.

5. Veronica Ions, *Indian Mythology* (London: Paul Hamlyn, 1967), 115.

6. Some accounts put the actual number of wives that he had at above three hundred fifty.

7. Before the birth of Rama, for a long time Dasaratha had tried vainly to sire an heir. One of the methods he employed to break this dry spell was to sacrifice a horse. It seems to have worked as well as some of our fertility drugs.

8. Sita was the incarnation of Lakshmi, Visnu's wife.

9. Valmiki and Anonymou, *The Ramayana and The Mahabarata*. Trans. Romesh C. Dutt (London: J.M. Dent & Sons, 1963), 4.

10. There are scholars who believe that Laksmana's interest in Sita was more than brotherly. Even Sita indicated at one point that she had her doubts about her brother-in-law. When Rama went out to catch the enchanted deer, he ordered Laksmana not to leave Sita's side. After Rama mortally wounded it, however, the deer assumed his voice and cried out for Laksmana to help him. The latter suspected that it was a trick and refused to go, but Sita made him change his mind by insinuating that he wanted to stay there with her only so that he could possess her after his brother died.

11. In the work *Nose*, by the great nineteenth century Russian writer Nikolai Gogol, a character named Kovalev wakes up one morning to learn that his nose is gone.

12. Mareecha was actually Ravana's uncle. He tried in vain to get out of this assignment since he knew that Rama would kill him when he discovered the truth. Finally, Ravana warned him that if he did not do it, he would save Rama the trouble and kill him himself. Mareecha decided that it would be better to be killed by an enemy than by a nephew, and so gave in to Ravana's demands.

13. Jatayu was an incarnation of Vishnu's horse, Garuda.

14. What Rama did not know was that Ravana had already had bad luck with monkeys. At one time he had tried to assault the powerful monkey Vali, but the latter simply picked him up and carried him around under his arm. Three men, Austen H. Layard, Hormuzd Rassam, and George Smith, found the bulk of the material in the ruins of two ancient libraries: the temple library of the god Nabu and the palace library of the king Ashurbanipal (668–633 B.C.). The location was Nineveh, the later capital of the Assyrian empire.

15. Vibhishana, who was as good as Ravana was evil, reminded Ravana that it was improper to kill a messenger. As evil as he was, Ravana did adhere to certain rules.

16. Ravana was able to gain favor from Brahma by sacrificing nine of his original ten heads. A third brother, Vibhishana, also took part in this period of penance. He was the moral opposite of the other two, however, and was granted his request that he never be allowed "...to swerve from righteousness even under the most trying circumstances."

17. There is another version to this myth that tells of a battle between the thunder god, Indra, and Kumbhakarna. It was going so badly for Indra at one point that Brahma was forced to intervene. He commanded that Kumbhakarna sleep for six months at a time and awake for only one day thereafter.

18. He demoralized the monkeys at one point by creating a phantom Sita and killing her before their horrified eyes.

19. R.K. Narayan, *Gods, Demons and Others* (New York: Viking Press, 1964), 125.

20. J.L. Brockington, *Righteous Rama: The Evolution of an Epic* (Oxford Press: Bombay, 1984), 163.

21. For the most part, mythology has an anti-female bias. When one adds to this the fact that Indian society had less than an enlightened attitude toward its women, Rama's actions toward his wife are understandable.

22. There is a modern Japanese superhero of the comics named "Rapeman," who follows in his Babylonian prototype's footsteps.

23. See Chapter V: The Trojan War.

24. Narayan, 124.

25. Wendy Doniger O'Flaherty, *The Origins of Evil in Hindu Mythology* (Berkeley: University of California Press, 1976), 65.

26. Gilgamesh demonstrated this when his partner, Enkidu, died. His life thereafter was barren. And Rama stated directly that Laksmana was the only one in his life who was irreplaceable.

27. See Chapter I.

28. Heracles, Theseus, Odysseus and Leminkäinen, to name a few.

Chapter 4

1. Dennis Neville was replaced by Sheldon Moldoff, who drew Hawkman from late 1940 to 1945. Towards the end of 1944, however, he was assisted by Joseph Kubert, who then became the chief illustrator until the first demise of the strip in 1949. Except for several episodes during the period from 1947 to 1949 that were written by Robert Kanigher, Fox was the primary writer.

2. For a more thorough discussion of Hawkman see *The World Encyclopedia of Comics*, edited by Maurice Horn (New York, Chelsea House Publishers, 1976), 307–308. A more up to date history is on the internet: http://www.en.wikipedia.org/wiki/Hawkman/.

3. Moses was said to have studied at the temple school in Heliopolis, training ground for the elite Egyptian priest corps, considered among the most learned in the world.

4. *The Book of the Dead*, trans. E.A. Wallis Budge (New York: University Books, 1960), 99.

5. In the tomb of Pharaoh Thutmosis III there are 740 gods listed.

6. *New Larousse Encyclopedia of Mythology*, trans. Richard Aldington and Delano Ames (London: Hamlyn, 1974), 11.

7. The reason for Ra's disapproval of the marriage between his children is not as clear as one might assume. Since it was the rule rather than the exception for brothers and sisters to marry, it does not seem that incest was at the root of his attitude.

8. The Egyptians divided their year into thirty-six sections of ten days each, the remaining five days being counted separately. These five days were designated as the birthdays of the major gods: Osiris on the first day, the elder Horus on the second, Seth on the third, Isis on the fourth and Nephthys on the fifth.

9. Norma Lorre Goodrich, *The Ancient Myths* (New York: Mentor Books, 1960), 28.

10. *Plutarch's Writings: Miscellanies,* ed. A.H. Clough and William W. Goodwin (New York: Little, Brown, 1909), p. 75.

11. To this day, redheads are considered bad luck by many Egyptians.

12. The former was an undertaker on the old Fred Allen radio program. The latter was the leading character in a more recent television series by the same name.

13. According to Plutarch, during her stay in Phoenicia, Isis agreed to become nursemaid to King Malcander's and Queen Astarte's baby. She nursed it with her finger, and every evening would put the baby over a flame so as to make it immortal. The queen happened to see her holding it over a flame one evening and began to shriek, thus robbing her baby of immortality.

14. The Egyptian god of wisdom. He was also a moon god, a patron of science and literature, the god of inventions, and spokesman for and official record keeper of the gods. Thoth is portrayed with the head of an Ibis, the sacred bird of Egypt.

15. Kriemhild personally exacts revenge on her husband's murderer.

16, Horus ruled as Pharaoh and had four sons. Due to him, the hawk became a protected species in Egypt; anyone who dared to kill one and was caught was punished by death.

17. Hephaestos was crippled when Zeus threw him from Mt. Olympus for siding with Hera during a marital dispute. In the *Iliad*, Zeus is deceived by Hera; Aphrodite and Ares are wounded by Diomedes (aided by Athena), and there is a constant undertone of bickering between those divinities who support the Trojan side and those who favor the Greeks.

18. Two recent television series come immediately to mind: *Knight Rider* and *Airwolf*. In the former, the automobile (named Kitt) performed the more spectacular feats, while the helicopter after which the show was named is the true hero in the latter. Such popular modern superheroes as Batman and James Bond also rely heavily on "gadgets" to achieve their goals. The fact is that superheroes mirror the times from which they come. One need only review the media coverage of modern warfare to see that "smart" bombs and guided missiles are given more credit for victories than the warriors.

Chapter 5

1. Who has not heard of an Oedipal or Elektra complex, an Achilles heel, the ill-fated Titanic, Herculon, Titanium, aphrodisiacs, Poseidon missiles, Saturn rockets, Trident toothpaste, the Olympic games — the list is endless.

2. One wonders how she was able to bring Kronus to her surface, and why she did not do the same with all of the other Titans.

3. Hesiod, *The Poems of Hesiod*, trans. R.M. Frazer (Norman: University of Oklahoma Press, 1983), 36.

4. The Erinnyes, or their Roman counterparts, the Furies, were the feared goddesses of vengeance. Their role was to punish any transgression against the natural order, both on earth and after death. Although their number was not always fixed, Euripides set it at three: Allecto (she who never rests), Tisiphone (avenger of murder) and Megaera (the jealous one).

5. A minor myth names Gaea the creatress of man, while still another gives Epimetheus credit. In Ovid's *Metamorphosis*, the human race was destroyed by Zeus, who had grown tired of man's wicked ways. The only survivor was Deucalion (son of Prometheus) and his wife, Pyrrha (daughter of Epimetheus). With the aid of their grandmother, Themis, the two survivors re-created the human race (Book I).

6. The creation of woman is also discussed in Hesiod's *Theogeny* (lines 570ff) but not in such detail.

7. Athena, the goddess of "just" wars and wisdom, was

one of the super virgin goddesses of Greek mythology. (Artemis was the other.) Athena's birth was miraculous: Zeus had been suffering from severe headaches and so he went to his son, Hephaestos. The latter dealt him such a hard blow on the head that his head split open and Athena emerged, full grown and in shining armor. Another version is that she was the daughter of Zeus and his first wife, Metis. Gaea warned Zeus that a child of Metis would surpass him in wisdom and become leader of the gods, and so he swallowed her whole, thus absorbing all of her wisdom. In this version, too, Athena was born from Zeus' head. We have already discussed the birth of Aphrodite from the severed genitals of Uranus; Homer's version designates her the daughter of Zeus and Dione, an ancient sky-goddess.

8. The standard number is nine: Calliope (epic poetry), Clio (history), Erato (love poetry), Euterpe (tragedy and flute playing), Melpomene (also tragedy and lyre playing, Terpsichore (choral dancing), Polyhymnia (sacred music and dancing), Thalia (comedy) and Urania (astronomy).

9. The three fates were Clotho, who spun out the thread of a person's life; Lachesis, who measured the length of the thread; Atropos, who cut the thread at the appropriate time.

10. The son of Zeus and Semele, a princess of Thebes. Zeus came to her in human form and impregnated her. When Hera found out, she was furious. She went to Semele disguised as an old woman and tricked the latter into persuading Zeus to appear to her in his true form. Finally, Zeus gave in and did as requested. The sight of the king of the gods was too much for her; she was reduced to ashes. Zeus acted quickly to save the fetus, which he sewed into his thigh until it could come to term. Thus, Dionysus, the god of the orgy, was appropriately born from Zeus' thigh.

11. Zeus made love to the Spartan princess Leda in the form of a swan. Leda later produced Helen, Castor and Pollux. This myth has been the theme of countless paintings.

12. Paris appeared one year at the funeral games that Priam held annually to celebrate his supposed death. Paris was so skilled in the various contests that he defeated everyone, including Hector. Envious, the losers plotted Paris' murder, but Cassandra recognized him as the brother they thought was dead and thus made the reconciliation possible.

13. Homer, *The Homeric Hymns*, trans. Apostolos N. Athanassakis (Baltimore: Johns Hopkins University Press, 1976), 31.

14. This does not appear in the *Iliad*. As could be expected, Helen had no lack of suitors, including Achilles and Odysseus. Odysseus convinced Helen's father, Tyndarios, that it would be wise to have all of the suitors swear that if Helen ever were abducted they would come together to aid her husband, whoever he might be, in the quest to recover her.

15. Palamedes is often listed as the inventor of the alphabet and the system of weights and measures. Odysseus respected and even envied his brilliance.

16. It has never been established that there was any one major Trojan War; the most educated thinking today is that there were many economically motivated clashes between the Greeks and Trojans. If, indeed, one of these far overshadowed the other, the time was probably somewhere between 1334 B.C. and 1150 B.C.

17. Homer, *The Iliad*, trans. Richmond Lattimore (Chicago: University of Chicago Press, 1959), 63, lines 149–151.

18. Zeus sends Thetis down with the order that Achilles allow Priam to retrieve Hector's body and give it proper funeral rites.

19. Homer goes out of his way to present Thersites as an unpleasant character. His physical description borders on caricature: "This was the ugliest man who came beneath Ilion. He was/ bandy-legged and went lame of one foot, with shoulders/ stooped and drawn together over his chest, and above this/ his skull went up to a point with the wool grown sparsely upon it" (82, lines 216–219).

20. Without Athena in the chariot next to him, guiding his spear hand, Diomedes would not have been able to wound both Aphrodite and Ares. That the gods were able to deceive even each other is evident in this scene: Ares was unable to see Athena because she was wearing the "helm of Death," the magic helmet of Hades that rendered the wearer invisible.

21. The name of an American program during the golden age of radio. Don Ameche and Francis Langford portrayed a married couple whose sole form of communication was bickering. It is no surprise that the Olympian number one couple did not get along that well. According to one account, Zeus got Hera to marry him only by means of forcible rape, which was to become his trademark in later relationships with goddesses and human females who caught his fancy.

22. She told Aphrodite that she needed it for Tethys, who has not slept with her husband, Okeanos, for quite some time because of an argument. The wearer of this bra-like garment (sometimes referred to in translation as a girdle) became irresistible.

23. Of course, from a realistic standpoint it seems improbable that the two never fought each other before. After all, the Greeks had already been there for ten years.

24. As we have seen, Paris satisfied this archetype.

25. The *destructive female archetype* scenario reads like this: Eris initiated the tragic course of events by playing on the pride of Hera, Athena and Aphrodite. As a result of the beauty contest, Helen was abducted, which led to the war in which the captivity of Chyrseis fostered the demand that Briseis be returned, which caused Achilles to withdraw from the battlefield, thus provoking the near destruction of the Greek armies, the ensuing death of Patroklos, and the final clash that sees Hector killed.

26. There are several versions of Achilles' death. The most popular is that Paris shot him in his vulnerable heel. (His mother had dipped him in the river Styx, holding him by the heel.) A second myth has Apollo, disguised as Paris, fire the fatal arrow. Yet a third version has Achilles betrayed by Polyxena, daughter of Priam and Hekuba. In this myth, Achilles has secretly entered Troy and is deceived by the young princess into telling where his vulnerable spot is. Polyxena then passes the information on to Paris, who either shoots or stabs him in the heel.

27. There were those who believed that the *Iliad* and the *Odyssey* were written by different authors, and even some who say that there was no Homer. Since we are dealing with mythology, though, a mythical Homer seems as valid as the material he presented.

28. Before Agamemnon was able to get the Greek expeditionary force moving from the port of Aulis, he had to appease the goddess Artemis. It seems that he had killed one of her sacred stags during an earlier hunting trip. Clytemnestra never forgave him for offering up their eldest daughter, Iphigenie, as a sacrifice.

29. Agamemnon sent out spies to learn whom the Trojans considered a greater hero, Ajax or Odysseus. The spies overheard a group of young girls praising Odysseus

and based their report on that conversation. In addition, Agamemnon polled his own leaders, who all cast their vote for the more popular Odysseus.

30. Homer, *The Odyssey,* trans. S.H. Butcher and A. Lang (New York: Modern Library, 1950), 1.

31. Ino had at one time been mortal. Due to a fit of madness, her husband, Athamas, chased her and their infant son, Melicertes, to a cliff, from which she and the boy threw themselves. They were rescued by a passing dolphin and transformed into divinities.

32. The use of drugs abounds in *The Odyssey.* Alcohol (wine) flows freely at all times, but it is by far not the only chemical crutch that is used. When Telemachus visited Helen in Sparta, the first thing she did was to supply them all with a super tranquilizer (Odyssey 51); the episode in which Odysseus' men strayed onto the island of the Lotus Eaters (128) is also an example of "hard" drug usage. Suffice it to say, the modern era was not the first in which humans tried to escape reality by using drugs.

33. Akin to souls.

34. Both Heracles and Agamemnon give him an account of their bloody deaths. Ajax is still brooding over the fact that Odysseus was awarded Achilles' armor and refused to speak to him. The list of the others he encounters during his brief visit to the Underworld reads like a Who's Who of Greek mythology.

35. He did spare the minstrel, Phemius, and his son's former tutor, Medon. This could be less a proof of Odysseus' leniency than that of Homer's bias for men of learning.

36. While in the court of King Alcinous in Phaeacia he was moved to tears when he heard the local minstrel sing the story of the Trojan Horse and the fall of Troy.

37. Mark Morford points out in his work, *Classical Mythology,* that it is very difficult to distinguish between Heracles the man and Heracles the god, since a great deal of ambiguity exists in the various myths associated with him. The historian, Herodotus, saw him as two separate entities: Heracles the Greek hero, and Heracles one of the twelve ancient gods of Egypt (332–336).

38. There are many myths connected with Tiresias. One of the most popular was that Hera blinded him for siding with Zeus in an argument between himself and Hera. He asserted, as Zeus had, that women enjoyed sex more than men (he had been a woman for a short time). Another myth has Athene blind him because he saw her bathing in the nude. At any rate, Zeus gave him the gift of insight and prophecy to compensate for his loss of physical vision.

39. An extremely interesting study of the moral and psychological implications of this entire episode is to be found in the work *Amphitryon* by the nineteenth century German writer, Heinrich von Kleist. The question of whether Alcmene was guilty of adultery in having willingly slept with Zeus (some critics insist that she must have realized that something was out of the ordinary) is one that cannot be answered with any certainty.

40. Another version has Hera going to Eileithyia, who was often given credit for being the goddess in charge of birth and requesting a delay in the birth of Heracles.

41. A second version has him sleeping with the fifty girls on consecutive nights, while yet a third claims that he slept with only forty-nine, the fiftieth having chosen to remain a virgin so that she could become a priestess. Regardless of which version one accepts, one must admit that it was a remarkable performance. From these unions, the daughters of King Thespius bore fifty-one sons. (Two gave birth to twins.)

42. One can also view Achilles' or Aeneas' unique armor as costumes.

43. For the sixth labor, Heracles had to kill a flock of murderous birds, and for the seventh capture a bull and bring it back to Eurystheus. Nothing significant transpired during both operations.

44. In the Amazon society, women were in charge of the government and the military. Captive males were used to perform all the household and other menial chores, and as studs to keep the population stable. The arms and legs of infant boys were broken to prevent them from causing trouble. It is only in later myths that the Amazons removed one breast to be better able to fire their arrows.

45. Hera had entrusted the care of the apples to the Hesperides, daughters of Atlas, but since they began to help themselves to the apples instead of guarding them, Hera gave the job to Ladon.

46. Graves provides an excellent short summary and bibliography in his work *The Greek Myths* 2:158–200.

47. He gave his first wife to his nephew/sidekick, Iolaus.

48. The World Encyclopedia of Comics, 254. For a full discussion of the Flash see http:www.//my.execpc.com/-icicle/GAFLASH.html.

49. "Wonder Woman Revisited," *Ms.* (July 1972), 55.

50. Phyllis Chesler, "An Interpretive Essay," in *Wonder Woman* (New York: Bonanza Books, 1969), unpaginated.

51. Phyllis Chesler, ed. *Wonder Woman* (New York: Bonanza Books, 1969). See the introduction by Gloria Steinem (unpaginated).

52. The original short skirt was replaced by skin tight shorts; she began to wear more lipstick and rouge in the sixties and sported the latest hair styles.

53. Even Penthesilea, the great Amazon who was said to have defeated Achilles in single combat, pales next to Wonder Woman. Had Penthesilea had the advantage of technology, however, it might have been quite a different story.

Chapter 6

1. They also incorporated the characteristics of Egyptian, Persian, Syrian, and Celtic divinities into their state religion, but the primary influence was Greek.

2. Nonetheless, he was made one of the chief gods by Augustus, who had a temple built for him on the Palatine.

3. The original Roman calendar began on March 1. In 153 it was changed to the present configuration.

4. Alba Longa was founded by Aeneas' son, Ascanius.

5. The wolf and the woodpecker were animals sacred to Mars.

6. The Sabines, a neighboring tribe, figured prominently in the development of Rome. When Romulus had difficulty attracting women to his new city, he invited the Sabines to the circus games and had all the unmarried Sabine women seized. In the ensuing war, Romulus was on the verge of defeat, but the Sabine women themselves intervened to put an end to the war. Thereafter, the Sabines moved to Rome and became an integral part of the new society.

7. See Chapter I, pp. 14–17.

8. See Chapter II, note 6.

9. The so-called Golden Age is actually divided into two major periods: the Ciceronian (106–63 B.C.) and the Augustan (63 B.C.–A.D. 14). The earlier period, marked

by the great orations of Cicero, was characterized by independent, republican ideas, the latter by imperial, conservative thinking.

10. Virgil, *The Aeneid,* trans. Allen Mandelbaum (New York: Bantam, 1972), 16 (Book I, lines 601–610).

11. Juno and Venus had opposite reasons for their wish to unite Aeneas and Dido. Juno wanted to keep Aeneas from founding Rome, Venus to protect him.

12. Thus setting up the ongoing enmity between Rome and Carthage that culminated in the destruction of the latter city by Rome in 146 B.C.

13. Achises asked for and was given what he considered an omen: sudden thunder and a shooting star pointing out their course.

14. The exact origin and meaning of "Sibyl" is uncertain. In Roman mythology there were as many as ten major oracles who were referred to as "Sibyl," the Sibyl of Cumae being the most famous. In 1932, the actual chamber of the Cumaen Sibyl was discovered at Mount Cuma, in the vicinity of Naples.

15. Roman name for Persephone, the wife of Pluto (Hades) and queen of the Underworld.

16. Those who were not buried properly had to wait for one hundred years before they could be granted the trip across.

17. Aeneas' encounter with Dido is parallel to that of Odysseus and Ajax. This is but one of the scenes "borrowed" and reshaped by the Roman poet.

18. Again, a most similar scene to the one in *The Odyssey* where Odysseus attempts to embrace his mother's shade.

19. Vulcan must have been quite liberal when it came to his wife's infidelities. After all, Aeneas was the product of one of Venus' "dalliances."

Chapter 7

1. It is called the *Prose Edda* to distinguish it from a collection of poems which bears the same name.

2. Saxo's work, *Gesta Danorum,* is a sixteen volume history of the Danes which, although rich in legend, mythology and religion, lacks all objectivity because it has the glorification of the Danes as its primary goal. Saxo was one of those who considered those beings who are referred to as the ancient Germanic gods to be nothing more than shrewd men who were able to delude the populace into thinking them gods.

3. That is to say, the blood of Ymir = the ocean.

4. Another version is that Niflheim and Muspellsheim were regions to the north and south of the Ginungagap. Muspellsheim had rivers containing a bitter poison that gradually solidified and began to fill up the Ginungagap. The warm air from Muspellsheim blew north and melted the ice blocks, forming Ymir.

5. The Frost Giants were a warlike race who grew under the left arm of Ymir. For their sake, one hopes that Ymir followed a strict regimen of personal hygiene.

6. The two that escaped, Bergelmir and his wife, went on to propagate a new race of giants.

7. Petre-Turville, E.O.G., *Myth and Religion of the North* (New York: Holt, Rinehart and Winston, 1964), 33. (See note 2.)

8. The number of the Aesir is uncertain, ranging from twelve to fourteen, depending on the source.

9. Interestingly enough, there was gender segregation in Asgard. The gods lived in a mansion called Gladsheim, while the goddesses occupied one by the name of Vingolf.

10. He was known among that group as Wotan or Woden (from the German word wüten = to rage). The Germanic peoples believed that thunder was the sound of Wotan's troop of dead warriors riding across the sky.

11. Similarly, the worshipers of Zeus credited him with the creation of man and the universe, although these were late additions to his list of accomplishments.

12. According to some accounts, the ancient Germanic peoples identified him with the Roman god Mercury, god of commerce, inventor of the arts, guide of travelers, and supreme in the area of commerce.

13. The Valkyries were visible only to those who were destined to fall in battle. In addition to their duty of escorting the dead heroes to Valhalla, these mounted Amazons often fought furiously in the battles on one side or the other.

14. This power of Odin's was not emphasized. Thor was better known as the god of storms and wind.

15. The so-called *Merserberger Zaubersprüche,* or "Merseberg Incantations," are examples. These two incantations, in clumsy alliterative verse, give a glimpse of the Germanic "Idisi," the equivalent of the Valkyries. The first incantation is a formula for breaking one's chains when imprisoned by an enemy, the second a charm that was used by Wodan to cure Balder's horse of lameness. Anyone who could recite it could do the same should his horse go lame.

16. See Petre, 42–43, for a detailed discussion of the similarities between what Jesus suffered at Cavalry and this experience of Odin.

17. Thursday was named after Thor. In German, the word for Thursday is "Donnerstag" (the day of thunder), after Donar. In Swedish Thursday is "Thorsday," in Danish Torsdag.

18. John Arnott MacCulloch, *The Mythology of All Races,* vol. 2 (Boston: Marshall Jones, 1929), 70.

19. Another myth tells that Mjöllnir was made from a piece of a meteorite.

20. In Snorri's *Edda,* Odin is Thor's father. He did not feel that Magni deserved to have such a gift because he was Thor's son by a giantess, Jarnsaxa. Apparently, Thor's hatred of giants did not prevent him from satisfying his lust with one of their females from time to time.

21. The explanation for this seems to be that the magical powers of the hammer worked only for Thor. Thus the theft was aimed at depriving Thor of the weapon rather than securing it for use against the Aesir.

22. The necklace in question was no ordinary one. It had been made by four dwarves and was so beautiful that Freyja consented to sleep with each one of them, the price they had set for it.

23. As in the myth where Loki cut off all of Sif's hair. Thor forced Loki to get the dwarves to replace the stolen hair with gold locks that actually grew.

24. It is no accident that in Mario Puzo's novel *The Godfather* the most loyal subject of Don Corleone was the consigliore named Hagen.

25. Anonymous, *The Nibelungenlied,* trans. A.T. Hatto (Middlesex: Bantam Books, 1970), 49.

26. In mythology, an Amazon's loss of virginity resulted in a loss of strength.

27. Since their father was dead, as the eldest brother this was his right.

28. Because a woman was not considered important enough a target of vengeance, Hagen had to direct his anger at Siegfried.

29. The battle in question was a sham. Gunther had seen to it that false reports of an enemy declaration of war

were delivered by his messengers so as to get Siegfried to offer his assistance.

30. J.G. Robertson, *A History of German Literature* (Edinburgh: William Blackwood & Sons, 1953), 78.

31. The Germans call such behavior *Schicksalsbereitschaft*, the readiness to give oneself over to one's fate. Hagen went even further at one point; he burned the ferry which could have taken them back home. His only concern at that point was that his king not disgrace the crown by any cowardly retreat.

32. At the beginning of the battle, Hagen cruelly kills the only son of Etzel and Kriemhild. He throws the boy's head on the table before the stunned couple.

33. Hagen almost killed Hildebrand at one point. Hildebrand barely managed to escape death by putting his shield on his back and running away.

Chapter 8

1. See Superman origin story, page 162.

2. Philip Wylie, *Gladiator* (CT: Hyperion Press, 1974), unpaginated foreword.

3. Philip Wylie, *Gladiator* (New York: Lancer Books, 1958), 5. (All future quotes will be from the Lancer edition of *Gladiator*.)

4. He was prepared to fly a plane into Germany, kill the emperor and his entire general staff and pull the city of Berlin apart with his bare hands.

5. Voltaire wrote the story *Micromegas* in that year. It was about a visitor from another planet.

6. The initial reason for Superman's dual identity was that he was a fugitive from the police, having taken the law into his own hands in the course of his struggle against the criminal element. This was also the case with Batman and other such American superheroes of that period.

7. The Nazi government recognized what they were up against and banned *Superman* comic books in the Third Reich. Strangely enough, however, Superman remained a favorite of Emperor Hirohito of Japan even after the Man of Steel began wreaking havoc on the armed forces of the Japanese Empire.

8. The three themes he refers to are the visitor from another planet, the superhuman being, and the dual identity.

9. As has already been pointed out, Heracles' costume was also indestructible, since it was made from the skin of the invulnerable Nimean Lion.

10. The idea of super vision goes back as far as ancient Greece, where at least one character (Lynkeus) had the ability to see things that were underground.

11. Kryptonite was first mentioned on the Superman radio program. Later it became a standard theme of the comic books and films. Eventually, different hues of kryptonite were credited with the power to produce varied deleterious effects on the Man of Steel.

12. Steranko places the number at 18, while E. Nelson Bridewell asserts that there were 17: *Superman: From the Thirties to the Seventies* (New York: Crown, 1972), 11.

13. This villain's name changed later (probably as the result of a typist's error) to Mxyzptlk.

14. In 1953, Superman and Batman appeared together (*Superman* #76), sharing the knowledge of each other's secret identities as they battled evil. They later began to operate as a team in *World's Finest Comics* #71.

15. Reruns of this series are still shown on television today.

16. Supergirl did not come in a rocket ship, but on a large fragment of the planet that had remained intact after the planet exploded.

17. The "new" Superman has more limited powers. When he performs his superhuman feats of strength, he often feels the effects. His alter-ego, Clark Kent, has gained confidence and respectability, and is now a feature writer who writes novels and works out on a Nautilus machine in his spare time. Lois Lane also has changed with the times. She is much more independent and career oriented, and does not depend on Superman's attentions to feel fulfilled.

18. This has changed in the television series just mentioned.

19. During the 1950s, there was a time when the relationship between Lois and Clark changed into a romantic one. They even married. This, however, happened only in the newspaper strip and was temporary. The author escaped from the situation by declaring that the entire episode had been nothing more than a dream. From time to time in the comic book version (at present Lois and Superman are married), and more recently in the films, there have been short-lived attempts to bring Lois Lane and Superman together in something more than a platonic relationship. Ultimately, however, the story reverts to the original dilemma.

20. Larry Niven, *All the Myriad Ways* (New York: Ballantine Books, n.d.).

21. Leslie Fiedler, "Up, up and away — the rise and fall of comic books," *The New York Times Book Review*, September 5, 1976.

22. In the original origin story Mrs. Kent's name was Mary. They have also been referred to as Eben and Sarah (*Superman from the Thirties to the Seventies*, 11).

23. Although in the 1978 Superman film he does see and hear his father's electronic message while in his "Fortress of Solitude."

24. In the 1978 film *Superman I*. He reversed time by flying faster than the speed of light, and brought Lois Lane, who had died when her car was buried by a landslide, back to life.

25. Of course, Superwoman could have survived such a mating, but she is a relative. Were Superman an Egyptian hero this would not be taboo, but a romantic alliance between the two Kryptonians would not be in keeping with the American standards of morality. One wonders why the writers never considered pairing the Man of Steel with Mary Marvel.

26. Actually, Captain Marvel had record sales in the period directly following the war. For a detailed account of the legal proceedings in the copyright infringement suit see Steranko's *History of Comics 2*, 17 and 20–21.

27. Otto Binder, the chief author of the Marvel series, stated the following during the time of the litigation: "This I can state categorically — not one story idea was ever 'lifted' from Superman." He went on to assert that when the stories of the two superheroes were compared, more of Superman's adventures seemed to be copied from Captain Marvel than the reverse. He attributed this to coincidence. We know better. Archetypes are not coincidental; they are universal.

28. Ibac was another acronym, albeit an evil one: **I**van the Terrible (terror); the **B**orgia family (cunning); **A**ttila the Hun (fierceness); and **C**aligula (cruelty).

29. Republic came out with a Captain Marvel serial in 1941. To this day it is considered one of the finest superhero film productions of all time.

30. *Captain Marvel* #1, published by Country Wide Comics in April, 1966.

31. She appeared in the December, 1942 issue of *Captain Marvel Adventures* #18. She soon became a regular in *Wow* comics, finally getting her own book in 1945. For whatever reason, the *Mary Marvel* series (as well as *Wow*) was cancelled in 1948. She did continue to appear in *The Marvel Family* until 1953, and was also part of the Marvelous revival in 1973.

32. In the Captain Marvel saga, the letters in the word SHAZAM stood for **S**olomon (wisdom), **H**ercules (strength), **A**tlas (stamina), **Z**eus (power), **A**chilles (courage), **M**ercury (speed). In Mary's case the letters stood for **S**ilena (grace), **H**ippolyta (strength), **A**riadne (skill), **Z**ephyrus (fleetness), **A**urora (beauty), **M**inerva (wisdom).

33. This, as we know, is not unprecedented in mythology. The Greek goddess Athena was born, fully grown, from Zeus' head. It is interesting to note that the three Marvels come into being via a thunderbolt, a medium under the control of Zeus.

34. That the Batson twins become the Marvel brother and sister team does not contradict this contention. Although the authors might not have had it in mind, they could have been chosen as hosts simply because they were parallel counterparts.

35. We will have to view metaphorically the fact that, although he sees and knows everything, Shazam does not seem to be clever enough to get out from under the huge granite slab before it comes crashing down. His time was apparently up.

36. The rotund Uncle Marvel had no super powers, but because of his good nature and burning desire to be one of them, the superhero Marvels pretended not to know that he was a fake. He wore a version of the Captain Marvel costume under his clothes, which could be unzipped very quickly to create the illusion that he was metamorphosing. He usually did this under the cover of the lightning bolt called down by Billy, Mary or Freddie when they uttered their respective magic words.

37. The original shield had three stars and was triangular in shape. This developed quickly into a round, one-starred version.

38. In a later episode, President Franklin Roosevelt personally replaces this shield with one made of iron, vibranium and a secret alloy. This new shield has a single star and is indestructible. No longer simply a defensive weapon, the shield is light enough to be hurled at an enemy and, like the Hammer of Thor, it has a boomerang quality: it returns to Captain America's hand after demolishing the target.

Chapter 9

1. The *Kalevala* has since been translated into virtually every major language. It is the most important single source of Finish mythology. The edition used for this study is W.F. Kirby's translation: *Kalevala*, trans. W.F. Kirby (London: Athlone Press, 1985).

2. The eagle was grateful to Väinämöinen for having left a birch tree standing so that the eagle and its feathered friends could rest and nest.

3. Ukko was often identified with Thor. Missionaries later used his name to refer to the Christian God.

4. A parallel to Dorothy's journey to Oz in the funnel of a tornado.

5. This is similar to the Greek myth of the wedding celebration of Peleus and Thetis, from which Eris, the goddess of discord, was excluded.

6. The Sampo had roots that extended nine fathoms below the earth.

7. Apparently, Väinämöinen had forgotten that Lemínkäinen was the creator of the Sampo.

8. *Mandrake the Magician* first appeared in 1934, written by Lee Falk and drawn by Phil Davis. It began as a daily strip and later became a Sunday offering (February 1935). *Mandrake* inspired a great number of imitators, both in the comic pages and in comic books.

Chapter 10

1. In the Egyptian and Norse myths already recounted, the gods served as superheroes although they were mortal and quite restricted in their powers. A very small number of modern superheroes also can claim divine ancestry, including Captain Marvel and Wonder Woman.

2. For the most part, the gods of yesteryear have been fused into a single Supreme Being, free from flaws, omniscient, and omnipotent. To be sure, each major religion, whether it be Buddhism, Christianity, Islam, or Judaism, has at its core an extraordinary figure in the form of a leader-guide (Moses), a prophet (Mohammed), a philosopher-teacher (Buddha) and even a man-god (Jesus), each of whom satisfies a number of the heroic archetypes already established for the superhero: *miraculous birth, abandonment to water, conquest of death, archenemy, divine intervention, sidekick.* Because of the complexity of contemporary belief associated with these figures, however, a closer scrutiny of them would necessitate a detailed theological discussion, which is beyond the scope of this present study.

3. The most famous of the alchemists were Paracelsus, Agrippa, Albertus Magus and Konrad Dippel. The Church obviously opposed such ventures strenuously, seeing them as attempts to play God.

4. As was shown in Chapter IX, a variation on this theme can be found in the Finish epic *Kalevala*, where the hero, Lemínkäinen, is re-created by his mother after having been literally chopped to pieces (*Kalevala*, Runo XV).

5. Faust's assistant, Wagner, created a being named Homunculus. Although limited to the confines of the test tube, Homunculus had the ability to speak and reason (Johann Wolfgang von Goethe, *Faust II*, lines 6819–7004).

6. None of these ideas is original. In Greek mythology, the birth of Aphrodite can be viewed as an early cloning success, while Hephaestos regularly designed and manufactured robots. In more recent times there have been notable accomplishments in the field of mechanical beings made by such diverse men as the Jesuit Jacques de Vaucanson (1709–1782) and the Swiss engineer Pierre Jaquet-Droz (1721–1790).

7. Radu Florescu, *In Search of Frankenstein* (Boston: New York Graphic Society, 1975), 2

8. Mary's father was the philosopher John Godwin. In 1792, her mother, Mary Wollstonecraft, wrote one of the first comprehensive works advocating women's rights, *Vindication of the Rights of Women*.

9. Mary Shelley, *Frankenstein* (New York: New American Library, 1965), 213.

10. Compare this to the movie version of the "monster," who plods along like a football player with an overextended knee.

11. Again, the contrast with the film version is striking. The early celluloid Frankenstein could, at best, grunt like a bear poked with an umbrella.

12. The influence of Robert Louis Stevenson's *Dr. Jekyll and Mr. Hyde* and Victor Hugo's *The Hunchback of Notre Dame* were also very evident, particularly in the early issues.

13. He was only gray in the first issue; the reason was technical rather than aesthetic.

14. http://www.samcci.comics.org/reviews/review017.htm/.

15. Bram Stoker, born in Dublin in 1847, suffered from a childhood illness that confined him to his bed until he was eight years old. Some critics see this as a factor that enabled him to understand a being who spent most of his time in a coffin. As for the actual writing of *Dracula*, there is an apocryphal story to the effect that one evening Stoker ate a meal of shellfish (either lobster or crab, depending on the biography) and as a result of a disturbed digestive system dreamed the story of Dracula.

16. Martin Riccardo, *Vampires Unearthed* (New York: Garland, 1983), 3.

17. Orsen Welles' *Mercury Theater* production of Stoker's classic and the 1980s film with Frank Langella in the lead role are two of the best renditions of a sexually attractive Dracula.

18. The translation of Dracula is "son of Dracul." In Germany he was called *Trakle* or *Dracole* and in Venice, Italy, *Dragulia*. The Hungarians called him *Dracula*.

19. *The Dracula Scrapbook*, ed. Peter Haining (New York: Bramhall House, 1976), 40.

20. Sigismund had a hidden personal agenda. The *Societas Draconis* was to be a means of making the house of Luxemburg the most powerful political force in Europe.

21. A detailed discussion of Dracul's shifting alliances can be found in Donald Glut's *The Dracula Book* (NJ: Scarecrow Press, 1975). Also in Florescu and McNally's work, *Dracula: Prince of Many Faces* (Boston: Little, Brown, 1989).

22. See Basil Copper, *The Vampire in Legend and Fact* (NJ: The Citadel Press, 1974), 29.

23. Montague Summers, *The Werewolf* (NY: Bell, 1966), 1.

24. Bralm Stoker, *Dracula* (NY: Signet Classics, 1965), 27.

25. The 1992 Dracula movie, starring Robert De Niro, contains state-of-the-art special effects.

26. In his 1983 book *Vampires Unearthed*, Martin Riccardo counted 33 anthologies, 173 novels, 172 short stories, 196 films, 6 television series, 35 plays, 7 socio-analytical treatises and 97 comic book features. Since that time the number of all has likely increased significantly.

27. Article in the newspaper *Reveille*, March 14, 1975. Reproduced in *The Dracula Scrapbook*, 69.

28. After more than six months of negotiations, the Treaty of Versailles (1919) marked the end to World War I. According to its terms, Germany took full responsibility for the war and had to make reparations to the other combatants. Among other penalties, Germany ceded portions of its territory, relinquished its colonies, and had severe restrictions placed on the size of its military forces.

29. Fredric Wertham, *Seduction of the Innocent* (New York: Reinhart, 1954).

30. E. Nelson Bridwell, *Batman: From the Thirties to the Seventies* (New York: Crown, 1971), 12.

31. See page 177.

32. This is a relatively new genre: a hybrid comic book/novel. The Batman entry into the field is *The Dark Knight Returns* by Frank Miller (Warner Books). In this existential work, an ageing Batman confronts his mortality.

33. Jack Nicholson's portrayal of the Joker in the 1989 feature film *Batman* is one of the classic villain roles in the history of cinema.

34. Two Face was a variation of Jekyll and Hyde, who, unlike Robert Louis Stevenson's creation, was both good and evil simultaneously. His dichotomous nature was not only evident in his face, one half of which had been horribly disfigured when a criminal threw acid into it, but in his clothes. The suit he wore was perfect on one side, torn and gaudy on the other. The Riddler was a bizarre psychopath whose subconscious need for punishment manifested itself in his need to leave a clue after every crime.

35. He appeared in Marvel Comics' *Fantasy* #4, the brain-child of Stan Lee.

36. In recent times, some critics have criticized the Spider-Man series for resorting to a series of crises, "...an endless string of cheap stunts and shock-value tactics to increase sales," http://www.en.wikipedia.org/wiki/Spiderman.

37. The relationship between Dracula and Spider-Man was noted in the July 1974 issue of *Giant-Size Spider Man*. The story entitled "Ship of Fiends" appeared in that issue.

Epilogue

1. Joseph Campbell, *The Hero with a Thousand Faces* (Cleveland & New York: World Publishing, 1970). See Chapter I, "Myth and Dream," 3–25.

2. Friedrich Nietzsche, *Menschlich, Allzumenschliches*, vol. 1 (München: Carl Hanser Verlag, 1956), 454–456.

3. Mircea Eliade, *The Sacred and the Profane* (New York: Harper and Row, 1961), 95.

4. Carl Jung, *Psyche and Symbol* (New York: Doubleday, 1958).

Bibliography

Anonymous. *The Nibelungenlied*. Middlesex: Bantam Books, 1970.

Bhaktivedanta Swami Prabhupada. *Bhagavad-Gita as It Is*. Los Angeles: Bhaktivendanta Book Trust, 1976.

Bowen, J.C.E., ed. *Poems from the Persian*. Philadelphia: Richard Clay, 1964.

Bridwell, E. Nelson. *Batman: From the Thirties to the Seventies*. New York: Crown, 1971.

_____, ed. *Superman: From the Thirties to the Seventies*. New York: Crown, 1972.

Brockington, J.L. *Righteous Rama: The Evolution of an Epic*. Bombay: Oxford Press, 1984.

Budge, Wallis, ed. *The Book of the Dead*. New York: University Books, 1960.

Bullfinch, Thomas. *Mythology*. New York: Dell, 1964.

Campbell, Joseph. *The Hero with a Thousand Faces*. Cleveland: Meridian Books, 1970.

Chesler, Phyllis. "An Interpretive Essay." In *Wonder Woman*. New York: Bonanza Books, 1969.

Clough, A.H., and William W. Goodwin, eds. *Plutarch's Writings: Miscellanies*. Vol. 4. New York: Little, Brown, 1909.

Collodi, Carlo. *The Adventures of Pinocchio*. New York: Lancer Books, 1968.

Copper, Basil. *The Vampire in Legend and Fact*. New Jersey: The Citadel Press, 1974.

Eliade, Mircea. *The Sacred and the Profane*. New York: Harper and Row, 1961.

Fiedler, Leslie, "Up, up and away: the rise and fall of comic books." *The New York Times Book Review*, September 5, 1976.

Firdowsi. *The Epic of the Kings*. Translated by Reuben Levy. Chicago: University of Chicago Press, 1967.

Goethe, Johann Wolfgang von. *Faust I and II*. Hamburg: Christian Wegner Verlag, 1963.

Goodrich, Norma Lorre. *The Ancient Myths*. New York: Mentor Books, 1960.

Graves, Robert. *The Greek Myths*. Vols. 1 and 2. Baltimore: Penguin Books, 1955.

Haining, Peter, ed. *The Dracula Scrapbook*. New York: Bramhall House, 1976.

Hawthorne, Julian, ed. *The World's Great Classics: Persian Literature: The Shah Nameh*. London/New York: Colonial Press, 1900.

Heidel, Alexander. *The Gilgamesh Epic and Old Testament Parallels*. Chicago: University of Chicago Press, 1946.

Hesiod. *The Poems of Hesiod*. Oklahoma: University of Oklahoma Press, 1983.

Homer. *The Iliad*. Chicago: University of Chicago Press, 1959.

_____. *The Odyssey*. New York: Modern Library, 1950.

Homer. *The Homeric Hymns*. Baltimore: Johns Hopkins University Press, 1976.

Horn, Maurice. *The World Encyclopedia of Comics*. New York: Chelsea House, 1996.

http://www.en.wikipedia.org/wiki/Hawkman/.

http://www.my.execpc.com/~icicle/GAFLASH.html/.

http://www.samcci.comics.org/reviews/review017.htm/.

Hugo, Victor. *The Hunchback of Notre Dame*. New York: Bantam Books, 1981.

Ions, Veronica. *Indian Mythology*. London: Paul Hamlyn, 1967.

Jung, Carl. *Psyche and Symbol*. New York: Doubleday, 1958.

Kirby, W.F., ed. *Kalevala*. London: Athlone Press, 1985.

Kleist, Heinrich von. *Amphitryon*. Munich: Wilhelm Goldmann Verlag, 1961.

MacCulloch, John Arnott. *The Mythology of All Races*. Vol. 2. Boston: Marshall Jones, 1929.

Martin, Riccardo. *Vampires Unearthed*. New York: Garland, 1983.

McNally, Raymond. *Dracula: Prince of Many Faces*. Boston: Little, Brown, 1989.

Miller, Frank. *The Dark Knight Returns*. New York: Warner Books, 1986.

Morford, Mark, and Robert Lenardon. *Classical Mythology*. New York: David McKay, 1971.

Murray, Henry A., ed. *Myth and Mythmaking*. New York: George Braziller, 1960.

Narayan, R.K. *Gods, Demons and Others*. New York: Viking Press, 1964.

New Larousse Encyclopedia of Mythology. London: Hamlyn, 1974.

Nietzsche, Friedrich. *Menschlich, Allzumenschliches*. München: Carl Hanser Verlag, 1956.

Niven, Larry. *All the Myriad Ways*. New York: Ballantine Books, 1968.

O'Flaherty, Wendy Doniger. *The Origins of Evil in Hindu Mythology*. Berkeley: University of California Press, 1976.

Petre-Turville, E.O.G. *Myth and Religion of the North*. New York: Holt, Rinehart and Winston, 1964.

Rank, Otto. *The Myth of the Birth of the Hero*. Translated by F. Robbins and S.E. Jellife. New York: Vintage Books, 1964.

Robertson, J.G. *A History of German Literature*. Edinburgh: William Blackwood & Sons, 1953.

Shelley, Mary. *Frankenstein*. New York: New American Library, 1965.

Spencer, Katherine. *Mythology and Values*. Memoir 48. Philadelphia: American Folklore Society, 1957.

Steranko, James. *History of Comics 1*. Reading, PA: Supergraphics, 1970.

_____. *History of Comics 2*. Reading, PA: Supergraphics, 1972.

Stevenson, Robert Louis. *Dr. Jekyll and Mr. Hyde*. London: Penguin Classics, 2003.

Stoker, Bram. *Dracula*. New York: Signet Classics, 1965.

Sturlson, Snorri. *The Prose Edda*. Los Angeles and London: University of California Press, 1973.

Summers, Montague. *The Werewolf*. New York: Bell, 1966.

Valmiki and Anonymous. *The Ramayana* and *The Mahabarata*. London: J.M. Dent & Sons, 1963.

Virgil. *The Aeneid*. New York: Bantam, 1972.

Wertham, Fredric. *Seduction of the Innocent*. New York: Reinhart, 1954.

Wollstonescraft, Mary. *Vindication of the Rights of Women*. London: Penguin Putnam, 2006.

World Encyclopedia of Comics. Edited by Maurice Horn. New York: Chelsea House, 1976.

Wylie, Philip. *Gladiator*. CT: Hyperion Press, 1974.

Index